Once Upon a Time

Using Storytelling, Creative Drama, and Reader's Theater with Children in Grades PreK-6

Judy Freeman

LIBRARIES
U N L I M I T E D
A Member of the Greenwood Publishing Group

Westport, Connecticut · London

Introduction

This book was supposed to be a simple little handbook to go along with a series of workshops I was preparing to present on storytelling, creative drama, and Reader's Theater, sponsored by my publisher, Libraries Unlimited, for teachers and librarians. (As my mother would have said, its gruesome). I decided to cull my best storytelling advice, with supporting materials from my books, the <u>Books Kids Will Sit Still For</u> series; from other workshops and articles and reviews I had done; and from my notes for the graduate courses in storytelling I have given at Rutgers and at Pratt Institute over the years. I gathered up some of my favorite stories, songs, chants, and children's books, and added ideas for using all of those things with children. When I pulled it all together, I found myself with a book. If you'd like to borrow some of these techniques and tales to use with your children, go right ahead. Stories work best when they're shared.

It is one thing to read aloud to children. I have been a read-aloud advocate throughout my life, from my childhood when my parents read to me, through my many years as a school librarian, and now as an advocate of children's books in the programs, speeches, and children's assemblies I present across the country. But reading aloud is just one of many ways to immerse children in stories.

As we age, we often lose a lot of our spontaneity, our ability to fool around and act silly that we had as children. "Acting like a child" is considered undesirable when you're past 30. Even the Bible weighs in on the subject, with Paul stating, "When I was a child, I spake as a child, I understood as a child, I thought as a child: but when I became a man, I put away childish things."

Still, working with children as a teacher or librarian or parent is very different from working in an office. If you spend time with children, it's vital to stay connected with childhood. We adults want children to grow up literate, industrious, conscientious, and selfless. Good stories help children internalize attributes like these.

Children are natural actors. They love acting foolish and falling over with laughter. We chide them to stop fooling around and to stop acting like children. There must be a happy medium. That's where stories come in, yet again. Want to see a roomful of children get happy? Tell them you're going to read or tell them a story and then they're going to act it out.

Now you may have your own ulterior motives here. You want your children to recall the story's sequence, to envision the setting, to understand why each character behaved as he or she did. You want them to read aloud with expression, to decode difficult words, to comprehend text. They, on the other hand, would like to laugh and have a good time. The two are not mutually exclusive.

Acting out stories in creative drama or using a written script to reread a story will help children achieve the skill levels they need in their reading lives. And they will have a whopping good time.

So what you'll find in this book is information on how to learn and tell stories; activities for using folklore in the classroom and library; a collection of songs and chants for spicing up your storytimes; some of my easiest-to-tell, most tried-and-true stories to get you started; instructions on how to organize, write, and perform creative drama exercises and Reader's Theater scripts, with suggestions of fail-safe stories and children's books to use; an annotated booklist, 400+ Children's Books Every Storyteller Should Know; and a bibliography of professional books and websites for storytelling, creative drama, and Reader's Theater.

Telling stories to children at school? Why bother? Because it's life-changing. They may forget the spelling tests and the worksheets, but they'll remember the stories, the poems, the songs, and the drama forever.

Getting Started with Storytelling

In the olden days, people told stories. People assumed that by now, in today's modern times, storytellers would become obsolete. Actually, we thought books would become obsolete, too. Some administrative types say, "Why do we need libraries? We have the Internet." As it turns out, neither storytelling nor books has died out. We've only begun to see how much richer our lives will be with computers and their added accessibility to facts, answers, and knowledge.

And, as it turns out, the Internet is full of stories, too. We need stories. We crave stories, whether we find them in books, on recordings, or live. Still, people look upon storytellers as magicians. "How do you do that?", they ask when a storyteller makes a twitchy class of children stop squirming with a well-told tale. "It doesn't look hard, but it must be."

Each of us has stories to tell—what happened the day the toaster caught on fire, the bat got into the attic, the cat fell into the bath (all things that have happened on my watch). Family goings-on, funny jokes, the latest TV episode or movie, what the neighbors did, what the government's up to, the latest news, a book you're reading; all of these are fodder for stories. Some of these stories you tell once, and they're over. Others become part of your personal store, told at get-togethers with relatives or friends or even strangers. "Something like that happened to me once . . ."

There are the stories we've heard all our lives—how our parents met, pivotal events that changed our lives like what you were doing when Kennedy got shot or on 9/11, or bedtime tales heard over and over. We hone these stories, passing them down to our children who, if we are lucky, remember to pass them down to theirs.

Storytellers are active seekers of stories to tell. Some people do this naturally, but it is also an art that can be learned. There's an endless archive of stories out there, and all we need to do is dig in to find the stories that speak to us, that define us, that change us.

Children take their stories very seriously, wanting to hear or read the same story over and over, and learning it by heart. One of my favorite episodes in Tomie dePaola's autobiographical chapter book, *26 Fairmount Avenue* (Penguin, 1999), is when six-year-old Tomie goes to see that very scary new movie, *Snow White and the Seven Dwarfs*, a full-length cartoon feature. At first, he thinks it's the best movie he's

1

ever seen, even though kids all around him, including his big brother Buddy, are crying and screaming in terror. But then he gets mad. He knows this story; his mother has read it to him. It seems Mr. Walt Disney has taken some liberties with the story. The movie has left out the part where the Evil Queen pulls the laces in Snow White's vest so tight that she faints. And there's no poison comb. When "The End" appears on the screen, he stands up in outrage and hollers, "The story's not over yet . . . Where're the red-hot iron shoes that they put on the Evil Queen so she dances herself to death?" He figures that Mr. Walt Disney never read the true story. Kids are sticklers for details and getting it right.

Let's begin with the basics. How do you learn to tell stories? And what are some practical ways we can use use folk and fairy tales with children?

How to Learn and Tell a Story:
A Refresher Course

Original recipe and inspiration from storyteller Laura Simms; recipe tinkered with and adapted by
Alice H. Yucht and Judy Freeman, and updated and revised by Judy Freeman.

Reprinted from *Books Kids Will Sit Still For 3: A Read-Aloud Guide* by Judy Freeman
(Libraries Unlimited, 2006).

In the past decade, I've taught courses on storytelling at Rutgers University and Pratt Institute, and I continue to see the advantages when librarians and teachers add storytelling to their teaching repertoires. All of the skills and concepts we seek to reinforce—including listening, comprehension, and higher-level thinking skills; character education and behavior issues; understanding story structure and recalling sequence and details through retelling; and making text-to-text, text-to-self, and text-to-world connections—can be introduced and reinforced with simple storytelling.

Are you worried it might be hard or too time consuming to learn stories? I've seen my graduate students arrive the first day of class, jittery and apprehensive about telling stories in front of a group, and without fail and without exception, they gain confidence and find personal and professional satisfaction in their new endeavor. On your way to work, instead of listening to talk radio, you could instead listen to a tape or CD you've made of yourself reading the stories you want to learn, and make it a new part of your commute.

Here are the tips I give my adult students to get them started. They also work with children, who learn stories far faster than us grown-ups and love to tell them to other classes or groups. There are many stellar books on how to tell stories that go into far more detail. See the Bibliography of Professional Books on page 179 for my favorites.

Storyteller Laura Simms says, "Storytelling is like baking a cake." You gather the ingredients, mix them together in the proper order, and adjust the seasonings to make the flavor suit you. Let it bake until it's ready and then present it to your eager, hungry public.

PREPARATION

1. Choose a story you truly love, one with real staying power that you won't find boring or meaningless after spending a lot of time and energy learning it. Folk and fairy tales are a natural source, of course, but often you will find a perfect picture book that tells as well as or better than it reads aloud. (For lots of suggestions, see STORIES TO TELL in each Subject Index of Judy Freeman's <u>Books Kids Will Sit Still For</u> series.) Photocopy the story, including the title and author of the book, for your Storytelling File. (Keep an ongoing file of stories you want to learn, and another one of stories you already know.)

2. Read the story at least three times, including at least once out loud so you can judge if it sounds as good as it looks. Talk about the story and retell the sequence of events aloud to yourself or a friend.

3. Think about what the story means to you. What is so special about it? How does it fit your own style, personality, and needs? How do you expect children will respond to it?

4. Time the story. How long does it take you to read it out loud? (As a general rule, if you're new at storytelling, don't start out with a story that takes more than 10 minutes. Keep it short and simple at first.)

5. Some people like to copy down the story in their own handwriting or typing (employing kinesthetic learning) and / or tape record it.

6. Put the story away for a day. Then, after at least 24 hours, sit down and outline as much as you can remember of the story without looking at it first, to see how much you've already internalized.

PRACTICE

1. Outline the sequence of events in the story: what happens first, second, third, etc. See if you can break it down into ten or so main events in the plot.

2. Describe (or draw) the characters in the story; how they look, what they wear, how they behave, and how they think.

3. Envision the places in the story. Draw a map of the setting.

4. If there are any special phrases or sentences or refrains in the story that have to be said in a specific way, or are intrinsic to the story, or that you just plain love, memorize them so you can recite them in your sleep. Learn the beginning and ending paragraphs by heart. You usually do not need to memorize the rest of the story per se; instead, internalize it and visualize it as you tell it.

5. Tell the story out loud—to a pet, a mirror, a compliant child, or a sympathetic "significant other." Keep a copy of the story with you at all times to read and reread. In the car, play your tape recorded version and try to recite along with your own narration. Be sure to keep your eyes on the road, though!

6. Assess the sections of the story you don't know as well and focus on them. Work hardest on the parts of the story that are weakest. Continue to tell the story to yourself dozens of times and in different ways. You might sing it or chant it. Sometimes you'll even dream about it at night.

7. Keep telling it to willing listeners—it gets easier each time! As you tell it, allow your mind's eye to work so you can "see" everything you are describing, like a movie playing in your head. If you stop visualizing the story, and think, say, about chocolate, you'll lose focus and forget what comes next.

8. Be aware of pitfalls—swaying, saying "uh" or "and" too much, telling a past tense story in the present tense, or losing your concentration. If you want to see how you look and sound, get out the video recorder and tape yourself. This can be a little scary to watch ("I can't *possibly* sound like that! And where did all those *wrinkles* come from?") but it is an honest way to assess your presentation on all fronts.

9. Prepare the final presentation: How long does it take to tell? Are there any special gestures or voices you need to practice? How will you introduce your story? Are there any props or supporting children's books you need to have with you? What will you do when you finish to wrap up the storytelling session? You want your story to have a good, strong beginning and ending.

PERFORMANCE

You can do it—even in front of an audience. Introduce your story with its title, origin, and background. The beginning of a story is vital. You're setting the stage for people to listen to you. Take charge of your audience and guide them through your story. Remember, when you tell stories to children, they are on your side. They love to hear stories of any kind and will consider you a magician for knowing how to tell them. Sure, it'll be uneven the first time you tell it. But once you're over that hump, your telling of the story will improve every time. The first five times you share it with an audience, you'll be aware of how much more fluid each successive performance is.

From *Once Upon a Time: Using Storytelling, Creative Drama, and Reader's Theater with Children in Grades PreK-6* by Judy Freeman. Westport, CT: Libraries Unlimited. Copyright © 2007.

20 More Storyteller's Performance Tips

1. Stand or sit still. Don't fidget, rock, sway, fiddle with keys or change in your pocket, wring your hands, or fool around with your hair, even if you feel nervous inside.

2. Make yourself the calm at the center of the story. Don't over-gesture or overact. Let the story tell itself. The story is more important than you, the teller.

3. Make eye contact. Finding friendly faces in the audience will give you reassurance, but look at everyone. Each person in your audience should feel as though you are telling the story directly to him or her.

4. Find the voices of each of your characters. Hear them and see them in your head. Concentrate, so you and your audience always know which character is speaking.

5. Speak clearly and with expression, empathy, and energy. Your audience is living the story through you. Enunciate so listeners can understand every word.

6. A loud voice can be effective when telling a story, but so can a soft one. Be sure to project so everyone can hear you clearly at all times, even if you whisper.

7. If you hear yourself overusing connecting words that make one sentence go on and on forever (such as *and*, *but*, *so*, and *well*) remind yourself to pause and take a breath instead. Don't worry that you've gone quiet for a moment—it will add space to your story.

8. Don't rush your telling, especially the ending. It's not a race. Breathe. The way you use pauses and pacing gives your story good timing, as the comedians all say. A skillfully told ending allows your audience to sit back, satisfied, and say, "Ahhh!"

9. If you lose your place or leave out something important, you don't need to stop and admit it. Don't apologize. Backtrack by saying, "And did I tell you . . ." or, "What I didn't tell you yet is that . . . ." If you stay cool and focused, your audience may never know the difference. And if they do, they usually don't care. They just want to hear a good story.

10. If you mess up a large section of the story, fix it as best you can, smile, and don't let yourself get demoralized. Get on with it. Think of yourself as an Olympic ice skater. They leap, twirl, and sometimes fall on their fannies, but they always pick themselves up and try to make it look as if nothing terrible has happened. The audience members may gasp, but when they see the skater jump back into the routine, they'll cheer at the end.

11. Tell folk and fairy tales in the past tense; jokes and current stories, on the other hand, are often told in the present tense. Avoid using modern colloquialisms or slang with old tales. They feel out of place and character. Keep your stories in the "once upon a time" past. You'll want to say, simply, "The frog said, 'Princess, why are you crying?' " and not, "So the frog goes, like, you know, 'Princess, why are you crying?' and she's like, 'I, like, dropped my golden ball in the well.' "

12. Yes, you can change a story to suit your storytelling style and personality, but be careful not to rob it of its own flavor and roots.

13. Have fun. Take time to enjoy your own telling of your story. As you relax into it, you'll realize that you are having as good a time as your eager listeners.

14. If you are telling a story with a chantable refrain ("Run, run, run, as fast as you can . . ."), with animal noises, or with any possibility of audience interaction, actively encourage your listeners to join in. If they're not used to hearing stories, they might think they're being rude if they speak out loud, so you'll want to say, "Help me tell this part," or "What did the dog say?"

15. Tell your story to more than one group, and note the improvements, strengths, and weaknesses in each rendition. It takes at least three tellings before you start to feel the story becoming yours. Each time you tell it, you'll be surprised at how much heart and meaning you continue to pull from it. Even the simplest stories can reveal profound meanings. It's like peeling an endless onion, but with a far better flavor. (The tears are up to you, depending on how deep you go.)

16. Pick another irresistible tale from your folder of Stories to Learn, and start the process all over again. Pretty soon, you'll have an interesting, eclectic, and varied repertoire that you can share with your children year after year—and a reputation as a magical person who knows how to spin a good yarn.

17. Immerse yourself in stories. Read widely in the folk and fairy tale section of your library—look for 398.2. Your library may also have professional storytelling CDs, DVDs, or videos that provide a source of new stories to tell and reveal how the experts do it.

18. Listen to other storytellers. Call your public library to see if they have a schedule of local storytelling performances in your area.

19. See if there are any storytelling groups in your area or start one with interested friends. Meet once a month and tell your new stories to each other. These groups give tellers incentive to learn and practice new stories or to hear good ones which you can borrow from other tellers.

20. Carry on the tradition. Teach other adults and / or children everything you have learned and keep storytelling alive in your neck of the woods.

Firsthand Advice from the Storytelling Class at Pratt Institute, New York City, 2007

Over the past batch of summers, I've had the privilege of teaching a graduate class in storytelling for the School of Information and Library Science at Pratt Institute in New York City. I hold the course off-campus, in the Central Children's Room at Donnell Library Center on West 53rd Street, where the original Winnie-the-Pooh is; right across from MoMA, the Museum of Modern Art. It's a most conducive place for learning and hearing and telling stories. The talented John Peters and his crackerjack staff of children's librarians, Elizabeth Bird, Rebecca Schosha, Aihui Liu, and Warren Truitt go out of their way to help us find needed resources and make us feel at home.

Each year, the dozen or so graduate students show up on the first day, nervous about learning to tell stories. One student said, "You mean we have to tell stories, not read them? How can we do that?"

We have our ways. Twice a week over the next five or six weeks, students dive into the vast pool of world literature: folk and fairy tales, picture books and fiction, family tales, life lessons from the ages, and all of the stories that have ever been; and emerge with three stories that they will learn by heart and love forever. They will tell their tales aloud to the class and to an audience of children. The learning time is short, with far too little time to process all those stories. It's impossible, really. But they do it anyway. Each year I'm astonished to see them turn into graceful, lyrical, accomplished, and sometimes brilliant tellers of tales with starting repertoires they can (and, I hope, will) use for the rest of their lives. It is magic.

What kinds of stories do they choose to tell? How do they find them? First off, they are expected to read widely through a list of titles I provide, a list you'll find in this book, "400+ Children's Books Every Storyteller Should Know," on page 111. They also wend their way through the classic collections of easy-to-tell stories by masters like Margaret Read MacDonald, Anne Pellowski, Martha Hamilton and Mitch Weiss, and Judy Sierra. Starting with simple stories to build confidence, they then continue to look for more complex tales with more impact.

As part of their coursework, there are three special assignments the students must complete. One is to begin assembling a lifelong folder of stories to learn. Each time I read a story I love and say to myself, "Boy, I'd could see myself telling that story," I photocopy it and put it in my "Stories to Learn" folder. On the first page, I note the title, author, publisher, and date of the book, or the source, if I got it off the Internet or from a colleague. If and when I take the time to learn it, I shift it over to my "Stories I Tell" folder. It's easier that way to go back and review an old story or pick a new one to tackle.

Next, students must go to see a real storyteller in concert. This can be a library storytelling program, or at a bigger venue. Luckily, in New York City it's easy to find storytellers. During the summer, every Wednesday and Saturday morning, children and grown-ups congregate at the Hans Christian Andersen Statue in Central Park for an hour-long program of stories told by professional storytellers. This tradition was started 25 years ago by the esteemed storyteller, Diane Wolkstein, author of *The Magic Orange Tree and Other Haitian Folktales* (Knopf, 1978) and dozens of picture books.

Afterwards, students write up a paper describing and critiquing, in detail, the programs they observed and the storyteller(s). They must consider: How was the program structured? Who were the tellers and what did you find out about them? How did they begin and end their stories? What stories were told and how effective were the tellings? What was the audience's (and your) reaction? Who was in the audience? What did you learn from the experience and how can you apply it to your own situation?

One summer Saturday, back in 2004, Pratt student Angie Ungaro went to Central Park, sat on a bench on the periphery of the audience assembled there, and started taking notes. A woman approached, sat down beside her, and asked what she was doing. Angie described her assignment for her storytelling class and showed her our syllabus.

From *Once Upon a Time: Using Storytelling, Creative Drama, and Reader's Theater with Children in Grades PreK-6* by Judy Freeman. Westport, CT: Libraries Unlimited. Copyright © 2007.

The next day, Sunday, I was eating breakfast when the phone rang. "Hi, Judy. This is Diane Wolkstein. I met one of your students yesterday."

I almost dropped my spoon. I had never met Diane but had seen her perform and had read all of her books. She wanted to know about our class, and I asked if she'd like to come over and tell us a few stories. She graciously accepted and spent a most delightful and instructive hour with the group. Storytellers are a special breed.

When critiquing a storytelling session, it is easy to draw lessons of what one should and shouldn't do as a teller. But seeing someone tell stories and then doing it yourself are two very different experiences. That brings the class to their third special project: go out and tell the three stories you've learned to the people for whom they're intended—actual children.

Where does one find children in the summertime? Some students arrange to put on a brief storytime at their local library, summer school, or daycare center, or they gather up a group of neighborhood children or family members.

In the summer of 2007, when Lisa Von Drasek, the librarian goddess at the Bank Street College of Education's elementary school, came to class as a venerable guest to tell stories and give the students a crash course in how to integrate storytelling across the curriculum in a school library, she regaled them with her personal experiences and observations. She told them how she brings bags of new children's books to read on the subway going to and from work every day, and sometimes gets so engrossed, she misses her stop. She related the time she was on the train when a group of campers, en route from uptown out to Coney Island, entered the car with, as she said, "50 kids in identical t-shirts, lots of noise and energy and young counselors, almost out-of-control." She stood up and announced that she needed to practice a new story on them. If you can get the attention of children riding on a subway, you can do anything. Lisa is fearless.

She said, "If there's a mom with her kids riding nearby, I say, 'Do you mind if I tell your kids a story? What stop are you getting off?' This way you can gauge how long you have and time your stories accordingly."

Candice Sheerer, one of the Pratt grad students, took Lisa's advice to heart. When she couldn't find a venue for her third project, she made a sign—"Storytelling by Candice"—went into a local park, and corralled a willing group of young children and their grateful parents. She was such a hit, one of the adults offered her a job as a storyteller in a local daycare.

After presenting their programs, students write up critiques and descriptions of the experience, including their own self-assessment and the reactions of their audiences. They've been so intent on finding, learning, and telling their stories in class, they don't think about how these stories will be received. For many of them, it's a revelation to find that they can relax and have fun and that children love hearing their stories.

One of the things that drives me crazy in modern life is the casual use of language that passes for conversation. These days, children spend their days hearing and repeating sentences like this one: "So I'm like at the mall, and, y'know, I was, like, with my friend, and she's like, 'Why are you doing that?' and I'm like, 'Whatever.' "

It's so lax, our language. Is it worse than when I was growing up? I think so, because it's not just the young who speak like this these days. Watching CNN one morning, I was stunned to hear one of the news anchors use "like" and "you know" repeatedly in her patter. The sloppy language of teens has filtered into adults' conversational styles, mine included, and it's not easy to stop it.

How can we model better English with our youngsters? When children hear narrative and dialogue read aloud, and then practice reading it aloud themselves, they hear and use speech patterns that are not strewn with slang and lazy language, and see words arranged in many gorgeous and felicitous ways.

So in my storytelling classes, I ban casual speech in stories. I want students to be aware of how they sound. We tend to tell jokes in the present tense. Since many stories happened "once upon a time," they need to be told in the past tense. This is probably the toughest concept to get across. Once the students can hear themselves— "so, you know, Rapunzel lets down her hair, and the prince says . . ."—and recognize how jarring this sounds, the battle is won. They become storytellers.

When someone lapses into present tense during a story, the group gasps. But they are kind as evaluators, praising each teller for what worked in a story, and gently suggesting ways to strengthen a performance.

They walk out of that final class with three stories under their belts, ready to tell them to the world. What we need to become storytellers, really, is time and desire. OK, you know you'll never have enough time to learn all the stories you want to learn. That's not realistic. But if you can somehow learn one story a year and make it yours, your repertoire will grow.

The younger you are, though, the more stories you should learn each year. As you get older, it gets harder to find the time and energy to master and remember lots of stories. Sure, you can do it, but it takes more work to make all the details stick. The fastest story learners are children. They can learn stories and poems and songs effortlessly.

In the summer of 2007, the 10 students in my Pratt Institute storytelling class took a little time to reflect on their storytelling experiences. They compiled a list of their best advice, based on their own on-the-job training of telling stories and watching their fellow students tell stories. Here is their list.

WHAT WE DISCOVERED ABOUT TELLING STORIES

Advice and Observations by Paula Blount-Harris, Becca Dash, Kristy Raffensberger, Jill Rothstein, Julie Row, Lauren Scherer, Candice Sheerer, Kat Takach, Abbie Weinberg, and Stephanie Weiss

Selecting Stories

- Make a commitment to your story. Plan everything you want to say and do.

- Variation is good. Try not to learn the same type of stories each time. Challenge yourself.

- Give yourself some time to get to know the story. Sometimes it takes years to find the true heart of it, but that's OK.

- Pick stories you love. You'll be spending many years together. Sometimes you fall out of love, though. Don't force a story. You can drop it, unless you have another good reason to tell it.

- Stealing is good. Listen to lots of storytellers and appropriate the stories you love to tell yourself.

- Watching experienced storytellers can help us to learn (or to avoid) little mannerisms and different styles.

- Look for stories in unexpected places. You may find a significant episode in a fiction book or an anecdote in a biography or a history or science book that is just right to tell as a story.

- You can change a story to fit your audience. Be respectful of your source, but don't be scared to adapt a story to your audience. The Story Police won't come after you if you edit or tweak it.

- Booktalking is a type of storytelling. We need to do more in-depth booktalking with children. They love it.

Learning Stories

- Practice just like it's the real thing. No swearing when you mess up.

- Sometimes you're perfect in rehearsal, when no one else is watching you.

- Be mindful of how you treat stereotypes in stories, like the wicked stepmother. A whole lot more kids have stepmothers now than when these fairy tales were first told.

- Stick with voices you are comfortable with. A bad Irish accent is jarring; watch public TV to hear and practice the real thing.

- Accents can be great fun to try, but keep them consistent.

- It's easy to be a Backseat Storyteller, someone who hasn't done any telling but still has lots of advice. Don't think you know everything until you try doing it yourself.

- Stop saying "I can't," "It's too hard," "I'm no good." Just shut up and do it.

- Choreograph your movements so they flow naturally in the story. Watch your body language, though. Animation helps a lot, but not if you overdo it.

- Visualize the story as if it is happening to you.

From *Once Upon a Time: Using Storytelling, Creative Drama, and Reader's Theater with Children in Grades PreK-6* by Judy Freeman. Westport, CT: Libraries Unlimited. Copyright © 2007.

- Get under the skin of your characters. Characters who die in a story only die temporarily. Children understand this, such as when two of the three little pigs get eaten by the wolf. They'll be back the next time you tell it.

- Learn the first paragraph and any refrains by heart so you can say them in your sleep.

- Memorizing each word of a story is not critical, unless you're good at that and like to do it.

- Beginnings are easy; endings are not. Make sure you're as happy with the way you finish your story as you were when you started it. Perfect your last paragraph—if the printed story ending isn't satisfying when told out loud, work on making the words work. If you need to rewrite or add a better last sentence, do it.

- Once you figure out what methods work for you in learning a story, no story is impossible to learn.

Performing Stories

- Introduce your stories with their titles and a little bit about where they're from. If it's from a book, show the cover.

- If you're telling more than one story, figure out a natural and interesting segue from one story to the next so there's a thread or connection.

- Keep a list of your program near you so you won't forget what you want to do next. You may want to keep a notebook with your stories and program notes and put it on a music stand. (Those collapsible music stands, cheap and on sale at any music store, are easy to bring along, and nicely unobtrusive.)

- Don't let your audience see you look at your watch. If you need one, take an old watch face, put a piece of velcro on the back, and fasten it to the inside cover of your notebook.

- Plan for more than you have time to tell. If a story doesn't seem to fit the occasion, you'll be able to substitute.

- It's normal to be nervous. If your nervousness affects the quality of your telling, you need think about it and figure some ways to channel it or make it work for you instead of against you. No one has ever died from telling stories in public.

- If standing makes you too nervous, you can sit.

- If you mess up part of a story, you'll learn that kids are very forgiving.

- Don't stop, even if you forget something. If you can cover your tracks without anyone catching on, that's good. If you can't, and you have to say, "Whoops, I forgot to tell you something," don't let it throw you. Just keep going. Don't freak out. Keep on keeping on. Finish that story.

- If you don't know your story real well and you want to tell it anyway, go ahead. You can always keep a copy of the story, a cheat sheet, or an outline in the chair beside you if you need it. Kids won't notice, probably, and they won't care if they do. If you tell them you're working on a new story, they'll be even more supportive.

- No offense, but you are not more important than the story. Your audience doesn't care so much about you; they care about the story. You are just the vehicle for the story. Try to give them the best presentation you can.

- Don't interrupt your own story with "asides." You don't need to ask your listeners questions about the story unless they will enhance it or build up to something. If children say, "Could you just . . . tell . . . the story!" you've gone too far.

- Let your audience into a story. Get them involved, whether it's just listening or actively participating. Without them, your story has no life.

- You can always tell it better. Each time you tell it, think about what you want to improve this time.

- If you are comfortable with yourself and your story, the audience will know and will be comfortable watching and listening.

- Words to watch and stop saying over and over: and, like, you know, so, uh, said, guys, he goes, she went. (Add your own list here.)

- Don't fidget, rock, sway, bounce, or make those annoying tsk-ing noises with your tongue that you never knew you were doing.

- Know your audience. Don't tell spooky stories to three-year-olds or babyish stories to teenagers. But remember that people of all ages enjoy stories. Just because the teenagers are rolling their eyes doesn't mean they're not enjoying your stories inside.

- Make eye contact with your audience, and really look at them. If you just turn your head from side to side, you'll get whiplash. Slow down and connect with people.

- Take your time with a story. It's not a race to get finished. Don't be afraid of silence.

- You learn something about yourself every time you tell a story.

- Do something to make the world more beautiful. Tell stories.

Kids Tell Stories

Reprinted from *Books Kids Will Sit Still For: The Complete Read-Aloud Guide* by Judy Freeman (Libraries Unlimited, 1990).

Storytelling adds a refreshing slant to the teaching of listening, comprehension, and critical thinking skills, not to mention the huge benefits it offers in terms of vocabulary and language development, a sharpened sense of humor, and a working understanding of the basic components of all literature. Carried further, children can easily learn to tell stories, most likely with far less effort than it takes us grown-ups.

In a library project that I developed and conducted with fourth- and fifth-grade classes, the children spent ten weeks learning to be storytellers. My general goals in the "Kids Tell Stories" project were as follows:

1. To familiarize students and teachers with the background and traditions of oral literature,

2. To introduce children to a body of written literature (i.e., folktales),

3. To acquaint students with the skills of storytelling and oral expression,

4. To develop the ability of students to conceptualize, using the "mind's eye" to visualize a complete story,

5. To develop reading and writing skills as an outgrowth of storytelling, and

6. To enhance students' self esteem, poise, and ease in speaking before a group.

During our once-a-week, one-hour sessions, we explored the origins of storytelling and read folk and fairy tales from all over the world, noting the characteristics of tales from Japan, Africa, Germany, England, China, the United States, and other countries. We charted the types and themes of stories, and examined the characteristics of main characters.

Each week I told them at least one new story, and they dramatized some, outlined the plots, drew vivid portraits of main characters, and constructed detailed maps of the settings. Even after a week had passed, a class, sitting in a circle, could collectively retell an entire story round robin, almost line for line. When one child forgot a section, someone else was sure to recall it and fill in the missing details.

We read and contrasted variants of well-known stories, such as a French versus a German version of "Cinderella," Dang Manh Kha's *In the Land of Small Dragon* (Viking, 1979) from Vietnam, Ai-Ling Louie's *Yeh-Shen* (Philomel, 1982) from China, and "Cenerentola" from Virginia Haviland's *Favorite Fairy Tales Told in Italy* (Little, Brown, 1965).

Students performed exercises to hone their storytelling skills by using their bodies to fit the tone and point of view of each character, and by learning to breathe properly from the diaphragm and to project their voices. They drew up large charts listing and comparing folktale characters, story beginnings and endings, and common folktale motifs, such as the use of magical numbers 3, 7 and 12 (i.e., three wishes, three little pigs, seven dwarfs, twelve dancing princesses), and the occurrence of transformations and magical objects.

Back in the classroom each week, the classroom teacher supplemented my lesson by reading aloud a sampling of additional folktales and using the stories as a kickoff to writing. For instance, after hearing "Why Dogs Hate Cats" from Julius Lester's *The Knee-High Man and Other Tales* (Dial, 1972), students made up new stories to explain the ongoing rivalry between mutt and feline.

Reading and creating folktale parodies works here, once children know and respect the original stories on which the spoofs are based. After everyone has heard a sampling of "Cinderella" stories,

Bernice Myers' *Sidney Rella and the Glass Sneaker* (Macmillan, 1985) is a gas; you can discuss how the author constructed her spoof based on the original. Many teachers expect their students to write folktale satire without understanding its underlying structure, which misses the point. In Jon Scieszka's *The True Story of the 3 Little Pigs* (Viking, 1979), Alexander T. Wolf protests that he was an innocent victim, framed by the media. Students can retell other stories from another character's point of view.

After all this background, which is in and of itself a valid and lasting way to extend the language arts, social studies, and science curriculums, each child selected and learned a story to tell. All stories had to be approved by the teacher or me, as some children wanted to try long, involved dissertations, and we offered guidance in selecting good, tellable folk and fairy tales.

Once they made their selections, students outlined their stories, drew main character portraits and story maps—as they had already done with one of the stories I told—discussed them first with a partner and then a small group, and next, told them to their groups. Classroom teachers allowed their tellers to adjourn to the hallway with partners to practice their stories as time allowed.

As a final rehearsal, they told their now-learned tales to the rest of the class seated on the floor on the library Story Rug. After each person finished, the class offered positive encouragement and suggestions for improvement. Children in this situation will be helpful and supportive as long as you lay the ground rules for what constitutes a helpful critique. After telling stories themselves, students are far more courteous, sympathetic, and encouraging when listening to their peers

Since a storyteller is not fulfilled until an audience is enthralled, the final goal of the ten weeks was for each "trainee" to tell his or her story to other classes. We used kindergarten, first- and second-graders as our willing guinea pigs. For each library class, I asked three or four different tellers to be the guest storytellers, until each student had told his or her story at least twice, and usually three times. The younger classes were wonderfully receptive audiences, as the performers discovered once they got over their initial jitters. "I'm so nervous. My knees are knocking!" was a typical "before" comment. Afterwards, most children said, "When can we do that again?"

Yes, some of the tellers were not wonderful, at least the first time. Many were brilliant, though, and some were great surprises to us all. I'll never forget one girl who rarely spoke aloud, especially when adults were in earshot. Her teacher and I were sure she would never learn her story, as during rehearsals, she would not participate, and she seemed overwhelmed by what, to her must have seemed an ordeal. Imagine our shock when, during the final rehearsal for the entire class, she stood up and knocked us out with the best-told story in the entire class. Something clicked for her, and she was radiant with her success.

The program's results can be measured in part by the number of students who still remember their stories the following year, and the demystification of the folktale section of the library, made obvious by the number of books children of all grades check out.

In 1942, famed storyteller Ruth Sawyer wrote in her book *The Way of the Storyteller* (Viking Penguin, 1977, p. 167):

> Insecurity, disturbance, apathy, national distrust are everywhere today. If we can make the art of storytelling an applied art, by which we may bring the rich heritage of good books into the lives of children throughout our country, that they may find a universal eagerness toward life and an abiding trust, then I think we may truly help build for the future.

Children never tire of the magical stories that make them laugh or let them linger in an enchanted world. By giving them the chance to hear stories told and to become storytellers themselves, we are indeed providing for the next generation, continuing an age-old tradition that must not become a victim of progress.

Types of Folktales

Reprinted from *Books Kids Will Sit Still For 3: A Read-Aloud Guide* by Judy Freeman
(Libraries Unlimited, 2006).

Folklore encompasses all forms of narrative, written or oral, that have been passed down from generation to generation. These include epics, ballads, folk songs, riddles, myths, legends, fables, folktales, and tall tales, plus, of course, the well-known fairy tales. When we talk about folktales versus fairy tales, the differences can be murky. I think of folktales, encompassing all of the stories in the 398.2 section of the library, as an early form of fiction, whose authors have been lost to history. Fairy tales, with their magic and royalty, are a subset of folktales. (All fairy tales are folktales, but not all folktales are fairy tales.) But don't take my word for it. Every place I looked for a simple definition, from books to Internet sites, offers a different take on what constitutes a folktale.

Here is a breakdown of the most common types:

CUMULATIVE TALES
(Often humorous stories incorporate repetition, chantable refrains, and a predictable sequence of events.)
Examples: "The Old Woman and Her Pig"
"The Gingerbread Boy"

POURQUOI TALES
(How and why stories explain a natural phenomena and how it came to be.)
Examples: *Why Mosquitoes Buzz in People's Ears* by Verna Aardema
How the Ox Star Fell from Heaven by Lily Toy Hong

BEAST TALES
(Talking animals act like humans, with all their faults and foibles.)
Examples: "The Three Little Pigs"
"Brer Rabbit" stories

NOODLEHEAD, FOOL, OR NUMBSKULL STORIES
(Foolish, hapless characters, usually male, either get fooled or try to fool others; often the fool turns out to be the smartest one.)
Examples: Jack (England and U.S.), Uncle Bouki (Haiti), Juan Bobo (Puerto Rico),
Fools of Chelm (Jewish, from Poland), Nasreddin Hoca (Turkey)

TRICKSTER TALES
(Involving sly schemers and deliberate troublemakers; some tricksters are fools as well; tricksters often get tricked and tend not to learn their lessons.)
Examples: Coyote, Raven, Rabbit (Native American), Anansi the Spider (Africa),
Iktomi (Native American), Reynard the Fox (France), Brer Rabbit (African American)

FABLES

(Short tales with a stated or easily understood moral that often involve animals in human roles.)
Examples: Aesop (Greek), La Fontaine (France)

MYTHS

(All about the interactions of gods and goddesses with humans; myths also explain creation, or how the world came to be.)
Examples: Greek, Roman, Norse

LEGENDS

(Featuring heroic people, who may or may not have lived, who achieved legendary status for their real or supposed deeds.)
Examples: Johnny Appleseed, William Tell, Robin Hood, King Arthur

TALL TALES

(Exaggerated yarns with larger-than-life characters; in U.S. folklore, these include rugged, indefatigable superheroes, mostly male, from the working world and the American frontier.)
Examples: Paul Bunyan (logger), Pecos Bill (cowboy), John Henry (steel-driving railroad track builder)

FAIRY TALES

(Lush, detailed, and often sweepingly romantic sagas and adventures incorporating magic, enchantments, transformations, quests, tasks, and trials; and supernatural beings such as witches, ghosts, fairies, giants, and talking animals; fairy tales represent the fulfillment of human desires—virtues of generosity, love, kindness, and truth prevail, while greed, hate, wickedness, and evil are punished.)
Examples: "Snow White," "Cinderella," "Rumpelstiltskin," "Sleeping Beauty"

Using Folk & Fairy Tales: An Ideas List

Reprinted from *Books Kids Will Sit Still For 3: A Read-Aloud Guide* by Judy Freeman
(Libraries Unlimited, 2006).

Here are 20 basic ways to incorporate folk literature into your classroom or library program.

1.   Using a classroom world map, pinpoint tales and their places of origin. (This works well for world geography, or, more locally, with tall tales of U.S. regions.)

2.   *Retelling:* After reading or telling a story aloud, have your listeners put the whole story back together again. Retell it, round robin, with each child recalling a small bit, in sequence.

3.   Make an outline of the story sequence. This is vital to learning a story, as it helps one recall each scene. List the 10 key events of the story.

4.   *Maps:* Each child draws a map of a story's settings, plotting the movements of all the characters and envisioning the physical details of each place.

5.   *Portraits:* Draw detailed portraits of main characters. (Watch the mind's eye at work.) Make story character masks out of papier mâché or oak tag. Or make clay figures, puppets, flannel board figures, or dolls of main characters. Use them to retell and act out stories.

6.   Compile large charts listing types of characters, settings and / or motifs (i.e., patterns and objects common to stories such as long sleeps, the numbers 3, 7, or 12, magical objects, or magical powers) typical to the tales you are studying. (See Fairy Tale Activity below, on page 19, for details.)

7.   Compare variants of stories such as "Cinderella," "Rumpelstiltskin," or "Jack and the Beanstalk." As students read through fairy tale collections, have them look for other variants of stories they've heard. (See some lists of these variants, starting on page 23.)

8.   Design giant movie-style "Coming Attractions" posters or book covers advertising stories.

9.   Act out stories after telling or reading them. Write Reader's Theater plays adapted from folktales. Starting in second grade, children can do this too, working in small groups. Videotape them or perform them for another class, the whole school, or just yourselves.

10.   Rewrite a story as a ballad or a poem.

11.   Learn folk dances and songs of countries in which your stories take place, and look up pictures of cities, natural wonders, and monuments.

12.   Play "20 Questions" where the object is to guess a story title. Or play the Story Character Game: Pin the name of a familiar folktale character on the back of each student's shirt. By asking each other "yes" and "no" questions, each child must ascertain his or her "identity."

13.   Dress in costume as story characters. Each character tells the group a little about him- or herself and the rest try to guess each identity.

14.   Compile a class book of student folklore, including jokes, riddles, tongue twisters, games, songs, autograph verse, and chants. Have children ask relatives and friends for the oral folklore they recall.

15.   After hearing a wide variety of folktales and talking about the story elements, children can create their own. (Tall tales and fables work well.) Or just rewrite endings to traditional tales.

16. Rewrite well-known tales from another character's point of view as Jon Scieszka did in *The True Story of the 3 Little Pigs* (Viking, 1979), as described by Alexander T. Wolf, who claims he was framed.

17. Write fairy tale parodies à la *The Stinky Cheese Man and Other Fairly Stupid Tales* (Viking, 1992) by Jon Scieszka, or reset traditional tales in other places, as Helen Ketteman did with her *Armadilly Chili* (Albert Whitman, 2004), a Southwest version of "The Little Red Hen," with Miss Billie Armadilly in the title role. Consider updating tales to modern times as Patricia Santos Marcantonio did in *Red Ridin' in the Hood: And Other Cuentos* (Farrar, 2005).

18. Put together a folktale newspaper. Students can write articles about characters and their exploits. (Possible columns: Help Wanted, Headline News, Obits, Sports, Comics, Advice to the Lovelorn.) See *The Fairytale News* by Colin and Jacqui Hawkins (Candlewick, 2004) for inspiration.

19. Teach children storytelling skills so they can select, practice, and tell folktales to others.

20. Organize a school-wide Storytelling Festival as a showcase for students efforts.

Fairy Tale Activity (Grades 2-6)

Reprinted from *Books Kids Will Sit Still For 3: A Read-Aloud Guide* (Grades 2–6) by Judy Freeman (Libraries Unlimited, 2006).

Select a variety of fairy tale picture books from the 398.2 shelves of your library. Hand out one book per pair or trio of children. Each group will then spend five minutes looking over its story to locate and identify the following information:

1. *Beginnings* that differ from "Once upon a time."

2. *Endings* that differ from " . . . and they all lived happily ever after."

3. *Settings*, including the country of origin.

4. *Main characters*, both heroes and villains.

5. *Hero's quest and / or magical elements* he or she encounters on the way.

Starting with the first category, "Beginnings," ask each group to quickly identify aloud the title and author of its book, show the cover, and read aloud the beginning sentence. Then move on to "Endings," "Settings," "Characters," and "Quests."

Now break the class into five research groups, and assign each group one of the categories. Each group will be responsible for making a large illustrated poster showing at least ten interesting and varied examples of their category that they've found while reading widely through the stories in the fairy tale section of the library.

1. Beginnings

Example: "Once upon a time when pigs were called swine and monkeys chewed tobacco; and hens took snuff to make them tough and ducks went quack quack quack-o . . . "—Joseph Jacobs's original opening to "The Three Little Pigs"

2. Endings

Example: "So snip snap snout, this tale's told out."—"The Three Billy Goats Gruff"

3. Settings

Example: "Deep in the forest, in a house on chicken legs"—"Baba Yaga"

4. Characters

Example: "A girl with lonnnggg hair, a sorceress, and a prince"—"Rapunzel"

5. Quest or magic elements

Example: A sister who plans to avenge her two sisters who were taken away and then declared dead by a dashing but dastardly count—"Count Silvernose"

Cumulatively, by the end of these activities, each person in the class will have hands-on experience examining fairy tale books, looking for specific details, and will have been exposed to a range of fairy tales from many countries.

Create An Instant Tall Tale

Reprinted from *Books Kids Will Sit Still For 3: A Read-Aloud Guide* by Judy Freeman
(Libraries Unlimited, 2006).

How do you explain the humor and exaggeration of tall tales? I have observed that younger children have literal senses of humor, and the dry, straight-faced humor of tall tales often flies over their heads.

I learned the following simple yet, hilarious, and instructive activity, a composite story exercise, from one of my graduate students at Pratt Institute. I asked her if I could use it, and she said, "Oh, sure. I got it from someone else, though." So I fiddled with it and made it my own. It's magical doing this activity with children to introduce or culminate a tall tales unit. You're reinforcing the Five W's—who, what, where, when, and why—in a Mad Libs kind of way, and you're demonstrating how exaggeration works.

Third grade teacher Nancy Havran did this project with her students at Van Holten School in Bridgewater, New Jersey, and they laughed and laughed. When I came back to visit her classroom later that day, they all wanted to share their composite stories. What I didn't expect, as the children regaled me with their very silly tall tales, was that they could already recite them aloud from memory.

OBJECTIVE:

- To reinforce the Five W's: Who, What, Where, When, Why

- To introduce the concept of absurdity in tall tales

SUPPLIES NEEDED:

1 long strip of legal-sized paper, cut in half the long way (4" x 14"), for each person; a pencil for each person

PROCEDURE:

1. To construct an instant absurd tall tale, each person in a group of seven writes down a response to your first writing prompt (see p. 21) at the top of the page, folds over a small flap of the paper to cover up the writing, and passes it on to the person on the right. On receiving the paper from the person on the left, and without unfolding it, each person writes an answer for the second prompt, folds the paper over again, and passes it to the right again.

2. At the end of the exercise, each person will have written one answer to each prompt, but on seven different strips of paper. Each writer then unfolds his or her final paper and reads aloud the usually hilarious composite sentence to the group or entire class.

3. Children can copy their composite tall tales on a long piece of drawing paper—a piece of 24" X 36" paper, cut in half the long way, would work fine—and illustrate each line. This makes a very cute bulletin board, "Heard any *TALL* tales lately?"

LEADER'S PROMPTS

1. **Who?** (Think of a real or fictional person's name, from books, real life, or movies—or even your own mother—such as: **The Stinky Cheese Man** or **Elvis Presley**.)

2. **Did What?** (Describe an activity, using an action verb, such as: **climbed Mount Everest** or **baked a cake**.)

3. **With Whom?** (Think of another real or fictional person's name, and use the preposition "with", such as: **with Cinderella** or **with George Washington**.)

4. **Where?** (Think of a place or a location, and start with a preposition like "in" or "on", such as: **on the back of a chicken** or **in Nome, Alaska**.)

5. **When?** (Give a time, such as: **last Tuesday** or **in 1776**.)

6. **Why?** (Give a reason, starting with the word "because", such as: **because roses are red and violets are blue** or **because I said so**.)

7. **And all the people said. . .** (Think of a quote, and start it with the words, "And all the people said", such as: **And all the people said,"To be or not to be. That is the question."**)

8. Unfold your paper and let's share our new tall tales.

And here is the final, composite, cheerfully absurd, tall tale sentence, as composed by seven individual writers:

> **The Stinky Cheese Man**
>
> **climbed Mount Everest**
>
> **with Cinderella**
>
> **on the back of a chicken**
>
> **last Tuesday**
>
> **because roses are red and violets are blue**
>
> **and all the people said,**
>
> **"To be or not to be. That is the question."**

From *Once Upon a Time: Using Storytelling, Creative Drama, and Reader's Theater with Children in Grades PreK-6* by Judy Freeman. Westport, CT: Libraries Unlimited. Copyright © 2007.

A Sampling of Tales to Compare and Contrast

Take a well-known folktale that has been retold in many versions, such as "The Gingerbread Boy," "Little Red Riding Hood," or "Rumpelstiltskin," or, of course, "Cinderella." You can use the following ideas and the lists of versions, variants, and parodies below to get you started in planning a folklore unit.

ACTIVITIES:

1. Read aloud as many of the different variants of each story as you can find.   Ask your listeners to compare and contrast:

   a. details common to each stories
   b. similarities and differences in each story's plot
   c. illustrations in terms of style and appeal
   d. clothing and dress of the characters
   e. settings of each story
   f. regional or national characteristics
   g. chants or repeated phrases
   h. beginnings and endings
   i. characters

2. Have your children break into small groups to compare and contrast two or more versions of a story, making a chart or Venn diagram of the similarities and differences. Have them present their findings to the whole group.

3. Write up a story as a Reader's Theater for children to read and act out, or have each group act out one story and then put it on for the rest of the class. Children in grades two and up can write their own Reader's Theater adaptations from a story, too.

4. Read a modern day parody of the story and analyze the elements of it that were taken from the original story. How did the author change the story? What was the same?

5. After reading stories and their parodies, have children read another well-known folk or fairy tale and have them write and illustrate a parody.

Looking for Other Versions, Variants, & Parodies

"RUNAWAY FOOD" STORIES

***The Gingerbread Boy*. Egielski, Richard. Illus. by the author. HarperCollins, 1997. (Gr. PreK-1)**

Set in New York City, this urban rendition of "The Gingerbread Boy" is just right to act out.
GERM: There's even a gingerbread cookie recipe included in this version of the classic chasing story, which you might want to try as a group project.

SOME RELATED TITLES

Armour, Peter. *Stop That Pickle*. Houghton, 1993. (*parody*)

Aylesworth, Jim. *The Gingerbread Man*. Scholastic, 1998.

Cauley, Lorinda Bryan. *The Pancake Boy: An Old Norwegian Folk Tale*. Putnam, 1988.

Cook, Scott. *The Gingerbread Boy*. Knopf, 1987.

Esterl, Arnica. *The Fine Round Cake*. Four Winds, 1991.

Galdone, Paul. *The Gingerbread Boy*. Clarion, 1979.

Ginsburg, Mirra. *The Clay Boy*. Greenwillow, 1997.

Howland, Naomi. *The Matzah Man: A Passover Story*. Clarion , 2002.

Kimmel, Eric A. *The Gingerbread Man*. Holiday House, 1993.

Sawyer, Ruth. *Journey Cake, Ho!* Puffin, 1978.

Scieszka, Jon. *The Stinky Cheese Man and Other Fairly Stupid Tales*. Viking, 1992. (*parody*)

Sierra, Judy. "Runaway Cookies" from *Nursery Tales Around the World*. Clarion, 1996.

"SWALLOWING" STORIES

***Clay Boy*. Ginsburg, Mirra. Illus. by Jos. A. Smith. Greenwillow, 1997. (Gr. PreK-2)**

Grandpa fashions a little boy made of clay but the greedy creature demands more food and begins to swallow everything in sight.
GERM: Listeners can create their own children figures out of clay and act out the story together.

SOME RELATED TITLES

Baumgartner, Barbara. *Crocodile! Crocodile!: Stories Told Around the World*. DK, 1994.

Chase, Richard. "Sody Sallyraytus" from *Grandfather Tales*. Houghton, 1948.

Compton, Joanne. *Sody Sallyratus*. Holiday House, 1995.

Galdone, Paul. *The Greedy Old Fat Man*. Clarion, 1983.

Haviland, Virginia. "The Cat and the Parrot" from *Favorite Fairy Tales Told in India*. Little, Brown, 1973.

Jackson, Alison. *I Know an Old Lady Who Swallowed a Pie*. Dutton, 1997. (*parody*)

Karas, G. Brian. *I Know an Old Lady*. Scholastic, 1984.

Kent, Jack. *The Fat Cat*. Scholastic, 1972.

Kesey, Ken. *Little Tricker the Squirrel Meets Big Double the Bear.* Viking, 1990.

Polette, Nancy. *The Little Old Woman and the Hungry Cat.* Greenwillow, 1989.

Prelutsky, Jack. *The Terrible Tiger.* Macmillan, 1989.

Rascol, Sabina I. *The Impudent Rooster.* Dutton, 2004.

Rounds, Glen. *I Know an Old Lady Who Swallowed a Fly.* Holiday House, 1990.

Sierra, Judy. "Incredible Appetites" from *Nursery Tales Around the World.* Clarion, 1996.

Sloat, Teri. *Sody Sallyratus.* Dutton, 1997.

So, Meilo. *Gobble, Gobble, Slip, Slop: The Tale of a Very Greedy Cat.* Knopf, 2004.

Taback, Simms. *There Was an Old Lady Who Swallowed a Fly.* Viking, 1997.

Westcott, Nadine Bernard. *I Know an Old Lady Who Swallowed a Fly.* Little, Brown, 1980

"WHO IS THE STRONGEST OR SMARTEST?" STORIES

Mouse Match. **Young, Ed. Silver Whistle/Harcourt, 1997. (Gr. 1-6)**

Young presents a unique retelling of the Chinese variant of the folktale "The Mouse Bride," illustrated as a 16-foot mural in a codex or accordion book format.
GERM: As you read the story, you will open up each panel. Have children come up and help you hold the book. Then have them turn it over to examine the entire text written in Chinese characters. Lay the opened book on the floor or propped upon two long tables to display the whole mural.

SOME RELATED TITLES

Climo, Shirley. *The Little Red Ant and the Great Big Crumb: A Mexican Fable.* Clarion, 1995.

Cook, Joel. *The Rat's Daughter.* Boyds Mills, 1993.

Courlander, Harold. "The Marriage of the Mouse" from *Fire on the Mountain and Other Stories of Ethiopia and Eritrea.* Henry Holt, 1950.

Demi. *Buddha Stories.* Henry Holt, 1997.

Demi. *The Stonecutter.* Crown, 1995.

Dupré, Judith. *The Mouse Bride: A Mayan Folk Tale.* Knopf, 1993.

Hurlimann, Ruth. *The Proud White Cat.* Morrow, 1977.

Kimmel, Eric A. *The Greatest of All: A Japanese Folktale.* Holiday House, 1991.

Kimmel, Eric A. *Ten Suns: A Chinese Legend.* Holiday House, 1998.

Kwon, Holly H. *The Moles and the Mireuk.* Houghton Mifflin, 1993.

McDermott, Gerald. *The Stonecutter: A Japanese Folk Tale.* Puffin, 1978.

Olaleye, Isaac O. *In the Rainfield: Who Is the Greatest?* Scholastic, 2000.

"DISOBEYING MOTHER'S ADVICE" STORIES

Little Red Riding Hood. **Grimm, Jacob. Retold and illus. by Trina Schart Hyman. Holiday House, 1983. (Gr. PreK-2)**

This somber retelling of the German folktale won Hyman a Caldecott Honor for her lyrical illustrations.
GERM: In pairs, children can act out the climactic "But, Grandma" scene.

SOME RELATED TITLES

Artell, Mike. *Petite Rouge: A Cajun Red Riding Hood.* Dial, 2001. (*parody*)

Emberly, Michael. *Ruby.* Little, Brown, 1990. (*parody*)

Ernst, Lisa Campbell. *Little Red Riding Hood: A Newfangled Prairie Tale.* Simon & Schuster, 1995. (*parody*)

Galdone, Paul. *Little Red Riding Hood.* McGraw-Hill, 1974.

Grimm, Jacob. *Little Red Cap.* Illus. by Lisbeth Zwerger. Morrow, 1983.

Harper, Wilhelmina. *The Gunniwolf.* Dutton, 1978.

Lowell, Susan. *Little Red Cowboy Hat.* Henry Holt, 1997. (*parody*)

Marcantonio, Patricia Santos. *Red Ridin' in the Hood: And Other Cuentos.* Farrar, 2005. (*parody*)

Marshall, James. *Red Riding Hood.* Dial, 1987.

Meddaugh, Susan. *Hog-Eye.* Houghton Mifflin, 1995. (*parody*)

Young, Ed. *Lon Po Po: A Red Riding Hood Story from China.* Philomel, 1989.

"GOOD SISTER/BAD SISTER" STORIES

The Talking Eggs. San Souci, Robert D. Illus. by Jerry Pinkney. Dial, 1989. (Gr. K-4)

In an African American tale, sweet Blanche is rewarded for her kindness to a strange old woman, while mean sister Rose is punished for her nasty ways.

GERM: Have listeners predict what they think Rose will do when she meets the old woman and what the consequences will be.

SOME RELATED TITLES

Alexander, Lloyd. *How the Cat Swallowed Thunder.* Dutton, 2000.

Aliki. *The Twelve Months.* Greenwillow, 1978.

Bender, Robert. *Toads and Diamonds.* Dutton, 1995.

De Regniers, Beatrice Schenk. *Little Sister and the Month Brothers.* Clarion, 1976.

Huck, Charlotte. *Toads and Diamonds.* Greenwillow, 1996.

Levine, Gail Carson. *The Fairy's Mistake.* HarperCollins, 1999. (*parody*)

Marshak, Samuel. *The Month Brothers.* Morrow, 1983.

Onyefulu, Obi. *Chinye: A West African Folk Tale.* Viking, 1994.

Steptoe, John. *Mufaro's Beautiful Daughters.* Lothrop, 1987.

Watts, Bernadine. *Mother Holly.* Crowell, 1972.

Winthrop, Elizabeth. *Vasilissa the Beautiful.* HarperCollins, 1991.

"LOCKED IN A TOWER" STORIES

Rapunzel. Zelinsky, Paul O. Illus. by the author. Dutton, 1997. (Gr. 2-6)

Winner of the 1998 Caldecott Medal, this version of the fairy tale, with Italianate-style paintings, is breathtaking.

GERM: Compare and contrast the trials and tribulations of princesses and princess-like heroines, such as Rapunzel, Snow White, Sleeping Beauty, and Cinderella.

SOME RELATED TITLES

Berenzy, Alix. *Rapunzel.* Henry Holt, 1995.

Ehrlich, Amy. *Rapunzel.* Dial, 1989.

Kindl, Patrice. *Goose Chase.* Houghton, 2001. Gr. 4-8 (*parody*)

Napoli, Donna Jo. *Zel.* Dutton, 1996. Gr. 8-12

Nesbit, E. *Melisande.* Harcourt, 1989.

Nones, Eric Jon. *The Canary Prince.* Farrar, 1991.

Rogasky, Barbara. *Rapunzel.* Holiday House, 1982.

San Souci, Daniel D. *The Tsar's Promise.* Philomel, 1992.

Stanley, Diane. *Petrosinella: A Neapolitan Rapunzel.* Dial, 1995.

Vozar, David. *Rapunzel: A Happenin' Rap.* Doubleday, 1998. (*parody*)

Wilcox, Leah. *Falling for Rapunzel.* Putnam, 2003. (*parody*)

"GUESS MY NAME" STORIES
Rumpelstiltskin. **Zelinsky, Paul O. Illus. by the author. Dutton, 1986. (Gr. 2-6)**

Winner of a Caldecott Honor, here is another Grimm version of the fairy tale about the little gold-spinning man.

GERM: Children can retell the story from the point of view of Rumpelstiltskin, the miller's daughter, the king, and the fellow who discovers the little man's real name.

SOME RELATED TITLES

Galdone, Paul. *Rumpelstiltskin.* Clarion, 1985.

Hamilton, Virginia. *The Girl Who Spun Gold.* Blue Sky/Scholastic, 2000.

Haviland, Virginia. "The Widow's Lazy Daughter" from *Favorite Fairy Tales Told in Ireland.* Little, Brown, 1961.

Ness, Evaline. *Tom Tit Tot.* Scribner, 1965.

Sage, Alison. *Rumpelstiltskin.* Dial, 1990.

San Souci, Daniel D. *The Tsar's Promise.* Philomel, 1992.

Sierra, Judy. *Can You Guess My Name?: Traditional Tales Around the World.* Clarion, 2002.

Stanley, Diane. *Rumpelstiltskin's Daughter.* Morrow, 1997. (*parody*)

Tarcov, Edith. *Rumpelstiltskin.* Four Winds, 1973.

White, Carolyn. *Whuppity Stoorie: A Scottish Folktale.* Putnam, 1997.

Zemach, Harve. *Duffy and the Devil.* Farrar, 1986.

Looking at Cinderella

Reprinted and updated from *Books Kids Will Sit Still For 3: A Read-Aloud Guide* by Judy Freeman (Libraries Unlimited, 2006).

When you ask students to compare and contrast elements of stories, one of the most interesting fairy tales to delve into in some detail is the world's most ubiquitous: "Cinderella." Ask your listeners first to tell you the story as they know it. (This may be the Disney movie version.) Next, read or tell a standard, familiar version, followed with a version from a non-European country. Together, your class can compare and contrast characters, setting, plot, motifs, theme, and style of both stories. Finally, small groups can read other versions and make charts showing the differences and similarities. Below are some elements to consider.

COMPARE AND CONTRAST:

Characters

- Cinderella's name
- Cinderella's physical appearance
- Cinderella's personality
- "Prince Charming"
- Fairy godmother
- Other characters (father, stepmother as villain, stepsiblings, fairy godmother type, etc.)
- Relationship of main characters (names and relation to "Cinderella" character)

Setting

- Country of origin
- Cinderella's house
- Place the party or ball is held

Plot

- How Cinderella's life changes
- Cinderella's work and her place in the family; stepsisters' treatment of Cinderella
- Cinderella's assigned tasks to perform at home before or during the ball
- How the fairy godmother helps Cinderella

Climax

- What happens to Cinderella at the ball, party, dance, or celebration
- How Cinderella is found by the prince afterwards
- Endings (What happens to her and to her family)

Motifs

- Lost shoes (what they are made from: glass, gold, straw, etc.)
- Clothing (from rags to finery)
- Magical godmother (human or animal)
- Other magical objects or characters (wands, rats, pumpkins, etc.)
- Magical powers or transformations
- Beginnings and endings (Once upon a time; happily ever after, and variations)
- Use of magical numbers (3, 7, etc.)

Theme

- How does good win out over evil?
- What lessons or morals are stated or implicit in the story?

Style and Format of the Retelling

- Language style and how it reflects the country of origin
- Illustrations

ADDITIONAL CINDERELLA LESSON IDEAS

GEOGRAPHY: Keep a globe handy to show the origins of versions of Cinderella from other countries and ask listeners how the story changed in each particular country.

FOOD TIE-INS: For a quick story-related snack, hand out toasted pumpkin seeds.

CREATIVE DRAMA: Conduct interviews with students posing as characters in the story. Holding a real microphone (and taping the proceedings if you like), ask each character a variety of questions, giving students the opportunity to range from yes or no answers to ones that require synthesis and analysis of a character's motives. *If the Shoe Fits: Voices from Cinderella* by Laura Whipple, told in poetry, examines the story from each character's vantage point.

POINT OF VIEW: As a warm-up to interviewing, have children get into character by repeating the following statement from a variety of points of view:

"Cinderella went to the ball."

How would each of these characters utter that sentence: the prince, the stepsisters, the fairy godmother, Cinderella, a dancer at the ball, the stepmother, an innocent bystander?

Next have them repeat the same sentence, but using different emotional shadings. Have them say it: disgustedly, jealously, angrily, delightedly, indifferently, quizzically, sarcastically, disappointedly, pityingly, sadly, and eagerly.

WRITING ACTIVITY: Write a Cinderella story that takes place in another time and place, using research to get the supporting details right.

RESEARCH ACTIVITY: When students are researching countries of the world, have them also explore the folklore of their countries.

AND FINALLY, AN URBAN JUMP ROPE RHYME

Cinderella, dressed in yella,
Went downtown to meet her fella;
On her way, her girdle busted,
How many people were disgusted?

CINDERELLA VARIANTS: A BOOKLIST

Here are but a handful of the hundreds of Cinderella variants worldwide. For more information on the story and its variants, go to the SurLaLune Fairy Tales website at **www.surlalunefairytales.com.**

Adelita: A Mexican Cinderella Story by Tomie dePaola. Putnam, 2002. (Mexico)

Ashpet: An Appalachian Tale by Joanne Compton, illus. by Kenn Compton. Holiday House, 1994. (United States)

Cendrillon: A Caribbean Cinderella by Robert D. San Souci, illus. by Brian Pinkney. Simon & Schuster, 1998. (Martinique)

Cinderella by K. Y. Craft. SeaStar, 2000. (France)

Cinderella by Paul Galdone. McGraw-Hill, 1978. (France)

Cinderella by Nonny Hogrogian. Greenwillow, 1981. (Germany)

Cinderella by Barbara Karlin, illus. by James Marshall. Little, Brown, 1989. (France)

Cinderella by Barbara McClintock. Scholastic, 2005. (France)

Cinderella: or, The Little Glass Slipper by Marcia Brown. Scribner, 1954. (France)

The Egyptian Cinderella by Shirley Climo, illus. by Ruth Heller. HarperCollins, 1993. (Egypt)

Favorite Fairy Tales Told in Italy by Virginia Haviland. Little, Brown, 1965. ("Cenerentola"; Italy)

The Gift of the Crocodile: A Cinderella Story by Judy Sierra, illus. by Reynold Ruffins. Simon & Schuster, 2000. (Indonesia)

The Golden Sandal: A Middle Eastern Cinderella Story by Rebecca Hickox, illus. by Will Hillenbrand. Holiday House, 1998. (Iraq)

In the Land of Small Dragon by Dang Manh Kha, illus. by Tony Chen. Viking, 1979. (Vietnam)

The Irish Cinderlad by Shirley Climo, illus. by Loretta Krupinski. HarperCollins, 1996. (Ireland)

Jouanah: A Hmong Cinderella by Jewell Reinhart Coburn, illus. by Anne Sibley O'Brien. Shen's Books, 1996. (Laos)

Kong and Potgi: A Cinderella Story from Korea by Oki S. Han and Stephanie Haboush Plunkett, illus. by Oki S. Han. Dial, 1996. (Korea)

The Korean Cinderella by Shirley Climo, illus. by Ruth Heller. HarperCollins, 1993. (Korea)

Moss Gown by William H. Hooks, illus. by Donald Carrick. Clarion, 1987. (United States)

Mufaro's Beautiful Daughters by John Steptoe. Lothrop, 1987. (Africa)

Oryx Multicultural Folktale Series: Cinderella by Judy Sierra. Oryx, 1992. (Various countries)

The Persian Cinderella by Shirley Climo, illus. by Robert Florczak. HarperCollins, 1999. (Iran)

Princess Furball by Charlotte Huck, illus. by Anita Lobel. Greenwillow, 1989. (United States)

The Rough-Face Girl by Rafe Martin, illus. by David Shannon. Putnam, 1992. (Native American)

Smoky Mountain Rose: An Appalachian Cinderella by Alan Schroeder, illus. by Brad Sneed. Dial, 1997. (United States)

Sootface: An Ojibwa Cinderella Story by Robert D. San Souci, illus. by Daniel San Souci. Doubleday, 1994. (Native American)

Sukey and the Mermaid by Robert D. San Souci, illus. by Brian Pinkney. Four Winds, 1992. (United States)

Tattercoats: An Old English Tale by Flora Annie Steele, illus. by Diane Goode. Bradbury, 1976. (England)

The Turkey Girl: A Zuni Cinderella Story by Penny Pollock, illus. by Ed Young. Little, Brown, 1996. (Native American)

The Way Meat Loves Salt: A Cinderella Tale from the Jewish Tradition by Nina Jaffe, illus. by Louise August. Henry Holt, 1998. (Jewish)

Wishbones: A Folk Tale from China by Barbara Ker Wilson, illus. by Meilo So. Bradbury, 1993. (China)

Yeh-Shen by Ai-Ling Louie, illus. by Ed Young. Philomel, 1982. (China)

From *Once Upon a Time: Using Storytelling, Creative Drama, and Reader's Theater with Children in Grades PreK-6* by Judy Freeman. Westport, CT: Libraries Unlimited. Copyright © 2007.

SOME CINDERELLA PARODIES AND UPDATES

Bella at Midnight by Diane Stanley. HarperCollins, 2006.

Bigfoot Cinderrrrrella by Tony Johnston, illus. by James Warhola. Putnam, 1998.

Bubba the Cowboy Prince: A Fractured Texas Tale by Helen Ketteman, illus. by James Warhola. Scholastic, 1997.

Cinder Edna by Ellen Jackson, illus. by Kevin O'Malley. Lothrop, 1994.

Cinderella by William Wegman. Hyperion, 1993.

Cinderella Skeleton by Robert D. San Souci, illus. by David Catrow. Harcourt, 2000.

Cinder-Elly by Frances Minters, illus. by G. Brian Karas. Viking, 1993.

Cinderlily: A Floral Fairy Tale by Christine Tagg, illus. by David Ellwand. Candlewick, 2003.

Cindy Ellen: A Wild Western Cinderella by Susan Lowell. Orchard, 1997.

Dinorella: A Prehistoric Fairy Tale by Pamela Duncan Edwards, illus. by Henry Cole. Hyperion, 1997.

Ella Enchanted by Gail Carson Levine. HarperCollins, 1997.

Ella's Big Chance: A Jazz-Age Cinderella by Shirley Hughes. Simon & Schuster, 2004.

Fanny's Dream by Caralyn Buehner, illus. by Mark Buehner. Dial, 1996.

I Was a Rat by Philip Pullman, illus. by Kevin Hawkes. Knopf, 2000.

If the Shoe Fits: Voices from Cinderella by Laura Whipple; illus. by Laura Beingessner. McElderry, 2002.

Prince Cinders by Babette Cole. Putnam, 1997.

"Prinderella and the Cince", retold by Judy Freeman in *Hi Ho Librario!: Songs, Chants and Stories to Keep Kids Humming*. Rock Hill Press, 1997. (For the text, see page 105 of this book.)

Sidney Rella and the Glass Sneaker by Bernice Myers. Macmillan, 1985.

CINDERELLA WEBSITES

FOLKLORE AND MYTHOLOGY ELECTRONIC TEXTS

On D. L. Ashliman's comprehensive folklore site, find the texts to 16 Cinderella variants worldwide. **http://www.pitt.edu/~dash/type0510a.html.**

SURLALUNE FAIRY TALES

Includes an annotated version of the tale from Andrew Lang's *The Blue Fairy Book* published in 1889; from the book *Cinderella* by Marian Roalfe Cox, published in 1893, detailed abstracts of 345 Cinderella variants; dozens of reproductions of classic illustrations and cover art of scores of children's books of the story. **http://www.surlalunefairytales.com/cinderella/index.html.**

WIKIPEDIA

Quite a thorough analysis of origins and history, plot and variations, a discussion of the story, and a list of adaptations. **http://en.wikipedia.org/wiki/Cinderella.**

Creating Literature Teaching Guides

I require my graduate students in the children's literature and storytelling classes to do a literature teaching guide so they can see what it's like to delve into a book and think of viable possibilities to try with children. Keep a file of your own guides and use it like a recipe book. It's always rewarding to go back and try something new. It's helpful to write up a guide to a book or a story you know you'll be using again and again with children.

Use the format below to clarify the discussion points and questions, ideas and activities, and related titles and stories to use with children. This doesn't mean you will ask every question or do every creative activity or share every book. It's up to you as a teacher to figure out just how much you plan to do.

Here's a sample.

LITERATURE TEACHING GUIDE

AUTHOR: Salley, Coleen
TITLE: *Epossumondas*
ILLUSTRATOR/PUBLISHER & DATE: Illus. by Janet Stevens. Harcourt, 2002.
GRADE and / or INTEREST LEVELS: Grades PreK-2
GENERAL THEMES AND RELATED TOPICS: ANIMALS. AUNTS. BEHAVIOR. CHANTABLE REFRAIN. CREATIVE DRAMA. FOLKLORE—U.S. FOOLS AND JESTERS. HUMOROUS STORIES. MISTAKES. MOTHERS AND SONS. NOODLEHEAD STORIES. OPOSSUMS. READER'S THEATER.

PLOT SUMMARY/DESCRIPTION OF ILLUSTRATIONS:

Every time sweet little patootie, Epossumondas, visits his auntie, she gives him something to take home, and each time he carries it home the wrong way. His exasperated Mama says, "Epossumondas, you don't have the sense you were born with." Storyteller and former children's literature professor Coleen Salley has refashioned the noodlehead story "Epaminondas" to reflect her New Orleans background, with an alligator, a raccoon, a nutria, and an armadillo each encountering the foolish opossum as he heads on home. In her huge affable watercolor and color-pencil illustrations, Janet Stevens has depicted Coleen herself, in large flowered dress, pillbox hat, and purple specs, in the parts of Mama and Auntie.

DISCUSSION POINTS AND / OR POSSIBLE QUESTIONS:

- As you read the story aloud, each time Epossumondas tries to bring something home, ask your listeners to predict what they think he will do with that object.

- Why does Epossumondas keep making mistakes?

- What does his mother mean when she says, "You don't have the sense you were born with."?

- Before finishing the story, ask: What does Auntie mean when she says, "Well, Epossumondas, you be careful about stepping on those pies." What do you think he'll do now?

- Have children retell the story and describe, in sequence, each mistake Epossumondas makes.

- Have you ever misunderstood directions and done something all wrong? What happened?

ACTIVITIES:

- This uproarious story will have your listeners chiming in on every refrain. It begs to be retold with props and puppets and a story apron to put them in, which you can make or buy from Mimi's Motifs at **www.mimismotifs.com**. It's also a natural to act out in creative drama or script as a Reader's Theater.

- Listeners can talk about what it means to take something literally. Bring in a nice pie so everyone can have a bite.

- Once the children have heard the story, have them retell it, and then break them into groups of three. (While either boys or girls can take the part of Epossumondas, boys will be more comfortable changing their parts to be fathers or uncles. The person who plays the aunt or uncle can also play all the animals who meet Epossumondas on his way home.) Have each trio find a private spot in the room where they can act out the whole story together, with dialogue.

- Ask your children, "What do you think his Mama will say or do when she gets home and sees those six pies with footprints in them?" Have them draw a picture of her reaction. Have them caption it: "When his mama came home, she said, . . ." and then finish the sentence.

- Sing "I'm Bringing Home a Baby Bumblebee." (See page 51 for Judy Freeman's updated verses).

- Marisa Montes's *Juan Bobo Goes to Work* is a Puerto Rican variant. Follow up with Salley's sequels, *Why Epossumondas Has No Hair on His Tail* (a reworking of a Brer Rabbit story) and *Epossumondas Saves the Day* (a new version of the old story "Sody Sallyratus").

RELATED BOOKS &/OR MATERIALS:

For more about the author, Coleen Salley, go to **www.coleensalley.com.**

For more about the illustrator, Janet Stevens, go to **www.janetstevens.com**.

Birdseye, Tom. *Soap! Soap! Don't Forget the Soap!: An Appalachian Folktale.* Holiday, 1993.

Edwards, Roberta. *Five Silly Fishermen.* Random House, 1989.

French, Vivian. *Lazy Jack.* Candlewick, 1995.

Maitland, Anthony. *Idle Jack.* Farrar, 1979.

Miranda, Anne. *To Market, To Market.* Harcourt, 1997.

Montes, Marisa. *Juan Bobo Goes to Work: A Puerto Rican Folktale.* HarperCollins, 2000.

Pitre, Felix. *Juan Bobo and the Pig: A Puerto Rican Folktale.* Lodestar, 1993.

Salley, Coleen. *Epossumondas Saves the Day.* Harcourt, 2006. (Go to www.harcourtbooks.com, type in the title or author in the search bar, and you can listen to the author tell the story.)

Salley, Coleen. *Why Epossumondas Has No Hair on his Tail.* Harcourt, 2004.

Schaefer, Carole Lexa. *The Biggest Soap.* Farrar, 2004.

Snyder, Dianne. *The Boy of the Three-Year Nap.* Houghton, 1988.

Stevens, Janet. *Tops & Bottoms.* Harcourt, 1995

Stevens, Janet, and Susan Stevens Crummel. *And the Dish Ran Away with the Spoon.* Harcourt, 2001.

Stevens, Janet, and Susan Stevens Crummel. *Cook-a-Doodle-Doo!* Harcourt, Brace, 1999.

How Well Do You Know Your Fairy Tales?

Many children have no concept as to what makes a story a fairy tale, so you may need to start from scratch. After you ask each question below, whether or not your listeners know the answer, hold up a book version of that tale and hand it out to interested readers. Notice how Eurocentric these tales are, for the most part? Be sure to introduce your students to fairy tales from all of the other continents (except for one). (And ask them if they can name the continent that has no stories. Penguins don't tell tales.)

1. IN WHAT FAIRY TALE does a princess spend her formative years locked in a tower growing her hair?

2. IN WHAT FAIRY TALE does a princess prick her finger on a spindle on her 16th birthday and take a very long nap?

3. IN WHAT FAIRY TALE does a boy steal a giant's harp and a hen that lays golden eggs?

4. IN WHAT FAIRY TALE does a princess accidentally drop her golden ball into a well, and accept the help of an amphibian to retrieve it?

5. IN WHAT FAIRY TALE does a soldier use his cloak of invisibility to follow a king's daughters at night to find out why their shoes keep wearing out?

6. IN WHAT FAIRY TALE does a Russian witch with iron teeth live in a house on chicken legs and ride through the sky in a mortar and pestle?

7. IN WHAT FAIRY TALE does a boy outsmart a powerful magician pretending to be his uncle, and summon a genie who makes him rich.

8. IN WHAT FAIRY TALE does a girl set off to find her true love, a white bear by day and a man by night, before he can marry a troll princess?

9. IN WHAT FAIRY TALE does a miller's idle boast lead to his daughter being locked in a room at the local castle to spend the night with a spinning wheel?

10. IN WHAT FAIRY TALE does a girl's stepmother arrange to have her taken into the forest by a woodsman and killed, just because a talking mirror said the girl was the fairest of them all?

11. IN WHAT FAIRY TALE do a brother and sister get lost in a forest and find a gingerbread house belonging to a witch?

12. IN WHAT FAIRY TALE does a poor young lad pass himself off to the king as the Marquis of Carabas, take over an ogre's castle, and win the hand of a princess, thanks to his clever cat?

13. IN WHAT FAIRY TALE does a man open the door to a robbers' cave with the words, "Open, Sesame"?

14. IN WHAT FAIRY TALE does an enchanted fish give an ungrateful woman a new house, which only makes her want more?

15. IN WHAT FAIRY TALE does a merchant's youngest daughter agree to move to the palace of a hideous creature who wants her to say she'll marry him?

From *Once Upon a Time: Using Storytelling, Creative Drama, and Reader's Theater with Children in Grades PreK-6* by Judy Freeman. Westport, CT: Libraries Unlimited. Copyright © 2007.

HOW WELL DO YOU KNOW YOUR FAIRY TALES? ANSWERS

1. "Rapunzel"
2. "Sleeping Beauty"
3. "Jack and the Beanstalk"
4. "The Frog Prince"
5. "The Twelve Dancing Princesses"
6. "Baba Yaga"
7. "Aladdin and the Magic Lamp"
8. "East of the Sun and West of the Moon" (or its American variant, "Whitebear Whittington")
9. "Rumpelstiltskin"
10. "Snow White"
11. "Hansel and Gretel"
12. "Puss in Boots"
13. "Ali Baba and the 40 Thieves"
14. "The Fisherman and His Wife"
15. "Beauty and the Beast"

Judy Freeman's Songbook

Including Songs, Chants, Riddles, and Plenty of Nonsense

I've been collecting stories, songs, chants, jokes, tongue twisters, and crazy bits of nonsense all my life. (Knock knock. Who's there? Cargo. Cargo who? Cargo BEEP BEEP.) I come from a family where everyone loved to sing and we all could carry a tune. Singing was just something we did.

My mother warbled standards from the 30s and 40s. She knew them all. She made up her own words when she couldn't recall a phrase, or threw in foreign ones, so I grew up thinking that a lot of songs had some pretty strange lyrics. There was "I've been around the world in a plane, seen revoluciones in Spain," and "The little breeze avec the trees tendrement." (What a surprise when I learned the real words: "The evening breeze caressed the trees tenderly.)

In the last years of her life, when emphysema rendered her voice breathless, she could still produce a piercing whistle for surprising lengths of time, which drove everyone crazy as she went through her repertoire. Every time I hear one of her many favorite tunes on the radio, I stop and listen. "That's a Gladys song," I say, wistfully.

My father whistled, too, and was the best joke teller I knew, with an endless supply. He was a traveling dress salesman, and, as such, felt obligated to regale the buyers at the stores he visited with outrageous jokes on a regular basis. He tried them out on us, too, which we often appreciated.

My brother Richard, the jazz nut, played guitar, clarinet, and sax, and spent lots of time pounding on old upright pianos. When I was in seventh grade, he came home from college for a visit, his hair shaggy and wild, and played guitar and sang at my birthday party. Most of my friends looked stunned. They'd never heard singing and growling all mingled like that, I guess. I thought he was amazingly cool.

My sister Sharron and I both played the guitar, too. We went to summer camp together, and became counselors in our teens, and played hundreds of camp songs at campfires and in our bunks. We haven't forgotten too many of them. These days, I can't remember new lyrics to save my life, but I can sing every verse of "The Cat Came Back" and "Andy Koochy Katchy Kama Tosaneera Tosanova Sammy Kammy Wacky Brown," a song most reminiscent of the story "Tikki Tikki Tembo."

When I became an elementary school librarian, I incorporated music, songs, poetry, and drama into every aspect of my program. I harvested all of those songs from my youth and sang them with my students. It seems to me the most effective way to get children reading is to immerse them in language in as many ways as possible.

If you want your children to work on their fluency, or, as my mother used to put it, "Don't-read-it-one-word-at-a-time," then start singing. Every time you sing a song, hand out the words for children to follow as they sing, even if it's a song they know. They can't sing it one word at a time; keeping up with the song ensures that their eyes will move more quickly and efficiently from left to right over the printed page. You've heard of Reader's Theater? Call this version Singer's Theater.

I've included lots of my favorite songs and chants and nonsense here, which you can borrow and try out with your kids. (If you play the guitar, I've put in chords, too.) And maybe they'll remember them when they grow up and pass them along to their kids.

LOOK FOR 398.2

By Judy Freeman, © 1980.

If you want a good story, let me tell you what to do—
LOOK FOR 398.2, LOOK FOR 398.2!

Prince or princess in hot water, trouble with a witch's brew—
LOOK FOR 398.2, LOOK FOR 398.2!

Fierce and fire-breathing dragons, shiny scales of green and blue—
LOOK FOR 398.2, LOOK FOR 398.2!

Ogres, leprechauns, and goblins all are waiting just for you—
LOOK FOR 398.2, LOOK FOR 398.2!

Find a tale from every country, from Australia to Peru—
LOOK FOR 398.2, LOOK FOR 398.2!

STORYTELLER'S NOTE

Snap your fingers as you recite this tongue-twisting little rap, and have children chant the refrain with you each time. When I was a school librarian, every child in my school knew "Miss Freeman's favorite number, 398.2." This chant helped them remember the number and why it was important. Fairy tales tend to be be overlooked on the shelves unless you make sure children know they're there and they're wonderful. I call folk and fairy tales "the original fiction" from back in the days before people wrote everything down. Make them a regular part of your literature program and across the curriculum.

FOOLING AROUND WITH NURSERY RHYMES

ROCKABYE BABY

(First verse traditional; second verse by Sarah Vesuvio's grandfather; third verse by Judy Freeman)

```
D                        A7
Rockabye baby, on the treetop

                         D      A7
When the bough bends, the cradle will rock;

D           A7      D        G
When the bough breaks, the cradle will fall,

    D                E7   A  D
And down will come baby cradle and all.
```

Rockabye baby, upon the moon
Eating her cornflakes, with a big spoon;
When the wind blows, the moon it will break,
And down will come baby on a cornflake.

Rockabye baby, up in the stars
Waving to Earth, and waving to Mars;
When the stars shine, the sky will be bright,
And down will come baby with a night light.

STORYTELLER'S NOTE

Sarah Vesuvio, then a fifth grader, sang to me a new verse of "Rockabye Baby" that she said her grandfather had written. So I wrote a verse, too, just for fun. See if you and your students can write a new one to sing.

IT'S RAINING, IT'S POURING

(First verse traditional; second and third verse by Judy Freeman, © 2004. You can hear an instrumental version online at: **www.nurseryrhymes4u.com/NURSERY_RHYMES/Page_339.html**.)

      A
It's raining, it's pouring, the old man is snoring;
Bumped his head when he went to bed,
And he couldn't get up till the morning.

D A D A   D A   E A
Rain, rain, go away, come again some other day.

It's thundering, it's lightning, it's loud and it's frightening;
But I'm not scared and you're not scared,
For the sky will soon be brightening.
Rain, rain, go away, come again some other day.

It's stopping, it's drying, the rain has gone goodbye-ing;
No more storm, now the sun is warm;
And the birds are up there flying.
Rain, rain, go away, come again some other day.

STORYTELLER'S NOTE

Sing this song on a rainy day. Follow up with a rain-based story or two like Manya Stojic's *Rain* (Crown, 2000) or Amy Hest's *In the Rain with Baby Duck* (Candlewick, 1995). Then tell the paperfolding story on page 94, "The Rainhat." The rainstorm activity on page 56 will round out the program nicely with a nice bit of noise.

THREE MYOPIC RODENTS

(First verse anonymous, second verse © 1980 by Judy Freeman; to the tune of "Three Blind Mice")

```
A    E   A      E    A
Three myopic rodents, three myopic rodents,

          E      A                E     A
Observe how they perambulate, observe how they perambulate;

              E            A          E
They all circumnavigated the agriculturalist's spouse;

       A            E       A      E
She excised their extremities with a carving utensil;

         A   E        A            D
Did you ever observe such an occurrence in your existence

       A   E  A
As three myopic rodents.
```

Now take your thesaurus, now take your thesaurus,
Find a dictionary, find a dictionary;
Pick a nursery rhyme that appeals to you;
Take out all the words, put in synonyms, do;
Set Mother Goose on her beak and you'll have written an erudite poem.

TWINKLE, TWINKLE?

(Anonymous)

D   G   D
Scintillate, scintillate, globule aurific,

G   D   A   D
Fain would I fathom thy nature specific;

          G   Em   A
Loftily poised in the ether capacious,

D   G   Em   A
Strongly resembling a gem carbonaceous;

D   G   D
Scintillate, scintillate, globule aurific,

G   D   A   D
Fain would I fathom thy nature specific.

STORYTELLER'S NOTE

Children can write, illustrate, and read aloud their erudite rewritten nursery rhymes for others to identify. The two ditties above should get them inspired. Using a thesaurus or **www.thesaurus.com**, send them off to fool around with and discover new words. When they read aloud their retooled nursery rhymes, others will need to identify the original rhyme and recite it. With older children, this is an ideal way to reinforce familiarity with the old rhymes, which far too many children don't hear these days. As I always say, if you don't know your nursery rhymes, you will never be able to do the *New York Times*'s crossword puzzles.

INTERACTIVE SONGS WITH MOTIONS

I'M A LITTLE TEAPOT (ALTERNATE VERSION)

(Source unknown)

[SING:] I'm a little teapot, short and stout;
Here is my handle [*put one fist on hip*]
Here is my . . . [*Put other fist on hip. Look puzzled. Shake head; shrug shoulders. Take arms down.*]
[SPOKEN:] Let's try that again.

[SING:] I'm a little teapot, short and stout;
Here is my handle [*put one fist on hip*]
Here is my . . . [*Put other fist on hip. Look baffled. Shake head; look from side to side, examining your "handles"; shrug shoulders. Take arms down.*]
[SPOKEN:] Let's try that again. [*smile, hopefully; nod head*]

[SING:] I'm a little teapot, short and stout;
Here is my handle [*put one fist on hip*]
Here is my . . . [*Put other fist on hip. Look baffled. Then look enlightened.*]
[SPOKEN:] **Oh my goodness, oh my soul, I'm not a teapot, I'm a SUGAR BOWL!**

STORYTELLER'S NOTE

You may think you already know that Little Teapot song. Never assume. I learned this one from my big sister Sharron when I was three and she was a sophisticated seven, back in the Fabulous Fifties. I still think it's hilarious. What's so much fun about it is the way people (especially adults) feel they need to correct you while you're singing this, as if you were just too dim to know you were supposed to put out one arm as a spout.

I never tire of teaching this to young children—showing them how to pause and act puzzled, and how they should never give away the ending too soon. "Go home and try this on your parents. See if they crack up." I tell them. And they do, and they do.

I love doing both versions of the teapot song, traditional and parody, before reading aloud the book *Livingstone Mouse* by Pamela Duncan Edwards (HarperCollins, 1996). Livingstone wants to explore the world and is looking for China. Finally, he finds a white overturned teapot on the ground. "What's that?" he asks. "It's just some old china," he is told, and that's where he makes his home. Children aren't always familiar with the word "china" as a synonym for dishes. I have an old China teapot I bring out to show so we can talk about the difference between the country called China and the white porcelain we also call china. In this we can examine and understand the wordplay of the story. What about kids who don't know what a sugar bowl looks like? Bring one in and have it ready to show.

If you like, you can talk about the difference between Turkey and turkey. Or Thailand and ties. Kids find all of this infinitely amusing.

PEANUT BUTTER AND JELLY

(This version courtesy of Hester Stephenson.)

Do you know how to make a peanut butter and jelly sandwich?
Can you copycat me? (Can you copycat me?)
Can you say what I say? (Can you say what I say?)
Can you do what I do? (Can you do what I do?)
Are you hungry? (Are you hungry?)
Let's go! (Let's go!)

1. First you grow the peanuts and you pick 'em, you pick 'em
First you grow the peanuts and you pick 'em, you pick 'em
For the PEANUT, PEANUT BUTTER. . . and JELLY
PEANUT, PEANUT BUTTER . . . and JELLY

2. Then you take the peanuts and you mash 'em and smash 'em
Then you take the peanuts and you mash 'em and smash 'em
For the PEANUT, PEANUT BUTTER . . . and JELLY
PEANUT, PEANUT BUTTER . . . and JELLY

3. Then you pick the grapes and you SQUEEZE 'em, you SQUEEZE 'em
Then you pick the grapes and you SQUEEZE 'em, you SQUEEZE 'em
For the PEANUT, PEANUT BUTTER . . . and JELLY
PEANUT, PEANUT BUTTER . . . and JELLY

4. Then you take the bread and you spread it, you spread it
Then you take the bread and you spread it, you spread it
For the PEANUT, PEANUT BUTTER . . . and JELLY
PEANUT, PEANUT BUTTER . . . and JELLY

5. Then you take the sandwich and you munch it and crunch it
Then you take the sandwich and you munch it and crunch it
(sing refrain with mouth full of peanut butter)
For the PEANUT, PEANUT BUTTER . . . and JELLY
PEANUT, PEANUT BUTTER . . . and JELLY

6. Then you take the sandwich and you swallow it and swallow it
Then you take the sandwich and you swallow it and swallow it
For the PEANUT, PEANUT BUTTER . . . and JELLY
PEANUT, PEANUT BUTTER . . . and JELLY

[SPOKEN:] And *that's* how you make a peanut butter and jelly sandwich!

From *Once Upon a Time: Using Storytelling, Creative Drama, and Reader's Theater with Children in Grades PreK-6* by Judy Freeman. Westport, CT: Libraries Unlimited. Copyright © 2007.

STORYTELLER'S NOTE

There are many versions of this delightful call-and-response chant out there, including a picture book version, *Peanut Butter and Jelly; a Play-Rhyme* by Nadine Bernard Westcott (Dutton, 1987). I learned my version from Hester Stephenson, a former New Jersey librarian, many years ago.

When you do this with children, have them pantomime picking the peanuts; then mashing and smashing them (which I do by making a pounding motion with one fist in the palm of the other hand); picking and squeezing the grapes, one hand at a time; and spreading the pb&j onto the bread, with one palm outstretched as the bread, and the other holding an invisible knife.

The fun part comes when you "munch it and crunch it." Use your eyes here—look a little frantic as you become aware that your mouth's stuffed up with peanut butter. Speak with your mouth full, all muffled, not getting your palate fully clear until the final refrain.

About that refrain. To do the chant for maximum aerobic effect, push both arms up to the left above your head (for the peanut, peanut butter), and then down to the right, by your hips (and jelly). Here's how it looks:

"For the peanut, peanut butter . . . and jelly."

And here's how it sounds:

Is this chant meant just for little kids? Certainly not. Think about those older kids, working on that procedural writing assignment: How to make something. This chant is perfect for introducing that topic.

Ask students how one makes a peanut butter and jelly sandwich. They can write down the procedure, step by step. Bring in a loaf of bread, a jar of peanut butter, a jar of jelly, a plate, and a knife. Have one student read aloud his or her written instructions, while another student follows them to the T.

Then teach them the chant. It's truly fun for all ages. Ask if anyone suffers from *arachibutyrophobia.* What's that? Morbid fear of having peanut butter stick to the roof of your mouth.

WHO TOOK THE COOKIES FROM THE COOKIE JAR?

(Unknown)

GROUP:	Who took the cookies from the cookie jar?
LEADER:	Judy took the cookies from the cookie jar.
JUDY:	Who, me?
GROUP:	*Yes, you!*
JUDY:	Couldn't be!
GROUP:	*Then who?*
JUDY:	Izzy took the cookies from the cookie jar.
IZZY:	Who, me?
GROUP:	*Yes, you!*
IZZY:	Couldn't be!
GROUP:	*Then who?*

(And so on until you go all around the circle, with each child as accused and accuser. I like to end it like this:)

GROUP:	My teacher *(or use your name:* Miss Freeman*)* took the cookies from the cookie jar!
TEACHER:	Who, me?
GROUP:	*Yes, you!*
TEACHER:	Couldn't be!
GROUP:	*Then who?*
TEACHER:	I admit it! I took all the cookies! And they were DELICIOUS!

STORYTELLER'S NOTE

This is a another chant I learned from my big sister, Sharron way back when. It's perfect for getting to know everyone's name and getting your little ones to talk up with attitude. Standing in a big circle, each child gets a turn, going around the circle until it comes back to you and you claim responsibility. Be forewarned—you may need to take a little cookie break.

Children can go around the circle again and say, "My name is _____ and my best cookie ever is . . ." and name the types they love best.

A delectable book to use with this chant is *Cookies: Bite-Size Life Lessons* by Amy Krouse Rosenthal (HarperCollins, 2007), where you see how children interact with each other in the making, tasting, and sharing of cookies.

OH, MY AUNT CAME BACK

(Courtesy of librarian friend, Diane Model, who saw it on TV. Revised words by Judy Freeman to cover each continent; to the tune of "Old Hogan's Goat" or "How Dry I Am." Not sure of the tune? Listen to it here: **http://members.lycos.nl/catchytune/ohappyda.mid**.)

Oh, my aunt came back (oh, my aunt came back)
From old Japan (from old Japan),
And brought with her (and brought with her)
A hand-held fan (a hand-held fan). *[Motion: fan face with hand]*

Oh, my aunt came back from:
. . . the Sydney fair . . . a rocking chair. *[Motion: rock back and forth]*
. . . the London piers . . . . a pinking shears. *[Motion: scissor with two fingers]*
. . . the South Pole loop . . . a hula hoop. *[Motion: rock hips in circle]*
. . . from darkest Peru . . . a golden shoe. *[Motion: hold up foot]*
. . . a Cairo shed . . . a mummy's head. *[Motion: roll head]*
. . . the New York Zoo . . . a nut like YOU! *[Motion: stop all other motions and point to others]*

STORYTELLER'S NOTE

Been sitting too long? Need to get the blood flowing again? This is a jaunty call-and-response song that might help you all burn off a couple of calories. You sing the line and do the motion; your audience will sing it back to you. Keep doing each old motion as you add on each new one, and by the end you'll all be nodding and rocking and swaying like dancing dolls, though not quite so coordinated.

I rewrote some of the verses so the song would take singers around the globe to each continent. Have listeners identify each country and continent on the globe afterwards. You could also have them rewrite the song to identify places in one country, state, or town.

GEORGE WASHINGTON BRIDGE

(To the tune of the chorus of "Over the Waves," or "The Loveliest Night of the Year." Don't think you know it? Bet you do. Listen to it at: **http://members.lycos.nl/catchytune/sobrelas.mid**)

E   B7
George Washington Bridge, George Washington Washington Bridge.

                                                                    E
George Washington Bridge, George Washington Washington Bridge.

                                                    E7   A
George Washington Bridge, George Washington Washington Bridge.

                            E   B7   E
George Washington Bridge, George Washington Washington Bridge.

Sound Effects

Group 1: *Sing the words; hold arms in bridge-like arc over head, sway in time to music*

Group 2: *SPOKEN:* Plank chisel chisel, plank chisel chisel (*slap thighs, snap fingers twice*)

Group 3: *SPOKEN:* Um pea soup, um pea soup (*clap hands, tap left foot, tap right foot*)

STORYTELLER'S NOTE

Here's a silly song I learned at summer camp—either Camp Dark Waters in Medford, New Jersey where I was a camper, ages 8-9, and then a counselor for two summers (during the second of which I met my future husband, Izzy!); or Camp Echo Hill on the Chesapeake Bay in Maryland.

What you do is divvy your audience into three groups. Group 1 starts by singing the song with great gusto, arms overhead, swaying from left to right. As they start into the second round, group 2 says, in time to the music, "Plank chisel chisel," which gives the song good percussion. Then next time around, group 3 joins in, on the same beat as group 2, with their "Um pea soup." It sounds quite lovely.

Now, if you want to add a wrinkle, have each group sing the song again, with each group responsible for singing one word. And have them stand up and sit down again each time they sing their word. Group 2 has the most relaxed job, because they sing the word Washington twice, which means they get a little breather, having more time to stand there.

Do let them know that there is really such a thing as the George Washington Bridge, which spans the Hudson River quite magnificently between New York and New Jersey.

BABY JAWS

(Learned from New Jersey first grade teacher, Loreli Stochaj.)

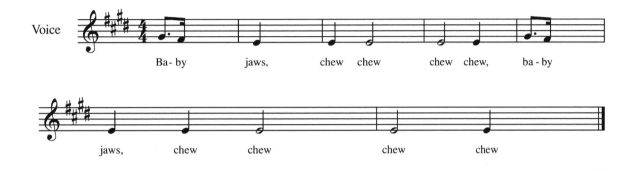

Baby jaws (chew chew chew chew)
[palms together, hinged at base of hands; open and close hands like a mouth]
Baby jaws (chew chew chew chew)

Mama jaws (chew chew chew chew)
[arms together at waist; palms outstretched together, horizontal to floor, forearms held together at elbows; open and close stiffly, like big jaws]
Mama jaws (chew chew chew chew)

Daddy jaws (chew chew chew chew)
[arms outstretched, bottom arm stiff, bottom palm facing sky; raise and lower other arm and hand, open and shut]
Daddy jaws (chew chew chew chew)

Grandma jaws (gum gum gum gum)
[like daddy jaws, but hands held in fists to signify toothlessness; sing this part with lips pulled over teeth, as if you were not wearing your dentures]
Grandpa jaws (gum gum gum gum)

Lady swim (swim swim swim swim)
[do the crawl with arms]
Lady swim (swim swim swim swim)

Shark attack (doo doo doo AUUUGHH!)
[lean head forward eagerly, eyes glittering, hands held like little paws in front of you; scream the AUUUGHH and throw both hands up in the air]
Shark attack (doo doo doo AUUUGHH!)

Swim away (swim swim swim swim)
[do a backstroke with arms]
Swim away (swim swim swim swim)

[Spoken:] **Whew. I made it!**
[pull hand across brow in relief]

STORYTELLER'S NOTE

Whenever I sing this three-note song during a school concert, children rush up to me after the program to sing the different versions they know. It's a wonderful interactive little story that is suprisingly visual, and children of all ages enjoy doing it together.

The first time, have children join in as a call-and-response with both words and motions. They'll do the motions and mostly sing the "doo doo" parts. Then tell them to join in a second time, this time doing both the motions and all the words. I tell them, "It's twice as hard that way, and twice as fun."

If you're telling shark stories, like *Punia and the King of Sharks: A Hawaii Folktale* by Lee Wardlaw (Dial, 1997) or *The Shark God* by Rafe Martin (Scholastic, 2001), this is a natural. Don't have any shark stories on your agenda? Then change the words from "shark attack" to "croc attack" instead and use it with alligator or crocodile stories like "Wide Mouth Frog" on page 75.

I'M BRINGING HOME A BABY BUMBLEBEE

(Traditional, with additional verses by Judy Freeman.)

```
     E              A      E
I'm bringing home a baby bumblebee,

B7                 A          B7
Won't my mommy be so proud of me,

             E           A   E
'Cause I'm bringing home a baby bumblebee;

Buzzy, buzzy, buzzy—

            B7
OOOOOOH, it bit me!
```

Oh, I'm bringing home a baby tur-ur-tle,
Won't my mommy really pop her girdle,
'Cause I'm bringing home a baby tur-ur-tle;
Snappy, snappy, snappy—
OOOOOOH, it *bit* me!

Oh, I'm bringing home a baby rattlesnake,
Won't my mommy shiver and shake,
'Cause I'm bringing home a baby rattlesnake;
Rattle, rattle, rattle—
OOOOOOH, it *bit* me!

Oh, I'm bringing home a baby great white shark,
Won't my mommy run into the dark,
'Cause I'm bringing home a baby great white shark;
Splashy, splashy, splashy—
OOOOOOH, it *bit* me!

Oh, I'm bringing home a baby grizzly bear,
Won't my mommy tear out all her hair,
'Cause I'm bringing home a baby grizzly bear;
Grrr, grrr, grrr—
OOOOOOH, it *bit* me!

From *Once Upon a Time: Using Storytelling, Creative Drama, and Reader's Theater with Children in Grades PreK-6* by Judy Freeman. Westport, CT: Libraries Unlimited. Copyright © 2007.

Oh, I'm bringing home a baby Tyrannosaur,
Won't my mommy fall right through the floor,
'Cause I'm bringing home a baby Tyrannosaur;
Gobble, gobble, gobble—
OOOOOOOOOOOHHHHHHHHH, it *ate* me!

STORYTELLER'S NOTE

This is an interactive song where children can really ham it up. At the start of each verse, they hunch over and pretend to cradle the new animal. Then they "become" the animal, shaking their fists together like a bumblebee, opening and closing their two hands like a snapping turtle, navigating their hands in a snakelike way, making big splashing motions for the shark, and growing and showing their grizzly bear claws.

Then, when they say the final line each time—OOOOOOH, it *bit* me!—they become themselves again, sitting straight up in indignation.

I love to use this song when showing the oversized nonfiction picture book, *Actual Size* by Steve Jenkins (Houghton Mifflin, 2004), which is full of many lovely fearsome creatures, including the Nile Crocodile and the goliath bird eater tarantula. Inspired, children can brainstorm a list of other dangerous animals they love and fear and make up new verses to sing and act out.

THE SWIMMING POOL SONG

(Anonymous; to the tune of "Sailing, Sailing, Over the Bounding Main".)

Swimming, Swimming *[arms do crawl]*
In my swimming pool *[draw big rectangle in the air with index fingers]*
When days are hot *[fan face with hands]*
When days are cold *[hug arms]*
In my swimming pool *[draw big rectangle with index fingers]*
Side stroke *[do side stroke with arms]*
Breast stroke *[do breast stroke with arms]*
Fancy diving, too *[with hands together, pantomime diving up and down]*
Don't you wish that you had *[wag index finger]*
Nothing else to do *[hold palms open]*
But . . .

STORYTELLER'S NOTE

The first time, sing the whole song as you do each motion. The second time, leave off the first line ("Swimming, swimming") and just do the pantomime. Each time you repeat the verse, leave off one more line, and just pantomime the actions instead of singing them. By the time you sing it ten times, you will be pantomiming the entire song silently (except for all the giggles), and end with only one word spoken: **"BUT."**

CREEPING, CREEPING

(By Judy Freeman; to the tune of "Sailing, Sailing, Over the Bounding Main")

Creeping, creeping, *[use hands as if they're feet, creeping at waist level]*
In my haunted house, *[draw house shape with index fingers]*
See ghosts that zoom, *[zoom with both hands]*
A witch's broom, *[hold imaginary broomstick & fly]*
In my haunted house; *[draw house shape with index fingers]*
Pumpkins grinning, *[hold chin in hands, grin, nod side to side]*
Skeletons are near, *[hold arms to sides, floppy, like skeleton]*
Don't you wish that you had *[wag index finger]*
Nothing else *[throw up hands in a shrug]*
to fear—*[hug arms with hands in a shiver]*
BOO! *[throw out hands towards audience]*

STORYTELLER'S NOTE

One Halloween, I was looking for an interactive song to do with my classes, and remembered the "Swimming Pool" song. Using that same framework, I simply penned new lyrics and off we flew. If you want another interactive activity for the holiday, see also "It's Halloween" on page 88.

The first time through, sing the whole song as you do each motion. The second time, leave off the first line ("Creeping, creeping") and just do the pantomime. Each time you repeat the verse, leave off one more line, and just pantomime the actions instead of singing them. By the time you sing it ten times, you will be pantomiming the entire song silently (except for all the giggles), and end with only one word spoken: "**BOO!**"

And then do the classic spooky call and response poem, "In a Dark, Dark Woods" on page 55.

IN A DARK, DARK WOODS

(Traditional)

In a dark, dark woods,
There was a dark, dark path. *[pantomime a path]*
And down that dark, dark path,
There was a dark, dark house. *[pantomime house]*

And in that dark, dark house,
There was a dark, dark door. *[pantomime door]*
Behind that dark, dark door, *[pantomime opening door]*
There was a dark, dark room.

And in that dark, dark room,
There was a dark, dark closet *[pantomime door]*
And in that dark, dark closet, *[pantomime opening door]*
There was a dark, dark shelf. *[pantomime shelf]*

And on that dark, dark shelf,
There was a dark, dark box. *[bring out box]*
And in that dark, dark box,
There was a . . . **GHOST!** *[shout this word to make your listeners JUMP!]*

STORYTELLER'S NOTE

You can bring in a box to use with this chant, a jump tale for even the youngest listeners. I have a little ghost made out of a bit of a white sheet tied around a tennis ball, with eyes and mouth drawn in black marker. When I get to the last line, I open the box and out pops the little ghost. Children still jump and scream. It's loads of fun to do.

Develop motions to go along with each line, and encourage children to chime in on each "dark, dark" line. Make your voices spooky and mysterious. Then have your group recall the sequence and retell the whole story with you. This is a good story they can bring home to try on their families.

David A. Carter illustrated a picture book version of this chant, *In a Dark, Dark Wood* (Little Simon, 2002), that incorporates a final pop-up page with a spooky green, sheeted ghost that will make everyone jump and then laugh and laugh.

From *Once Upon a Time: Using Storytelling, Creative Drama, and Reader's Theater with Children in Grades PreK-6* by Judy Freeman. Westport, CT: Libraries Unlimited. Copyright © 2007.

RAINSTORM

RUB / SNAP / CLAP / STAMP / CLAP / SNAP / RUB

STORYTELLER'S NOTE

The Rainstorm activity is a happening in sound, evoking the ambiance of a summer storm. I learned it many years ago when taking a memorable graduate course in Creative Drama at the Rutgers School of Communications, Information and Library Studies, taught by the amazing Joan Robinson, now the associate director for school programs at the Flynn Center for the Performing Arts in Burlington, Vermont. Go to **www.google.com** and look up the key words rainstorm, rub, snap, and clap, and you'll find scores of versions.

To begin, prepare your audience. If you have a small group of 25 or fewer, have them sit in a big circle, either on chairs or on the floor. With a larger group of children, divide them into Groups 1 to 4—left, left middle, right middle, and right.

Next go over the rules:

1. Tushies must stay on the floor (or on the chair) at all times.

2. No talking.

In fact, entreat your entire group to refrain from making any noise at all that comes from their mouths. This will seem like an alien concept to some children who can't imagine that you mean them when you tell everyone not to talk. I say, "We're going to be making a tremendous amount of noise. The trick is, none of it comes from your vocal cords. So if you feel yourself about to turn to your friend and say, 'This is cool,' don't do it. You'll break the magic. Try not to cough, sneeze, or even laugh."

3. Use your mind's eye to hear, see, smell, taste, and feel the rainstorm.

Do we really have an extra eyeball in the middle of our brains? Ask children to tell you what we mean by the mind's eye, and someone will say it's another name for the imagination. And if we really concentrate during this exercise, that rainstorm will sound like the real thing.

Next, I go over the hand signals I use. If I want them to be louder, I use a "come here" motion with the four fingers of my hand. To be very very loud, I cup my ear with my hand.

If I put my index finger up to my mouth in a classic shushing motion, it means someone is talking and breaking the magic and they need to stop. And finally, to motion each group to be silent, I hold out my hand, palm to the floor, and push it to one side in a straight line.

If the children are sitting in a circle, explain that you are going to begin the actions by rubbing your hands together. When you do, the first child to your left will start rubbing his hands together, and then, one at a time, the children to his left will do the same, until, one by one, the motion travels around the circle and everyone is rubbing hands. Then you'll start a new motion—snapping your fingers. The trick is, each person must keep rubbing hands (doing the old motion) until the *new* motion travels around to him or her.

With a bigger group, you'll start the first motion with group one, then point to group two to begin, and then group three, and finally, group four. It's a bit like doing The Wave at a baseball game. When you begin the new motion with group one, the others continue doing the old motion until you point to them, one group at a time.

Now it's time for the weather to begin. Wait till everyone is silent, and then somberly intone "Rainstorm."

RUB

Begin rubbing your hands with group one. By the time everyone is rubbing hands, you'll notice the lovely shushy sound, like the start of a misty rain.

SNAP

Next, snap your fingers in a random way. You don't want everyone snapping or clapping in unison. Notice that some littler children who can't snap will start clucking their tongues instead. It's fun to watch them figure out how they're going to do that motion.

CLAP

When you get to the clapping, exaggerate your motions to show you're not doing applause-like clapping, but varying the sound and rhythm. Use your hand motions to get them to do it louder and then louder still. It'll sound like rain hitting the rooftops.

STOMP

With their legs in front of them, children will stomp their feet. This is the best part, and some will laugh and even scream. Do that shushing motion here so they stay in control. Use your hand motions again. It's the loudest and most joyous part of the storm, with the rain pounding and drumming down like that. You'll be amazed at how real it sounds.

Now you reverse the actions, going first to *CLAP*, then *SNAP*, and finally *RUB*.

The storm is over. You say, "Wow! Rainstorm! Did you hear it? Did you see it? Did you smell it? Did you taste it? Did you feel it?"

Want to do it again? Bring out your tape recorder. When you play back the rainstorm your group has created, it sounds amazingly like the real thing. Even the most skeptical kids will be delighted at the results.

Sure, you can do this exercise with children when studying weather in science. Or after you tell the story "The Rainhat" (see page 94) or act out the Reader's Theater script for Aaron Shepard's *Master Man: A Tall Tale of Nigeria* (HarperCollins, 2001). Or when it's raining. Or when it's not raining. Or when you have five minutes to fill. I've done this with a whole auditorium full of children, and it's magical.

What has happened to you in the rain? Children can then tell or write true rain stories from their own experiences.

TANGUE TONGLING NONSENSE
TONGUE TWISTER SONG

(Anonymous; to the tune of "Battle Hymn of the Republic" or "John Brown's Body".)

G
One slick snake slid up the stake, and the other slick snake slid down.
C   G   D
One slick snake slid up the stake, and the other slick snake slid down.
G   B7   Em
One slick snake slid up the stake, and the other slick snake slid down.
Am   D   G
One slick snake slid up the stake, and the other slick snake slid down.

CHORUS:
Glory, glory, how peculiar,
Glory, glory, how peculiar,
Glory, glory, how peculiar;
One slick snake slid up the stake,
And the other slick snake slid down.

One cute king's kite caught quite quick, and the other cute king's kite couldn't.
One rich witch's wrist watch itched, and the other rich witch's didn't.
One eager eagle eased under the eaves, and the other eager eagle eased east.
One sick sheik's sixth sheep was sick, and the other sick sheik's was not.
One drunk duck dropped into the ditch, and the other drunk duck dropped dead.

STORYTELLER'S NOTE

The alliteration in this song is so satisfying. The trick to singing this without getting your tangue all tungled is to visualize each verse. Make a mental picture of the slick snake, sliding up a stake, and another snake sliding down. If you can picture it in your mind's eye, it seems to be easier to sing.

My favorite verse is the last one, but it's a tad irreverent, so I don't sing it with children younger than third graders. Invariably, kids love that verse, too.

As a warm-up, have children try some of your (and their) favorite killer tongue twisters, five times, fast. Mine include: Unique New York; Good Blood, Bad Blood; Lemon Liniment; Toy Boat (remembering the first season of *Saturday Night Live* with Chevy Chase); Red Leather, Yellow Leather.

And as a follow up to the song, children can write new verses to illustrate and sing together.

THE LIMERICK SONG

(Traditional; First and last verses by Judy Freeman; Chorus to the tune of "Celito Lindo." Don't recognize it? Go to **www.smickandsmodoo.com/stardust/stardust.shtml** and listen to the melody online.)

If poetry's your cup of tea,

Then take this suggestion from me:

Choose your favorite ditty,

A limerick so witty,

And sing it magnificently.

From *Once Upon a Time: Using Storytelling, Creative Drama, and Reader's Theater with Children in Grades PreK-6* by Judy Freeman. Westport, CT: Libraries Unlimited. Copyright © 2007.

CHORUS:

Aye-aye-aye-aye
In China they never grow chilly;
So sing me another verse that's worse than the first verse,
Make sure that it's foolish and silly.

A tutor who tutored the flute,
Tried to tutor two tooters to toot;
Said the two to the tutor,
"Is it tougher to toot or
To tutor two tooters to toot?"

There was an old man from Peru,
Who dreamed he was eating his shoe;
He awoke in a fright,
In the dark of the night,
And found it was perfectly true.

There was a young fellow of Perth,
Who was born on the day of his birth;
He was married, they say,
On his wife's wedding day,
And he died when he quitted the earth.

A man who was dining at Crewe,
Found quite a large mouse in his shoe;
Said the waiter, "Don't shout,
Or wave it about, or the rest will be wanting one, too."

And now that you've heard quite a few,
From both sides and all points of view,
Climb down from your shelf,
And write one yourself,
And see what a poet can do.

STORYTELLER'S NOTE

This is just the right song to demonstrate the workings of a limerick and to inspire children to write and illustrate their own and then sing them for the rest of the group. Look on the 821 shelf in the poetry section of your library and introduce your rhymesters to the limericks of the venerable Edward Lear, whose *Book of Nonsense* was first published in 1845.

MCTAVISH

(Anonymous; To the tune of "The Irish Washerwoman." If you don't recall this tune offhand, go to **http://webpages.marshall.edu/~irby1/laura/frames.html** and listen to a fiddle version of it.)

      D
Old McTavish is dead and his brother don't know it;

      A7
His brother is dead and McTavish don't know it;

      D
They're both of them dead and they're in the same bed,

      A7   D
And neither one knows that the other is dead.

Oh, McTavish he died of peritonitis;
His brother he died of chronic arthritis;
How both of them cried and both of them sighed,
When each of them found that the other had died.

STORYTELLER'S NOTE

I love singing this one on St. Patrick's Day. It's such a ridiculous bit of nonsense. You'll need to explain what peritonitis is (which killed Harry Houdini, you know), and chronic arthritis (which won't kill you but hurts a lot just the same).

From *Once Upon a Time: Using Storytelling, Creative Drama, and Reader's Theater with Children in Grades PreK-6* by Judy Freeman. Westport, CT: Libraries Unlimited. Copyright © 2007.

Judy Freeman's Storybook: Tales You Can Hear Today and Tell Tomorrow

In the book *The Storyteller's Guide* by Bill Mooney and David Holt (August House, 1996), storyteller Elizabeth Ellis has ingeniously categorized the types of stories one can choose to tell. She updated her comments from that book for me as follows:

There are four types of stories. What determines the type of story is the response the audience gives to it. Children need a doorway to step into the land of story. So, if you're presenting a program, the first type of story would be:

Ha Ha. This is the funny story from the most slapstick to the most subtle, from the noodlehead story to the sophisticated literary tale that is comic because of its plotting.

The next kind of story is:

Ah Ha. This is a story that has some element of surprise. It could be a story that explains where things come from, like a *pourquoi* story. It could be a ghost story. It could be a story like the ones O'Henry wrote. The broadest type would be the jump tale. The most subtle would be, "Oh, I get it! They're talking about why raccoons have rings on their tails."

The third type of story is:

Ah. If you are telling to a large audience, you can physically hear that sound, "Aaah!" It may be a fairy tale, a personal experience story, or a story from the Bible. It encompasses a wide variety of tales. But the thing they all have in common is that "Ah!" reaction. It requires listening at a much deeper level of concentration than the "Ha Ha" or "Ah Ha" stories. When the story ends, the audience is usually a long way out of their bodies, and it takes them a while to hike back.

The last type is:

Amen. Amen literally means "so be it." "Yes! Let my life be lived that way." "This is the way life should be lived." An "Amen" story is any story that speaks to the spirit. It could be

63

from one of the world's great religions or from your own experience. These stories give great closure and meaning to a storytelling program.

So when you're setting up a program, this is a blueprint for a program, starting with "Ha Ha" and ending with "Amen." Each successive category requires listening at a deeper level and asks more of your listener. Occasionally you hit on a story that has each of these elements in it. If it is a long story, you would ideally want all four elements in it.

When I'm planning a program, I pick two or more stories from "Ha Ha" and one story from each of the other categories. It is a circle. It is my intention, if I can, to get all the way around the circle. I don't always accomplish it, but that's my goal. I go as far as the situation allows me to go."

It occurs to me that while Elizabeth Ellis came up with her designations to categorize the stories she tells, they also apply to the books we read. Some books we choose for the sheer fun of them, and some books change our lives, the way we think about the world, and feel about ourselves.

The next time you plan to share books or stories with your students, write the four categories on the board. Booktalk and discuss examples of each category. Ask readers to talk about the "Ah" and the "Amen" books that have had an impact on their lives.

In this chapter, I offer up some of my easiest and most reliable stories to tell. Most of them have been part of my life for years, and some for decades. I can tell these stories at a moment's notice—they are part of my psyche—and after all these years, somehow I'm still not tired of them. I still get great pleasure from telling them to children, and hope you will, too. True, they're all "Ha Ha" and "Ah Ha" stories, not "Ah" and certainly not "Amen" stories. (To find those more complex tales that speak to your soul, start reading widely and living large. They take a lifetime to find.) But they'll get you started and give you confidence in your new identity as a storyteller, enchanter of children everywhere.

WE'RE GOING ON A LION HUNT

(A call-and-response chant adapted by Judy Freeman, © 2006.)

REFRAIN:
We're going on a lion hunt. *[march in place; slap alternating thigh with hands]*
Looking for a big cat. *[make roaring sound; hold hands up as claws]*
We're not scared. *[shake head from side to side; hands on hips]*
Now what do you think of that? *[throw out hands to sides]*

Say goodbye to our tent. *[wave goodbye, hand and forearm going side to side like a windshield wiper]*
Climb up a tree. *[pantomime climbing up]*
Looking for a lion. *[one hand holding tree; other hand shading eyes, look all around]*
But he won't catch me. *[hold on to tree with one arm, point boldly to self with other thumb]*

Look at that hill. *[point]*
Too high to fly over it. *[make an "over" motion with both hands]*
Too hard to tunnel under it. *[make an "under" motion with both hands]*
Too wide to go around it. *[make a "wide" motion with arms]*
Let's climb over it. *[marching motion with arms]*
OOH, UNH, OOH, UNH *[climbing motions to the top; run down the other side]*

REFRAIN

Look at that water hole. *[point]*
Too wide to fly over it. *[make an "over" motion with both hands]*
Too hard to tunnel under it. *[make an "under" motion with both hands]*
Too wide to go around it. *[make a "wide" motion with arms]*
Let's swim through it. *[jump in water and swim across]*
SPLISH, SPLASH, SPLISH, SPLASH

REFRAIN

Look at that long grass. *[point]*
Too high to fly over it. *[make an "over" motion with both hands]*
Too hard to tunnel under it. *[make an "under" motion with both hands]*
Too wide to go around it. *[make a "wide" motion with arms]*

Let's walk through it. *[marching motion with arms]*
SWISH, SWASH, SWISH, SWASH *[use hands to part the tall grass]*
OOOOHHHH. *[with grass parted, stop and peer out; look alarmed]*

Look at that cave. *[point with shaky finger and scared voice]*
It's dark and it's cold. *[clutch arms and shiver]*
Let's go in. *[shake head yes]*
We're brave and bold. *[wave fist in air]*

Oops. What's that? *[move body back from the waist, startled]*
It's furry and warm. *[pat the big kitty all over]*
With a great big tongue. *[slurp with big tongue]*
It's licking my arm. *[look at arm, alarmed]*

Turn on the flashlight. *[click it on]*
What's that I see? *[shine it around; stop, shocked]*
It's a great a great big lion. *[lick your lips and smile]*
Coming after me! *[Open mouth to yell]*
ROOOAARRRRRR!!!

RUN!!! AAAAHHHHHH!!!! *[slap thighs with hands]*

In the grass we'll hide. *[use hands to part the tall grass]*
SWISH, SWASH, SWISH, SWASH *[crouch down and hide head in hands]*
ROOOAARRRRRR!!!
In the water hole *[jump in water]*
SPLISH, SPLASH, SPLISH, SPLASH *[swim across, fast]*
ROAARRR!!! *[a little softer]*
Over the hill—OOH, UNH, OOH, UNH *[fast climbing motions to the top]*
ROAR. *[softer still]*
Down the other side—OOH, UNH, OOH, UNH *[run down the other side, fast]*
ROAR. *[whisper]*

Make a run for our tent. *[look both ways, run]*
Say hello to our tree. *[wave hello]*
We found a mighty lion. *[roar]*
But he didn't catch me. *[point to self in triumph]*

We went on a lion hunt. *[march in place]*
Found a big cat. *[roar]*
We're not scared. *[shake head from side to side]*
Now what do you think of that? *[throw out hands to sides]*

 From *Once Upon a Time: Using Storytelling, Creative Drama, and Reader's Theater with Children in Grades PreK-6* by Judy Freeman. Westport, CT: Libraries Unlimited. Copyright © 2007.

STORYTELLER'S NOTE

Have your children do this interactive call-and-response story with you. You say a line and do the accompanying motions, and they copycat you. At the climax of the story, when the lion turns and looks at you and roars, expect a bit of controlled pandemonium. What you're doing from this point is reversing all of the motions as everyone scrambles to get away from the lion and back to the campsite.

As a school librarian, I loved to do the chant as "We're Going on a Bear Hunt" and follow up with a good bear story. Some good choices from the bibliography, "400+ Children's Books Every Storyteller Should Know," starting on page 111, include *How Chipmunk Got His Stripes: A Tale of Bragging and Teasing* by Joseph and James Bruchac, *Pancakes for Supper* by Anne Isaacs, *Swamp Angel* by Anne Isaacs, *Tops & Bottoms* by Janet Stevens, and, of course, *Goldilocks and the Three Bears* by Jim Aylesworth or by James Marshall.

Michael Rosen's picture book, *We're Going on a Bear Hunt* is a classic picture book version of the story. Feel free to improvise and make the story fit other occasions, such as your own version of "We're Going on a Witch Hunt" at Halloween time.

Which puts me in mind of two true stories. Many years ago, I announced to a kindergarten class, "It's almost Halloween. Let's go on a witch hunt!"

"Yay!" the children cheered. But one girl, a timid but earnest redhead named Janet, started to cry. "I don't want to go on a witch hunt. I'm afraid of witches!"

Oh, my. What do you do? I explained to her that this was just a pretend witch hunt and that she would be perfectly safe and have fun, too. She did just fine, and emerged from the story unscathed and unscared. Whew.

Many years later, I took a class of first graders on a Lion Hunt, with lots of roaring and laughing, and after we finished, one little boy said indignantly, "But you said we were going to go on a lion hunt. Where was the lion? There wasn't a real lion!"

A little girl turned to him, exasperated, and said, "We did, too, go on a lion hunt! I saw the lion!"

Other children said, "Yeah, we saw the lion!"

And I thought, wistfully, too much TV . . . So many kids these days don't get a chance to exercise their mind's eye, their imagination. TV fills in all the pictures. Storytelling lets children conjure up their own pictures and envision themselves as the hero of the story.

So when you finish your lion hunt, ask your listeners to describe what the lion looked like. Have them describe and / or draw their favorite scene and relive the story.

You'll find other versions of this chant online, including the one in the teacher's guide for Michelle Knudsen's irresistible picture book *Library Lion* (Candlewick, 2006; **www.candlewick.com**), where you'll also find directions for making lion masks on paper plates and a pattern for lion finger puppets.

THE LITTLE ROUND RED HOUSE

(Adapted and retold by Judy Freeman, © 1996.)

On a cold, rainy, and windy Saturday in October, a little boy was bored. He went down to the kitchen where his mother was reading the newspaper and he said, "Mom, I don't know what to do. I'm bored, bored, bored."

His mother looked up from her paper and smiled. "Why don't you draw a picture with your new crayons?"

"I already drew a hundred pictures," he said. "I'm bored, bored, BORED."

"Well, why don't you read one of your new library books?" she suggested.

"I already read all of my books a thousand times. I'm bored, BORED, BORED!" he said.

"How about playing with your toys?" she said.

"I already played with a million toys. I'm **BORED, BORED, BORED**!"

Most of the time, mothers don't like it when their children say they are bored. "I was never bored when I was your age," they say, though this can't be true, can it?

The little boy's mother thought for a bit, and then she said, "I remember one day when I was your age and I was bored. My mother—your grandmother—sent me out to search for the strangest little house. If you'd like, I can tell you just what she told me to do."

The little boy looked up. His mother was bored once. That was interesting.

She said, "First you need to put on your raincoat and your hat and your scarf and your mittens and your boots. Then you need to go outside. And then you need to walk up the block and down the block and around the block to look for that little house.

"What kind of little house?" the little boy asked.

"It's a little round red house with no windows and no doors, a chimney on top, and a star in the middle," she said.

The little boy stared at her. "I never saw a house like that before. Where is it?"

His mother said, "I can't tell you. But if you keep your ears open and your eyes open, and you look hard, you should find it not too far from here. You won't even need to cross the street."

"I'll do it," he said.

He bundled up in his raincoat and his hat, his scarf and his mittens, and his boots, too, and set out to find the little round red house with no windows and no doors, a chimney on top, and a star in the middle.

He walked down his long block, all the way to the corner. He saw white houses and blue houses and yellow houses and green houses. Then he saw a red house.

"There it is," he cried. But wait. The house was square, not round. It had a chimney, all right, but also lots and lots of windows. It had a door, too. He couldn't tell if there was a star. The windows had curtains on the inside.

"That can't be it," he said, and continued his march, around the corner, up the long block and to the next corner. There were yellow houses and brown houses and many-colored houses, but not one of them was a little round red house with no windows and no doors, a chimney on top, and a star in the middle.

As he was standing on the sidewalk feeling puzzled, the little white mail truck pulled up. The mail carrier poked his head out of the window and said, "Little boy, are you lost?"

"Oh, no," the little boy replied. "I live at 331 Ivy Rock Lane, Bridgewater, New Jersey."

"That's right around the corner," the mail carrier said. "No, you're not lost."

The little boy asked, "Do you know where everyone lives around here? I'm looking for a special house."

The mail carrier said proudly, "Of course I do, little boy. That's my job. What house do you want to find?"

The little boy said, "My mother sent me to find a little round red house with no windows and no doors, a chimney on top, and a star in the middle."

"Little boy," the mail carrier said, "I've been to every house in town, but I've never seen a house like that before. Are you sure your mother isn't pulling your leg?"

"Oh, no," the little boy answered. "My mother wouldn't tease me. She said she found the same house when she was just my age, so I know it's real."

The mail carrier shook his head sorrowfully and said, "Sorry I can't help you, my friend. I've got to be getting on my way. It's time to deliver the mail."

Waving goodbye, he drove off down the road.

The little boy tromped around the next corner and down the block. Every house had windows and doors. Some were red. Some had chimneys. But not one of them was a little round red house with no windows and no doors, a chimney on top, and a star in the middle.

He stopped again to think and looked up to see a police car cruising down the street. It pulled up alongside him and a police officer poked her head out of the window. "Little boy, are you lost?"

"Oh, no," the little boy replied. "I live at 331 Ivy Rock Lane, Bridgewater, New Jersey."

"That's right around the block," the police officer said. "No, you're not lost."

The little boy asked, "Do you know where everyone lives around here? I'm looking for a special house. I asked the mail carrier, and he didn't know where it was."

The officer said, "Little Boy, I know this neighborhood like the back of my hand. I drive up these streets and down these streets every day, making sure things are safe around here. What house do you want to find?"

The little boy said, "My mother sent me to find a little round red house with no windows and no doors, a chimney on top, and a star in the middle."

"Little boy," the officer said, "I've been past every house in this town, but I've never seen a house like that before. Are you sure that's what your mother said?"

"Oh, yes," the little boy answered. "She said she found the same house when she was just my age, so I know it's real."

The police officer said, "Sorry I can't help you, buddy. I've got to be getting back to my street patrol."

Waving goodbye, she drove off down the road.

The little boy was getting discouraged. His mother said he wouldn't even need to cross the street, but no matter how hard he looked, he could not find the house he was looking for. There was just one more house to check, and that was Mr. Fetzer's house, at the end of the block.

Mr. Fetzer had lived in the neighborhood longer than anyone. Years and years ago, there were many farms in Bridgewater, but one by one, the land had been sold, and houses were built where there had once been fields of Jersey tomatoes and white corn. Mr. Fetzer's farm was the last one left in the neighborhood. He ran a small farm stand and sold the fresh fruits and vegetables he grew in his gardens and orchards.

"If anyone knows where that house is, he should," the little boy reasoned. So up he trudged to Mr. Fetzer's barn and peered inside.

There was the farmer, packing apples into boxes. He looked up. "Why, hello there, young feller. What can I do for you? Come for a taste of my apple cider?"

He poured a cup and handed it to the little boy. The little boy drank it down gratefully. Hunting for houses was thirsty work. The cider tasted sweet and tart all at the same time.

"Thanks for the cider," the little boy said. "Mr. Fetzer, can you help me? I'm looking for a house. It's a little round red house with no windows and no doors, a chimney on top, and a star in the middle. My mother says you've lived here longer than anybody, and she found the house when she was my age, so I thought you might know where it is."

Mr. Fetzer smiled. "Seems to me I remember your mother when she was just a little girl. Seems to me she came to find me on a day just like today. Seems to me that she was looking for a house, too, just like the one you've described. And seems to me, I knew just where to send her."

The farmer walked outside and pointed to his orchards, up on a little hill. "See those trees? Run up there and take a look around, and I think you'll find what you're looking for."

The little boy ran across the field and up the hill. He stood under one of the apple trees and looked all around. The wind was blowing a dancing breeze and it blew a red apple right off the tree. Thunk. The apple landed at his feet. Picking it up, the little boy took a closer look.

"A little round red house with no windows and no doors," he said, turning it and looking at its shiny round red surface. "A chimney on top," he said, touching the stem. "A star in the middle?"

He put the apple in his raincoat pocket and ran all the way home.

"Mom! Mom!" he cried. "I think I found it."

His mother smiled when he took the apple out of his pocket and handed it to her. "I think you did, too," she said. "A little round red house with no windows and no doors, and a chimney on top."

"But where's the star?" he asked.

She picked up a sharp knife from the table. Placing the apple on its side on a plate, she cut it in half, right through its middle. And there, in the center, was a star. *(NOTE: Have an apple, a knife, and a plate at hand so you can cut the apple open with great fanfare and show children the star within.)*

She sliced the little boy a plate of apple star cookies to eat. They were delicious. Then he filled a little pot with potting soil, planted the apple seeds, watered them a little bit, and placed the pot on the sunny windowsill. And he wasn't bored one bit.

STORYTELLER'S NOTE

This is what you'd call a teaching story. I've heard and read dozens of versions, and mine is just one more. We all want our preschoolers through second graders to know their addresses and phone numbers by heart, and how to ask for help. This story can be a kickoff point to having children memorize their vital information and to talk about community helpers. It's also perfect to use with another apple story, "T for Tommy," which you'll find on page 81 of this handbook. Studying trees or apples or fall? Use it with Steven Kellogg's picture book biography, *Johnny Appleseed* (Morrow, 1998).

The first thing you want to do after telling this story, however, is to hand out Apple Star cookies. They're the ideal after-story snack, tasty and nutritious. You can get four or five of them out of each apple. Just turn the apple on its side and cut it into thin apple rings. Children eat around the stars in the middle made by the seeds. Pour out mini cups of apple cider for all to try. And cook up a nice pot of applesauce.

Want another great prop story about a bored child, a girl this time? Try the paperfolding story, "The Rainhat" on page 94.

HOIMIE THE WOIM

(Adapted & retold by Judy Freeman from Megan Moskaluk's telling in 1996.)

I was sitting on a fence,
Chewing my bubblegum (chomp chomp chomp chomp) *[loud chewing noise]*
Playing with my yo-yo (doo-wop, doo-wop), *[Push down index finger and pull it up, like you're using a yo-yo]*
When along came **HOIMIE THE WOIM**.
He was **THIS BIG**. *[show with hands 12" apart]*
I said, "**HOIMIE THE WOIM**, what happened?"
He said, " **I ATE a RAT!**"
I said, "Ohhhhh."
And off he went. *[hold out fist, thumb up, and move arm to the side, extending it past your shoulder, as if you're hitchhiking]*

I was sitting on a fence,
Chewing my bubblegum (chomp chomp chomp chomp) *[loud chewing noise]*
Playing with my yo-yo (doo-wop, doo-wop), *[yo-yo motion]*
When along came **HOIMIE THE WOIM**.
He was **THIS BIG**. (show with hands 18" apart)
I said, "**HOIMIE THE WOIM**, what happened?"
He said, " **I ATE a CAT!**"
I said, "Ohhhh." And off he went. *[hitchhiking motion]*

I was sitting on a fence,
Chewing my bubblegum (chomp chomp chomp chomp) *[loud chewing noise]*
Playing with my yo-yo (doo-wop, doo-wop), *[yo-yo motion]*
When along came **HOIMIE THE WOIM**.
He was **THIS BIG**. *[show with hands 2' apart]*
I said, "**HOIMIE THE WOIM**, what happened?"
He said, " **I ATE a DOG!**"
I said, "Ohhhh." And off he went. *[hitchhiking motion]*

I was sitting on a fence,
Chewing my bubblegum (chomp chomp chomp chomp) *[loud chewing noise]*
Playing with my yo-yo (doo-wop, doo-wop), *[yo-yo motion]*
When along came **HOIMIE THE WOIM**.
He was **THIS BIG**. *[show with arms wide apart]*
I said, "**HOIMIE THE WOIM**, what happened?"

He said, "**I ATE a COW!**"

I said, "**Ohhhh.**" And off he went. *[big hitchhiking motion, past your head]*

I was sitting on a fence,

Chewing my bubblegum (chomp chomp chomp chomp) *[loud chewing noise]*

Playing with my yo-yo (doo-wop, doo-wop), *[yo-yo motion]*

When along came **HOIMIE THE WOIM.**

He was **THIS** *[extend arms all the way apart]* **BIG.** *[Bring arms back together and stop with hands 6" apart; then show finger and thumb, about 4" apart]*

I said, "**HOIMIE THE WOIM**, what happened?"

[sniff sadly] " **I . . . BOIPED!**"

STORYTELLER'S NOTE

I first heard the story of Hoimie the Woim many years back, and somehow forgot all about it. I then learned this even better version of the story from a first grader, Megan Moskaluk, though she called him Hermie the Worm, or maybe it was Hermie the Wormie. You may find your students know other variants of the story. In some versions, the worm eats breakfast, lunch, and dinner. In others, he eats his whole family. And at the end, he burps. Google "Herman the Worm," "Hermie the Worm," and "Hermie the Wormie" and you'll find a zillion versions.

For this version, my very favorite, you'll need to use your best New Yawk accent. I like to start off the story by asking the kids if they speak New Yawk-ese. I ask if they can translate these sentences into standard English:

So I'm standin' at the cawnah of Toity-toid Street and Toid Avenue. I'm lookin' at awl the liddle boidies up in the trees. So I sez to myself, I sez, 'The oily boid catches da woim!'

Many children will call out, "The early bird catches the worm!"

"Oh, you know about woims! Let me tell you a story about one hungry, hungry woim. His name was Hoimie the Woim. Can you say his name with me?"

And off you go. Children will start to chime in on the refrains, and by the end, they'll know the whole sequence.

When you say the final line ("I BOIPED!") , some children will get it, and some won't. Ask your group, "What happened to Hoimie?" Someone will call out, "He burped!"

And you'll say something akin to this: "That's exactly right. But he's a woim, isn't he? So he didn't just BURP, he BOIPED!" And have them repeat the last line with you.

This is a simple and very funny interactive story to tell. I taught it to all of the students at my school, kindergarten through fifth grade. I remember watching a class of kids sauntering down the hall on their way to lunch, all of them stepping in unison, chanting, "doo-wop, doo-wop," their fingers going up and down as they tossed their invisible yo-yos. I've told it hundreds of times, and always entreat audiences to tell it to everyone they know.

Basically, this is what is called a "swallowing story." Young children love swallowing stories where everyone or everything gets eaten, only to be regurgitated safely at the end.

Include in your story hour the following swallowing stories, listed by author in the bibliography, "400+ Children's Books Every Storyteller Should Know" on page 111: *Clay Boy* by Mirra Ginsburg, *Sody Sallyratus* by Teri Sloat, *Gobble, Gobble, Slip, Slop: The Tale of a Very Greedy Cat* by Meilo So, and, of course, everyone's favorite singable ditty, *There Was an Old Lady Who Swallowed a Fly* by Simms Taback.

WIDE MOUTH FROG

(As adapted and told by Judy Freeman, who first heard it from her niece, Myra Feldman, and her nephew, Charlie Feldman, and sister-in-law, Margaret Feldman, who heard it told at a performance by Mary Murphy, a storyteller in Albany, New York, in 1986 or so.)

Once upon a time there was a Wide Mouth Frog and it was his birthday. Wide Mouth Frog woke up early and hopped to the kitchen. His mother was already there, cooking something that smelled delicious.

"Good morning, Mother dear," said the Wide Mouth Frog.

"Happy birthday, my sweet little Wide Mouth Frog," said his mother.

"Mother dear," said the frog, "what are you making for birthday dinner?"

"I'm making you your favorite—mashed sweet potatoes and crunchy little black flies."

"Hooray!" cried the Wide Mouth Frog.

"Now listen, my boy. I need you to get out from under flipper so I can concentrate on my cooking," his mother said. "Why don't you go outside for a little while."

"Certainly, Mother dear," said the Wide Mouth Frog. Wide Mouth Frog hopped outside. The sun was shining. The sky was blue. Wide Mouth Frog was happy to be alive. He closed both his eyes, opened his mouth as *wiiiide* as he could, and he started to sing this song:

Wide Mouth Frog, Wide Mouth Frog,
Gee, it's great to be a Wide Mouth Frog.

He hopped and he hopped until he came to the tree where Mrs. Squirrel lived. He looked up. High in the tree, he could see Mrs. Squirrel and her little squirrel babies.

He called out, "Oh, Mrs. Squirrel! Oh, Mrs. Squirrel! It's my birthday! My mother's making me my favorite—mashed sweet potatoes and crunchy little black flies. Tell me, Mrs. Squirrel, what do you feed your babies for birthday dinner?"

Mrs. Squirrel looked down at the frog below. She said, "I feed my babies roasted acorns and mashed honeynuts. As a matter of fact, I'm making some right now. Would you like a taste?"

Wide Mouth Frog wrinkled up his nose. "Eeuuuuwww," he said. But then he remembered his manners. "Ah, I mean, no thank you, Mrs. Squirrel. But thanks for asking. I need to save my appetite for later. Give the babies a pat for me."

And off he hopped. The sun was still shining. The sky was still blue. Wide Mouth Frog was happy to be alive. He closed both his eyes, opened his mouth as *wiiiide* as he could, and he started to sing that song again:

Wide Mouth Frog, Wide Mouth Frog,
Gee, it's great to be a Wide Mouth Frog.

He hopped and he hopped until he came to the tree where Mrs. Monkey lived. He looked up. High in the tree, he could see Mrs. Monkey and her little monkey babies.

He called out, "Oh, Mrs. Monkey! Oh, Mrs. Monkey! It's my birthday! My mother's making me my favorite—mashed sweet potatoes and crunchy little black flies. Tell me, Mrs. Monkey, what do you feed your babies for birthday dinner?"

Mrs. Monkey looked down at the frog below. She said, "I feed my babies mashed bananas and little chocolate chips. As a matter of fact, I'm making some right now. Would you like a taste?"

Wide Mouth Frog wrinkled up his nose. "Eeuuuuwww," he said. But then he remembered his manners. "Ah, I mean, no thank you, Mrs. Monkey. But thanks for asking. I need to save my appetite for later. Give the babies a pat for me."

And off he hopped. The sun was still shining. The sky was still blue. Wide Mouth Frog was happy to be alive. He closed both his eyes, opened his mouth as *wiiiide* as he could, and he started to sing . . . that . . . song again:

Wide Mouth Frog, Wide Mouth Frog,
Gee, it's great to be a Wide Mouth Frog.

He hopped and he hopped until he came to the cave where Mrs. Lion lived. He hopped inside. It was dark. It was damp. It was spooky. It was smelly. At the back of the cave, he could see Mrs. Lion and her little lion cubs.

He called out, "Oh, Mrs. Lion! Oh, Mrs. Lion! It's my birthday! My mother's making me my favorite—mashed sweet potatoes and crunchy little black flies. Tell me, Mrs. Lion, what do you feed your babies for birthday dinner?"

Mrs. Lion looked down at the Wide Mouth Frog. She licked her lips. She said, "I feed my babies little moles and little voles and nice little mice and other small squishy creatures like that."

Wide Mouth Frog said, "Oh. Oh, you do? Oh, you do! Well, that's very interesting, Mrs. Lion. Small squishy creatures." He puffed himself up to look a little bigger. "Very interesting indeed. I'd love to stay here and chat, Mrs. Lion, but I think I hear my mother calling me."

He started to back out of the cave. "Nice talking with you, Mrs. Lion. Give my regards to the cubs. No, no, Mrs. Lion, don't get up. I can see myself out."

And he backed out of the cave, with his heart pounding out to here, for he knew full well that he was a small squishy creature, too. He backed up and he backed up and he backed up until he was at the mouth of the cave. Then he turned and hopped away as fast as he could.

Wide Mouth Frog couldn't believe his eyes. The sun was still shining. The sky was still blue. Wide Mouth Frog was happy to be alive. He closed both his eyes, opened his mouth as *wiiiide* as he could, and he started to *sing...that...song* again:

Wide Mouth Frog, Wide Mouth Frog,
Gee, it's great to be a Wide Mouth Frog.

He hopped and he hopped until he came to the swamp where Mrs. Crocodile lived. He hopped to the bank of the water. It was dark. It was damp. It was spooky. It was smelly. Stretched out on the bank, sound asleep, was Mrs. Crocodile.

Wide Mouth Frog hopped over to Mrs. Crocodile. He hopped closer and closer until he was right beside her long, bumpy, green snout.

Wide Mouth Frog said, "Oh, Mrs. Crocodile! Oh, Mrs. Crocodile! It's my birthday! My mother's making me my favorite—mashed sweet potatoes and crunchy little black flies. Tell me, Mrs. Crocodile, what do you feed your babies for birthday dinner?"

Mrs. Crocodile opened first one eye, and then the other. She looked down at the small, squishy creature standing before her. She licked her lips. She grinned a sharp toothy grin. She said, "I feed my babies *wide...mouth...frogs*!"

Wide Mouth Frog said, "Oh. Oh, you do?"

From *Once Upon a Time: Using Storytelling, Creative Drama, and Reader's Theater with Children in Grades PreK-6* by Judy Freeman. Westport, CT: Libraries Unlimited. Copyright © 2007.

It suddenly dawned on Wide Mouth Frog what Mrs. Crocodile had just said. He pulled close his wide-open mouth into a very, very, small mouth, and pursed his lips together in a little circle, like a fish.

With his little fishlike lips, he said, "Oh, you do! Well, that's very interesting, Mrs. Crocodile. Wide mouth frogs. As you can see, I myself am what you'd call a small mouth frog. But if I happen to run into any wide mouth frogs out there, why, I'll send them right over."

Wide Mouth Frog started to back away from Mrs. Crocodile. With his lips still puckered he said, "Nice talking with you, Mrs. Crocodile. I'd love to stay here and chat, but I think I hear my mother calling me. No, no, Mrs. Crocodile, don't get up. I can see myself out."

He started to back away from the swamp, with his heart pounding out to here. He backed up and he backed up and he backed up until he was far from Mrs. Crocodile. Then he turned and hopped away as fast as he could.

Wide Mouth Frog couldn't believe his eyes. The sun was still shining. The sky was still blue. Wide Mouth Frog was happy to be alive. He closed both his eyes, and he started to *sing . . . that . . . song again*. **BUT**, he didn't sing it the same way this time! Keeping his mouth as small as he could and his lips pursed, he sang:

Wide Mouth Frog, Wide Mouth Frog,
Gee, it's great to be a Wide Mouth Frog.

Then he hopped and he hopped until he got all the way home. His mother gave him a delicious dinner of mashed sweet potatoes and crunchy little black flies. He opened all his presents and they were all just what he wanted. And it was the best birthday he ever had.

STORYTELLER'S NOTE

As with all stories, this one has evolved since I first started telling it. My niece and nephew and sister-in-law came back all excited from a storytelling program at the Bethlehem Public Library in Delmar, New York, and said, "We heard this really funny story and we think you'd love it." They didn't know the name of the storyteller they had seen. So I asked the three of them to retell the story, and they were right. I loved it. Since they couldn't recall all of the details, I added some of my own. Over the years, in telling the story to children, the story has evolved. Stories are not statues—they change a bit every time you tell them.

I use my guitar with this story, adding sound effects and playing the chorus as follows:

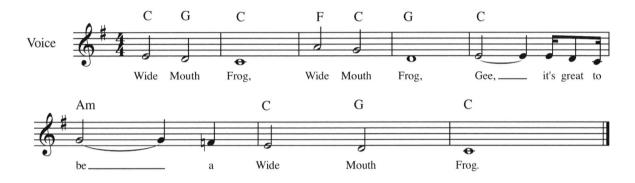

Feel free to play around with this story, and tailor it to fit your audience. You can have the Wide Mouth Frog looking forward to Christmas or Thanksgiving dinner, if you need a good story before a holiday. Be prepared, however, for many hours of nonstop refrains sung by your children. As one of the dopiest stories I know, it's also one of my very favorites.

Here's one way the story has changed to fit my audiences. I used to say, "And he started to sing that song," and then go right into the chorus. After the second time, some children would say, "Oh, no, not again!" and act like they were tired of singing. So now I say, "And he started to sing . . . that . . . *song* again," emphasizing the word "song." When I do that, I acknowledge their exasperation, and celebrate it, and children laugh and join in. It's startling, the difference one word can make.

For 20 years, I wondered who the storyteller was who first told this story. Late one night, I Googled "Wide Mouth Frog" to see what other versions I could find. And there it was online—a recorded version by Mary Murphy. I listened to it with growing delight, realizing that this was indeed the storyteller my family had gone to see in Albany. Oh, the power of the Internet!

I called Mary the next day and she told me that she, too, had originally heard the story from another storyteller—a woman named Louise Kessel from North Carolina. Mary is still a storyteller in the Albany area. You can hear her version of "Wide Mouth Frog" at **www.murphywong.net/marymurphy/frog.htm**.

I found another hilarious rendition told by Larry N. Swenson at **http://cdbaby.com/cd/swenson**. He tells it twice, with the first time being merely funny, and the second time, when he adds an "ob" to every syllable ("Thob-a Wob-ide Mob-outh Frob-og), fall-on-the-floor hilarious.

There is also a very cute children's book of the story called *The Wide-Mouthed Frog: A Pop-Up Book* by Keith Faulkner and Jonathan Lambert (Dial, 1996).

And there are two more retellings I found—one called "The Big, Wide-Mouth Frog" in Martha Hamilton and Mitch Weiss's *Children Tell Stories: A Teaching Guide* (Richard C. Owen, 1990) and one called "Wide-Mouth Frog" in Hiroko Fujita's *Stories to Play With: Kids' Tales Told with Puppets, Paper, Toys, and Imagination* (August House, 1999).

Apparently, everyone has a version of this story, which started, I surmise, as a funny joke. I even found that there is such a creature called the wide mouth frog that lives in South America. Who knew?

T for Tommy

(An American Folktale, retold by Judy Freeman, © 2004.)

Once upon a time, there was a boy named Tommy. And here is a T for Tommy.

Tommy lived in a two room house. There was one room over here, just like this.
And another room over here. Just like that.
Tommy's house had two windows, just like this.
And it had two doors, together, just like that.

Now, it was lovely in Tommy's house in the summer, when the sun was shining. But in the winter, it got pretty cold. It got very cold. Since Tommy lived a long, long, time ago, what do you think he used to heat his house?

Fire? Yes, you are right. He kept a fire going in his fireplace. In fact, if you peered inside his windows, you could see two fireplaces. There was one fireplace in this room, and one in that room, too.

If you have two fireplaces in your house, then what do you need on the roof to let out all that smoke?

That's right. A chimney. In fact, Tommy's house had two chimneys. There was one chimney over here, just like this. And another one over there, just like that.

Tommy's house was just about perfect. But every time he stepped out his front door, **BAM**, he'd fall in the mud, because it was so far from the doorway down to the ground. What a mess.

"Hamm," Tommy said, "I think I need to build me some . . ."

Steps? That's right. That's just what he said. And that's just what he did. So Tommy built three steps, just like this.

But there was still plenty of mud on either side of the steps, and it didn't look very nice. So Tommy thought, and then he said, "Hamm. I think I need to plant something green that grows fast."

And so he planted some . . .

Grass! That's exactly right. That's just what he said. And that's just what he did. It grew and it grew and it grew like crazy, and pretty soon, it looked just like this.

Tommy had a best friend, and her name was Sally. And here's a big **S** for Sally.

One day, Tommy decided he would go and pay a visit to Sally. He walked out the front door, down the steps, and looked at the tall, tall grass. "I really should cut that," he said.

He walked across the field, over the meadow, until he got to Sally's house.

"Sally," he said, "You should see how I've fixed up my house. I have new steps and I planted grass. It's wonderful."

"Well, Tommy," said Sally, "I have a whole basket of apples in my basement. Why don't we go down to the basement, get the apples, and bring them over to your house. We'll have a party!"

"That's a great idea!" said Tommy.

So they went down to the basement, and they picked up the apples, and they walked up the basement steps, and out the basement door, just like this.

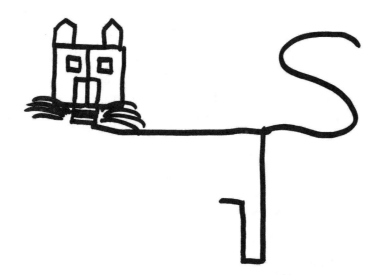

Tommy took one step, and **BAM**, down he went. He must've tripped over a rock or something. Well, Tommy wasn't hurt, and the apples weren't hurt, but Tommy went rolling, and the apples went rolling, and they had to pick up the apples and put 'em in the basket and pick up the apples and put 'em in the basket and pick up the apples and put 'em in the basket.

Then Tommy and Sally walked up the little hill he'd just rolled down. They walked and they walked, across the field, over the meadow, talking and laughing, when, all of a sudden, **BAM**. Tommy tripped *again*! Down he went.

He must've tripped over a rock or something. Well, Tommy wasn't hurt, and the apples weren't hurt, but Tommy went rolling, and the apples went rolling, and they had to pick up the apples and put 'em in the basket, and pick up the apples and put 'em in the basket, and pick up the apples and put 'em in the basket.

Then Tommy and Sally walked up the little hill he'd just rolled down. Sally said, "Tommy, you keep falling. Why don't I carry the apples now?"

"Okay," said Tommy, and he handed the basket of apples over to Sally.

Sally took one step and . . . (You know what's going to happen, don't you? Let's do it together.) **BAM**. Down she went.

She must've tripped over a rock or something. Well, Sally wasn't hurt, and the apples weren't hurt, but Sally went rolling, and the apples went rolling, and they had to pick up the apples and put 'em in the basket and pick up the apples and put 'em in the basket and pick up the apples and put 'em in the basket.

They walked all the way up the little hill she'd just rolled down, and all the way up to Tommy's house. But when they got there, Sally stopped short. "I can't go in there!" she said. "There's a big black cat on the doorstep!"

And there's the cat.

And that's why they call this story "**The Tale of a Black Cat.**"

STORYTELLER'S NOTE

I have been drawing and telling this story since the early 1970s when I found Carl Withers's little picture book *The Tale of a Black Cat* (Henry Holt, 1966) in my school library's collection, along with his *The Wild Ducks and the Goose* (1968). This story has been around since the 1880s, and passed down from generation to generation by children. Over the years, my telling of the story has changed, though I can't say I always did it consciously. I added repetition, audience participation, and even a little bit of equal rights ("Let me carry the apples," says Sally, apparently exasperated over Tommy's ability to hold on to the basket. Of course, she falls, too. Equal time, that.) I did what storytellers do—I made the story my own. That happens when you tell a story over and over.

When you introduce this story, never say the actual title, "The Tale of a Black Cat," or you'll give away the whole surprise of what you're going to be drawing. When I tell it to children, whether it's to a single class or an assembly, I start like this:

"This is an old, old story. It's an antique. An antique is an object that is more than a century old. School kids have been telling this story and passing it along for more than 100 years, so I think of it as a real antique.

"Not only will I be telling you this story, I'll be drawing it here, on this easel, as well. Observe my beautiful black magic marker. Blue won't do. Or green, or yellow, or orange. Forget about pink and purple. Black is what you need for this story. A black marker or pen or crayon. Remember that when you tell this story to your mother, father, grandmother, grandfather, sister, brother, aunt, uncle, cousin, and all your friends and neighbors. You'll want to tell it to everyone. Don't let me stop you.

"I can't tell you the real title of this story. Not yet, anyway. If I do, I'll give too much away. For now, we'll just call it 'T for Tommy.'"

"I can't tell you the author of this story, either. No, I didn't write it. I'm just the teller. No one knows who made it up, a long time ago. That's folklore for you. Someone, somewhere, sometime made this story up and started to tell it and started to draw it. Wish we knew who and where and when. But we don't. At least we still have a good story."

And then I launch into the story, my marker at the ready.

Some of the changes in my telling of this story came about because of the kids. One day, I was giving an assembly program to first and second graders. At the end of the story, when I said, "And THERE'S the CAT!" I heard a little voice in the audience.

"Where?"

I was taken aback. Were there other children who couldn't tell that what I had just drawn was a cat? I asked, "How many of you can see the cat?" Most raised their hands, but not all. Could it be that some children were so focused on the steps of the story that they didn't put all of the pieces together?

For some children, it's easy. As soon as you put in the windows and doors, some will call out, "It looks like a head," or "I see a cat." For others, they don't see it at all, even at the end. What could I do to make sure everyone "got it"?

So I made some changes. At the end of the story, when you say, "And that's why they call this story 'The Tale of a Black Cat,' " I always write the title in the torso of the cat, so listeners can see it as well as hear it.

After that, I now say, "Can you see the cat? Tell me, what are the cat's EYES made of?"

They call out, "Windows!"

"What are the cat's EARS made of?" "Chimneys!" "What are the cat's WHISKERS made of?" "Grass!" "And what is the cat's TALE made of?" "An S, for Sally."

"That's right. And THERE'S the cat!"

When you do this, you'll hear excited murmurs of recognition. "I see it! It's a cat!"

Through this simple story, you can see the spectrum of learners we teach every day, from the ones who get everything the first time to the ones who need lots of help. We try to reach every child.

Richard Thompson, whose terrific website **www.drawandtell.com** is packed with his own original, clever draw-and-tell stories, has some ideal advice for what to do when children interrupt during a story—what he calls "Put your finger on your nose . . .":

> Part of the fun of listening to a draw-and-tell story is trying to guess what the picture will be at the end.
>
> The fact that there is a "puzzle" element to the story is part of the fun of telling one of these stories as well, but it can create a bit of a problem for you, the storyteller.
>
> Almost inevitably, someone in the audience is going to figure out what the picture is before you get to the end of the story. And especially if that someone is in Kindergarten or Grade One, that someone is going to want to let you . . . and the rest of the people in the room . . . know that she has figured out what the picture is going to be.
>
> She will probably yell out in a nice clear voice: "I know what it is! I know what it is! It's an alligator!"
>
> And now everyone in the audience knows, and everyone in the audience wants to let you know that they know . . .
>
> So . . . here is a little trick that can help you get around that problem. Before you start the story, say to the children in your audience:
>
> "As I am telling this story, I will be drawing lines and shapes. Those lines and shapes are going to turn into a picture. Now, you won't be able to tell what the picture is right away, but I know that some of you will figure it out before I get to the end of my story. If you do figure it

out, I am going to ask you to do me a favor . . . don't call out and tell me what it is. Wait until the end of the story to tell. There will probably be some people who need a little more time to figure it out, and we want to give them a chance. BUT . . . you can tell me that you have the picture figured out by sending me a silent signal. If I see you put your finger on your nose . . . once . . . like this . . . I will know that you have figured out the picture . . . And then at the end of the story, we will see if you were right."

(By the way, she was wrong . . . that wasn't an alligator that I was drawing there . . .)

If you are telling a draw-and-tell story to a small group, say one class, then hand out paper and black crayons and have them draw the whole story while you tell it. I used to do it with my first graders every year. It's great for sequence skills and retelling and you can also see which children are having perceptual problems.

By first grade, most children will be able to follow the sequence and draw along with you. Watch them make the first T. If it's too close to the top of the page, leaving no room for the rest of the head, or the T is too small, have them turn over the page and start again on the other side.

There is another wonderful side effect to the drawing component. At the end of the story, ask children to hold up their cat pictures and to look at everyone else's. They'll notice that no two cats look the same. Some cats will be skinny, and others rotund. Each cat will have its own personality. From this you can discuss illustrations and how no two artists draw the same way, even when they draw the same thing. Show a variety of picture books about cats, and look at the different styles of illustration.

My favorite cat book to read along with this story is Nick Bruel's *Bad Kitty* (Roaring Brook, 2005) which is wonderful to act out in creative drama as well. (See page 239 in this handbook.) See also the Reader's Theater script for *The Barking Mouse* by Antonio Sacre (Albert Whitman, 2003) on page 230. There's a big bad cat in that story, too.

It's also a good way to open a discussion on homonyms, talking about the difference between the tale of a black cat and the tail of a black cat.

And finally, if you can find a copy of the delightful but out-of-print picture book, *The Maid and the Mouse and the Odd-Shaped House: A Story in Rhyme* by Paul O. Zelinsky (Dutton, 1993), you'll discover it's a variant of the black cat story that was found written in a teacher's notebook from 1897. It's interesting to compare and contrast the two.

From *Once Upon a Time: Using Storytelling, Creative Drama, and Reader's Theater with Children in Grades PreK-6* by Judy Freeman. Westport, CT: Libraries Unlimited. Copyright © 2007.

IT'S HALLOWEEN

(By Laura Coughlin and Judy Freeman, © 1990.)

GROUP	CUE	(RESPONSE)
1.	WITCHES	(Heh heh heh)
2.	GHOSTS	(Oooohhhhh)
3.	GOBLINS	(Ee-ee-ee)
4.	SKELETONS	(Tap tap tap)
5.	BLACK CATS	(Mee-owww)
All	TRICKS AND TREATERS	(Ding dong)

It's Halloween! It's Halloween!
The night for **TRICKS AND TREATERS** (Ding dong).
We'll walk down blocks, wear out our socks,
For miles and feet and meters.

There's a house upon the hilltop;
We will not go inside,
For that is where the **WITCHES** (Heh heh heh) live,
Where **GHOSTS** (Oooohhhhh) and **GOBLINS** (Ee-ee-ee) hide.

The **SKELETONS** (Tap tap tap) arise tonight,
White bones clatter in the cold moonlight.
The **BLACK CATS** (Mee-owww), black as blackest coal,
Are out upon their midnight stroll.

The **GHOSTS** (Oooohhhhh) they host a party;
The lights are burning bright,
While all the grinning **GOBLINS** (Ee-ee-ee)
Squeal with main and might.

WITCHES (Heh heh heh) whiz on magic brooms,
While **SKELETONS** (Tap tap tap) rise up from tombs.
The sleek **BLACK CATS** (Mee-owww) with eyes of gold
Have come to revel, I am told.

We **TRICKS AND TREATERS** (Ding dong) will not ring
That bell upon the door;
For inside, all the **WITCHES** (Heh heh heh) whirl
The **GHOSTS** (Ooooohhhhh) across the floor.

They dance and sing their eerie songs;
The **GOBLINS** (Ee-ee-ee) bang the dinner gongs.
The **SKELETONS** (Tap tap tap) dish up batwing stew;
The **BLACK CATS** (Mee-owww) are the cleanup crew.

We do not want, we do not wish
To tempt them as a dinner dish.
Instead we roam the silent streets,
Playing tricks and getting treats.

It's late and we are weary,
The air is cold and still.
But now it's time to go to bed
And dream of winter's chill.

We'll dream of **GHOSTS** (Ooooohhhhh) in attics,
and **GOBLINS** (Ee-ee-ee) on the wall;
We'll dream of **WITCHES** (Heh heh heh) gliding
On their broomsticks in the hall;

And **BLACK CATS** (Mee-owww) in the alley,
And **SKELETONS** (Tap tap tap) in tombs,
While we the **TRICKS AND TREATERS** (Ding dong)
Lie safe within our rooms.

Oh what we've seen, oh where we've been
This spooky, scary **HALLOWEEN**!

STORYTELLER'S NOTE

Some years back, Laura Coughlin, a teacher at Van Holten School in Bridgewater, New Jersey, where I was then the school librarian, asked me if I knew any good Halloween stories where kids could join in on the sound effects. I recalled the story "The King with the Terrible Temper," from Virginia Tashjian's collection of story hour stretches, *With a Deep Sea Smile* (Little, Brown, 1974), and showed it to her. (If you don't have a copy of that long-out-of-print treasure, you can find the individual story at many Boy Scout sites online, if you Google it.) In that story, each group is responsible for making a sound effect, including the horse (slapping hands on thighs), the king ("Grrr"), and several other characters.

"This is a great one, but it's not scary. Maybe you want to write your own for Halloween?" I suggested.

Laura did just that, and gave me her first draft. We worked on it back and forth, and the resulting poem has been just the ticket for involving a group in some Halloween revelry.

Divide your audience into the five groups listed above, and go over each of the sounds. Have each group think up a physical motion to go with its sound effect. For instance, the skeletons may decide to tap their fingernails on a book to make their sound; the witches may want to rub their hands together in glee as they cackle their "heh-heh-heh."

As you recite the poem, each time you say the words "tricks and treaters," everyone will say, "ding dong!" When you say "witches" or "ghosts" or "goblins" or "skeletons" or "black cats" though, each group will respond only to its assigned sound effect. You might want to practice with the children, doing the first verse to make sure they understand their parts.

After reading aloud or reciting the poem the first time, hand out copies for all to perform aloud the second time as a choral reading. You could do the whole poem in unison, and then read it yet again, with each group reading a verse in turn.

Another fun Halloween participation story is the song "Creeping, Creeping" on page 54.

Putting together a story hour? Stir in Erica Silverman's *Big Pumpkin* (Macmillan, 1992) and Linda Williams's *The Little Old Lady Who Was Not Afraid of Anything* (Crowell, 1986), both of which you'll find listed in "400+ Children's Books Every Storyteller Should Know" on page 111.

THE VIPER

(An old story retold by Judy Freeman.)

Once I was home waiting for my friend Bonnie to come over. The phone rang. (Can you help me with the phone sound effects in this true story? BRRRIIING! Thank you. That's very good.)

I picked up the telephone. "Bonnie?" I said. "Is that you?"

A voice on the other end said, "Hello. Theese eese Theee Viperrr. I am coming to your house in vone year."

"Very funny, Bonnie," I said into the phone. She didn't say anything. And then she hung up.

"Nice phony phone call," I told her when she came over a few minutes later.

"What?" she said. "What phony phone call?"

"Never mind," I said. "I know it was you."

But 11 months later, the telephone rang again. BRRRIIING!

"Hello?"

"Hello. Theese eese Theee Viperrr. I am coming to your house in vone month."

"Bonnie? Is that you? Is this some kind of joke?"

But she hung up. I didn't think anything about it. When I saw Bonnie and asked her about the call, she said, "I don't know what you're even talking about."

Three weeks later, the telephone rang again. BRRRIIING!

"Hello?"

"Hello. Theese eese Theee Viperrr. I am coming to your house in vone veek."

It didn't sound like Bonnie. It didn't sound like Bonnie at all.

"Vone veek? I mean, one week? Who is this? Why are you calling me? What do you want with me?"

The line went dead. I tried not to think about it.

Six days later, the telephone rang again. BRRRIIING!

"Hello?"

"Hello. Theese eese Theee Viperrr. I am coming to your house in vone day."

"One day? You're coming to my house in one day? Oh, no!"

I couldn't sleep at all that night. I was tossing and turning, tossing and turning, tossing and turning all night. Why, oh why, was The Viper coming to my house? What did he want? What was a viper, anyway?

Twenty-three hours after the last call, the telephone rang again. BRRRIIING!

From *Once Upon a Time: Using Storytelling, Creative Drama, and Reader's Theater with Children in Grades PreK-6* by Judy Freeman. Westport, CT: Libraries Unlimited. Copyright © 2007.

"Hello. Theese eese Theee Viperrr. I am coming to your house in vone hour."

"One hour. Yup. I see. One hour. Right. One hour. Great. Thanks. See you."

I bit my nails. I paced the floor. I worried. I waited.

Fifty-nine minutes later, the telephone rang again. BRRRIIING!

"Hello?"

"Hello. Theese eese Theee Viperrr. I am coming to your house in vone minute."

"One minute? You're coming to my house in one minute? Oh, no!"

Fifty-nine seconds later, the doorbell rang. DINGGGGG DONGGGG. I didn't want to answer the door. I didn't *want* to answer the door. But I *had* to answer the door. With shaking hands, I turned the doorknob. I opened the door. SQQQQUUUEEEAAAKKK.

And there he stood.

"Hello," he said. "I am Theee Viper. Theee Vindow Viper. I've come to Vash and Vipe your Vindows!"

STORYTELLER'S NOTE

When I was a child, my good friend Bonnee Zabell, now Bonnee Bazin, and I used to tell each other scary jump tales for the fun of it. We'd spook ourselves out. This is one we always loved. Put your own name into this story if you like. Personalize it as something that happened to you. If you want to be dramatic, bring in a small pail and a squeegee to pull out for the last line of the story.

Lisa Thiesing did a cute version of the story as an easy reader, making the main character of *The Viper* (Dutton, 2002) the very nervous Peggy the Pig. It would be very effective to write up as a two-person Reader's Theater for pairs to read together.

I took the old "Will You Remember Me" knock-knock joke and turned it into a math joke, below. Try it as a call-and-response follow-up to "The Viper."

WILL YOU REMEMBER ME?

(An old joke adapted by Judy Freeman, 2000.)

Q: *Will you remember me in a thousand years?*
A: A millennium? YES.

Q: *Good. Will you remember me in a hundred years?*
A: A century? YES.

Q: *Good. Will you remember me in ten years?*
A: A decade? YES.

Q: *Good. Will you remember me in 365 days or 12 months?*
A: One year? YES.

Q: *Good. Will you remember me in 30 days or 4 weeks?*
A: A month? YES.

Q: *Good. Will you remember me in 7 days?*
A: A week? YES.

Q: *Good. Will you remember me in 24 hours?*
A: A day? YES.

Q: *Good. Will you remember me in 60 minutes?*
A: An hour? YES.

Q: *Good. Will you remember me in 60 seconds?*
A: A minute? YES.

Q: *Good. Will you remember me in one second?*
A: YES.

Q: *KNOCK, KNOCK.*
A: WHO'S THERE?

Q: *YOU FORGOT ME ALREADY???!!!*

THE RAINHAT

(A paperfolding story inspired by the version in Nancy Schimmel's *Just Enough to Make a Story: A Sourcebook for Telling,* 2nd. ed. (Sisters Choice Press, 1992), and by the telling of Alice H. Yucht, and then another 15 years of tinkering.)

Once upon a time there was a girl named Minka who was bored, bored, bored. It was Saturday, it was raining, and she wanted to go out and play in the rain. But her mother wouldn't let her.

"No," her mother told her, "you can't play in the rain. You don't have a rainhat. You'll get all wet."

Minka was so annoyed. She was aggravated, aggrieved, and angry. She stomped up the stairs to her bedroom.

"It's not fair," she fumed. "I want to go outside and play in the rain, but Mother says no, I'll get all wet, just because I don't have a rainhat. It's not fair."

She picked up a big piece of paper. "All I have is this big boring piece of paper."

She took that piece of paper and folded it in half, like a hamburger, just like this.

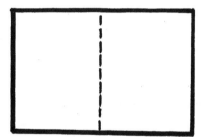

1. Fold paper in half, like a hamburger.

Minka looked at the folded paper. "It looks like a party invitation. But no one has invited me to a party. Even if they had, I probably couldn't go because it's raining and I don't have a raincoat. It's not fair."

But she liked folding that piece of paper in half. She liked it so much, she folded it in half again.

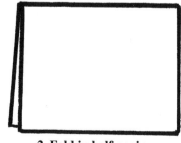

2. Fold in half again.

"Now it looks like a book. But I don't feel like reading a book right now. What I really want to do is go outside and play in the rain. But Mother says I can't play in the rain because it's raining and I don't have a rainhat. It's not *fair!*"

Minka took that piece of paper and opened it up, like an open book. Then she folded down the corner of the left side of the paper into a big triangle, right down the middle crease. And she liked doing that so much, she folded down the right corner into another triangle down the middle crease to match it.

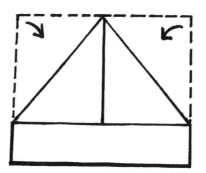

3. Open like an open book, with fold at the top. Then fold down left corner along center crease; then fold down right corner, too.

And when she did, what did she have but a . . . space shuttle? A house? That was no good. Then she noticed that at the bottom there were two flaps. She folded the front flap over the two triangles, and opened it up at the bottom.

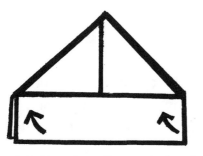
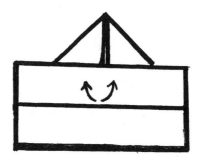

4. Fold up front flap over triangles.   **5. Pull front flap open from center—PILGRIM HAT.**

She put it on her head, and when she did, what did she have but a . . . *PILGRIM HAT?* "That's no good. It's not even Thanksgiving!" she exclaimed.

So Minka took the hat off. Then she noticed there was still another flap on the other side. Turning the hat over to the other side, she folded up the other flap. And when she did, and she slid her thumbs and opened up the two sides, what did she have but a *RAINHAT*! And a mighty fine rain hat it was. She put it on her head.

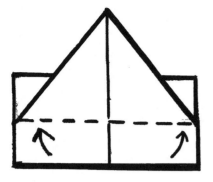

6. Close hat and turn around to other side. Fold flap up to match flap on other side.

7. Hook thumbs under either sides of opening at bottom, pull open—RAIN HAT.

So Minka ran outside to play in the rain. She splashed in the puddles and had a marvelous time. She sang,

"I'm singing in the rain, just singing in the rain;
What a glorious feeling, I'm happy again . . ."

But then the rain stopped and the sun came out. "Oh, no," cried the girl. "The sun's out. That's no good."

Just then, something terrible happened to the house next door. The house next door caught . . . on . . . *fire!*

"Oh, no," Minka said. "The house next door is on fire. I have to fight the fire! It's all up to me."

She stopped. "Wait a minute. I can't fight that fire! I'm wearing a rainhat. If I'm going to fight that fire, I need a . . . *firefighter's hat!*"

So she took off her rainhat and she opened it all the way and pushed it flat into a diamond shape. She tucked under the loose flaps on the bottom of each side. Then she folded up the front flap of the diamond until it met the point at the top and became a triangle.

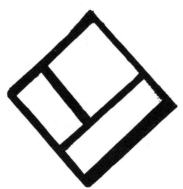

8. Open rain hat all the way; flatten into a new diamond. Tuck under flaps at bottom in front and back.

From *Once Upon a Time: Using Storytelling, Creative Drama, and Reader's Theater with Children in Grades PreK-6* by Judy Freeman. Westport, CT: Libraries Unlimited. Copyright © 2007.

With her thumb, she pulled the opening at the bottom of the triangle, until what did she have but a . . . *FIREFIGHTER'S HAT!* That's right. And a mighty fine firefighter's hat it was.

 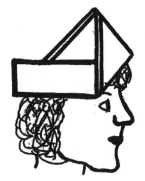

9. Fold up the front half of the diamond into a triangle to meet the top point. Pull out from middle and open—FIREFIGHTER'S HAT.

Minka put that hat on her head, picked up the hose in her back yard, turned on the water, and she started to fight that fire. She fought that fire—Psssshhhhhh—and she fought that fire—Psssshhhhhh—and she fought that fire—Psssshhhhhh—until she put that fire out!

But she was having such a good time with the hose and all that water, she just kept right on spraying. Psssshhhhhh. Until she flooded the back yard. PSSSHHHHH! Until she flooded the neighborhood. *PSSSSSHHHHHHHHHH*! Until she flooded *everything*!

She was stomping in the water, and splashing in the water, and getting all wet. "Wow," she said. "I feel like a pirate on the seven seas!"

Suddenly, she stopped. "Wait a minute. I can't be a pirate on the seven seas! I'm wearing a firefighter's hat. If I'm going to be a pirate on the seven seas, I need a . . . *pirate hat*!"

So she took off her firefighter's hat and she pushed on the front triangle until it was flat. She turned it over to diamond shape on the other side. Then she folded up the bottom flap of the diamond until it met the point at the top and became a triangle.

From *Once Upon a Time: Using Storytelling, Creative Drama, and Reader's Theater with Children in Grades PreK-6* by Judy Freeman. Westport, CT: Libraries Unlimited. Copyright © 2007.

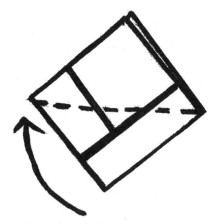

10. Flatten out firefighter's hat back into a diamond; turn over and fold diamond up to top point to make a triangle to match the other side.

She hooked her thumbs on either side of the opening at the bottom of the triangle, and she pulled, until what did she have but a . . . *PIRATE HAT!* And a mighty fine pirate hat it was.

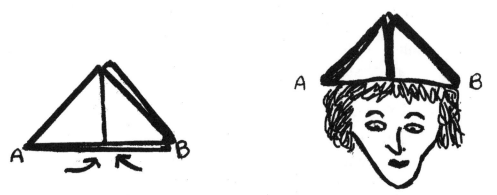

11. Hook thumbs under either side in the center; pull out and open—PIRATE HAT.

Minka put that hat on her head. "Yo ho ho, and a bottle of pop!" she sang. "Ahoy there, matey!"

She was stomping in the water, and splashing in the water, and getting even wetter. Suddenly, she stopped.

"Hold on," she said. "It's all well and good to be a pirate on the seven seas wearing my pirate hat. But if I'm really going to be a pirate on the seven seas, what I need is a pirate . . . *SHIP!*"

She took off her pirate hat and hooked her thumbs under the middle of each side. She pulled all the way until it became another diamond.

12. Push bottom corners of pirate hat together to make a new diamond shape; flatten.

Then she took hold of the two flaps on either side at the top of the diamond. She pulled and she tugged, she tugged and she pulled, until what did she have but a pirate . . . *SHIP!* And a mighty fine pirate ship it was, too.

13. Carefully pull flaps on either side of the point, and open up into a SHIP. Flatten ship at bottom.

So she climbed aboard. And she went . . .
Sailing, sailing, over the bounding main,
For many a stormy wind shall blow,
Till we come home again,
Sailing, sailing, over the bounding main,
For many a stormy wind shall blow,
Till we come home again.

Yes, she went sailing, sailing, over the bounding main,
For many a stormy wind shall blow,
Till we come home again,

Sailing, sailing, over the bounding main,
For many a stormy wind shall blow,
Till we come home again.
Yes, she went Sailing, sailing, over the bounding . . .

CRASH! She crashed her boat into the brick wall of South Mountain School. She bashed off the bow, the front, of the boat.

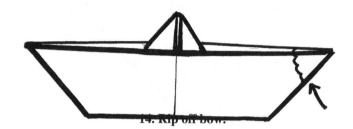

14. Rip off bow.

"Oh," she said, "that's not good. The bow is gone. Oh, well. I still have the stern."

And turning the front of the boat, the bow, around to the back of the boat, the stern, she went . . .

Sailing, sailing, over the bounding main,
For many a stormy wind shall blow,
Till we come home again,
Sailing, sailing, over the bounding . . .

CRASH! She crashed her boat into the brick wall of South Mountain School again. She dashed, she crashed, she smashed, she gashed, she trashed, she bashed off the stern, the back, of the boat.

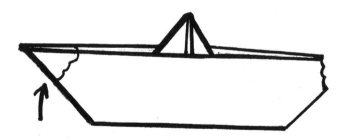

"Ohhhhh," she said, "that's not good. The bow is gone. The stern is gone. Oh, well. It still floats."

So she went . . .
Sailing, sailing, over the bounding main,
For many a stormy wind shall blow,
Till we come home again,
Sailing, sailing, over the bounding . . .

CRASH!

She hit a rock. She gashed a hole in the bottom of the boat.

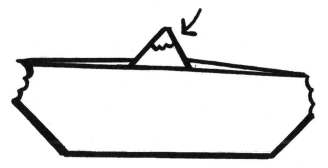

16. Carefully reach inside center and tear off top of tip.

[hold up the boat and open it a little at the bottom so your audience can see the hole]

Everyone knows, if you gash a hole in the bottom of your boat, that boat is going . . . to . . . *SINK! [show boat sinking lower and lower]* That's right. Right down to the bottom of Davy Jones's locker!

But Minka didn't drown. No! She didn't drown. And why?

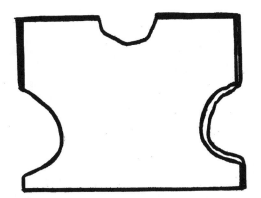

17. Unfold carefully; undo and pull out bottom flaps; shake out your LIFE JACKET.

[as you say this next part, carefully unfold the boat and, on the last line, shake it out and hold it up] Because she . . . was wearing . . . her . . . **LIFE JACKET!**

And that's how you tell a story out of a simple piece of *PAPER!* *[open up paper into one big piece again]*

STORYTELLER'S NOTE

In storytelling, the most important part is making a story your own. That's what happened with "The Rainhat" for me. I acquired the story after seeing my friend and colleague Alice Yucht tell it, using a sheet of newspaper. I looked up the instructions in Nancy Schimmel's book, *Just Enough to Make a Story,* and, after a few tries, mastered the paperfolding sequences. And then the story started to grow.

Over years of telling, the story somehow acquired a couple of songs; a justifiably pouty but resourceful child, indignant because she wasn't allowed outside; and satisfying language, including all that crashing, bashing, and smashing into the school's brick wall. One day, I reread Nancy Schimmel's story and was startled to see the many ways in which my telling of it had evolved. It had become personal, with lots of humor, sound effects for children to join in on, and audience interaction.

When you tell this story to children, they love seeing the different hats, but you can see them getting ho hum-ish around the time you start singing the "Sailing, Sailing" song. You can see them thinking, OK, that's all there is? Big deal. Impress me.

Then CRASH. The boat hits the wall and they sit right up. That crazy storyteller is destroying her own boat! Now you have their attention and their involvement again.

So you think you're paper-impaired and can't master all the folding in this story? Give it a try anyway. Keep the instructions in front of you, and after four or five tries, using a piece of computer paper, you'll see that each object you fold will flow into the next one. If you're having problems, find a ten year old to show you. Once you have the basics, you can graduate up to a large piece of chart paper, such as 24" x 30". You want the hats to fit on your head.

I used to tell this story to kindergarten classes in my school library every year, and it was a huge favorite. The following week, I would ask children to help me retell it and then have them do the paper folding with me, using manila paper or white computer paper. Is this too hard for kindergarten? Yes and no. Their manual dexterity hasn't quite kicked in, but with some help from an adult at each table or an older child, it's quite doable.

My favorite part is always when you demonstrate how to run your hand along a crease of the paper on the table to flatten it. Kindergartners will, instead, hit at the paper with their hands, thinking, somehow, that this will work. This is very cute and amusing to watch, and yes, they'll need assistance with that part. The looks on their faces when they make each hat and then the boat are wonderful to behold.

I prefer not to have them do the paper-ripping part of the story. Instead, stop when the ships are sailing over the bounding main, and then bring out the crayons for them to decorate both sides. They'll want to put the ship's name on the side—The S.S. *Amy,* for instance.

From *Once Upon a Time: Using Storytelling, Creative Drama, and Reader's Theater with Children in Grades PreK-6* by Judy Freeman. Westport, CT: Libraries Unlimited. Copyright © 2007.

Mind you, this story should not be restricted to the very young. Older children like it just as much, and they quickly become proficient at the paperfolding. Once they discover that a half-piece of paper produces a smaller ship, they'll experiment with smaller and smaller pieces of paper. These could even be used as Christmas tree decorations.

If you're building a storytime program around "The Rainhat" for young children, start with an interactive chant like:

Rain on green grass, *[fingers wiggling, like rain, waist-high]*
And rain on the tree. *[fingers wiggling, like rain, arms up high over head]*
Rain on the rooftop, *[fingers wiggling as you pantomime a high slanted roof]*
But not upon me! *[both hands cover head]*

Or sing a rain song. I wrote a few new verses to the traditional song, "It's Raining, It's Pouring," which you'll find on page 39.

PRINDERELLA AND THE CINCE

(This retelling is a composite based on several versions from New Jersey folks, including Carol Phillips, head of Children's Services at East Brunswick Public Library; teacher Betty Butler; author and librarian consultant, Alice Yucht, who originally "cranstribed" all three versions together; and further edited and tampered with by Judy Freeman.)

Reprinted from *Books Kids Will Sit Still For 3: A Read-Aloud Guide* by Judy Freeman
(Libraries Unlimited, 2006).

Tonce upon a wime there lived a gritty little pearl named Prinderella. She lived in a hovely louse with her stugly sep-isters and her sticked wep-mother. All lay dong Prinderella had to do all the hork of the wousehold; wean the clindows, flub the scroor, pine the shots and shans, and do all the other wirty dirk, while her sugly isters and sticked wep-mother dept all slay on beather feds. Prinderella was treated bery vadly and had to wear roppy slags that fidn't dit. Isn't that a shirty dame?

Done way, the Quing and Keen prade a mocklimation that there would be a brand drancy-fess gall in honor of the Cince, and all the gelligible irls of the kole wingdom were invited. So the kole whingdom prepared for the brand gall. Prinderella's stugly sep-isters and sticked wep-mother made Prinderella murk all day to wake their drancy fesses.

Then poor Prinderella, in her roppy slags that fidn't dit, had to hay stome as her stugly sep-isters and sticked wep-mother went off to the gall in a covely larriage. Wasn't that a shirty dame!

Prinderella dat in the soorway, crobbing and sying till her gairy fodmother, who lived in a laraway fand, heard her and came to see mat was the whatter.

"Oh! Gairy Fodmother," cried Prinderella, "I feel so serribly tad! Why can't I bo to the gall, and pree the Cince?"

Near fot, chy mild. You *shall* bo to the gall!" said the gairy fodmother. "Now, so to the geller and bring me some pice, a mumpkin, and three rat fats."

When Prinderella brought the pice, the mumpkin, and the rat fats, the gairy fodmother fapped her sningers, touched them with her wagic mand, and changed the mumpkin into a hoach, the pice into corses, and the rat fats into moachcen.

But Prinderella still had nothing to wear but roppy slags that fidn't dit. Wasn't that a shirty dame? So the gairy fodmother quickly fapped her sningers again, winkled her tye, and there was a garkling spown of gilver and sold, all covered with pubies and rearls. It was the bost dreautiful mess in the kole whingdom! And for her feet, there was a painty dair of slass glippers.

As the gairy fodmother clelped Prinderella himb into the covely larriage, she warned her: "Don't gorfet: you must beave lefore the moke of stridnight, for the brell will be spoken when the twock clikes strelve."

Prinderella was the bost meautiful baiden at the mall. When the Cince saw her fovely lace and her dreautiful bess, all covered with pubies and rearls, he lell in fove with her. They nanced all dight, until the calace plock chegan to bime. Then, just before the last moke of stridnight, Prinderella dan out the roor to her waiting harriage and courses. But as she durried hown the stalace peps, she slopped her dripper! Now wasn't that a shirty dame?

The dext nay, the Ping issued a krocklamation that the Cince was lesperately dooking for the meautiful baiden who had slopped her dripper as she left the brand gall. The Cince hent to the wouses of all the gelligible earls of the kole whingdom in gearch of the sirl he had lallen in fove with, and now manted to warry.

When the Cince came to Prinderella's house, her stugly sep-isters all tried to tit their foes into the slass glipper, but it fidn't dit!

But whuess gat? When Prinderella flipped her soot into the slass glipper, it fid dit! So Prinderella and the Cince mere warried. She wore a gedding wown of wharkling spite, all covered with pubies and rearls. And Prinderella and the Cince hived lappily ever after. That wasn't such a shirty dame, was it?

STORYTELLER'S NOTE

Finish off your Cinderella unit with Prinderella. (For resources, see the "Looking at Cinderella" section of this book on page 27, for lots of ideas, activities booklists, and websites.) I introduce it to children, grades three and up, by saying, "Do you kids like tairy fails?"

"What?" they always answer. "Do we like what?"

"Tairy fails! Everyone loves tairy fails! You know, like Whow Snite and the Deven Swarves? And Gansel and Hretel? And what about Beeping Sleuty! Everyone loves Beeping Sleuty!"

At which point, someone always says, "Sleeping Beauty! She means Sleeping Beauty!"

"Exactly. Tairy fails. Just like I said. I'm going to tell you a really famous one." And then I launch into Prinderella.

After you read or tell this story, ask listeners just what it was you were doing with the words. They'll observe that you were switching initial consonants.

You can segue into a lesson on Spoonerisms, based on the legendary tips of the slongue, er, slips of the tongue, made by the Reverend William Archibald Spooner (1844-1930), the Oxford Dean and Warden of New College in Oxford, England. He called a well-oiled bicycle "a well-boiled icicle." He once reprimanded a student who, as he said, "hissed my mystery lecture." Officiating at a wedding, he proclaimed, "Son, it is now kisstomary to cuss the bride." And, in church one day, he said, "Mardon me padam, this pie is occupewed. Can I sew you to another sheet?"

The Greeks called this metathesis, or the act of switching things around.

"Prinderella and the Cince" is a prime example of metathesis, and a case of phonics run amok. After you share it aloud, hand out copies of the text and have children pair up and try reading it to each other. They can orally transpose each sentence back into English. And then ask them to bring the story home and read it aloud to their parents.

You can also use the story to fool around with other well-known fairy tales. Have them work in pairs or trios (humor is most satisfying when shared) to read a fairy tale—"Snow White and the Seven Dwarfs," "Hansel and Gretel," and "Sleeping Beauty" do come to mind, among others— and then write a one or two sentence synopsis of it. Then have them switch some of the consonants. Finally, have each group read aloud its description for the rest of the children to identify. It's an effective way to familiarize children with classic fairy tales we assume they know but often do not.

Shel Silverstein's *Runny Babbit* (HarperCollins, 2005) is an entire book of witty poetry filled with Spoonerisms, ideal to read aloud and share. Children love writing their own rhyming poems about the further exploits of Runny Babbit and his animal friends, and doing Silverstein-like pen and ink line drawings to go along.

For more fun with wordplay, including anagrams, palindromes, Tom Swifties, Malapropisms, mnemonic devices, and more, you and your students will love this site: **www.fun-with-words.com**.

IF YOU ASK YOUR MOTHER TO
TELL YOU A STORY

(By Judy Freeman.)

NOTE: To tell this story about stories, I use a 7-piece set of wooden Russian nesting dolls, called matrioshka or matreshka dolls, that opens up into seven dolls, graduated in size from 6" tall down to a tiny 1/2" tall. As I tell the story, I open the doll, show the doll within, and place the opened doll on a table next to the previous one. I end up with seven dolls in a line, and then the children help me to retell the story verbally as I put the doll back together. It's an effective way to demonstrate the power and longevity of a story. Here's what I say to children.

There's nothing better than hearing a good story. People have been telling stories and passing them along forever. Your own parents and grandparents know lots of stories, including some I bet they've never thought to tell you: folktales and fairy tales, stories about their parents and about what it was like when they grew up, and stories about how they fell in love, and stories about you from when you were too little to remember.

[Hold up big matrioshka doll.] If you go home tonight and say to your mother, "Mom, tell me a story, an old story you knew when you were a little girl," perhaps she will remember a story she hasn't thought about for years; a story that she once heard night after night, time after time, from her mother—your grandmother. *[Open doll, place on table, and hold up new smaller doll.]*

And, maybe, your grandmother heard that same story, night after night, time after time, from her mother—your great-grandmother. *[Open doll, place on table, and hold up new smaller doll.]*

And, maybe, your great-grandmother heard that same story, night after night, time after time, from her mother—your great-great-grandmother. *[Open doll, place on table, and hold up new smaller doll.]*

And, maybe, your great-great-grandmother heard that same story, night after night, time after time, from her mother—your great-great-great-grandmother. *[Open doll, place on table, and hold up new smaller doll.]*

And, maybe, your great-great-great-grandmother heard that same story, night after night, time after time, from her mother—your great-great-great-great-grandmother. *[Open doll, place on table, and hold up new smaller doll.]*

[Pause.] And, maybe, your great-great-great-great-grandmother heard that same story, night after night, time after time, from her mother—your great-great-great-great-great-grandmother. *[Open doll, place on table, and hold up smallest doll; children will scream.]*

Now let's put the story back together again with words. Help me by telling it with me.

If your great-great-great-great-great-grandmother told a story to your great-great-great-great-grandmother *[Enclose tiny doll in bigger one.]*. . .

And she told that story to your great-great-great-grandmother *[Enclose doll in bigger one.]* . . .

And she told that story to your great-great-grandmother *[Enclose doll in bigger one.]* . . .

And she told that story to your great-grandmother *[Enclose doll in bigger one.]* . . .

And she told that story to your grandmother *[Enclose doll in bigger one.]* . . .

And she told that story to your mother *[Enclose doll in biggest one.]* . . .

Maybe tonight, your mother will tell that story to you, and tell it to you night after night, time after time. And when you grow up, you'll tell it to your children, and when they grow up, they'll tell it to their children, and that story will live on, forever, passed down from one generation to the next, from now until the end of time.

STORYTELLER'S NOTE

My friend Lois Farrah went to Russia one summer, and brought me back a hand-painted matreshka or matrioshka, or nesting doll, about six inches tall. One of my mantras of education is "Never throw anything out. If you do, someone will write a book about it." And its companion, "Hmmm. What can I use this for?"

So I began to show it to children, and gradually, as I opened each doll, the story emerged. This little interactive recitation works wonders in getting children to go home and ask their families for stories.

As the doll gets smaller and smaller, children of all ages are entranced. They have the same reaction when I get to the tiniest doll. They open their mouths and scream. Aaaaaaaahhhh. It's very satisfying.

You can find nesting dolls at many sites online, including **www.goldengrail.com/goods/47.html** where there's a good selection of seven-piece sets, priced at $10 and up. There's even a set of unpainted dolls that you can design yourself at **www.grandrivertoys.com/Pages/products/Matrioshka_Doll_ Kit.htm.**

400+ Children's Books Every Storyteller Should Know

Adapted in part from entries in *Books Kids will Sit Still For* (Libraries Unlimited, 1990), *More Books Kids will Sit Still For* (1995), and *Books Kids will Sit Still For 3* (2006) by Judy Freeman.

In putting together the titles for this bibliography, I looked for memorable children's stories to read, share, and tell from many countries and cultures. I included a judicious sampling of my favorite books whether they were in print or not. Books of folktales seem to go out of print faster than fiction, which is unhelpful, inconvenient, and most unfortunate. Hooray for librarians who know that the dustier and mustier a book of folktales is, the more precious. Check your library to see if some of the older classic treasures listed below are still on the shelves.

For more collections, ideas, and advice, see the "Professional Bibliography" on page 179. You'll find thousands of exemplary folktales and stories to read aloud and retell in the *Books Kids will Sit Still For* series.

I've attempted to categorize each title on the list into basic categories, as defined below. See also page 159 for "Types of Tales: A Booklist," a list of all of the titles, sorted by categories.

KEY TO CATEGORIES

BEAST: beast or animal folktales where the animals talk and interact like humans

COLLECTION: collections of folktales, instead of one single story

CUMULATIVE: cumulative, sequence, or circular stories with repetition and chantable refrains

EASY FICTION: easy fiction picture books, many of which are also great to tell as well as to read aloud

FABLE: fables

FAIRY TALE: folktales with magical elements

FICTION: chapter books, most of them fantasies dealing with folklore themes

FOLKTALE: old tales about ordinary people without a component of magic (You'll find those under FAIRY TALE. See also BEAST for folktales about animals and COLLECTIONS for anthologies of folktales.)

LEGEND: about legendary figures who may have lived; this category overlaps with MYTHS

MYTHS: tales of gods and goddesses that explain ancient religious beliefs, including Greek, Roman, Norse, African, and Native American; this category overlaps with LEGENDS

NONFICTION: informational books

NOODLEHEAD: noodlehead or fool stories about simpletons who usually come out ahead

PARODY: parodies of folktales, including updates and rewrites

POETRY: Mother Goose and other nursery rhymes or poetry

POURQUOI: how and why tales that explain how something came to be

SCARY: stories that give kids the chills

TALL TALE: exaggerated stories about larger-than-life characters

TRICKSTER: trickster tales about folks who try to get away with something and often do.

Aardema, Verna. *Misoso: Once Upon a Time Tales from Africa*. Illus. by Reynold Ruffins. Knopf, 1994. Gr. 2-6 (beast, collection)

The dozen tellable folktales in this attractive collection introduce us to characters like Anansi; the hungry spider trickster who meets up with talking foods; the Sloogey Dog; and an ape who repays in kind the man who removes a thorn from its foot.

Aardema, Verna. *Traveling to Tondo: A Tale of the Nkundo of Zaire*. Illus. by Will Hillenbrand. Knopf, 1991. Gr. 1-4 (beast, cumulative)

Bowane the civet cat invites his friends the pigeon, the snake, and the tortoise to go with him to meet his beautiful bride-to-be, but they procrastinate so long, they arrive years too late.

Aardema, Verna. *Why Mosquitoes Buzz in People's Ears*. Illus. by Leo and Diane Dillon. Dial, 1975. Gr. PreK-2 (beast, cumulative, pourquoi)

In this Caldecott winner, a cumulative African pourquoi tale, the lie mosquito tells to iguana sets off a chain of trouble among the animals.

Alexander, Lloyd. *How the Cat Swallowed Thunder*. Illus. by Judith Byron Schachner. Dutton, 2000. Gr. PreK-3 (easy fiction)

When Mother Holly leaves her rascally cat alone for the first time, with strict orders to tidy up the cottage, everything goes awry for the overwhelmed puss.

Andersen, Hans Christian. *The Nightingale*. Retold by Stephen Mitchell. Illus. by Bagram Ibatoulline. Candlewick, 2002. Gr. 2-6 (easy fiction)

The Emperor of China is incensed to hear that travelers consider the nightingale, which he never knew existed, to be the loveliest attraction in his land, and he demands the bird be presented to sing for him.

Andersen, Hans Christian. *The Nightingale.* **Retold and illus. by Jerry Pinkney. Putnam, 2002. Gr. 2-6 (easy fiction)**

With lush watercolor and gouache paintings, Pinkney reset from China to Northwest Africa the classic Andersen story of the Emperor who loves and then forsakes a nightingale.

Andersen, Hans Christian. *The Tinderbox.* **Adapted and illus. by Barry Moser. Little, Brown, 1990. Gr. 4-6 (easy fiction)**

Andersen's classic tale has been reset in the post–Civil War South, where Yoder Ott, a young soldier returning home, braves three huge-eyed dogs to fetch a magic tinderbox.

Anderson, Leone Castell. *The Wonderful Shrinking Shirt.* **Illus. by Irene Trivas. Albert Whitman, 1983. Gr. K-3 (easy fiction)**

Each time Elbert's fine yellow flannel shirt with the purple stripes gets washed, it shrinks and must be passed down to a smaller family member to wear.

Anholt, Catherine, and Laurence Anholt. *Chimp and Zee.* **Illus. by the authors. Putnam, 2001. Gr. PreK-1 (easy fiction)**

Two naughty little chimpanzees disobey their Mumkey and get lost in Jungletown, when the gray stones on which they are hiding turn out to be elephants. The equally fun sequel is *Chimp and Zee and the Big Storm* (2002).

Arkhurst, Joyce Cooper. *The Adventures of Spider: West African Folk Tales.* **Illus. by Jerry Pinkney. Little, Brown, 1992, c1964. Gr. 1-4 (beast, trickster)**

Do read aloud the introduction to these six good-natured trickster tales from Liberia and Ghana.

Asbjørnsen, P. C. *The Three Billy Goats Gruff.* **Illus. by Marcia Brown. Harcourt, 1957. Gr. PreK-2 (beast, cumulative)**

Here's the classic Norwegian tale of a nasty troll who gets what he deserves.

Auch, Mary Jane. *The Princess and the Pizza.* **Illus. by Mary Jane Auch and Herm Auch. Holiday House, 2002. Gr. K-5 (easy fiction, parody, pourquoi)**

Missing her former life as a princess, Paulina heads for the castle to compete with eleven other princesses to become the royal bride to drippy Prince Drupert, and in the process, invents a winning new recipe for something she calls "pizza."

Aylesworth, Jim. *Aunt Pitty Patty's Piggy.* **Illus. by Barbara McClintock. Scholastic, 1999. Gr. PreK-1 (cumulative, folktale)**

Aunt Pitty Patty's niece enlists the help of everyone and everything—the dog, stick, fire, water, ox, butcher, rope, rat, cat, and farmer—in order to make that stubborn new piggy enter her gate, but they all refuse.

Aylesworth, Jim. *The Gingerbread Man.* **Illus. by Barbara McClintock. Scholastic, 1998. Gr. PreK-1 (cumulative, folktale)**

In this traditional folktale, the Gingerbread Man runs away from everyone he meets, leading them on a frantic and merry chase, until he encounters a sneaky fox.

Aylesworth, Jim. *Goldilocks and the Three Bears.* **Illus. by Barbara McClintock. Scholastic, 2003. Gr. PreK-1 (beast, folktale)**

Old-fashioned but comical watercolor, sepia ink, and gouache illustrations portray a proper little moppet, the saucy, impetuous Goldilocks who disregards her mother's warnings about breaking and entering.

Aylesworth, Jim. *The Tale of Tricky Fox: A New England Trickster Tale.* **Illus. by Barbara McClintock. Scholastic, 2001. Gr. PreK-2 (cumulative, folktale, trickster)**

Tricky Fox boasts to Brother Fox that he can fool a human into putting a fat pig into his sack, and he almost succeeds, thanks to all the curious matrons who can't help peering into his sack after he warns them not to.

Babbitt, Natalie. *Ouch!: A Tale from Grimm.* **Illus. by Fred Marcellino. HarperCollins, 1998. Gr. 2-6 (fairy tale)**

Marco, a common but likable boy born with a birthmark that is shaped like a crown, is destined to marry the princess in spite of the king's many attempts to do him in.

Bader, Barbara. *Aesop & Company: With Scenes from His Legendary Life.* **Illus. by Arthur Geisert. Houghton Mifflin, 1991. Gr. 3-6 (beast, collection, fable)**

What's notable about this collection of 19 fables is the introduction, which details the influence Aesop's fables have had on the world of folklore and the facts known about the man.

Bang, Molly Garrett. *Wiley and the Hairy Man.* **Illus. by the author. Macmillan, 1976. Gr. K-3 (fairy tale, scary)**

In this scary (though easy-to-read) African American folktale, Wiley takes his mother's wise advice on how to fool the swamp-dwelling Hairy Man three times to be rid of him.

Bania, Michael. *Kumak's Fish: A Tall Tale from the Far North.* **Illus. by the author. Alaska Northwest, 2004. Gr. PreK-3 (easy fiction)**

Using his Uncle Aglu's amazing hooking stick, Kumak catches a huge fish from the great frozen lake and everyone in the family and the village helps him pull it out. Also wonderful is the companion story, *Kumak's House* (Alaska Northwest, 2002).

Bateman, Teresa. *Farm Flu.* **Illus. by Nadine Bernard Westcott. Albert Whitman, 2001. Gr. PreK-2 (easy fiction)**

Mom's out of town, so when all the farm animals start ka-choo-ing, her young son takes over and nurses them back to health just like Mom would have done.

Baumgartner, Barbara. *Crocodile! Crocodile!: Stories Told Around the World.* **Illus. by Judith Moffatt. DK, 1994. Gr. PreK-2 (beast, collection)**

Bright cut-paper collages accompany six great tales to tell that incorporate repetition, tricksters, swallowing themes, and, animals.

Beaumont, Karen. *I Ain't Gonna Paint No More.* **Illus. by David Catrow. Harcourt, 2005. Gr. PreK-2 (easy fiction)**

Caught painting pictures on the floor, ceiling, walls, curtains, and door by his exasperated Mama, an unrepentant little boy sneaks down the jars of paint she's hidden at the top of the closet and proceeds to cover himself in colors, one body part at a time.

Bernhard, Emery. *How Snowshoe Hare Rescued the Sun: A Tale from the Arctic.* **Illus. by Durga Bernhard. Holiday House, 1993. Gr. K-3 (Myth, pourquoi)**

Greedy demons who live under the earth steal the sun for themselves, leaving only the Northern Lights to dispel the gloom, until Snowshoe Hare volunteers to get it back.

Bertrand, Lynne. *Granite Baby.* **Illus. by Kevin Hawkes. Farrar, 2005. Gr. 1-4 (easy fiction)**

Five giant sisters from the Granite State of New Hampshire each have a special talent, but not one knows how to care for Lil Fella, the caterwauling baby one sister carves from a tiny piece of pink granite.

Billingsley, Franny. *The Folk Keeper.* **Simon & Schuster, 1999. Gr. 5-8 (fiction)**

Fifteen-year-old orphan, Corinna, disguised as Corin so no one will know she is a girl, is sought out by the dying Lord Merton as the new Folk Keeper on his island estate. Corin's job is to keep the underground Folk from destroying crops, livestock, and luck.

Birdseye, Tom. *Soap! Soap! Don't Forget the Soap!: An Appalachian Folktale.* **Illus. by Andrew Glass. Holiday House, 1993. Gr. K-4 (folktale, noodlehead)**

Plug Honeycut, a boy so forgetful he often doesn't recall his own name, gets in a heap of trouble the day his mama sends him to the store to buy some soap.

Black, Holly, and Tony DiTerlizzi. *The Spiderwick Chronicles, Book 1: The Field Guide.* **Illus. by Tony DiTerlizzi. Simon & Schuster, 2003. Gr. 2-5 (fiction)**

Nine-year-old Jared, his twin, Simon, and their 13-year-old sister, Mallory, having just moved with their mother to Great Aunt Lucinda's creepy old Victorian mansion, find a mysterious poem and an old book, a field guide to real faeries.

Bodkin, Odds. *The Crane Wife.* **Illus. by Gennady Spirin. Harcourt, 1998. Gr. 2-6 (fairy tale)**

In a breathtaking picture book version of the well-known Japanese folktale, a sailmaker named Osamu nurses an injured crane back to health and then meets and marries Yukiko, a mysterious woman who weaves him a magical sail.

Booth, David, comp. *Doctor Knickerbocker and Other Rhymes.* **Illus. by Maryann Kovalski. Ticknor & Fields, 1993. Gr. 2-5 (poetry)**

Each page is packed with children's rhymes and nonsense verses, some well-known, some not, and witty, detailed, Victorian-flavored pen and inks.

Brett, Jan. *Honey . . . Honey . . . Lion!* **Illus. by the author. Putnam, 2005. Gr. PreK-2 (easy fiction)**

After Honey Badger neglects to share his honeycomb with Honeyguide, the little bird leads him on a merry chase past the great gray baobab, across the water hole, and over to the lion's den.

Briggs, Raymond. *Jim and the Beanstalk.* **Illus. by the author. Coward-McCann, 1989. Gr. 3-6 (easy fiction, parody)**

After climbing the beanstalk outside his window, Jim finds the now-old, toothless, bald, son of the giant that Jack had met in the old folktale, and helps him acquire specs, teeth, and a wig.

Brown, Marcia. *Stone Soup.* **Illus. by the author. Scribner, 1947. Gr. 1-4 (cumulative, folktale)**

In a French village, some hungry soldiers teach the stingy villagers a lesson about cooking and sharing.

Bruchac, Joseph. *The Boy Who Lived with the Bears and Other Iroquois Stories.* **Illus. by Murv Jacob. HarperCollins, 1995. Gr. 1-6 (beast, collection)**

These six exciting and mostly humorous Native American animal tales from the Iroquois tradition are about tricksters, warriors, and friends.

Bruchac, Joseph, and James Bruchac. *How Chipmunk Got His Stripes: A Tale of Bragging and Teasing.* **Illus. by Jose Aruego and Ariane Dewey. Dial, 2001. Gr. K-2 (beast, pourquoi)**

In a lively Native American East Coast pourquoi tale, Brown Squirrel asks bragging Bear if he can stop the sun from rising in the morning and Bear takes the challenge.

Bruchac, Joseph, and James Bruchac. *Raccoon's Last Race: A Traditional Abenaki Story.* **Illus. by Jose Aruego and Ariane Dewey. Dial, 2004. Gr. PreK-2 (beast, pourquoi)**

Long-legged Azban the Raccoon, the fastest runner of all the animals, pushes Grandfather Rock off the mountain, races the heavy rock downhill, and is rolled flat.

Brusca, María Cristina, and Tona Wilson. *When Jaguar Ate the Moon: And Other Stories About Animals and Plants of the Americas.* **Illus. by María Cristina Brusca. Henry Holt, 1995. Gr. 2-6 (beast, collection)**

A well-chosen collection of folktales native to North and South America is arranged alphabetically by the names of plants and animals, from anteater to zompopo.

Buehner, Caralyn. *Fanny's Dream.* **Illus. by Mark Buehner. Dial, 1996. Gr. 1-6 (easy fiction, parody)**

Sturdy Wyoming farm girl Fanny Agnes works hard on her daddy's farm but yearns for a fairy godmother to help her marry a prince (or at least the tall, handsome mayor's son).

Burleigh, Robert. *Pandora.* **Illus. by Raúl Colón. Harcourt, 2002. Gr. 3-6 (myth)**

Burleigh's poetic and sober retelling of the classic Greek myth is well-served by formal, framed, textured watercolor and colored pencil illustrations.

Calmenson, Stephanie. *The Children's Aesop: Selected Fables.* **Illus. by Robert Byrd. Doubleday, 1988. Gr. 2-5 (beast, collection, fable)**

The conversational style of these 28 (mostly) animal fables lends itself to easy rewriting to turn them into Reader's Theater plays which your children can then act out.

Calmenson, Stephanie. *The Frog Principal.* **Illus. by Denise Brunkus. Scholastic, 2001. Gr. K-4 (easy fiction, parody)**

Hardworking principal Mr. Bundy, whom we first met in Calmenson's Hans Christian Andersen parody, *The Principal's New Clothes* (1989), is back, this time as an enchanted frog in the modern day model for the Grimm Brothers' "The Frog Prince."

Campoy, F. Isabel, and Alma Flor Ada. *Tales Our Abuelitas Told: A Hispanic Folktale Collection.* **Illus. by Felipe Dávalos, Viví Escrivá, Susan Guevara, and Leyla Torres. Atheneum, 2006. Gr. 1-6 (collection)**

A dozen sprightly folktales introduce American kids to a wide range of stories with roots in Spain and Latin America, each enlivened further with one or two full page color illustrations.

Carle, Eric. *Twelve Tales from Aesop.* **Illus. by the author. Philomel, 1980. Gr. K-3 (beast, collection, fable)**

The old favorite are retold, short and sweet, with one fable and one bright full-color painting per double-page spread.

Chase, Richard. *Grandfather Tales.* **Illus. by Berkeley Williams, Jr. Houghton Mifflin, 1948. Gr. K-6 (collection)**

There's a storyteller's feast in 18 Southern Appalachian folktales, many recognizable variants of well-known folktales which the author collected in North Carolina, Virginia, and Kentucky.

Chase, Richard. *The Jack Tales.* Illus. by Berkeley Williams Jr. Houghton Mifflin, 1943. Gr. 4-6 (collection, trickster)

Eighteen tales collected in North Carolina and Virginia follow the exploits of clever Jack, alternately hardworking and lazy, as he seeks his fortune from kings, farmers, and giants.

Cheng, Hou-Tien. *The Six Chinese Brothers: An Ancient Tale.* Illus. by the author. Henry Holt, 1979. Gr. PreK-2 (fairy tale, trickster)

Black and red scissors cuttings depict the saga of the identical brothers who can not be executed.

Chief Lelooska. *Echoes of the Elders: The Stories and Paintings of Chief Lelooska.* Illus. by the author. DK Ink, 1997. Gr. 3-6 (collection, myth)

Finding out that he was gravely ill, storyteller and artist Chief Lelooska recorded, wrote down, and illustrated five of his own traditional Northwest Coast Indian tales.

Child, Lauren. *Beware of the Storybook Wolves.* Illus. by the author. Scholastic, 2001. Gr. PreK-2 (easy fiction, parody)

On the night Herb's mother forgets to take the bedtime storybook out of his bedroom, he turns on the light to discover two menacing wolves hovering over him ready to gobble him up, right down to his little pink toes.

Child, Lauren. *Who's Afraid of the Big Bad Book?* Illus. by the author. Hyperion, 2003. Gr. K-3 (easy fiction, parody)

Herb may love his storybooks, but he takes terrible care of them until the night he falls asleep with his head in an open book of fairy tales.

Choi, Yangsook. *The Sun Girl and the Moon Boy.* Illus. by the author. Knopf, 1997. Gr. 1-4 (fairy tale, pourquoi)

In this Korean tale, a tiger eats a woman and the corncakes she is bringing home for her daughter and son, then disguises himself in the woman's clothes and sets off in pursuit of her children.

Christelow, Eileen. *Five Little Monkeys Jumping on the Bed.* Illus. by the author. Clarion, 1989. *Gr. PreK-1* (easy fiction)

One fell off and bumped his head in the well-known rhyme which children can recite along with you.

Christelow, Eileen. *Where's the Big Bad Wolf?* Illus. by the author. Clarion, 2002. Gr. PreK-2 (easy fiction, parody)

Police Detective Phineas T. Doggedly is on the trail of that low-down, no-good, chicken-chasing, pig-poaching rascal, the Big Bad Wolf, who always promises to stay out of trouble, but is now blowing down the houses of three delectable little piggies.

Climo, Shirley. *Atalanta's Race: A Greek Myth.* Illus. by Alexander Koshkin. Clarion, 1995. Gr. 3-5 (myth)

Not believing in love, Atalanta, a king's daughter who was cast off as a baby and raised by a she bear, agrees to wed the man who can outrun her in a race, declaring that the penalty for defeat is death.

Climo, Shirley. *The Egyptian Cinderella.* **Illus. by Ruth Heller. Crowell, 1989. Gr. 2-6 (fairy tale)**

One of the world's oldest Cinderella stories, first recorded in the first century B.C., this is loosely based on life of Rhodopis, a Greek slave girl whose rose-red gold slipper is dropped into the bored Pharaoh's lap by a falcon.

Climo, Shirley. *Stolen Thunder: A Norse Myth.* **Illus. by Alexander Koshkin. Clarion, 1994. Gr. 3-6 (legend, myth)**

Thor has lost Mjolnir, his thunder-making fiery hammer; trickster Loki finds it in the clutches of giant Thrym the Frost King, who offers to trade it for the hand of Freya, the Goddess of Love.

Cohn, Amy L. *From Sea to Shining Sea: A Treasury of American Folklore and Folk Songs.* **Illus. by 11 Caldecott Medal and 4 Caldecott Honor book artists. Scholastic, 1993. Gr. 1-6 (collection)**

There are more than 140 songs and stories to suit every taste in Cohn's impeccable and masterful compilation, plus an array of colorful and handsome illustrations by award-winning artists.

Cole, Joanna. *Best Loved Folktales of the World.* **Illus. by Jill Karla Schwarz. Doubleday, 1983. Gr. 1-6 (collection)**

With 200 tales, both familiar and lesser-known, broken down by continent, the cramped format makes it more appropriate as a sourcebook and a read-aloud than a book children will read on their own.

Cole, Joanna. *Bony-Legs.* **Illus. by Dirk Zimmer. Four Winds, 1983. Gr. K-2 (fairy tale, scary)**

In a simplified but nicely chilling Baba Yaga story, kind Sasha escapes her stew pot fate with the aid of the witch's gate, dog, and cat, who give her a magic mirror and comb to reward her kindness.

Cole, Joanna. *Don't Tell the Whole World!* **Illus. by Kate Duke. Crowell, 1990. Gr. K-4 (folktale, noodlehead)**

Finding a money box while plowing is a stroke of luck for John, but first he must figure out a way to keep his wife Emma from revealing their good fortune to their rich landlord, Old Mr. Snood.

Compestine, Ying Chang. *The Runaway Rice Cake.* **Illus. by Tungwai Chau. Simon & Schuster, 2001. Gr. PreK-2 (cumulative, folktale)**

"Ai yo! I don't think so!" cries the Chang family's rice cake as it pops out of the steamer, into the courtyard, and through the village on Chinese New Year.

Compestine, Ying Chang. *The Story of Chopsticks.* **Illus. by YongSheng Xuan. Holiday House, 2001. Gr. K-4 (easy fiction)**

Long ago when people in China ate with their hands, the youngest of three boys in the Kang family, Kùai, plucked two long sticks from the kindling pile to spear his too-hot dinner, thus inventing the first chopsticks.

Compton, Patricia A. *The Terrible Eek.* **Illus. by Sheila Hamanaka. Simon & Schuster, 1991. Gr. K-3 (folktale)**

On a rainy, windy night in the mountains, a boy asks his father what he fears the most. An eavesdropping wolf and a thief lurking near the small thatched-roof house are baffled by his misheard reply: "A terrible leak."

Courlander, Harold, and George Herzog. *The Cow-Tail Switch and Other West African Stories.* **Illus. by Madye Lee Chastain. Henry Holt, 1988. Gr. 2-6 (collection)**

Collected by the authors, these 17 folktales are superb for reading aloud, retelling, and discussing. Also look for *The Hat-Shaking Dance: And Other Tales from the Gold Coast* (Harcourt, 1957).

Cousins, Lucy, comp. *The Little Dog Laughed and Other Nursery Rhymes.* **Illus. by the author. Dutton, 1990. Gr. PreK-1 (poetry)**

This visually arresting collection 64 nursery rhymes, so childlike and fun, uses bold and splashy primary colors outlined in black.

Crews, Nina. *The Neighborhood Mother Goose.* **Illus. by the author. Greenwillow, 2004. Gr. PreK-1 (poetry)**

Travel to Nina Crews's Brooklyn neighborhood where she shot the extraordinary full-page color photos of a multicultural cast of real kids acting out 41 traditional Mother Goose rhymes.

Cronin, Doreen. *Click, Clack, Moo: Cows That Type.* **Illus. by Betsy Lewin. Simon & Schuster, 2000. Gr. K-6 (easy fiction)**

"Cows that type? Impossible!" Farmer Brown declares when his cows find an old typewriter in the barn and post on the barn door a typed demand for electric blankets.

Davol, Marguerite W. *The Paper Dragon.* **Illus. by Robert Sabuda. Atheneum, 1997. Gr. K-3 (easy fiction)**

Humble scroll-painting artist Mi Fei must answer three difficult questions when he volunteers to face the dragon, Sui Jen, newly awakened from his hundred years' sleep.

Day, Nancy Raines. *The Lion's Whiskers: An Ethiopian Folktale.* **Illus. by Ann Grifalconi. Scholastic, 1995. Gr. 2-5 (folktale)**

Seeking a magic potion that will cause her new stepson to love her, Fanaye visits a medicine man who instructs her to collect three whiskers from the chin of a fierce lion.

Dee, Ruby. *Two Ways to Count to Ten: A Liberian Folktale.* **Illus. by Susan Meddaugh. Henry Holt, 1988. Gr. K-3 (beast)**

Competing to win the title of future King, Elephant, Bush Ox, Chimpanzee, and Lion all try but fail to throw a spear that will remain in the air till the count of ten.

DeFelice, Cynthia C. *The Dancing Skeleton.* **Illus. by Robert Andrew Parker. Macmillan, 1989. Gr. 2-4 (folktale, scary)**

Though mean and ornery Aaron Kelly is dead and buried, he feels just fine, so he comes home to sit in his rocking chair until he turns into nothing but a skeleton.

Delaney, Joseph. *The Revenge of the Witch. (The Last Apprentice, Book One).* **Illus. by Patrick Arrasmith. Greenwillow, 2005. Gr. 5-8 (fiction)**

Thomas Ward, the left-handed 12-year-old seventh son of a seventh son, becomes the new apprentice to the Spook, a man who walks the County protecting it from witches, boggarts, ghosts, and gasts.

Demi. *A Chinese Zoo: Fables and Proverbs.* **Illus. by the author. Harcourt, 1987. Gr. 2-6 (beast, collection, fable)**

Both text and morals of these 13 Chinese fables will be certain to inspire thought and discussion, whether used in conjunction with Aesop or alone.

Demi. *The Hungry Coat: A Tale from Turkey.* **Illus. by the author. McElderry, 2004. Gr. 1-6 (folktale)**

After helping to catch a wayward little goat, Nasrettin Hoca does not have time to change his worn out, oily, smelly coat before he heads off to a banquet at the home of a rich friend.

Demi. *King Midas: The Golden Touch.* **Illus. by the author. McElderry, 2002. Gr. 2-5 (myth)**

Two droll Midas tales are retold in Demi's opulent, gold-loaded version of the Greek myths, including how the king tried to hide his donkey ears and how he got his golden touch.

Demi. *One Grain of Rice: A Mathematical Folktale.* **Illus. by the author. Scholastic, 1997. Gr. 2-6 (folktale)**

When Rani, a clever village girl, is offered a reward from the raja for a good deed, she teaches the greedy ruler a lesson, asking for a single grain of rice to be doubled each day for thirty days.

DePaola, Tomie. *Adelita: A Mexican Cinderella Story.* **Illus. by the author. Putnam, 2002. Gr. 1-6 (fairy tale)**

After Adelita's mother dies, her father marries a widow with two daughters who treat Adelita harshly, even sending away her beloved Esperanza, the housekeeper who raised her.

DePaola, Tomie. *The Comic Adventures of Old Mother Hubbard and Her Dog.* **Illus. by the author. Harcourt, 1981. Gr. PreK-2 (poetry)**

DePaola's rendition of the famous early-19th-century nursery rhyme by Sarah Catherine Martin will inspire listeners to act out the dog's role and intone the "but when she came back" refrain.

DePaola, Tomie. *Fin M'Coul, the Giant of Knockmany Hill.* **Illus. by the author. Holiday House, 1981. Gr. K-4 (fairy tale, trickster)**

Thanks to his clever wife Oonah, Finn, the famed Irish giant, is able to outsmart Cucullin, a rival giant whose great strength lies in his brass index finger.

DePaola, Tomie. *Jamie O'Rourke and the Big Potato: An Irish Folktale.* **Illus. by the author. Putnam, 1992. Gr. K-4 (fairy tale, trickster)**

With his wife, Eileen, off to visit her sister for a week, Jamie makes a mess of the cottage, but each night a donkey-like creature called a pooka cleans and sets everything right.

DePaola, Tomie. *The Mysterious Giant of Barletta: An Italian Folktale.* **Illus. by the author. Harcourt, 1984. Gr. 1-4 (fairy tale, trickster)**

A town's giant statue comes to life to dissuade an outside army from invading his peaceful village.

DePaola, Tomie. *Strega Nona.* **Illus. by the author. Simon & Schuster, 1975. Gr. K-4 (fairy tale, trickster)**

The Italian tale of lotsa pasta, a helpful witch, and Big Anthony, who doesn't listen, is one of the all time greats to read and tell.

DePaola, Tomie. *Tomie dePaola's Mother Goose.* **Illus. by Tomie dePaola. Putnam, 1985. Gr. PreK-2 (poetry)**

Along with Arnold Lobel's *The Random House Book of Mother Goose* and Iona Opie's *My Very First Mother Goose*, this is an essential collection of 200 rhymes with large cheerful watercolors.

DeRegniers, Beatrice S. *Little Sister and the Month Brothers.* **Illus. by Margot Tomes. Seabury, 1976. Gr. K-3 (fairy tale)**

This is a Slavic version of the tale about a hard-working, good-hearted young girl, sent out into the snow by her malicious stepmother and stepsister to find violets and strawberries.

Diakité, Baba Wagué. *The Hatseller and the Monkeys.* **Illus. by the author. Scholastic, 1999. Gr. PreK-2 (cumulative, folktale)**

Stopping under a mango tree for a nap, hatseller BaMusa is horrified when he wakes up and finds all his hats are gone, stolen by monkeys up in the tree. Compare this with Esphyr Slobodkina's classic version, *Caps for Sale* (HarperCollins, c1947, 1985) on page 250.

Diakité, Baba Wagué. *The Hunterman and the Crocodile.* **Illus. by the author. Scholastic, 1997. Gr. 1-5 (beast, folktale, trickster)**

In this West African variant of an oft-told folktale, Donso the Hunterman helps Bamba the crocodile across the river and then looks for a way out when the croc plans to eat him.

Diakité, Baba Wagué. *The Magic Gourd.* **Illus. by the author. Scholastic, 2003. Gr. 1-4 (beast, folktale)**

As a reward for freeing a chameleon from a thorny bush, Dogo Zan (Brother Rabbit) is given a gourd that, when commanded, fills itself with food and water, a gift that greedy Mansa Jugu, the king, finds irresistible.

DiCamillo, Kate. *The Tale of Despereaux: Being the Story of a Mouse, a Princess, Some Soup, and a Spool of Thread.* **Illus. by Timothy Basil Ering. Candlewick, 2003. Gr. 4-8 (fiction)**

Despereaux, a ridiculously small and sickly mouse with huge ears, falls madly in love with the Princess Pea, a human girl, and breaks three of the great ancient rules of mice.

Donaldson, Julia. *The Giants and the Joneses.* **Illus. by Greg Swearington. Henry Holt, 2005. Gr. 2-5 (fiction)**

Nine-year-old giant, Jumbeelia, loves her mij to read her that exciting bedtime story about the iggly plop who climbed up a bimplestonk into their own land of Groil. Mij says iggly plops don't exist, but Jumbeelia proves otherwise.

Doucet, Sharon Arms. *Why Lapin's Ears Are Long and Other Tales from the Louisiana Bayou.* **Illus. by David Catrow. Orchard, 1997. Gr. 1-4 (beast, pourqui, trickster)**

This collection of three Creole and Cajun Compère Lapin (Brother Rabbit) trickster tales will keep kids laughing, with Catrow's raucous watercolors adding much to the fun.

Early, Margaret. *William Tell.* **Illus. by the author. Abrams, 1991. Gr. 2-5 (legend)**

Meticulous gold leaf–filled paintings illuminate this unforgettable and dramatic retelling about the legendary medieval Swiss hero whose alleged revolt against a tyrant led to the unification of Switzerland.

Edwards, Pamela Duncan. *The Leprechaun's Gold.* **Illus. by Henry Cole. HarperCollins, 2004. Gr. K-3 (easy fiction)**

Humble Old Pat and Young Tom, the braggart, set out together to walk to the Royal Palace where they plan to enter the king's harping contest.

Edwards, Pamela Duncan. *The Neat Line: Scribbling Through Mother Goose.* **Illus. by Diann Cain Blumenthal. HarperCollins, 2005. Gr. PreK-2 (easy fiction)**

A baby scribble, after much practice, grows up to be a Neat Line, and heads off into the first page of a real book, *Mother Goose's Nursery Rhymes*, where it comes to the aid of Little Boy Blue, Jack and Jill, Little Miss Muffet, and more.

Egielski, Richard. *The Gingerbread Boy.* **Illus. by the author. HarperCollins, 1997. Gr. PreK-1 (cumulative, folktale)**

The talking cookie's loose in New York City! Chased by a rat, some construction workers, street musicians, and a police officer on horseback, the Gingerbread guy meets his end, thanks to a sly fox, in Central Park.

Ehlert, Lois. *Cuckoo: A Mexican Folktale/Cucú: Un Cuento Folklórico Mexicano.* **Illus. by the author. Harcourt, 1997. Gr. PreK-3 (beast, pourquoi)**

Beautiful, lazy Cuckoo irritates the other birds with her lovely but incessant singing until the day she saves them from a fire which scorches her feathers black and turns her voice hoarse.

Emberley, Michael. *Ruby.* **Illus. by the author. Little, Brown, 1990. Gr. K-3 (easy fiction)**

On her way to Granny's to drop off a batch of triple-cheese pies, red-cloaked mouse Ruby fails to heed her mother's advice not to talk to strangers, especially cats.

Emberley, Rebecca. *Three Cool Kids.* **Illus. by the author. Little, Brown, 1995. Gr. PreK-2 (easy fiction)**

Needing a change of scenery, the Three Cool Kids—Big, Middle, and Little—set out for the vacant lot down the city street, where they are confronted by a potbellied sewer rat.

Emrich, Duncan. *The Nonsense Book.* **Illus. by Ib Ohlsson. Four Winds, 1970. Gr. 2-6 (collection)**

This, plus companions *The Hodgepodge Book* (1972) and *The Whim-Wham Book* (1975), is a browser's paradise, jam-filled with jokes, riddles, puzzles, tongue twisters, and rhymes, all from American folklore.

Ernst, Lisa Campbell. *Little Red Riding Hood: A Newfangled Prairie Tale.* **Illus. by the author. Simon & Schuster, 1995. Gr. K-3 (easy fiction)**

Riding her bike across the prairie to bring warm wheat berry muffins and cold lemonade to her grandma, Red meets up with a muffin-craving wolf.

Esbensen, Barbara Juster. *The Star Maiden: An Ojibway Tale.* **Illus. by Helen K. Davie. Little, Brown, 1988. Gr. 2-5 (myth, pourquoi)**

Tired of wandering across the sky, a glowing star longs to live among people as a flower.

Farley, Carol. *Mr. Pak Buys a Story.* **Illus. by Benrei Huang. Albert Whitman, 1997. Gr. 1-4 (folktale)**

The power of a good story can't be measured by its price, as we learn in this amusing retelling of a Korean folktale about old Mr. and Mrs. Kim whose faithful servant, Mr. Pak, sets off to the distant city to buy a story.

Fisher, Leonard Everett. *Cyclops.* **Illus. by the author. Holiday House, 1991. Gr. 4-6 (myth)**

After ten years fighting in Troy, Odysseus and his Greek army set sail for home, but land instead on an island where the one-eyed giant Polyphemus takes them captive and begins eating them alive, one by one.

Fisher, Leonard Everett. *William Tell.* **Illus. by the author. Farrar, 1996. Gr. 2-5 (legend)**

"Neither I nor my son shall kneel before the hat of a bully," declares the legendary hunter and marksman, William Tell, when he learns of a restrictive new proclamation by the royal governor Herr Gessler in 1307.

Fleming, Denise. *The Cow Who Clucked.* **Illus. by the author. Henry Holt, 2006. Gr. PreK-1 (easy fiction)**

Cow awakes to find she has lost her moo (though she has, somehow, acquired a "cluck, cluck"), and sets off through the barnyard to find it.

French, Vivian. *Lazy Jack.* **Illus. by Russell Ayto. Candlewick, 1995. Gr. K-4 (folktale, noodlehead)**

Jack's mom hauls him out of bed and sends him off to work, but no matter what job he does, he brings home each day's payment in a foolish and ridiculous way.

Gackenbach, Dick. *Arabella and Mr. Crack.* **Illus. by the author. Macmillan, 1982. Gr. K-3 (folktale)**

In a comical English folktale, a new housekeeper must adapt to her master's eccentric vocabulary.

Gag, Wanda. *Tales from Grimm.* **Retold and illus. by Wanda Gag. Coward-McCann, 1936. Gr. 2-6 (collection, fairy tale)**

Along with *More Tales from Grimm* (1947), these classic collections, reprinted by the University of Minnesota Press in 2006, make a fine introduction to Grimm for children.

Galdone, Joanna. *The Tailypo: A Ghost Story.* **Illus. by Paul Galdone. Seabury, 1977. Gr. 2-4 (folktale, scary)**

A scruffy old man is terrified when a varmint, whose tail he has chopped off and eaten, returns to get him.

Galdone, Paul. *The Old Woman and Her Pig.* **Illus. by the author. McGraw-Hill, 1960. Gr. PreK-1 (cumulative, folktale)**

In a cumulative English folktale, an old woman needs the help of a dog, a stick, some fire, water, an ox, a butcher, a rat, and a cat to nudge her stubborn pig over a stile so she can get home.

Galdone, Paul. *The Three Sillies.* **Illus. by the author. Clarion, 1982. Gr. 1-4 (folktale, noodlehead)**

In a comical tale from England, a suitor sets out to find three people who are sillier than his sweetheart and her parents.

Garcia, Laura Gallego. *The Legend of the Wandering King.* **Translated by Dan Bellm. Scholastic, 2005. Gr. 5-8 (fiction)**

In ancient Arabia, when every Arab was a poet at heart, the dashing young prince of Kinda, Walid ibn Hujr, is consumed with jealousy when the poetry prize he expected to win is instead awarded to Hammad, a simple peasant and carpet weaver.

Garland, Sherry. *Why Ducks Sleep on One Leg.* **Illus. by Leo and Diane Dillon. Scholastic, 1993. Gr. 1-4 (folktale, pourquoi)**

In old Japan, a proud and cruel lord cares little for the drake he orders captured and caged so he can show it off, but he condemns to death a sympathetic kitchen maid and a former samurai for freeing the bird.

Gates, Frieda. *Owl Eyes.* **Illus. by Yoshi Miyake. Lothrop, 1994. Gr. K-4 (beast, myth, pourquoi)**

In this humorous Mohawk legend, we see how Raweno, Master of All Spirits and Everything-Maker created first the world and then the animals, allowing all the not-completed creatures to choose their own features except for nosy, overbearing Owl.

Gatti, Ann. *Aesop's Fables.* **Illus. by Safaya Salter. Gulliver/Harcourt, 1992. Gr. 1-6 (beast, collection, fable)**

The elaborately bordered watercolors will be savored by children as they predict and analyze the morals of these sixty lesser-known tales, and act them out in small groups.

Gerson, Mary-Joan. *Why the Sky Is Far Away: A Nigerian Folktale.* **Illus. by Carla Golembe. Little, Brown, 1992. Gr. K-4 (myth, pourquoi)**

Though the people are told never to break off more of the delicious-tasting sky than they can finish, one greedy woman, Adese, ignores that warning.

Gerstein, Mordicai. *Carolinda Clatter.* **Illus. by the author. Roaring Brook, 2005. Gr. PreK-2 (easy fiction)**

The people of Pupicktown are able to stay quiet so as not to disturb a sleeping giant mountain until the birth of a little girl named Carolinda Clatter who loves noise.

Gilman, Phoebe. *Something from Nothing.* **Illus. by the author. Scholastic, 1993. Gr. PreK-2 (cumulative)**

Joseph's wonderful blanket is wearing out, and his tailor grandfather fixes it, making first a jacket, then a vest, a tie, a handkerchief, a button, and finally, a story.

Ginsburg, Mirra. *The Chinese Mirror.* **Illus. by Margot Zemach. Harcourt, 1988. Gr. 1-4 (folktale)**

A Korean man brings home a magical treasure from his travels in China—a small hand mirror— which distress his wife, mother, father, and son when each sees a different unfamiliar face.

Ginsburg, Mirra. *Clay Boy: Adapted from a Russian Folk Tale.* **Illus. by Jos. A. Smith. Greenwillow, 1997. Gr. PreK-1 (cumulative, folktale)**

"More! I want more!" cries the ravenous clay boy after swallowing Grandpa and Grandma.

Goble, Paul. *Her Seven Brothers.* **Illus. by the author. Bradbury, 1988. Gr. 3-6 (myth, pourquoi)**

In a Cheyenne legend, a girl rejects the demands of the chief of the Buffalo People and escapes into the sky with her seven adopted brothers. Together they become part of the Big Dipper in the northern night sky.

Goble, Paul. *Iktomi and the Boulder: A Plains Indian Story.* **Illus. by the author. Orchard, 1988. Gr. K-3 (myth, pourquoi, trickster)**

When the clever but lazy trickster Iktomi is trapped by an angry bounding boulder, he enlists the help of the bats to help him.

Goldin, Barbara Diamond. *The Girl Who Lived with the Bears.* **Illus. by Andrew Plewes. Harcourt, 1997. Gr. 2-6 (legend, myth)**

In this somber Native American folktale of the Pacific Northwest, the spoiled and haughty daughter of the chief of the Raven clan speaks disrespectfully about bears and, as a punishment, is kidnapped by the Bear People.

Greene, Ellin. *Billy Beg and His Bull.* **Illus. by Kimberley Bulcken Root. Holiday House, 1994. Gr. 2-4 (fairy tale)**

Billy's stepmother claims that only the blood of Billy's beloved bull can heal her, which starts the young Irish prince on a quest where he fights many-headed giants, kills a princess-eating dragon, and, like Cinderella, loses a shoe.

Grey, Mini. *The Adventures of the Dish and the Spoon.* **Illus. by the author. Knopf, 2006. Gr. PreK-2 (easy fiction)**

When somebody puts on a phonograph record with that "Hey Diddle Diddle" tune, the Dish and the Spoon can't resist and run away once again, sailing together to New York City where they soon become a famous act in vaudeville.

Grifalconi, Ann. *The Village of Round and Square Houses.* **Illus. by the author. Little, Brown, 1986. Gr. K-4 (myth, pourquoi)**

A storytelling grandmother in the West African village of Tos describes the eruption of Old Naka long ago and how it lead to the villagers living in two types of houses: the men in square ones and the women in round ones.

Grimm, Jacob. *The Juniper Tree and Other Tales from Grimm.* **Selected by Lore Segal and Randall Jarrell. Illus. by Maurice Sendak. Farrar, 2003, c1973. Gr. 3-6 (collection, fairy tale)**

A small, handsome two-volume set includes some of Grimm's lesser known and more melancholy fairy tales.

Gryski, Camilla. *Cat's Cradle, Owl's Eyes; A Book of String Games.* **Illus. by Tom Sankey. Morrow, 1984. Gr. 2-6 (collection)**

Step-by-step introduction for making dozens of string figures from around the world will help children develop a sense of sequence and fine motor skills while they're having fun.

Haley, Gail E. *A Story, a Story.* **Illus. by the author. Atheneum, 1970. Gr. K-3 (myth, pourquoi, trickster)**

This Caldecott winner is an African tale of Anansi the Spider and how he spread the world's first stories.

Hamilton, Martha, and Mitch Weiss. *Scared Witless: Thirteen Eerie Tales to Tell.* **Illus. by Kevin Pope. August House, 2006. Gr. 3-6 (collection, scary)**

Humorous but spooky jump tales, with tips for telling each one, include old favorites like "The Hairy Toe" and "The Red Satin Ribbon." Also look for the author's *How & Why Stories* (1999) and *Noodlehead Stories* (2000).

Hamilton, Virginia. *Bruh Rabbit and the Tar Baby Girl.* **Illus. by James E. Ransome. Blue Sky/Scholastic, 2003. Gr. PreK-4 (beast, trickster)**

In this variant of the "tar baby" story from the Sea Islands of South Carolina, Bruh Wolf constructs first a scarecrow and then a Tar Baby Girl to stop Bruh Rabbit from stealing peanuts from his field.

Hamilton, Virginia. *The Girl Who Spun Gold.* **Illus. by Leo and Diane Dillon. Scholastic, 2000. Gr. 2-6 (beast, fairy tale)**

In a breathtaking and elegant West Indian variant of "Rumpelstiltskin," Young Quashiba's mother tells Big King that her daughter can spin the finest golden thread, which, of course, is not true.

Hamilton, Virginia. *The People Could Fly: The Picture Book.* **Illus. by Leo and Diane Dillon. Knopf, 2004. Gr. 3-6 (fairy tale)**

In the land of slavery, Sarah and her baby escape the Overseer's whip when she rises into the sky, thanks to the magic words of the old man, Toby, who helps all the slaves fly away to Free-dom.

Hamilton, Virginia. *When Birds Could Talk & Bats Could Sing.* **Illus. by Barry Moser. Scholastic, 1996. Gr. 2-5 (beast, collection, pourquoi)**

Sit yourselves down, relax, and enjoy eight old tales from back in the days when Bruh Sparrow liked to cause mischief, Miss Bat still had a long tail, and Hummer the hummingbird had a honey-sweet voice.

Han, Suzanne Crowder. *The Rabbit's Escape.* **Illus. by Yumi Heo. Henry Holt, 1995. Gr. 1-5 (beast, trickster)**

When the Dragon King of the East Sea becomes ill and is told only the fresh raw liver of a rabbit can cure him, Turtle brings back a live rabbit who has no intention of cooperating.

Hancock, Sibyl. *Esteban and the Ghost.* **Illus. by Dirk Zimmer. Dial, 1983. Gr. 2-4 (fairy tale, scary)**

On All Hallow's Eve, a merry tinker sets off to drive a ghost out of a haunted castle, for which he will receive a thousand gold reales—if he lives to tell the tale.

Harper, Wilhelmina. *The Gunniwolf.* **Illus. by William Wiesner. Dutton, 1978. Gr. PreK-1 (cumulative, folktale)**

Little Girl breaks her promise to her mother when she wanders into the jungle, meets up with the Gunniwolf, and sings him "that guten sweeten song again" to put him to sleep so she can get away.

Hartman, Bob. *The Wolf Who Cried Boy.* **Illus. by Tim Raglin. Putnam, 2002. Gr. K-2 (easy fiction)**

Detesting the lamburgers and Sloppy Does his mom makes for dinner, Little Wolf sets out to catch a nice boy so he can have a decent meal for once.

Hastings, Selina. *Sir Gawain and the Loathly Lady.* **Illus. by Juan Wijngaard. Lothrop, 1985. Gr. 3-6 (legend)**

Destined to die at the hands of the Black Knight unless he can answer the question, "What is it that women most desire," King Arthur learns the answer from a monstrous hag who wants, in return, one of Arthur's knights for a husband.

Hausman, Gerald, and Hausman, Loretta. *Dogs of Myth: Tales from Around the World.* **Illus. by Barry Moser. Simon & Schuster, 1999. Gr. 2-6 (beast, collection)**

In this masterful collection of 13 international folktales, we meet an array of notable and noble dogs who vanquish wolves, armies, and giants.

Haviland, Virginia. *Favorite Fairy Tales Told Round the World.* **Illus. by S. D. Schindler. Little, Brown, 1985. Gr. 1-4 (collection, fairy tale)**

Two or three tales have been culled from each of Haviland's 16 books in the "Favorite Fairy Tales" series, national collections of stories from countries including Ireland, Italy, India, and Sweden.

Haviland, Virginia. *North American Legends.* **Illus. by Ann Strugnell. Putnam, 1979. Gr. 4-8 (collection, myth)**

A meaty collection of 29 traditional American folk and tall tales encompasses Indians, Eskimos, European immigrants, and African Americans.

Hawkins, Colin, and Jacqui Hawkins. *The Fairytale News.* **Illus. by the authors. Candlewick, 2004. Gr. PreK-3 (easy fiction, parody)**

Old Mother Hubbard's son, Jack, gets a job delivering the Fairytale News. At the back of this ebullient book is a four-page, heavystock, newsprint copy of the paper, filled with news, sports, classified ads, and advice from Mother Goose herself.

Hayes, Sarah. *Robin Hood.* **Illus. by Patrick Benson. Henry Holt, 1989. Gr. 3-6 (legend)**

A most enthralling and romantic retelling of the Robin Hood legends spans Robin's first encounter with the maniacal Sir Guy and the Sheriff of Nottingham, his exploits with his green-clad fellows of Sherwood, and his tragic, untimely passing.

Henderson, Kathy. *Lugalbanda: The Boy Who Got Caught Up in a War.* **Illus. by Jane Ray. Candlewick, 2006. Gr. 3-8 (legend)**

In one of the oldest stories in the world, the youngest and weakest of the king's eight sons, Lugalbanda, is left behind when he falls ill on his way to help conquer the city of Aratta and encounters the terrifying Anzu bird.

Henkes, Kevin. *Kitten's First Full Moon.* **Illus. by the author. Greenwillow, 2004. Gr. PreK-1 (easy fiction)**

When she sees her first full moon, Kitten thinks it's a little bowl of milk in the sky, and she wants it.

Hewitt, Kathryn. *King Midas and the Golden Touch.* **Illus. by the author. Harcourt, 1987. Gr. 1-4 (myth)**

Hewitt's detailed golden watercolors are a treat in this retelling of the Greek myth about the king who finds out the hard way that gold isn't everything.

Hewitt, Kathryn. *The Three Sillies.* **Illus. by the author. Harcourt, 1986. Gr. 1-4 (folktale, noodlehead)**

A young girl (though in this version of the English tale, all the characters happen to be pigs) cries at the sight of an ax stuck in the cellar ceiling, envisioning the disaster it could bring.

Hicks, Barbara Jean. *Jitterbug Jam: A Monster Tale.* **Illus. by Alexis Deacon. Farrar, 2005. Gr. PreK-3 (easy fiction)**

Bobo, a little horned monster whose big brother calls him a fraidy-cat, is indeed scared of the human boy who hides in Bobo's closet at night and sneaks under his bed in the morning.

Hicks, Ray. *The Jack Tales.* **Illus. by Owen Smith. Callaway, 2000. Gr. 2-5 (collection, trickster)**

In an oversized volume with huge down-home illustrations and an accompanying CD, 78-year-old storyteller Ray Hicks regales us with three stories he learned from his grandfather about that trickster, Jack.

Hindley, Judy. *Do Like a Duck Does!* **Illus. by Ivan Bates. Candlewick, 2002. Gr. PreK-1 (easy fiction)**

Five little ducklings are following Mama Duck when up struts a long-tailed, furry stranger who claims he's a big, brown duck, too.

Ho, Minfong, and Saphan Ros. *Brother Rabbit: A Cambodian Tale.* **Illus. by Jennifer Hewitson. Lothrop, 1997. Gr. K-3 (beast, trickster)**

In typically devious fashion, Brother Rabbit promises to cure crocodile of his rough skin in exchange for a ride across the river where Rabbit hopes to feast on seedlings in a newly-planted rice field.

Hoberman, Mary Ann. *You Read to Me, I'll Read to You: Very Short Fairy Tales to Read Together.* **Illus. by Michael Emberley. Little, Brown, 2004. Gr. K-3 (fairy tale, poetry)**

Eight well-known fairy tales have been adapted into witty, easy to read, rhyming poems for two voices, with a series of endearing watercolor and pastel illustrations that accompany each stanza.

Hoberman, Mary Ann. *You Read to Me, I'll Read to You: Very Short Stories to Read Together.* **Illus. by Michael Emberley. Little, Brown, 2001. Gr. K-2 (poetry)**

Fourteen short and utterly enchanting rhymed poem stories with friendly pen-and-watercolor illustrations celebrate reading in easy-to-read dialogues for two voices.

Hodges, Margaret. *Saint George and the Dragon: A Golden Legend.* **Illus. by Trina Schart Hyman. Little, Brown, 1984. Gr. 3-6 (legend)**

In a Caldecott winning picture book adapted by Margaret Hodges from Edmund Spenser's sixteenth century epic poem "The Faerie Queen," Una recruits the Red Cross Knight to slay the mighty dragon that plagues her father's kingdom.

Hodges, Margaret. *Saint Patrick and the Peddler.* **Illus. by Paul Brett Johnson. Orchard, 1993. Gr. 1-4 (legend)**

After seeing Saint Patrick in his dream three times running, a poor peddler finally heeds his advice to travel to Ballymena and hear what he was meant to hear.

Hogrogian, Nonny. *One Fine Day.* **Illus. by the author. Macmillan, 1971. Gr. PreK-2 (beast, cumulative)**

A fox must barter for milk to give to an old woman before she will sew his tail back on.

Hong, Lily Toy. *How the Ox Star Fell From Heaven.* **Illus. by the author. Albert Whitman, 1991. Gr. K-6 (myth, pourquoi)**

In this Chinese picture book pourquoi tale, the Emperor of All the Heavens sends trusted Ox Star to earth to decree that hungry peasants will be permitted to eat once every third day, but the ox gets the message wrong.

Hong, Lily Toy. *Two of Everything: A Chinese Folktale.* **Illus. by the author. Albert Whitman, 1993. Gr. K-3 (folktale, noodlehead)**

After digging up a large pot in his garden, poor old Mr. Haktak is astonished to find whatever he throws in the pot automatically doubles, guaranteeing him and his wife instant wealth.

Hooks, William H. *Moss Gown.* **Illus. by Donald Carrick. Clarion, 1987. Gr. 2-6 (fairy tale)**

In this Southern U.S. variant of a Cinderella story, Candace tells her father, "I love you more than meat loves salt," but he misunderstands her and casts her out.

Hooks, William H. *The Three Little Pigs and the Fox.* **Illus. by S. D. Schindler. Macmillan, 1989. Gr. PreK-2 (beast)**

While her two brothers are captured and detained by that mean, tricky old drooly-mouth fox, Hamlet is sharp enough to trap him in a butter churn and make the forest safe for piglets leaving home to seek their fortunes.

Huck, Charlotte. *The Black Bull of Norroway.* **Illus. by Anita Lobel. Greenwillow, 2001. Gr. 2-5 (fairy tale)**

When Peggy Ann, youngest and merriest of three sisters, says she'd even be content to marry the Black Bull of Norroway, the bull comes to take her away.

Huck, Charlotte. *Princess Furball.* **Illus. by Anita Lobel. Greenwillow, 1989. Gr. 1-4 (fairy tale)**

Before she will marry the Ogre to whom her father has betrothed her, the princess insists on three fancy gowns and a coat made of a thousand kinds of fur.

Hyman, Trina Schart. *Little Red Riding Hood.* **Illus. by the author. Holiday House, 1983. Gr. PreK-2 (fairy tale)**

Many children have never heard the traditional version of the wolf in Granny's clothing, and this version is stellar.

Hyman, Trina Schart. *The Sleeping Beauty.* **Illus. by the author. Little, Brown, 1977. Gr. 2-5 (fairy tale)**

The prophecy of a wicked fairy comes true when Briar Rose pricks her finger and falls into a hundred-year sleep.

Isaacs, Anne. *Pancakes for Supper.* **Illus. by Mark Teague. Scholastic, 2006. Gr. PreK-2 (easy fiction, parody)**

Toby gives away her brand new clothes to a hungry wolf, a cougar, a skunk, a porcupine, and a bear, but gets them all back, and a bucket of pancake syrup, too, when the critters argue over who is the grandest animal in the forest.

Isaacs, Anne. *Swamp Angel.* **Illus. by Paul O. Zelinsky. Dutton, 1994. Gr. 1-6 (tall tale)**

Meet Angelica Longrider, Tennessee's greatest woodswoman and indefatigable giantess, who, the story claims, formed the Great Smoky Mountains during a five-day wrestling match with Thundering Tarnation, a bear to end all bears.

Jackson, Ellen. *Cinder Edna.* **Illus. by Kevin O'Malley. Lothrop, 1994. Gr. 1-6 (easy fiction, parody)**

Cinderella's next-door neighbor, take-charge, resourceful Edna, has too much on the ball to sit around waiting for a fairy godmother to solve her family problems, and finds Prince Charming "borrring."

Jenkins, Emily. *Toys Go Out: Being the Adventures of a Knowledgeable Stingray, a Toughy Little Buffalo, and Someone Called Plastic.* **Illus. by Paul O. Zelinsky. Schwartz & Wade, 2006. Gr. 1-4 (fiction)**

In six delectable chapters, get to know StingRay, Lumphy the buffalo, and Plastic, Little Girl's best toys, each of whom heads out of Little Girl's bedroom for an adventure.

Johnson, Paul Brett. *Fearless Jack.* **Illus. by the author. McElderry, 2001. Gr. K-5 (folktale, trickster)**

Killing ten yellow jackets at one whack inspires country boy Jack to call himself Fearless Jack; when he wanders into town, the sheriff offers him a hundred dollars cash money ree-ward to rid the town of some wild varmints.

Johnson, Paul Brett. *Jack Outwits the Giants.* **Illus. by the author. McElderry, 2002. Gr. K-5 (folktale, trickster)**

Stopping off at a farmhouse when a rainstorm catches him on the road, Jack is taken in by a two-headed giant and his one-headed wife who welcome him to spend the night in their loft.

Johnson, Paul Brett. *Little Bunny Foo Foo.* **Illus. by the author. Scholastic, 2004. Gr. PreK-1 (easy fiction)**

The traditional silly story-song is expanded a bit here and narrated by the Good Fairy herself, as she gives the bopping bunny three chances to behave before she turns him into a goon.

Johnson-Davies, Denys. *Goha the Wise Fool.* **Illus. by Hany El Saed Ahmed from drawings by Hag Hamdy Mohamed Fattouh. Philomel, 2005. Gr. 2-6 (collection, noodlehead)**

Fifteen short, droll tales introduce us to a staple of Egyptian folklore, Goha, a well-meaning fool, trickster, and sage who sometimes learns a lesson and sometimes doesn't.

Johnston, Tony. *The Tale of Rabbit and Coyote.* **Illus. by Tomie dePaola. Putnam, 1994. Gr. PreK-2 (beast, pourquoi, trickster)**

Stuck to a farmer's beeswax doll, Native American trickster Rabbit thinks fast and talks Coyote into taking his place, and then convinces him to hold back a rock to keep it from crushing the world.

Juster, Norton. *The Hello, Goodbye Window.* **Illus. by Chris Raschka. Hyperion, 2005. Gr. PreK-1 (easy fiction)**

In her stream-of-consciousness narrative, a little girl describes a special overnight at Nanna and Poppy's house.

Kajikawa, Kimiko. *Yoshi's Feast.* **Illus. by Yumi Heo. DK Ink, 2000. Gr. K-4 (folktale)**

Too stingy to buy his neighbor Sabu's broiled eels, Japanese fan-maker Yoshi enjoys their marvelous aromas as he eats his boiled rice each night until Sabu presents him with a bill for all the eels he has smelled.

Keats, Ezra Jack. *John Henry: An American Legend.* **Illus. by the author. Knopf, 1987. Gr. 1-4 (tall tale)**

Compare this version of how the steel-driving man beat the steam drill and died with his hammer in his hand with the one by Julius Lester on page 134.

Kellogg, Steven. *Johnny Appleseed.* **Illus. by the author. Morrow, 1988. Gr. 1-4 (tall tale)**

The legendary John Chapman walked through Pennsylvania, Ohio, and Indiana, planting and selling his apple trees to pioneer families and inspired tall tales about his backwoods exploits.

Kellogg, Steven. *Sally Ann Thunder Ann Whirlwind Crockett: A Tall Tale.* **Illus. by the author. Morrow, 1995. Gr. 1-4 (tall tale)**

Even as a baby, Sally Ann Thunder Ann Whirlwind can "out-talk, out-grin, out-scream, out-swim, and out-run" anyone in Kentucky, including her nine older brothers, though she later meets her match in her future husband, Davy Crockett.

Kesey, Ken. *Little Tricker the Squirrel Meets Big Double the Bear.* **Illus. by Barry Moser. Viking, 1990. Gr. 1-4 (easy fiction, parody)**

Ravenous bear, Big Double swallows up Sally Snipster the marten, Longrellers the Rabbit, and Charlie Charles the Woodchuck until he is outdone and overcome by the wily ways of Little Tricker, a red squirrel who claims he can fly.

Ketteman, Helen. *Armadilly Chili.* **Illus. by Will Terry. Albert Whitman, 2004. Gr. K-2 (easy fiction, parody)**

With a blue norther a-blowin', Miss Billie Armadilly asks her pals, tarantula Tex, bluebird Mackie, and horned toad Taffy to help her make a pot of hot armadilly chili, but they're all too busy to help.

Kimmel, Eric A. *Anansi and the Magic Stick.* **Illus. by Janet Stevens. Holiday House, 2001. Gr. PreK-2 (beast, trickster)**

Anansi, that lazy, greedy, lovable trickster spider from West Africa, steals Hyena's Magic Stick so he can clean up his own ramshackle house without having to do any work.

Kimmel, Eric A. *Anansi and the Moss-Covered Rock.* **Illus. by Janet Stevens. Holiday House, 1990. Gr. PreK-2 (beast, trickster)**

Every time Anasi the Spider prompts another animal to say, "Isn't this a strange moss-covered rock," he falls down senseless for an hour, leaving the cunning spider free to steal its food supply.

Kimmel, Eric A. *Anansi and the Talking Melon.* **Illus. by Janet Stevens. Holiday House, 1994. Gr. PreK-2 (beast, trickster)**

Anansi the Spider eats so much of the inside of a ripe orange cantaloupe, he's too fat to squeeze back out. To pass the time, he insults Elephant, Hippo, Warthog, and even the king, all of whom believe the melon can talk.

Kimmel, Eric A. *Anansi Goes Fishing.* **Illus. by Janet Stevens. Holiday House, 1992. Gr. PreK-2 (beast, trickster)**

Spider Anansi's plans to let Turtle do all the work backfire when Turtle offers his own irresistible strategy: one will work while the other will get tired.

Kimmel, Eric A. *Baba Yaga: A Russian Folktale.* **Illus. by the author. Holiday House, 1991. Gr. K-2 (fairy tale, scary)**

Little Tishka, son of elderly parents who were granted their wish for a child, is captured by Baba Yaga for her supper.

Kimmel, Eric A. *Boots and His Brothers: A Norwegian Tale Retold.* **Illus. by Kimberly Bulcken Root. Holiday House, 1992. Gr. 2-6 (fairy tale)**

Boots' kindness to an old beggar woman nets him useful advice in return: "Whenever you ask a question, do not rest until you find the answer."

Kimmel, Eric A. *Cactus Soup.* **Illus. by Phil Huling. Marshall Cavendish, 2004. Gr. K-4 (folktale)**

In a lively retelling of "Stone Soup" set in Mexico at the time of the Mexican Revolution (1910-1922), a troop of soldiers arrive at a town where the mayor has urged the townsfolk to hide their food and pretend to be poor.

Kimmel, Eric A. *Count Silvernose: A Story from Italy.* **Illus. by Omar Rayyan. Holiday House, 1996. Gr. 3-6 (fairy tale)**

When a dashing count with a silver nose takes away two beautiful but flighty sisters to be his washerwomen and then claims to their mother that they have died, their plain but loyal sister Assunta vows to avenge them.

Kimmel, Eric A. *The Gingerbread Man.* **Illus. by Megan Lloyd. Holiday House, 1993. Gr. PreK-1 (cumulative, folktale)**

A delightful telling, with large, genial illustrations perfect for story-hour, reminds us that "Gingerbread men return, it's said / When someone bakes some gingerbread."

Kimmel, Eric A. *The Hero Beowulf.* **Illus. by Leonard Everett Fisher. Farrar, 2005. Gr. 4-8 (legend)**

Adapted from the oldest surviving epic poem in English literature, composed in the 8th century, this gloriously creepy tale covers the first of three parts, where hero Beowulf slays five sea serpents and takes on Grendel, a man-devouring monster.

Kimmel, Eric A. *Ten Suns: A Chinese Legend.* **Illus. by Yongsheng Xuan. Holiday House, 1998. Gr. 1-6 (myth)**

The emperor of the eastern sky, Di Jun, must take drastic measures when his ten sons, each a sun whose daily walk across the sky brings light and heat to the earth below, decide to walk together.

Kimmel, Eric A. *The Three Princes: A Tale from the Middle East.* **Illus. by Leonard Everett Fisher. Holiday House, 1994. Gr. 1-4 (fairy tale)**

Given the task of going out in the world and bringing back the rarest thing they find in their travels, three cousins set out on camelback across the desert to win the princess's hand, but rush home to save her life when she becomes ill.

Kimmel, Eric A. *Three Samurai Cats: A Story from Japan.* **Illus. by Mordicai Gerstein. Holiday House, 2003. Gr. K-4 (fairy tale)**

When the damyo, a powerful Japanese lord, is unable to rid his castle of a savage, rampaging rat, he seeks a tough, fighting samurai cat to chase it.

Kirstein, Lincoln. *Puss in Boots.* **Illus. by Alain Vaïs. Little, Brown, 1992. Gr. 1-4 (fairy tale)**

Robin fits his cat Puss with stout cowhide boots, and the cat, in return, arranges for his master an audience with the King and a whole new identity.

Knutson, Barbara. *Love and Roast Chicken: A Trickster Tale from the Andes Mountains.* **Illus. by the author. Carolrhoda, 2004. Gr. K-3 (beast, trickster)**

The quick thinking of Cuy the guinea pig helps him escape from Tió Antonio, the hungry but gullible fox, who believes Cuy's warnings about the sky falling and the world ending in a rain of fire.

Kurtz, Jane. *Pulling the Lion's Tail.* **Illus. by Floyd Cooper. Simon & Schuster, 1995. Gr. 2-6 (folktale)**

Seeking a way to make her new stepmother love her, Almaz follows Grandfather's instructions to bring him some hair from the tail of a lion.

Kurtz, Jane. *Trouble.* **Illus. by Durga Bernhard. Gulliver/Harcourt, 1997. Gr. K-2 (cumulative, folktale)**

In a comical Eritrean folktale from the east coast of Africa, young Tekleh has a hard time keeping clear of trouble as he takes his gabeta game board and heads to the hills to graze his goats.

Lang, Andrew. *The Blue Fairy Book.* **Viking, 1978. Gr. 2-6 (collection)**

The first of 12 marvelous "color" collections of international folk and fairy tales compiled by English folklorist Andrew Lang in the late 19th century contains 32 stories, many familiar. Publishers Peter Smith and Dover have reprinted the others.

Langrish, Katherine. *Troll Fell.* **HarperCollins, 2004. Gr. 5-8 (fiction)**

After his carpenter father's funeral, Peer Ulfsson and his beloved little dog, Loki are carried of by Peer's brutish twin uncles, Grim and Baldur Grimsson, to their house and mill up on bleak Troll Fell where he is worked like a slave.

Larry, Charles. *Peboan and Seegwun.* **Illus. by the author. Farrar, 1993. Gr. 1-4 (myth)**

At the end of winter, in an Anishinabe or Ojibwa lodge where an old man sits listening to the wind, a young man comes to visit, share a pipe, and swap stories of their power over the seasons.

Leach, Maria. *The Thing at the Foot of the Bed and Other Scary Tales.* **Illus. by Kert Werth. Putnam, 1987. Gr. 2-6 (collection, scary)**

Get out your flashlight to read or tell these 35 short, easy-to-learn, ghostly folktales.

Lester, Julius. *John Henry.* **Illus. by Jerry Pinkney. Dial, 1994. Gr. 1-4 (tall tale)**

Based on several versions of the folk song, this large sized picture book version has majestic watercolors and a narrative line bursting with humor and wonder combined.

Lester, Julius. *The Knee-High Man and Other Tales.* **Illus. by Ralph Pinto. Dial, 1972. Gr. 2-5 (collection)**

These six boisterous and humorous African American folktales and pourquoi tales about animals and humans are perfect for telling.

Lester, Julius. *Sam and the Tigers: A New Telling of Little Black Sambo.* **Illus. by Jerry Pinkney. Dial, 1996. Gr. PreK-3 (cumulative, easy fiction)**

Lester and Pinkney have taken the essence of Helen Bannerman's controversial *The Tale of Little Black Sambo* about a boy who outsmarts tigers, and replaced it with a verbally and visually dazzling story about Sam from Sam-sam-sa-mara.

Lester, Julius. *The Tales of Uncle Remus: The Adventures of Brer Rabbit.* **Illus. by Jerry Pinkney. Dial, 1990. Gr. 2-5 (collection, trickster)**

Liberated from Joel Chandler Harris's use of heavy dialect, these 48 retellings of famous African American trickster tales are made even more comical through the use of more modern day slang. The second volume is *More Tales of Uncle Remus* (1988).

Levine, Gail Carson. *Ella Enchanted.* **HarperCollins, 1997. Gr. 4-7 (fiction)**

Cursed at birth by the interfering fairy Lucinda's "gift" of obedience, Ella, now 14, relates how she is shipped off to finishing school with her two cloddish and manipulating future stepsisters.

Levine, Gail Carson. *The Fairy's Mistake.* **Illus. by Mark Elliott. HarperCollins, 1999. Gr. 4-7 (fiction)**

Good sister Rosella is rewarded by a fairy with diamonds and jewels that fall from her mouth; bad sister Myrtle is punished with snakes and spiders, but in this sly turnaround tale, the bad sister comes out on top.

Lewin, Ted. *The Storytellers.* **Illus. by the author. Lothrop, 1998. Gr. 1-3 (easy fiction)**

In the ancient, walled city of Fez, Morocco, Abdul and his grandfather set off through the bustling cobblestoned market to their job—telling stories to the people in the medina.

Lin, Grace. *The Year of the Dog.* **Illus. by the author. Little, Brown, 2006. Gr. 3-5 (fiction)**

Sprinkled throughout Grace Lin's winsome autobiographical fiction book, based on her own experiences growing up as a Taiwanese American girl in upstate New York, are the family stories her mother tells about growing up in Taiwan.

Little, Jean, and Maggie de Vries. *Once Upon a Golden Apple.* **Illus. by Phoebe Gilman. Viking, 1991. Gr. PreK-2 (easy fiction, parody)**

The bedtime story dad tells his two nay-saying children is all mixed up, though Briar Rose, Prince Valiant, and their Rock-a-bye baby still end up living happily ever after.

Lobel, Arnold. *Fables.* **Illus. by the author. HarperCollins, 1980. Gr. 3-6 (beast, easy fiction, fable, parody)**

Twenty original animal fables, wise and insightful little jewels, with sophisticated and sly morals, won Arnold Lobel a Caldecott Medal.

Lobel, Arnold. *The Random House Book of Mother Goose.* **Illus. by Arnold Lobel. Random House, 1986. Gr. PreK-2 (poetry)**

This visual feast with over five hundred rhymes is a book for all core collections.

Long, Sylvia, comp. *Sylvia Long's Mother Goose.* **Illus. by Sylvia Long. Chronicle, 1999. Gr. PreK-1 (poetry)**

Sylvia Long's delightful detailed watercolors bring warmth to her graceful and elegant Mother Goose collection.

Louie, Ai-Ling. *Yeh-Shen: A Cinderella Story from China.* **Illus. by Ed Young. Philomel, 1982. Gr. 3-5 (fairy tale)**

A magic fish is the girl's confidant in this Chinese Cinderella variant tale that predates by 1,000 years the earliest-known European version.

Lum, Kate. *What! Cried Granny: An Almost Bedtime Story.* **Illus. by Adrian Johnson. Dial, 1999. Gr. PreK-1 (easy fiction)**

At bedtime, Granny chops down a tree to make a bed for her grandson Patrick, plucks chickens for his pillow, shears sheep to weave him a blanket, and sews him a gargantuan teddy.

Lunge-Larsen, Lise, retel. *The Troll with No Heart in His Body: And Other Tales of Trolls from Norway.* **Illus. by Betsy Bowen. Houghton Mifflin, 1999. Gr. 2-5 (collection)**

The nine troll stories in this delightful collection, some old favorites, some not so familiar, are all storyteller-worthy and illustrated with large, troll-filled woodcuts.

Lupton, Hugh, and Daniel Morden. *The Adventures of Odysseus.* **Illus. by Christina Balit. Barefoot, 2006. Gr. 3-7 (collection, myth)**

Washed ashore on an island kingdom, Odysseus is invited to King Alcinous's feasting hall to describe his arduous journey toward home since the end of the Trojan War nine years before.

MacDonald, Margaret Read. *Mabela the Clever.* **Illus. by Tim Coffey. Albert Whitman, 2001. Gr. PreK-2 (beast, trickster)**

Foolish mice can't wait to join the cat's secret Cat Society, heedlessly following her into the forest, until the smallest but smartest mouse, Mabela, recalls her father's advice to listen, look around, pay attention, and move fast.

Maddern, Eric. *The Fire Children: A West African Creation Tale.* **Illus. by Frané Lessac. Dial, 1993. Gr. K-3 (myth, pourquoi)**

Two spirit people, Aso Yaa and Kwaku Ananse, propelled to Earth when sky-god Nyame sneezes, get lonely and shape, bake, and breathe life into an array of little clay children.

Mahy, Margaret. *The Seven Chinese Brothers.* **Illus. by Jean Tseng and Mou-sien Tseng. Scholastic, 1990. Gr. K-4 (fairy tale)**

In mending a hole in the Great Wall, seven siblings each have one amazing power that saves them from being killed by the Celestial Emperor.

Manushkin, Fran. *The Shivers in the Fridge.* **Illus. by Paul O. Zelinsky. Dutton, 2006. Gr. PreK-2 (easy fiction)**

Brrr! It's cold and dangerous in the place where Papa Shivers and his family live, all huddled together for warmth in their cardboard box. Zelinsky's deliciously busy pastels show a whole other side of the refrigerator—the inside.

Marcantonio, Patricia Santos. *Red Ridin' in the Hood: And Other Cuentos.* **Illus. by Renato Alarcão. Farrar, 2005. Gr. 4-8 (fiction)**

Taking eleven traditional fairy tales, Marcantonio has reset them in the barrios of the United States and given them an utterly original and contemporary Latino flavor.

Marshall, James. *Goldilocks and the Three Bears.* **Illus. by the author. Dial, 1988. Gr. PreK-1 (beast, folktale)**

An irreverent romp takes the blonde-haired scamp through scalding porridge, unsuitable chairs, and a comfy bed.

Marshall, James. *Old Mother Hubbard and Her Wonderful Dog.* **Illus. by the author. Farrar, 1991. Gr. PreK-1 (poetry)**

Rats, cats, and chickens run riot in the background while the feisty bulldog plays dead, dances, and reads the news in this Mother Goose rhyme, always perfect for creative dramatics.

Marshall, James. *Red Riding Hood.* **Illus. by the author. Dial, 1987. Gr. PreK-2 (fairy tale)**

In this almost-slapstick rendition, Granny is furious at having her reading interrupted by the wolf who swallows her.

Marshall, James. *The Three Little Pigs.* **Illus. by the author. Dial, 1989. Gr. PreK-1 (beast)**

While sticking closely to the story about the three little porkers and the wolf, Marshall injected hilarious touches into his dialogue and illustrations.

Martin, Rafe. *Foolish Rabbit's Big Mistake.* **Illus. by Ed Young. Putnam, 1985. Gr. PreK-2 (beast)**

Like the main character in the folktales about Chicken Little or Henny Penny. Foolish Rabbit thinks the earth is breaking up when he hears a loud noise and runs off to warn the other animals.

Martin, Rafe. *The Rough-Face Girl.* **Illus. by David Shannon. Putnam, 1992. Gr. 2-6 (fairy tale)**

In this solemn Algonquin Indian Cinderella variant, a young girl, scarred and burned from tending the fire, sets out in tattered moccasins and a dress fashioned from birch bark to meet the Invisible Being only she can see.

Martin, Rafe. *The Shark God.* **Illus. by David Shannon. Scholastic, 2001. Gr. 1-6 (fairy tale)**

When a brother and sister touch the king's drum, which is kapu (forbidden), and the hardhearted king refuses to lift his sentence of death, the children's parents visit the cave of Kauhuhu, the fearsome Shark God, to ask for help.

Mathews, Judith, and Fay Robinson. *Nathaniel Willy, Scared Silly.* **Illus. by Alex Natchev. Bradbury, 1994. Gr. PreK-2 (easy fiction)**

Even the cat, dog, pig, and cow his grandmother dumps in his bed one night can't keep Nathaniel from being scared of his squeaky old door until the wise old woman from down the road oils it.

McCaughrean, Geraldine. *The Bronze Cauldron: Myths and Legends of the World.* **Illus. by Bee Willey. McElderry, 1998. Gr. 4-8 (collection, myth)**

Poring over McCaughrean's mesmerizing collection of 27 myths and legends from five continents, one realizes that Greece and Rome were not the only places with gods, powerful animals, bizarre creatures, and brave heroes and heroines.

McCaughrean, Geraldine. *Gilgamesh the Hero: The Epic of Gilgamesh.* **Illus. by David Parkins. Eerdmans, 2003. Gr. 6-8 (collection, legend)**

This collection of twelve epic adventures of mighty King Gilgamesh and his friend Enkidu, the Wild Man, sent to him by the gods, is the first of all buddy stories, dating back to Mesopotamia (now Iraq) sometime between 3200 B.C. and 2700 B.C.

McClements, George. *Jake Gander, Storyville Detective.* **Illus. by the author. Hyperion, 2002. Gr. PreK-2 (easy fiction, parody)**

In "The Case of the Greedy Granny," dim bulb detective Jake Gander knows there's something strange about Red R. Hood's Granny—fur pajamas, really sharp teeth, rabbit breath—but can't put his finger on what's wrong.

McClintock, Barbara. *Animal Fables from Aesop.* **Illus. by the author. Godine, 1991. Gr. 2-6 (beast, collection, fable)**

Nine animal tales, all illustrated in 19th century style of pen and ink and watercolors, focus mainly on sly foxes and wolves.

McClintock, Barbara. *Cinderella.* **Illus. by the author. Scholastic, 2005. Gr. K-4 (fairy tale)**

Based on Charles Perrault's original telling from the 16th century, this version is set in 18th century France and illustrated with delicate pen, india ink, and watercolors that look like old Albrect Dürer engravings.

McCormick, Dell J. *Paul Bunyan Swings His Axe.* **Illus. by the author. Caxton, 1936. Gr. 3-6 (collection, tall tale)**

Share these 17 tall tales of the legendary U.S. logger and his blue ox, Babe.

McCully, Emily Arnold. *Beautiful Warrior: The Legend of the Nun's Kung Fu.* **Illus. by the author. Scholastic, 1998. Gr. 1-4 (easy fiction)**

Sent to tutors to learn as if she were a son, Jingyong becomes a master at kung fu, joins the Shaolin Monastery as a Buddhist nun, and is renamed Wu Mei, meaning beautiful warrior.

McDermott, Gerald. *Coyote: A Trickster Tale from the American Southwest.* **Illus. by the author. Harcourt, 1994. Gr. PreK-2 (beast, trickster)**

In a comical Zuni Indian legend, trickster Coyote follows his nose for trouble and attempts to fly with the crows.

McDermott, Gerald. *Jabutí the Tortoise: A Trickster Tale from the Amazon.* **Illus. by the author. Harcourt, 2001. Gr. K-2 (trickster)**

Jabutí, a trickster who hails from the Amazon rain forest, once had a smooth and shiny shell and played sweet music on his flute which all the birds loved to hear, except for jealous Vulture.

McDermott, Gerald. *Musicians of the Sun.* **Illus. by the author. Simon & Schuster, 1997. Gr. 2-5 (myth, pourquoi)**

This magnificently illustrated pourquoi tale of how color and sound began on Earth is a fragment of an ancient Aztec myth collected in the 16th century by a Spanish missionary.

McDermott, Gerald. *Raven: A Trickster Tale from the Pacific Northwest.* **Illus. by the author. Harcourt, 1993. Gr. K-4 (myth, pourquoi, trickster)**

Sad for the humans who live in the dark and cold, trickster Raven arranges to be born as a boy child of the Sky Chief's daughter so he can steal the sun that is kept hidden in a box in the lodge and give it to all the people.

McDermott, Gerald. *Zomo the Rabbit: A Trickster Tale from West Africa.* **Illus. by the author. Harcourt, 1992. Gr. PreK-1 (myth, pourquoi, trickster)**

Not satisfied with his own cleverness, Zomo asks Sky God for wisdom, and is told he can earn it by completing three impossible and dangerous tasks.

McGill, Alice. *Sure as Sunrise: Stories of Bruh Rabbit & His Walkin' Talkin' Friends.* **Illus. by Don Tate. Houghton Mifflin, 2004. Gr. K-5 (beast, collection, trickster)**

Retold by a master storyteller who recalls each story from her North Carolina childhood, these five lively African American folktales about the crafty trickster Bruh Rabbit and his animal pals and rivals will get your listeners laughing.

McGovern, Ann. *Too Much Noise.* **Illus. by Simms Taback. Houghton Mifflin, 1967. Gr. PreK-2 (cumulative)**

Similar to Marilyn Hirsch's *Could Anything Be Worse* (Holiday House, 1974) and Margot Zemach's *It Could Always Be Worse* (Farrar, 1990), this story about a man who couldn't sleep in his noisy house until he brought inside an even noisier array of barn animals is the easiest to tell.

McKissack, Patricia C. *Flossie & the Fox.* **Illus. by Rachel Isadora. Dial, 1986. Gr. K-3 (easy fiction)**

On her way to deliver a basket of eggs, a little girl encounters and outwits a fox.

McKissack, Patricia C. *Porch Lies: Tales of Slicksters, Tricksters, and Other Wily Characters.* **Illus. by André Carrilho. Schwartz & Wade, 2006. Gr. 4-8 (collection)**

McKissack's 10 original funny tall tales introduce a cast of silver-tongued tricksters who charm their victims while bamboozling or outsmarting them.

McKissack, Patricia C., and Robert L. McKissack. *Itching and Twitching: A Nigerian Folktale.* **Illus. by Laura Freeman. Scholastic, 2003. Gr. PreK-1 (beast)**

When Rabbit and Monkey have dinner together at Monkey's house, Monkey can't stop itching, and Rabbit can't stop twitching, which leads to a contest: the first to scratch or twitch must do the dishes.

McKissack, Patricia, and Onawumi Jean Moss. *Precious and the Boo Hag.* **Illus. by Kyrsten Brooker. Atheneum, 2005. Gr. 1-4 (easy fiction)**

Precious, a young African American girl staying home alone while her mamma and big brother are working in the fields, fends off the tricky, scary, and none-too-smart Pruella the Boo Hag who will do or say anything to get inside the house.

McMullan, Kate. *I Stink!* **Illus. by Jim McMullan. HarperCollins, 2002. Gr. PreK-1 (easy fiction)**

A no-nonsense, tough-talking, cheerful, grinning, sometimes scowling New York City garbage truck explains how he scarfs down your bags of trash each night while you sleep, listing an alphabet of the smelly contents of a typical night's haul.

McVitty, Walter. *Ali Baba and the Forty Thieves.* **Illus. by Margaret Early. Abrams, 1989. Gr. 3-6 (fairy tale)**

"Open sesame" are the words a poor woodcutter overhears that lead him into a robber's den in this famous tale from the Arabian Nights, illustrated with Persian miniature-like paintings.

Meddaugh, Susan. *Hog-Eye.* **Illus. by the author. Houghton Mifflin, 1995. Gr. K-3 (easy fiction)**

A young pig regales her horrified parents and siblings with her melodramatic saga of being captured by a soup-hungry but illiterate wolf, whom she outwits with the help of a patch of poison ivy.

Meddaugh, Susan. *The Witch's Walking Stick.* **Illus. by the author. Houghton Mifflin, 2005. Gr. PreK-3 (easy fiction)**

On a walk in the woods, a cantankerous old witch is thinking about using her magic walking stick to turn a stray dog into a cat, when the dog grabs the stick and runs off.

Medearis, Angela Shelf. *Seven Spools of Thread: A Kwanzaa Story.* **Illus. by Daniel Minter. Albert Whitman, 2000. Gr. K-4 (easy fiction)**

In this pourquoi tale that reads like an African folktale but was written by the author especially for Kwanzaa, we learn how seven quarreling sons must learn to work together, after their father dies, to weave the first multicolored Kente cloth.

Minard, Rosemary. *Womenfolk and Fairy Tales.* **Illus. by Suzanne Klein. Houghton Mifflin, 1975. Gr. 3-6 (collection, fairy tale)**

Eighteen stories introduce heroines from the Chinese Red Riding Hoods to Kate Crackernuts, and all of these female protagonists save the day.

Mollel, Tololwa M. *Ananse's Feast: An Ashanti Tale.* **Illus. by Andrew Glass. Clarion, 1997. Gr. K-3 (beast, trickster)**

Before they begin eating, greedy Ananse the Spider, the West African trickster, sends his friend Akye the Turtle down to the river three times to wash his four hands and devours all the food himself before Akye gets back.

Mollel, Tololwa M. *The Orphan Boy: A Maasai Story.* **Illus. by Paul Morin. Clarion, 1991. Gr. 1-4 (myth, pourquoi)**

A childless old man is overjoyed with the companionship of a boy who calls himself Kileken, though he becomes increasingly driven to discover how the child manages to complete each day's difficult chores.

Mollel, Totolwa M. *Subira Subira.* **Illus. by Linda Saport. Clarion, 2000. Gr. 1-6 (folktale)**

After Mother dies, and Tatu cannot get her little brother Maulidi to obey her, she seeks out a spirit woman who instructs her to pluck three whiskers from a lion.

Mora, Pat. *Doña Flor: A Tall Tale About a Giant Woman with a Great Big Heart.* **Illus. by Raúl Colón. Knopf, 2005. Gr. PreK-3 (easy fiction)**

Gentle giantess Doña Flor who can speak every animal language, welcomes everyone in her pueblo to her mountain-sized casa, even the roaring mountain lion who is causing her neighbors to hide in fear.

Morimoto, Junko. *The Two Bullies.* **Illus. by the author. Crown, 1999. Gr. K-2 (folktale, pourquoi)**

Huge Ni-ou, the strongest fellow in Japan, sets off for China to challenge strong man, Dokkoi, to a fight to see who is more powerful.

Morpurgo, Michael. *The McElderry Book of Aesop's Fables.* **Illus. by Emma Chichester Clark. McElderry, 2005. Gr. K-5 (beast, collection, fable)**

Twenty-one fables, some familiar, introduce the usual assortment of misbehaving and misguided rats, dogs, foxes, crows, and other animal friends and enemies, all of whom learn their lessons.

Mosel, Arlene. *The Funny Little Woman.* **Illus. by Blair Lent. Dutton, 1972. Gr. Pre-K-3 (fairy tale)**

In Old Japan, when the funny little woman drops her rice dumpling and it rolls into the underworld, she runs after it only to be captured by wicked oni who order her to cook for them.

Mosel, Arlene. *Tikki Tikki Tembo.* **Illus. by Blair Lent. Henry Holt, 1968. Gr. PreK-3 (cumulative, folktale)**

In a classic folktale set in China, Chang runs for help when his brother falls into a well. Your listeners will not be able to resist chanting his great long name along with you.

Moser, Barry. *The Three Little Pigs.* **Illus. by the author. Little, Brown, 2001. Gr. PreK-1 (beast)**

Moser's rotund pigs, rendered in splendid watercolors, meet up with that wolf who eats the first two and gets boiled into wolf stew by the third.

Moser, Barry. *Tucker Pfeffercorn: An Old Story Retold.* **Illus. by the author. Little, Brown, 1994. Gr. 3-6 (easy fiction, parody)**

Believing that Bessie Grace Kinzalow, a young widow-woman, can spin cotton into gold, mean mine owner Hezakiah Sweatt locks her in a room until she does.

Moses, Will. *Mother Goose.* **Illus. by the author. Philomel, 2003. Gr. PreK-K (poetry)**

Delicate, convivial folk art paintings, in an early 19th century New England-ish style, accompany 70 mostly familiar nursery rhymes.

Musgrove, Margaret. *The Spider Weaver: A Legend of Kente Cloth.* **Illus. by Julia Cairns. Scholastic, 2001. Gr. K-4 (pourquoi)**

Heading home through a forest in Ghana late one night, master weavers Koragu and Ameyaw come across an extraordinarily colorful and intricate web, which inspires them to develop a new kind of colorful woven cloth they name kente.

Muth, Jon J. *Stone Soup.* **Illus. by the author. Scholastic, 2003. Gr. K-2 (folktale)**

Three Chinese monks arrive in an inhospitable village and help show the people the way to happiness by making soup from a stone.

Muth, Jon J. *Zen Shorts.* **Illus. by the author. Scholastic, 2005. Gr. 1-6 (easy fiction)**

Karl, Michael, and Addy meet their new neighbor, Stillwater, a giant panda who speaks with a slight panda accent and tells them thoughtful stories taken from traditional Buddhist and Taoist tales.

Myers, Tim. *Basho and the Fox.* **Illus. by Oki Sittan. Marshall Cavendish, 2000. Gr. 1-4 (easy fiction)**

In a humorous, fictional story about Basho—Japan's renowned hermit-like poet, who lived from 1644-1694—a fox challenges the poet to write one good, not even great, haiku in exchange for the sweet cherries the fox has taken from Basho's tree. The sequel is *Basho and the River Stones* (2004).

Napoli, Donna Jo. *The Prince of the Pond: Otherwise Known as De Fawg Pin.* **Illus. by Judith Byron Schachner. Dutton, 1992. Gr. 3-6 (fiction)**

"Hep me," the frog stranger implores Jade, the female frog narrator, who not only helps him elude the vindictive witch who has just enchanted him, but instructs him in frog behavior, and even falls in love with him.

Nodelman, Perry. *The Same Place But Different.* **Simon & Schuster, 1995. Gr. 5-8 (fiction)**

Johnny Nesbit sets out to find the fairies or Strangers who stole away his baby sister Andrea and replaced her with a look-alike Changeling and to close the door between the two worlds.

Nolan, Dennis. *Androcles and the Lion.* **Illus. by the author. Harcourt, 1997. Gr. 1-6 (myth)**

Androcles, an escaped slave, pulls a thorn from a lion's paw, thus gaining the animal's undying gratitude.

Ogburn, Jacqueline K. *The Bake Shop Ghost.* **Illus. by Marjorie Priceman. Houghton Mifflin, 2005. Gr. K-3 (easy fiction)**

After master baker Cora Lee Merriweather dies, she haunts and runs off each new owner of her bake shop until she meets her match in pastry chef Annie Washington.

Onyefulu, Obi. *Chinye: A West African Folk Tale.* **Illus. by Evie Safarewicz. Viking, 1994. Gr. K-3 (fairy tale)**

Sent by her stepmother to fetch water from the stream one night, Chinye meets an old woman who bids her to take home a small, quiet gourd which gives off great riches.

Opie, Iona, ed. *Here Comes Mother Goose.* **Illus. by Rosemary Wells. Candlewick Press, 1999. Gr. PreK-1 (poetry)**

The watercolor and ink illustrations in this oversized Mother Goose collection of 56 lesser-known rhymes are simply smashing.

Opie, Iona, and Opie, Peter, eds. *I Saw Esau: The Schoolchild's Pocket Book.* **Illus. by Maurice Sendak. Candlewick, 1992. Gr. 1-5 (poetry)**

In this small-sized book, there are lots of satisfying and irreverent chants, rhymes, riddles, tongue twisters, insults (the kind children say to each other when they think there are no grown-ups about), and marvelous watercolors, too.

Opie, Iona, ed. *My Very First Mother Goose.* **Illus. by Rosemary Wells. Candlewick, 1996. Gr. PreK-1 (poetry)**

While there are loads of wonderful Mother Goose collections out there, this oversized book will quickly become a home and classroom treasure with its 68 well-chosen verses and watercolors.

Osborne, Mary Pope. *American Tall Tales.* **Illus. by Michael McCurdy. Knopf, 1991. Gr. 3-6 (collection, tall tale)**

The exploits of nine uniquely American folklore heroes are recounted with exuberance and laugh-out-loud gusto, along with fascinating historical explanations of how these exaggerated characters first became part of our national heritage.

Osborne, Mary Pope. *The Brave Little Seamstress.* **Illus. by Giselle Potter. Atheneum, 2002. Gr. 2-6 (fairy tale)**

The main character of this re-sexed German tale, "The Brave Little Tailor," is a little seamstress who kills a swarm of flies, and then boldly outwits giants, a vicious wild unicorn, and a wild boar.

Osborne, Mary Pope. *Kate and the Beanstalk.* **Illus. by Giselle Potter. Atheneum, 2000. Gr. K-5 (fairy tale)**

Inspired by Andrew Lang's version of "Jack and the Beanstalk" published in 1890, Mary Pope Osborne has reworked the familiar tale to give us a female protagonist, the plucky Kate.

Osborne, Mary Pope. *Mermaid Tales from Around the World.* **Illus. by Troy Howell. Scholastic, 1993. Gr. 3-6 (collection, fairy tale)**

Twelve romantic stories from Japan, Nigeria, Ukraine, Greece, and elsewhere are accompanied with breathtaking paintings done in styles that evoke each country.

Osborne, Mary Pope. *New York's Bravest.* **Illus. by Steve Johnson and Lou Fancher. Knopf, 2002. Gr. PreK-6 (tall tale)**

Mose, New York City's mythical 19th century firefighter who stands eight feet tall, has hands as big as Virginia hams, and can swim the Hudson River in two strokes, disappears after rescuing people from a hotel fire, though his spirit lives on.

Osborne, Will, and Mary Pope Osborne. *Sleeping Bobby.* **Illus. by Giselle Potter. Atheneum, 2005. Gr. K-6 (fairy tale)**

Just as in "Sleeping Beauty," on which this turnaround fairy tale is based, Bob pricks his finger on a spindle on his eighteenth birthday, and falls into a 100-year snooze.

Palatini, Margie. *The Web Files.* **Illus. by Richard Egielski. Hyperion, 2001. Gr. K-3 (easy fiction, parody)**

Ducktective Web and his partner, Bill, are hot on the trail of missing about-to-be-pickled purple peppers in this deadpan barnyard takeoff on the old *Dragnet* TV show.

Parks, Van Dyke, and Malcolm Jones. *Jump!: The Adventures of Brer Rabbit.* **Illus. by Barry Moser. Harcourt, 1986. Gr. 2-5 (beast, collection, trickster)**

Retold here in an easygoing manner are five classic Southern black folktales with African roots, introducing Brers Fox, Rabbit, Wolf, and Bear.

From *Once Upon a Time: Using Storytelling, Creative Drama, and Reader's Theater with Children in Grades PreK-6* by Judy Freeman. Westport, CT: Libraries Unlimited. Copyright © 2007.

Paterson, Katherine. *The Tale of the Mandarin Ducks.* **Illus. by Leo and Diane Dillon. Dutton/Lodestar, 1990. Gr. 1-6 (fairy tale)**

A proud and cruel Japanese lord cares little for the drake he orders captured and caged, but when sympathetic kitchen maid, Yasuko, frees the duck, the lord condemns her and Shozu, a former samurai, to death by drowning.

Paxton, Tom. *Aesop's Fables.* **Illus. by Robert Rayevsky. Morrow, 1988. Gr. 3-6 (beast, collection, fable)**

Folksinger Paxton took 10 known and not-so-known fables and rewrote them in verse. Paxton's companion collections include *Androcles and the Lion and Other Aesop's Fables* (1991) and *Belling the Cat and Other Aesop's Fables: Retold in Verse* (1990).

Paye, Won-Ldy, and Margaret H. Lippert. *Head, Body, Legs: A Story from Liberia.* **Illus. by Julie Paschkis. Henry Holt, 2002. Gr. PreK-3 (folktale, pourquoi)**

Head, who can only eat the things he can reach on the ground, joins forces with Arms, Body, and Legs, attaching the parts together so they can work together to reach up high and pick mangoes to eat.

Paye, Won-Ldy, and Margaret H. Lippert. *Mrs. Chicken and the Hungry Crocodile.* **Illus. by Julie Paschkis. Henry Holt, 2003. Gr. PreK-1 (beast, trickster)**

Crocodile waits in the river for her chicken dinner, but Mrs. Chicken talks Crocodile out of eating her, promising to prove that they are really sisters.

Peck, Jan. *The Giant Carrot.* **Illus. by Barry Root. Dial, 1998. Gr. PreK-2 (cumulative, folktale)**

Papa Joe and Mama Bess plant a carrot seed, Brother Abel waters it, and sweet Little Isabelle sings and dances around it and gets it growing, but it takes some doing to pull that carrot up.

Perrault, Charles. *Puss in Boots.* **Illus. by Fred Marcellino. Farrar, 1990. Gr. 1-4 (fairy tale)**

This Caldecott Honor version is distinguished for its unforgettable and innovative front cover with the huge, handsome, behatted head of the famous cat; the title, author, and illustrator are relagated to the back cover.

Philip, Neil. *The Adventures of Odysseus.* **Illus. by Peter Malone. Orchard, 1997. Gr. 3-6 (collection, myth)**

Philip's elegantly told but easily digested account of Odysseus's trip home from Troy is a large, attractively illustrated, and accessible collection of 11 stories from *The Odyssey* that will whet children's appetites for more mythology.

Philip, Neil. *Odin's Family: Myths of the Vikings.* **Illus. by Maryclare Foa. Orchard, 1996. Gr. 3-6 (collection, myth)**

From the creation of the Earth and its rulers—Odin the All-father, and his brothers, Vili and Ve—to the death of Balder the Beautiful and the twilight of the gods, see how the mighty Viking gods held court in Asgard.

Pinkney, Andrea Davis. *Peggony-Po: A Whale of a Tale.* **Illus. by Brian Pinkney. Hyperion, 2006. Gr. 1-4 (easy fiction)**

After a monster whale named Cetus snaps Galleon Keene's whaling boat in two and bites off the whaler's leg to boot, Galleon carves himself a son out of the hunk of driftwood that saved his life and names the boy Peggony-Po.

Pinkney, Jerry. *Aesop's Fables.* **Illus. by the author. SeaStar, 2000. Gr. 2-8 (beast, collection, fable)**

Graced with Pinkney's signature lush watercolors are 60 well-told Aesop's fables, some beloved and others lesser known, all of which are natural read-alouds that lead into discussions of the morals, retelling, acting out, and writing new fables.

Pinkney, Jerry. *The Little Red Hen.* **Illus. by the author. Dial, 2006. Gr. PreK-1 (beast)**

Hunting for food for her chicks, the little red hen comes across some strange seeds which her neighbors—the short brown dog, the thin gray rat, the tall black goat, and the round pink pig—can't be bothered to help her plant.

Pitre, Felix. *Juan Bobo and the Pig: A Puerto Rican Folktale.* **Illus. by Christy Hale. Dutton, 1993. Gr. PreK-2 (folktale, noodlehead)**

Juan Bobo, or "Simple John," the well-loved lazy fool from Puerto Rican folklore, dresses the pig in his mother's finest and sends it off to church.

Pollock, Penny. *The Turkey Girl: A Zuni Cinderella Story.* **Illus. by Ed Young. Little, Brown, 1996. Gr. 2-5 (fairy tale)**

Wanting to attend the Dance of the Sacred Bird, the Turkey Girl is granted her wish by the turkeys she attends so faithfully, promising to come back to them before Father Sun returns to his sacred place.

Pratchett, Terry. *The Wee Free Men.* **HarperCollins, 2003. Gr. 6-8 (fiction)**

When nine-year-old Tiffany Aching is warned away from a sharp-toothed green-headed monster by two tiny redheaded blue men in a boat, it seems that she may be the new witch of the lowlands.

Prelutsky, Jack, comp. *Poems of A. Nonny Mouse.* **Illus. by Henrik Drescher. Knopf, 1989. Gr. K-4 (poetry)**

According to Prelutsky, all those poems written by Anonymous were actually composed by A. Nonny Mouse, a charming and clever rodent, and many of her best ditties are reproduced here. The companion volume is *A. Nonny Mouse Writes Again!* (1993).

Pullman, Philip. *I Was a Rat!* **Illus. by Kevin Hawkes. Knopf, 2000. Gr. 4-7 (fiction)**

Old Bob the cobbler and his washerwoman wife, Joan, take in a disheveled little boy in a page's uniform who shows up at their doorstep and tells them, "I was a rat."

Pullman, Philip. *The Scarecrow and His Servant.* **Illus. by Peter Bailey. Knopf, 2005. Gr. 4-7 (fiction)**

On the night lightning strikes the wheat field, a scarecrow with a big solid turnip head and nothing in the way of brains jolts to life and takes to the road with his new personal servant, a young boy named Jack.

Rascol, Sabina I. *The Impudent Rooster.* **Illus. by Holly Berry. Dutton, 2004. Gr. 1-4 (beast)**

Folk-art paintings bring out the humor of this Romanian cautionary tale of a poor old man's enterprising rooster who finds a purse with pennies in it only to have it stolen by a greedy nobleman.

Rex, Adam. *Frankenstein Makes a Sandwich: And Other Stories You're Sure to Like, Because They're All About Monsters, and Some of Them Are Also About Food. You Like Food, Don't You? Well, All Right Then.* **Illus. by the author. Harcourt, 2006. Gr. 2-6 (poetry)**

Meet garrulous creatures from the silver screen and your nightmares—including Frankenstein, the Phantom of the Opera, the Mummy, and Dracula—in a collection of 20 appealing poems that will have your kids screaming. With laughter.

Riordan, Rick. *The Lightning Thief.* **(Percy Jackson & the Olympians, Book 1) Miramax/Hyperion, 2005. Gr. 5-8 (fiction)**

In Book 1 of a crackling series, meet Percy, troubled dyslexic ADHD sixth grader who is about to find out out about his lineage: he is a half-blood, with a mother from New York City and a father who is a Greek god.

Rodanas, Kristina. *The Blind Hunter.* **Illus. by the author. Cavendish, 2003. Gr. 1-4 (easy fiction)**

When a young man offers to let the now blind Chirobo come hunting with him in the South African bush, Chirobo teaches him that there are many ways of seeing.

Root, Phyllis. *Rattletrap Car.* **Illus. by Jill Barton. Candlewick, 2001. Gr. PreK-1 (easy fiction)**

Poppa doesn't know if he and the hot hot hot kids—Junie, Jakie, and the baby—can make it all the way to the lake in his old jalopy, especially when the floor falls off, the gas tank falls off, and the engine falls out.

Rosen, Michael. *We're Going on a Bear Hunt.* **Illus. by Helen Oxenbury. Macmillan, 1989. Gr. PreK-1 (cumulative, easy fiction)**

Dad, four kids, and the dog all head out through the tall grass (Swishy swashy!), the deep, cold river (Splash splosh!), the thick, oozy mud (Squelch squerch!), and the big dark forest (Stumble trip!), till they find A BEAR!!!!

Ross, Gayle. *How Turtle's Back Was Cracked: A Traditional Cherokee Tale.* **Illus. by Murv Jacob. Dial, 1995. Gr. 1-4 (beast, pourquoi)**

Though it was really Possum who killed a persimmon-stealing wolf, when Turtle takes the credit, the other wolves threaten to throw him in the fire, boil him up for turtle soup, or throw him in the river.

Rostoker-Gruber, Karen. *Rooster Can't Cock-a-Doodle-Doo.* **Illus. by Paul Rátz de Tagyos. Dial, 2004. Gr. PreK-1 (easy fiction)**

Rooster wakes with a terrible sore throat and enlists the help of the hens, cows, sheep, and pigs to figure out a way to wake up Farmer Ted without cock-a-doodle-doo-ing.

Rounds, Glen. *Ol' Paul, the Mighty Logger.* **Illus. by the author. Holiday House, 1976. Gr. 4-6 (collection)**

The subtitle to these 11 tall tales says it all: Being the True Account of the Seemingly Incredible Exploits and Inventions of the Great Paul Bunyan."

Rounds, Glen. *The Three Billy Goats Gruff.* **Illus. by the author. Holiday House, 1993. Gr. PreK-2 (beast, cumulative)**

With its giant typefaces and scraggly black line and crayon illustrations, this version is so satisfying, though it tones down the original wording of the troll and biggest goat's final confrontation.

Rounds, Glen. *Three Little Pigs and the Big Bad Wolf.* **Illus. by the author. Holiday House, 1992. Gr. PreK-2 (beast)**

While this version is missing the second of three wolf-planned encounters—the apple tree scene—the rest of the tale is so mischievously told and illustrated that you won't mind.

Rowling, J. K. *Harry Potter and the Sorcerer's Stone.* **Illus. by Mary GrandPré. Scholastic, 1998. Gr. 4-8 (fiction)**

In the first book of a series that has captivated readers worldwide, ten-year-old Harry learns his parents were great wizards, killed by an evil wizard named Voldemort, and he is summoned to attend the Hogwarts School of Witchcraft and Wizardry.

Rumford, James. *Dog-of-the-Sea-Waves.* **Illus. by the author. Houghton Mifflin, 2004. Gr. 2-5 (easy fiction)**

In this literary folktale, written in both English and Hawaiian, we meet five brothers—the first to explore the Hawaiian Islands—and the wounded dolphin the youngest brother, Manu, rescues and befriends.

Ryan, Pam Muñoz. *Mice and Beans.* **Illus. by Joe Cepeda. Scholastic, 2001. Gr. PreK-2 (easy fiction)**

As Rosa María spends the week in her tiny casita (house) preparing a birthday party for Little Catalina, her youngest grandchild, she sets mousetraps for the mice, who are organizing their own birthday celebration.

Sabuda, Robert. *Arthur and the Sword.* **Illus. by the author. Atheneum, 1995. Gr. 2-5 (legend)**

Based on Sir Thomas Malory's 1485 retelling of the legend, "Le Morte D'Arthur," Sabuda's picture book version with illustrations that look like stained glass panels is a riveting introduction to the Round Table tales for younger children.

Sacre, Antonio. *The Barking Mouse.* **Illus. by Alfredo Aguirre. Albert Whitman, 2003. Gr. 1-4 (easy fiction)**

Mamá and Papá Ratón and their two children, Hermano and Hermana, are having a wonderful time on their picnic until they encounter a big mean gato, but brave Mamá thinks of just the right way to defend her familia.

Salley, Coleen. *Epossumondas.* **Illus. by Janet Stevens. Harcourt, 2002. Gr. PreK-2 (beast, noodlehead)**

Every time sweet little patootie, Epossumondas, visits his auntie, she gives him something to take home, and each time he carries it home the wrong way, according to his Mama.

Salley, Coleen. *Why Epossumondas Has No Hair on His Tail.* **Illus. by Janet Stevens. Harcourt, 2004. Gr. PreK-2 (noodlehead, pourquoi)**

When possum Epossumondas asks Mama why his tail is pink, naked, and funny looking, she tells him an old story about his great-great-great grandpa, Papapossum, whose love of persimmons got him in trouble.

San Souci, Robert D. *Cendrillon: A Caribbean Cinderella.* **Illus. by Brian Pinkney. Simon & Schuster, 1998. Gr. 2-6 (fairy tale)**

On the Caribbean island of Martinique, a nannin' or godmother explains how she came to be the helpmate for Cendrillon, whose mother has died and whose stepmother works her like a serving girl.

San Souci, Robert D. *The Faithful Friend.* **Illus. by Brian Pinkney. Simon & Schuster, 1995. Gr. 3-6 (fairy tale)**

On the Caribbean island of Martinique, Hippolyte's best friend Clement falls in love with a picture of Pauline, though she is the niece of a dangerous quimboiseur, or wizard, Monsieur Zabocat.

San Souci, Robert D. *Larger Than Life: The Adventures of American Legendary Heroes.* **Illus. by Andrew Glass. Doubleday, 1991. Gr. 3-6 (collection, tall tale)**

Get to know six straight-faced tall tale characters: John Henry, Old Stormalong, Slue-Foot Sue and her honey Pecos Bill, Strap Buckner, and Paul Bunyan.

San Souci, Robert D. *Sister Tricksters: Rollicking Tales of Clever Females.* **Illus. by Daniel San Souci. August House, 2006. Gr. 3-6 (beast, collection, trickster)**

In a jocular collection of eight tales from down South, meet Molly Hare, Miz Duck, Miz Grasshopper, and Miz Goose, sassy females who outsmart, outtalk, and outrage their less clever male opponents, tricksters Mistah Slickry Sly-fox and Mistah Bear.

San Souci, Robert D. *Sukey and the Mermaid.* **Illus. by Brian Pinkney. Four Winds, 1992. Gr. 2-6 (fairy tale)**

On a little island off the coast of South Carolina, a young hardworking girl who lives with her mother and harsh new step-pa, sings a song and summons up a "beautiful, brown-skinned, black-eyed mermaid" who gives her gold pieces.

San Souci, Robert D. *The Talking Eggs.* **Illus. by Jerry Pinkney. Dial, 1989. Gr. K-3 (fairy tale)**

Sweet and kind and sharp as 40 crickets, Blanche is rewarded for her kindness to an old woman, while mean sister Rose, who doesn't know beans from birds' eggs, is punished for her nasty ways.

San Souci, Robert D. *A Weave of Words: An Armenian Tale.* **Illus. by Raúl Colón. Orchard, 1998. Gr. 3-6 (folktale)**

The lovely weaver, Anait, won't marry Prince Vachagan until he learns how to read and write and earn a living by his own hands.

San Souci, Robert D. *Young Arthur.* **Illus. by Jamichael Henterly. Doubleday, 1997. Gr. 2-5 (legend)**

This majestic picture book of the first King Arthur tale takes us from Arthur's acquisition of the sword Excalibur to his first battle.

Sawyer, Ruth. *The Remarkable Christmas of the Cobbler's Sons.* **Illus. by Barbara Cooney. Viking, 1994. Gr. K-3 (fairy tale)**

After a poor cobbler must leave his three hungry sons on Christmas Eve to mend the boots of the soldiers, the boys open the door for a bad-tempered little man who hogs the bed but rewards them with a Christmas feast.

Say, Allen. *Kamishibai Man.* **Illus. by the author. Houghton Mifflin, 2005. Gr. 1-6 (easy fiction)**

On his first visit to the city in years, the elderly kamishibai man recalls how the children used to cluster about him, eager to listen to him tell his stories with his colorful storycards.

Schaefer, Carole Lexa. *The Biggest Soap.* **Illus. by Stacey Dressen-McQueen. Farrar, 2004. Gr. PreK-2 (easy fiction)**

On laundry day, when Mama sends Kessey to the store to get the biggest bar of soap he can find, he rushes off fast as a typhoon wind so he can get back in time to listen to Mama and her cousins tell stories.

Schanzer, Rosalyn. *Davy Crockett Saves the World.* **Illus. by the author. HarperCollins, 2001. Gr. K-3 (easy fiction, tall tale)**

In this literary tall tale, Davy Crockett, Tennessee frontiersman, hunter, and scout, is enlisted by the President to pull the tail off of Halley's Comet so it won't crash into the earth.

Schwartz, Alvin. *And the Green Grass Grew All Around: Folk Poetry from Everyone.* **Illus. by Sue Truesdale. HarperCollins, 1992. Gr. 2-6 (poetry)**

You'll find a meaty collection of over 300 poems, songs, riddles, and chants about people, food, school, teases and taunts, and other nonsense that will keep everyone humming and giggling all year.

Schwartz, Alvin. *Busy Buzzing Bumblebees and Other Tongue Twisters.* **Illus. by Kathie Abrams. HarperCollins, 1982. Gr. PreK-2 (poetry)**

Fun, garish, and easy to read and repeat, these tongue twisters, one per page, will get children laughing and writing their own.

Schwartz, Alvin. *I Saw You in the Bathtub and Other Folk Rhymes.* **Illus. by Syd Hoff. HarperCollins, 1989. Gr. K-3 (poetry)**

Over three dozen funny kid rhymes and chants, many of which you'll recall from your childhood, are presented in easy-to-read format.

Schwartz, Alvin. *Scary Stories to Tell in the Dark.* **Illus. by Stephen Gammell. HarperCollins, 1981. Gr. 4-8 (collection, scary)**

This book gets banned a lot, and it has very creepy illustrations, true, but the 29 tales are fabulous to tell, and older children adore them. Also look for *More Scary Stories to Tell in the Dark* (1984) and *Scary Stories 3* (1991).

Schwartz, Alvin. *Tomfoolery: Trickery and Foolery with Words.* **Illus. by Glen Rounds. Lippincott, 1973. Gr. 1-6 (noodlehead)**

This chuckle-filled volume of poetry, tricks, riddles, jokes, and word games, collected from American folklore, is ripe for trying out on unsuspecting students and friends. Just as great are *Flapdoodle* (1980), *Unriddling* (1983), and *Witcracks* (1973).

Scieszka, Jon. *The Frog Prince, Continued.* **Illus. by Steve Johnson. Viking, 1991. Gr. 2-6 (easy fiction, parody)**

In his frantic search for happy-ever-after-ness, and nostalgic for his frog-days, this discontented yuppie prince encounters an assortment of sarcastic and / or nasty witches from other folktales before he reconciles with his princess.

Scieszka, Jon. *Squids Will Be Squids: Fresh Morals, Beastly Fables.* **Illus. by Lane Smith. Viking, 1998. Gr. 2-6 (fable, easy fiction, parody)**

Those two funnymen, Scieszka and Smith, have taken on Aesop, with 18 hip, au courant, off-the-wall fables about "all kinds of bossy, sneaky funny, annoying dim-bulb people," transformed into animals to protect the "not-so innocent."

Scieszka, Jon. *The Stinky Cheese Man and Other Fairly Stupid Tales.* **Illus. by Lane Smith. Viking, 1992. Gr. PreK-Adult (easy fiction, parody)**

This frantic, insanely comic send-up of fairy tales presents nine masterpieces, rewrites of well-known tales, recounted by narrator Jack (of beanstalk fame), and spectacular collage paintings.

Scieszka, Jon. *The True Story of the 3 Little Pigs.* **Illus. by Lane Smith. Viking, 1989. Gr. 2-Adult (easy fiction, parody)**

You may think you know what happened to those three house-constructing pig brothers, but, as narrated and explained by Alexander T. Wolf, the whole thing started when he had a cold and tried to borrow a cup of sugar.

Seeger, Pete. *Abiyoyo.* **Illus. by Michael Hays. Macmillan, 1986. Gr. K-2 (easy fiction)**

Famed folksinger Seeger's original story-song about a ukulele-playing boy, his magician father, and a monster named Abiyoyo is based on an African lullaby.

Shannon, George. *Stories to Solve: Folktales from Around the World.* **Illus. by Peter Sis. Greenwillow, 1985. Gr. 2-6 (collection)**

Each of 14 brief folktales contains a problem, conundrum, or mystery which listeners must figure out, solve, and explain. *More Stories to Solve* (1991) and *Still More Stories to Solve* (1994) provide more puzzlers.

Shannon, George. *True Lies: 18 Tales for You to Judge.* **Illus. by John O'Brien. Greenwillow, 1997. Gr. 3-6 (collection)**

Challenge your children to figure out how each character in these 18 brief amusing international folktales and jokes manages to trick or mislead others while appearing to be honest and upstanding. Follow up with *More True Lies* (2001).

Shepard, Aaron. *King o' the Cats.* **Illus. by Kristin Sorra. Atheneum, 2004. Gr. 2-5 (scary)**

Father Allen is exasperated with his storytelling young sexton, Peter, who tells outlandish tales, but the night Peter witnesses a cat's funeral procession, the priest has no choice but to believe him. Go to **http://aaronshep.com/rt/** to print out Reader's Theater scripts for all of Aaron Shephard's stories to act them out after you read his books aloud.

Shepard, Aaron. *Master Man: A Tall Tale of Nigeria.* **Illus. by David Wisniewski. HarperCollins, 2001. Gr. K-5 (pourquoi, tall tale)**

Impressed with his own muscles, Shadusa decides to call himself Master Man, but soon finds out there are others far stronger than he in this comical West African pourquoi tale.

Shepard, Aaron. *The Princess Mouse: A Tale of Finland.* **Illus. by Leonid Gore. Atheneum, 2003. Gr. K-3 (fairy tale)**

Obeying his father's instructions on finding a sweetheart, Mikko cuts down a tree, follows where it points, and comes to a cottage with a bright-eyed talking mouse he comes to love.

Shulman, Lisa. *The Matzo Ball Boy.* **Illus. by Rosanne Litzinger. Dutton, 2005. Gr. PreK-2 (easy fiction, parody)**

On Passover morning, a lonely old bubbe (grandmother) makes a lovely little matzo ball boy, but he escapes from her chicken soup, runs through town, and no one can catch him.

Shulman, Lisa. *Old MacDonald Had a Woodshop.* **Illus. by Ashley Wolff. Putnam, 2002. Gr. PreK-1 (easy fiction)**

Old MacDonald, an industrious sheep, is busy with all the other animals—sawing, drilling, hammering, filing, and painting—in order to make a surprise out of wood.

Shute, Linda. *Momotaro, the Peach Boy: A Traditional Japanese Tale.* **Illus. by the author. Lothrop, 1986. Gr. K-4 (fairy tale)**

This folktale of a brave young man and his monkey, dog, and pheasant companions who roust a castleful of ugly oni dates back to eighth century Japan.

Sierra, Judy. *Can You Guess My Name?: Traditional Tales Around the World.* **Illus. by Stefano Vitale. Clarion, 2002. Gr. PreK-2 (collection)**

You'll find three compelling variants for each of five well-known European folktales—"The Three Pigs," "The Bremen Town Musicians," "Rumpelstiltskin," "The Frog Prince," and "Hansel and Gretel"—in a collection representing 13 countries.

Sierra, Judy. *The Gift of the Crocodile: A Cinderella Story.* **Illus. by Reynold Ruffins. Simon & Schuster, 2000. Gr. K-4 (fairy tale)**

In a Cinderella story from the Moluccas or Spice Islands in Indonesia, Damura is maltreated by her stepmother, but protected by Grandmother Crocodile who repays her kindness with a silver sarong.

Sierra, Judy. *Nursery Tales Around the World.* **Illus. by Stefano Vitale. Clarion, 1996. Gr. PreK-2 (collection)**

Compare and contrast 18 easy-to-tell stories, arranged in groups of three variants on the themes of Runaway Cookies; Incredible Appetites; Victory of the Smallest; Chain Tales; Slowpokes & Speedsters; and Fooling the Big Bad Wolf.

Sierra, Judy. *Schoolyard Rhymes: Kids' Own Rhymes for Rope Skipping, Hand Clapping, Ball Bouncing, and Just Plain Fun.* **Illus. by Melissa Sweet. Knopf, 2005. Gr. 1-5 (poetry)**

Chant along with the almost four dozen wacky children's rhymes, many of which will be familiar, spiced up with perfectly silly watercolors of kids.

Sierra, Judy. *Tasty Baby Belly Buttons: A Japanese Folktale.* **Illus. by Meilo So. Knopf, 1999. Gr. K-3 (fairy tale, trickster)**

When bad oni kidnap the babies of the village, bellybutton-less Uriko-hime or "melon princess" sets out with the her dog, a pheasant, and a monkey to rescue them.

Sierra, Judy. *Wild About Books.* **Illus. by Marc Brown. Knopf, 2004. Gr. PreK-2 (easy fiction)**

Springfield librarian, Molly McGrew, mistakenly drives her bookmobile to the zoo, where all of the animals go simply wild for all the wonderful books.

Silverman, Erica. *Big Pumpkin.* **Illus. by S. D. Schindler. Macmillan, 1992. Gr. PreK-2 (easy fiction)**

Though the witch tugs and pulls, she can not pull her pumpkin off the vine, and must accept assistance from the ghost, vampire, mummy, and bat who offer their services in hopes of a taste of pumpkin pie.

Simms, Laura. *The Squeaky Door.* **Illus. by Sylvie Wickstrom. Crown, 1991. Gr. PreK-2 (cumulative, folktale)**

Every night at bedtime when his grandmother turns out the light and closes the squeaky door to his room, a little boy gets scared, jumps under the bed and starts to cry, even with the addition of animals in his bed.

Singer, Isaac Bashevis. *When Shlemiel Went to Warsaw & Other Stories.* **Illus. by Margot Zemach. Farrar, 1979. Gr. 4-6 (collection, noodlehead)**

Both the foolish and the unfortunate prevail in these eight folklore-based Jewish stories told by a master of Yiddish literature. Also don't miss Singer's companion volume, *Zlateh the Goat and Other Stories* (HarperCollins, 1966).

Singh, Vandana. *Younguncle Comes to Town.* **Illus. by B. M. Kamath. Viking, 2006. Gr. 3-5 (fiction)**

In small Indian village, nine-year-old Sarita and her younger brother and baby sister are smitten with their father's unconventional youngest brother, Younguncle, who moves in during the monsoon season and regales them with stories of his escapades.

Sloat, Teri. *Sody Sallyratus.* **Illus. by the author. Dutton, 1997. Gr. PreK-3 (cumulative, folktale)**

For a delightful swallowing story, try this American folktale about a big black bear who eats up two children and two oldsters before their pet squirrel stops him in his tracks.

Snyder, Dianne. *The Boy of the Three Year Nap.* **Illus. by Allen Say. Houghton Mifflin, 1988. Gr. 2-5 (folktale, noodlehead)**

While lazy Japanese boy Taro tricks a rich merchant into arranging a marriage with his daughter, Taro's mother has her own agenda when she convinces the merchant to fix up her house and give her son his first real job.

So, Meilo. *Gobble, Gobble, Slip, Slop: The Tale of a Very Greedy Cat.* **Illus. by the author. Knopf, 2004. Gr. PreK-3 (beast, cumulative)**

In a folktale from India, a cat and a parrot decide to take turns preparing meals for each other, but when the parrot serves the cat a feast of five hundred delicious little cakes—gobble, gobble, slip, slop—the cat eats them all and the parrot, too.

Souhami, Jessica. *The Leopard's Drum: An Asante Tale from West Africa.* **Illus. by the author. Frances Lincoln, 2005. Gr. PreK-2 (beast, trickster)**

Nyame, the Sky-God, promises a reward to anyone who can bring him the drum belonging to fierce, proud, and boastful Oseba, the Leopard.

Souhami, Jessica. *Mrs. McCool and the Giant Cuhullin: An Irish Tale.* **Illus. by the author. Henry Holt, 2002. Gr. K-4 (fairy tale, trickster)**

In this full-bodied account of Finn's dealings with the brutish bully, Cuhullin, Finn's wife Oonagh, who has learned magic from the faeries, saves her husband from a beating, proving that "Big is big. But brains are better!"

Souhami, Jessica. *No Dinner!: The Story of the Old Woman and the Pumpkin.* **Illus. by the author. Cavendish, 2000. Gr. PreK-2 (cumulative, folktale)**

In this Indian folktale variant of "The Three Billy Goats Gruff," with elements of "Hansel and Gretel," "The Three Little Pigs," and other well-known European folktales, an old woman tricks a wolf, a tiger, and a bear into not eating her.

Stamm, Claus. *Three Strong Women: A Tall Tale from Japan.* **Illus. by Jean Tseng and Mou-Sien Tseng. Viking, 1990. Gr. 1-4 (tall tale)**

On his way to wrestle before the Emperor, Forever-Mountain meets up with a young girl, her mother, and grandmother, all of whom are stronger than he and who make him over into a truly powerful guy.

Stanley, Diane. *Bella at Midnight.* **HarperCollins, 2006. Gr. 5-8 (fiction)**

In this novel, a new take on the Cinderella story, after Bella's mother dies in childbirth, Sir Edward casts off his baby daughter who is then raised by the blacksmith and his kind wife, Beatrice.

Stanley, Diane. *The Giant and the Beanstalk.* **Illus. by the author. HarperCollins, 2004. Gr. PreK-2 (easy fiction, parody)**

When a human comes a-calling and steals Otto's pet hen, the golden egg-laying Clara, the giant heads down the beanstalk to find that boy named Jack.

Stanley, Diane. *Goldie and the Three Bears.* **Illus. by the author. HarperCollins, 2003. Gr. PreK-1 (easy fiction, parody)**

Goldie, a little blonde girl looking for a friend she can love with all her heart, wanders into a house with three sandwiches, three chairs, and three beds, where she finds the perfect friend.

Stanley, Diane. *Rumpelstiltskin's Daughter.* **Illus. by the author. Morrow, 1997. Gr. 2-5 (easy fiction, parody)**

According to this updated account, Meredith, the miller's daughter who was ordered by the king to spin straw into gold, ran off with that little man Rumpelstiltskin and had a daughter who, 16 years later, is kidnapped by the still-greedy king.

Steptoe, John. *Mufaro's Beautiful Daughters: An African Tale.* **Illus. by the author. Lothrop, 1987. Gr. 1-4 (fairy tale)**

The sumptuous stately paintings of this Caldecott Honor Book are unforgettable in this Cinderella variant where one good daughter and one bad set off to appear before the king hoping to be chosen as his queen.

Stevens, Janet, and Susan Stevens Crummel. *And the Dish Ran Away with the Spoon.* **Illus. by Janet Stevens. Harcourt, 2001. Gr. K-3 (easy fiction, parody)**

When Dish and Spoon don't come back after their performance of "Hey diddle diddle," Cat, Dog, and Cow set off to find them.

Stevens, Janet, and Susan Stevens Crummel. *Cook-a-Doodle-Doo!* **Illus. by Janet Stevens. Harcourt, 1999. Gr. PreK-2 (easy fiction, parody)**

Sick of eating chicken feed, Big Brown Rooster finds the cookbook of his famous great-grandmother, the Little Red Hen, and, with the help of pals, Turtle, Potbellied Pig, and Iguana, undertakes baking a strawberry shortcake.

Stevens, Janet. *Coyote Steals the Blanket: A Ute Tale.* **Illus. by the author. Holiday House, 1993. Gr. PreK-3 (beast, pourquoi, trickster)**

Though Hummingbird warns him not to, Coyote runs off with one of the blankets he finds draped over rocks in the middle of the desert, and now a huge rock is rumbling after him.

Stevens, Janet. *Tops & Bottoms.* **Illus. by the author. Harcourt, 1995. Gr. PreK-3 (trickster)**

When the poor hungry hare down the road proposes to plant and harvest crops on Bear's land and split the profit down the middle, it seems too good a deal for the lazy bear to pass up.

Sturges, Philemon. *The Little Red Hen (Makes a Pizza).* **Illus. by Amy Walrod. Dutton, 1999. Gr. PreK-1 (easy fiction, parody)**

The duck, the dog, and the cat are too busy to help the industrious hen construct her magnificent pizza, but she generously allows them to help her eat it anyway.

Sunami, Kitoba. *How the Fisherman Tricked the Genie: A Tale Within a Tale Within a Tale.* **Illus. by Amiko Hirao. Atheneum, 2002. Gr. 2-6 (easy fiction)**

When a genie threatens to kill the poor fisherman who has rescued him from a brass bottle in the Arabian Sea, the fisherman tells him three interconnected stories to convince the genie that he should never repay a good deed with an evil one.

Sutcliff, Rosemary. *Black Ships Before Troy!: The Story of the Iliad.* **Illus. by Alan Lee. Delacorte, 1993. Gr. 5-8 (collection, myth)**

Included in this huge, stately volume, a prose retelling of Homer's epic (and remarkably bloody and violent) poem "The Iliad," are magnificent sweeping paintings.

Sutherland, Zena. *The Orchard Book of Nursery Rhymes.* **Illus. by Faith Jaques. Orchard, 1990. Gr. PreK-1 (poetry)**

An all-around lovely collection sports 77 nursery rhymes on large, luxurious pages decorated with delicate late eighteenth century-style watercolors.

Swope, Sam. *Jack and the Seven Deadly Giants.* **Illus. by Carll Cneut. Farrar, 2004. Gr. 3-5 (fiction)**

In a wild yarn inspired by Jack tales of old, young Jack sets off down the road and encounters and outwits seven giants, each of whom embodies one of the seven deadly sins.

Taback, Simms. *Joseph Had a Little Overcoat.* **Illus. by the author. Viking, 1999. Gr. PreK-1 (cumulative)**

Tailor Joseph turns his old and worn overcoat into a succession of smaller garments, in this Caldecott Medal picture book, an adaptation of an old Yiddish folksong.

Taback, Simms. *Kibitzers and Fools: Tales My Zayda (Grandfather) Told Me.* **Illus. by the author. Viking, 2005. Gr. 1-4 (noodlehead)**

Meet kibitzers (know-it-alls) and a variety of fools, including nebbishes, nudniks, schmendriks, and schnooks, in this uproarious collection of 13 short tales from the Jewish tradition.

Taback, Simms. *There Was an Old Lady Who Swallowed a Fly.* **Illus. by the author. Viking, 1997. Gr. PreK-2 (cumulative, poetry)**

A die-cut hole in each page reveals the fly, spider, bird, and other creatures in the belly of the ravenous old woman as she devours creature after creature.

Taback, Simms. *This Is the House That Jack Built.* **Illus. by the author. Putnam, 2002. Gr. PreK-1 (cumulative, poetry)**

Taback's signature collage illustrations are frantic and fun in this lively version of the children's chant, first published in 1755.

Tashjian, Virginia A. *Juba This and Juba That: Story Hour Stretches for Large or Small Groups.* Illus. by Nadine Bernard Westcott. Little, Brown, 1995. Gr. PreK-4 (collection)

A spectacular and fun collection of chants, poems, stories to tell, fingerplays, riddles, songs, tongue twisters, and jokes will make your story hours sparkle. You'll also want the companion volume, *With a Deep Sea Smile* (1974).

Thiesing, Lisa. *The Viper.* Illus. by the author. Dutton, 2002. Gr. K-2 (easy fiction)

Peggy the pig gets more and more frightened each time she gets a call from "zee Viper" who says he is coming to her house in one year, month, week, and minute.

Thomas, Shelley Moore. *Get Well, Good Knight.* Illus. by Jennifer Plecas. Dutton, 2002. Gr. PreK-1 (easy fiction)

After the Good Knight's three little dragon friends come down with sneezes, coughs, and fevers, he seeks a cure from the old wizard, but finds that his own mother has the best soup recipe to heal them.

Thompson, Lauren. *One Riddle, One Answer.* Illus. by Linda S. Wingerter. Scholastic, 2001. Gr. 2-6 (folktale)

Faced with choosing a suitable husband, the Persian sultan's youngest daughter, Aziza, who loves numbers and riddles, presents her suitors with a riddle that has only one true answer.

Thomson, Pat. *The Squeaky, Creaky Bed.* Illus. by Niki Daly. Doubleday, 2003. Gr. PreK-1 (cumulative, easy fiction)

Every night, when the little boy's bed goes "squeak, squeak, creak!," he cries until his grandfather comes to the rescue with, cumulatively, a cat, a dog, a pig, and a parrot to keep him company.

Tripp, Wallace, comp. *A Great Big Ugly Man Came Up and Tied His Horse to Me; A Book of Nonsense Verse.* Illus. by the author. Little, Brown, 1973. Gr. PreK-4 (poetry)

Tripp's endearingly nutty illustrations demand closer scrutiny; when reading these goofy rhymes, have everyone squeeze up close. Also look for the humorous companion, *Granfa' Grig Had a Pig and Other Rhymes without Reason from Mother Goose* (1976).

Tucker, Kathy. *The Seven Chinese Sisters.* Illus. by Grace Lin. Albert Whitman, 2003. Gr. K-4 (fairy tale)

This is an amusing feminist reworking of the traditional tale about those identical Chinese brothers, who now meet seven sisters, each with a special talent.

Untermeyer, Louis. *Aesop's Fables.* Illus. by Alice Provensen and Martin Provensen. Golden Press, 1965. Gr. K-3 (beast, collection, fable)

In this large, indispensable classic anthology, you'll find most of the 40 stories are ideal for acting out in pairs or small groups.

Van Laan, Nancy. *In a Circle Long Ago: A Treasury of Native Lore from North America.* Illus. by Lisa Desimini. Knopf, 1995. Gr. K-5 (beast, collection, pourquoi, trickster)

In this splendid collection of Native American animal fables, many of them pourquoi and / or trickster tales, the stories are grouped by region, starting with the Arctic, moving in a counterclockwise spiral, and ending with the Plains Indians.

Waldherr, Kris. *Persephone and the Pomegranate: A Myth from Greece.* **Illus. by the author. Dial, 1993. Gr. 2-6 (myth)**

When Demeter's daughter is kidnapped by Pluto, lord of the underworld, the anguished goddess of the harvests will not rest until she can rescue her child.

Walker, Paul Robert. *Big Men, Big Country: A Collection of American Tall Tales.* **Illus. by James Bernardin. Harcourt, 1993. Gr. 4-6 (collection, tall tale)**

Boisterous, good-natured yarns about the usual guys—Davy Crockett, Paul Bunyan, John Henry and a few lesser knowns; detailed background notes about each story; and grand full page paintings make this a collection hard to beat.

Wardlaw, Lee. *Punia and the King of Sharks: A Hawaii Folktale.* **Illus. by Felipe Davalos. Dial, 1997. Gr. K-3 (folktale, trickster)**

Punia, a poor, hungry, but clever young boy whose fisherman father was devoured by lobster-hoarding sharks, tricks the King of Sharks four times, stealing his sweet and tasty lobsters each time.

Washington, Donna L. *A Pride of African Tales.* **Illus. by James Ransome. HarperCollins, 2004. Gr. 4-8 (collection)**

A rich collection of six thoughtful stories from West Africa, illustrated with full-bleed watercolor paintings, includes an Anansi tale, a pourquoi tale, a cautionary tale, a story about anger and forgiveness, a taboo story, and a fable.

Wattenberg, Jane. *Henny-Penny.* **Illus. by the author. Scholastic, 2000. Gr. PreK-2 (beast, cumulative)**

"CHICKABUNGA!" Henny-Penny squawks when an acorn smacks her on top of her fine red comb, and the eye-popping, color photo-based collages will knock kids out of their seats, too.

Westcott, Nadine Bernard. *Peanut Butter and Jelly: a Play-Rhyme.* **Illus. by the author. Dutton, 1987. Gr. PreK-2 (poetry)**

Two children, a baker, and a batch of elephants show the real way to make a PB&J sandwich includes mashing the peanuts and squashing the grapes.

Wheeler, Lisa. *Old Cricket.* **Illus. by Ponder Goembel. Atheneum, 2003. Gr. PreK-1 (easy fiction)**

Cantankerous Old Cricket thinks up a good excuse for why he can't help his wife ready the roof for winter, but his clever plans go awry when a hungry crow comes after him, planning to eat him for lunch.

Whipple, Laura. *If the Shoe Fits: Voices from Cinderella.* **Illus. by Laura Beingessner. McElderry, 2002. Gr. 4-8 (poetry)**

All aspects of Cinderella's extraordinary story, accompanied by exquisite gouache illustrations, are rehashed in 33 free verse poems narrated by Cinderella and everyone else who was there at the ball that enchanted night.

White, Carolyn. *Whuppity Stoorie: A Scottish Folktale.* **Illus. by S. D. Schindler. Putnam, 1997. Gr. K-6 (fairy tale)**

In this charming Scottish variant of Rumpelstiltskin, Kate of Kittlerumpit and her mother are overjoyed when their pig Grumphie helps them discover a wild fairy woman's name.

Wiesner, David. *The Three Pigs.* **Illus. by the author. Clarion, 2001. Gr. PreK-2 (easy fiction, parody)**

This unexpected, surreal, and nontraditional take-off on the classic folktale won Wiesner his second Caldecott Medal.

Willems, Mo. *Knuffle Bunny: A Cautionary Tale.* **Illus. by the author. Hyperion, 2004. Gr. PreK-1 (easy fiction)**

Leaving the Laundromat with her daddy, toddler Trixie realizes she's forgotten her beloved stuffed animal, Knuffle Bunny, but Daddy can't understand her baby talk when she tries to tell him.

Willems, Mo. *The Pigeon Finds a Hot Dog.* **Illus. by the author. Hyperion, 2004. Gr. PreK-2 (easy fiction)**

About to wolf down the hot dog and bun he has just found, Pigeon is interrupted by a persistent yellow duckling who says, "I've never had a hot dog before . . . What do they taste like?"

Willey, Margaret. *Clever Beatrice: An Upper Peninsula Conte.* **Illus. by Heather Solomon. Atheneum, 2001. Gr. 1-4 (fairy tale, trickster)**

Sharp-as-a-tack little Beatrice outwits a rich giant who lives on the other side of the Michigan woods.

Williams, Linda. *The Little Old Lady Who Was Not Afraid of Anything.* **Illus. by Megan Lloyd. Crowell, 1986. Gr. PreK-2 (cumulative, easy fiction)**

On her way home, a little old lady encounters, in sequence: two clomping shoes, a wiggling pair of pants, a shaking shirt, two clapping gloves, a nodding hat and one scary pumpkin head.

Withers, Carl, comp. *A Rocket in My Pocket: The Rhymes and Chants of Young Americans.* **Illus. by Susanne Suba. Henry Holt, 1948. Gr. K-4 (poetry)**

Rhymes, riddles, chants for bouncing balls and jumping rope, autograph verse, tongue twister, and lots more from American folklore celebrate the poetry of children.

Withers, Carl. *Tale of a Black Cat.* **Illus. by Alan E. Cober. Henry Holt, 1966. Gr. PreK-2 (folktale)**

Hand out paper and black crayons so listeners can draw this story from American folklore as you draw and tell it. See "T for Tommy," Judy Freeman's version of this story in this handbook on page 81. Another good draw-and-tell story by Withers is *The Wild Ducks and the Goose* (1968).

Wolkstein, Diane. *The Day Ocean Came to Visit.* **Illus. by Steve Johnson and Lou Fancher. Harcourt, 2001. Gr. PreK-3 (folktale, pourquoi)**

In this pourquoi tale from Nigeria, Sun invites his new friend, Ocean, to visit him and his wife, Moon, at their large bamboo house, but, once inside, Ocean floods everything.

Wolkstein, Diane. *The Magic Orange Tree and Other Haitian Folktales.* **Illus. by Elsa Henriquez. Knopf, 1978. Gr. 2-6 (collection)**

Wolkstein collected all 27 tales on a research trip to Haiti; her impressive book provides excellent storytellers' notes and the music for each story.

Wood, Audrey. *The Bunyans.* **Illus. by David Shannon. Scholastic, 1996. Gr. 1-4 (easy fiction, parody)**

The extraordinary family of tall tale hero Paul Bunyan—his gigantic wife Carrie, and their two titanic tots, Little Jean and Teeny—are credited for creating America's natural wonders in this deliciously deadpan original tall tale.

Wrede, Patricia. *Dealing with Dragons.* **Harcourt, 1990. Gr. 5-8 (fiction)**

In this crackling first of four books in the Enchanted Forest Chronicles, Cimorene, a youngest princess, rebels against convention and runs off to become cavekeeper for dragon Kazul to escape marriage with a mindless prince.

Yep, Laurence. *The Dragon Prince: A Chinese Beauty and the Beast Tale.* **Illus. by Kam Mak. HarperCollins, 1997. Gr. 2-6 (fairy tale)**

In a Chinese variant of "Beauty and the Beast," a farmer's youngest daughter, Seven, agrees to marry a terrifying dragon so he will spare her father's life.

Yep, Laurence. *The Junior Thunder Lord.* **Illus. by Robert Van Nutt. BridgeWater, 1994. Gr. 1-4 (folktale, pourquoi)**

"Those at the top should help those at the bottom," is the lesson Yue lives by, which is why he befriends and feeds Bear Face, a gargantuan man who in return saves Yue from drowning in this seventeenth century Chinese folktale.

Yep, Laurence. *The Khan's Daughter: A Mongolian Folktale.* **Illus. by Jean Tseng and Mou-Sien Tseng. Scholastic, 1997. Gr. K-6 (folktale)**

Believing his late father's words about becoming rich someday and marrying the Khan's daughter, Mongolian shepherd Möngke heads for the great city of domed tents to seek his fortune.

Yolen, Jane, and Robert J. Harris. *Odysseus in the Serpent Maze.* **HarperCollins, 2001. Gr. 4-7 (fiction)**

Longing to be regarded as a hero, 13-year-old Odysseus sets out with his best friend Mentor to slay the deadly Boar of Parnassus and meets up with pirates, a satyr, and two girls—affable Penelope and devastatingly attractive and obnoxious Helen.

Yolen, Jane. *Passager: The Young Merlin Trilogy, Book One.* **Harcourt, 1996. Gr. 4-7 (fiction, legend)**

The poetic first book in the Young Merlin Trilogy introduces us to a nameless eight-year-old boy, abandoned by his mother in an English forest where he survives by himself but loses the knowledge of even his own name.

Yolen, Jane. *Pegasus, the Flying Horse.* **Illus. by Li Ming. Dutton, 1998. Gr. 2-8 (easy fiction, myth)**

In a story within a story, an old beggar relates the Greek myth about Bellerophon and the winged horse Pegasus to a little boy and his father.

Yolen, Jane. *Wings.* **Illus. by Dennis Nolan. Harcourt, 1991. Gr. 4-6 (easy fiction, myth)**

Yolen's picture book retelling of the tragic Greek myth of Daedalus and Icarus is powerful and impassioned.

Young, Ed. *Cat and Rat: The Legend of the Chinese Zodiac.* **Illus. by the author. Henry Holt, 1995. Gr. K-4 (beast, pourquoi)**

When the Emperor holds a race, offering to reward the first twelve animals across the finish line by naming a year in the Chinese calendar after them, best friends Cat and Rat plan to enter.

Young, Ed. *Lon Po Po: A Red-Riding Hood Story from China.* **Illus. by the author. Philomel, 1989. Gr. K-2 (fairy tale)**

Disguised as their grandmother, an old wolf plans to eat the three young sisters staying home alone, but he is undone by his greed and their resourcefulness.

Young, Ed. *Mouse Match: A Chinese Folktale.* **Illus. by the author. Harcourt, 1997. Gr. 1-6 (beast, cumulative)**

Papa and Mama mouse would like to find the greatest and most powerful one in the world as a suitor for their wonderful daughter.

Young, Ed. *Seven Blind Mice.* **Illus. by the author. Philomel, 1992. Gr. PreK-3 (fable)**

A recasting of the Indian fable "The Blind Men and the Elephant," using brightly-hued collage illustrations and simple language, this visually exciting Caldecott Honor book features seven different-colored blind mice and one big elephant.

Zelinsky, Paul O. *Rapunzel.* **Illus. by the author. Dutton, 1997. Gr. 3-6 (fairy tale)**

This somber, Caldecott Medal-winning version of the traditional fairy tale about the long-haired girl locked in a high tower by a jealous sorceress is visually breathtaking with its dignified Italianate-style paintings.

Zelinsky, Paul O. *Rumpelstiltskin.* **Illus. by the author. Dutton, 1986. Gr. 1-4 (fairy tale)**

Magnificent medieval-style paintings brought Zelinsky's radiant retelling a well-deserved Caldecott honor award.

Zemach, Harve. *Duffy and the Devil.* **Illus. by Margot Zemach. Farrar, 1973. Gr. 2-5 (fairy tale)**

Squire Lovel's new wife makes a deal with the squinty-eyed devil to do all her knitting and spinning too in an uproarious Cornish variant of "Rumpelstiltskin."

Types of Tales: A Booklist

Sorted by types of tales, all of the titles below are also listed by author in the bibliography "400+ Children's Books Every Storyteller Should Know" on page **XXX**.

BEAST TALES

Aardema, Verna. *Misoso: Once Upon a Time Tales from Africa.* Illus. by Reynold Ruffins. Knopf, 1994. Gr. 2-6

Aardema, Verna. *Traveling to Tondo: A Tale of the Nkundo of Zaire.* Illus. by Will Hellenbrand. Knopf, 1991. *Gr. 1-4*

Aardema, Verna. *Why Mosquitoes Buzz in People's Ears.* Illus. by Leo and Diane Dillon. Dial, 1975. *Gr. PreK-2*

Arkhurst, Joyce Cooper. *The Adventures of Spider: West African Folk Tales.* Illus. by Jerry Pinkney. Little, Brown, 1992, c1964. *Gr. 1-4*

Asbjørnsen, P. C. *The Three Billy Goats Gruff.* Illus. by Marcia Brown. Harcourt, 1957. *Gr. PreK-2*

Aylesworth, Jim. *Goldilocks and the Three Bears.* Illus. by Barbara McClintock. Scholastic, 2003. *Gr. PreK-1*

Bader, Barbara. *Aesop & Company: With Scenes from His Legendary Life.* Illus. by Arthur Geisert. Houghton Mifflin, 1991. *Gr. 3-6*

Baumgartner, Barbara. *Crocodile! Crocodile!: Stories Told Around the World.* Illus. by Judith Moffatt. DK, 1994. *Gr. PreK-2*

Bruchac, Joseph. *The Boy Who Lived with the Bears and Other Iroquois Stories.* Illus. by Murv Jacob. HarperCollins, 1995. *Gr. 1-6*

Bruchac, Joseph, and James Bruchac. *How Chipmunk Got His Stripes: A Tale of Bragging and Teasing.* Illus. by Jose Aruego and Ariane Dewey. Dial, 2001. *Gr. K-2*

Bruchac, Joseph, and James Bruchac. *Raccoon's Last Race: A Traditional Abenaki Story.* Illus. by Jose Aruego and Ariane Dewey. Dial, 2004. *Gr. PreK-2*

Busca, María Cristina, and Tona Wilson. *When Jaguar Ate the Moon: And other Stories About Animals and Plants of the Americas.* Illus. by María Cristina Brusca. Henry Holt, 1995. *Gr. 2-6*

Calmenson, Stephanie. *The Children's Aesop: Selected Fables.* Illus. by Robert Byrd. Doubleday, 1988. *Gr. 2-5*

Carle, Eric. *Twelve Tales from Aesop.* Illus. by the author. Philomel, 1980. *Gr. K-3*

Dee, Ruby. *Two Ways to Count to Ten: A Liberian Folktale.* Illus. by Susan Meddaugh. Henry Holt, 1988. *Gr. K-3*

Demi. *A Chinese Zoo: Fables and Proverbs.* Illus. by the author. Harcourt, 1987. *Gr. 2-6*

Diakité, Baba Wagué. *The Hunterman and the Crocodile.* Illus. by the author. Scholastic, 1997. *Gr. 1-5*

Diakité, Baba Wagué. *The Magic Gourd.* Illus. by the author. Scholastic, 2003. *Gr. 1-4*

Doucet, Sharon Arms. *Why Lapin's Ears Are Long and Other Tales from the Louisiana Bayou.* Illus. by David Catrow. Orchard, 1997. *Gr. 1-4*

Ehlert, Lois. *Cuckoo: A Mexican Folktale / Cucú: Un Cuento Folklórico Mexicano.* Illus. by the author. Harcourt, 1997. *Gr. PreK-3*

Gates, Frieda. *Owl Eyes.* Illus. by Yoshi Miyake. Lothrop, 1994. *Gr. K-4*

Gatti, Ann. *Aesop's Fables.* Illus. by Safaya Salter. Gulliver/Harcourt, 1992. *Gr. 1-6*

Hamilton, Virginia. *Bruh Rabbit and the Tar Baby Girl.* Illus. by James E. Ransome. Blue Sky/Scholastic, 2003. *Gr. PreK-4*

Hamilton, Virginia. *When Birds Could Talk & Bats Could Sing.* Illus. by Barry Moser. Scholastic, 1996. *Gr. 2-5*

Han, Suzanne Crowder. *The Rabbit's Escape.* Illus. by Yumi Heo. Henry Holt, 1995. *Gr. 1-5*

Hausman, Gerald and Hausman, Loretta. *Dogs of Myth: Tales from Around the World.* Illus. by Barry Moser. Simon & Schuster, 1999. *Gr. 2-6*

Ho, Minfong, and Saphan Ros. *Brother Rabbit: A Cambodian Tale.* Illus. by Jennifer Hewitson. Lothrop, 1997. *Gr. K-3*

Hogrogian, Nonny. *One Fine Day.* Illus. by the author. Macmillan, 1971. *Gr. PreK-2*

Hooks, William H. *The Three Little Pigs and the Fox.* Illus. by S. D. Schindler. Macmillan, 1989. *Gr. PreK-2*

Johnston, Tony. *The Tale of Rabbit and Coyote.* Illus. by Tomie dePaola. Putnam, 1994. *Gr. PreK-2*

Kimmel, Eric A. *Anansi and the Magic Stick.* Illus. by Janet Stevens. Holiday House, 2001. *Gr. PreK-2*

Kimmel, Eric A. *Anansi and the Moss-Covered Rock.* Illus. by Janet Stevens. Holiday House, 1990. *Gr. PreK-2*

Kimmel, Eric A. *Anansi and the Talking Melon.* Illus. by Janet Stevens. Holiday House, 1994. *Gr. PreK-2*

Kimmel, Eric A. *Anansi Goes Fishing.* Illus. by Janet Stevens. Holiday House, 1992. *Gr. PreK-2*

Knutson, Barbara. *Love and Roast Chicken: A Trickster Tale from the Andes Mountains.* Illus. by the author. Carolrhoda, 2004. *Gr. K-3*

Lobel, Arnold. *Fables.* Illus. by the author. HarperCollins, 1980. *Gr. 3-6*

MacDonald, Margaret Read. *Mabela the Clever.* Illus. by Tim Coffey. Albert Whitman, 2001. *Gr. PreK-2*

Marshall, James. *Goldilocks and the Three Bears.* Illus. by the author. Dial, 1988. *Gr. PreK-1*

Marshall, James. *The Three Little Pigs.* Illus. by the author. Dial, 1989. *Gr. PreK-1*

Martin, Rafe. *Foolish Rabbit's Big Mistake.* Illus. by Ed Young. Putnam, 1985. *Gr. PreK-2*

McClintock, Barbara. *Animal Fables from Aesop.* Illus. by the author. Godine, 1991. *Gr. 2-6*

McDermott, Gerald. *Coyote: A Trickster Tale from the American Southwest.* Illus. by the author. Harcourt, 1994. *Gr. PreK-2*

McDermott, Gerald. *Jabutí the Tortoise: A Trickster Tale from the Amazon.* Illus. by the author. Harcourt, 2001. *Gr. K-2*

McGill, Alice. *Sure as Sunrise: Stories of Bruh Rabbit & His Walkin' Talkin' Friends.* Illus. by Don Tate. Houghton Mifflin, 2004. *Gr. K-5*

McKissack, Patricia C. and Robert L. McKissack. *Itching and Twitching: A Nigerian Folktale.* Illus. by Laura Freeman. Scholastic, 2003. *Gr. PreK-1*

Mollel, Tololwa M. *Ananse's Feast: An Ashanti Tale.* Illus. by Andrew Glass. Clarion, 1997. *Gr. K-3*

Morpurgo, Michael. *The McElderry Book of Aesop's Fables.* Illus. by Emma Chichester Clark. McElderry, 2005. *Gr. K-5*

Moser, Barry. *The Three Little Pigs.* Illus. by the author. Little, Brown, 2001. *Gr. PreK-1*

Parks, Van Dyke, and Malcolm Jones. *Jump!: The Adventures of Brer Rabbit.* Illus. by Barry Moser. Harcourt, 1986. *Gr. 2-5*

Paxton, Tom. *Aesop's Fables.* Illus. by Robert Rayevsky. Morrow, 1988. *Gr. 3-6*

Paye, Won-Ldy and Margaret H. Lippert. *Mrs. Chicken and the Hungry Crocodile.* Illus. by Julie Paschkis. Henry Holt, 2003. *Gr. PreK-1*

Pinkney, Jerry. *Aesop's Fables.* Illus. by the author. SeaStar, 2000. *Gr. 2-8*

Pinkney, Jerry. *The Little Red Hen.* Illus. by the author. Dial, 2006. *Gr. PreK-1*

Rascol, Sabina I. *The Impudent Rooster.* Illus. by Holly Berry. Dutton, 2004. *Gr. 1-4*

Ross, Gayle. *How Turtle's Back Was Cracked: A Traditional Cherokee Tale.* Illus. by Murv Jacob. Dial, 1995. *Gr. 1-4*

Rounds, Glen. *The Three Billy Goats Gruff.* Illus. by the author. Holiday House, 1993. *Gr. PreK-2*

Rounds, Glen. *Three Little Pigs and the Big Bad Wolf.* Illus. by the author. Holiday House, 1992. *Gr. PreK-2*

Salley, Coleen. *Epossumondas.* Illus. by Janet Stevens. Harcourt, 2002. *Gr. PreK-2*

San Souci, Robert D. *Sister Tricksters: Rollicking Tales of Clever Females.* Illus. by Daniel San Souci. August House, 2006. *Gr. 3-6*

So, Meilo. *Gobble, Gobble, Slip, Slop: The Tale of a Very Greedy Cat.* Illus. by the author. Knopf, 2004. *Gr. PreK-3*

Souhami, Jessica. *The Leopard's Drum: An Asante Tale from West Africa.* Illus. by the author. Frances Lincoln, 2005. *Gr. PreK-2*

Stevens, Janet. *Coyote Steals the Blanket: A Ute Tale.* Illus. by the author. Holiday House, 1993. *Gr. PreK-3*

Stevens, Janet. *Tops & Bottoms.* Illus. by the author. Harcourt, 1995. *Gr. PreK-3*

Untermeyer, Louis. *Aesop's Fables.* Illus. by Alice Provensen and Martin Provensen. Golden Press, 1965. *Gr. K-3*

Van Laan, Nancy. *In a Circle Long Ago: A Treasury of Native Lore from North America.* Illus. by Lisa Desimini. Knopf, 1995. *Gr. K-5*

Wattenberg, Jane. *Henny-Penny.* Illus. by the author. Scholastic, 2000. *Gr. PreK-2*

Young, Ed. *Cat and Rat: The Legend of the Chinese Zodiac.* Illus. by the author. Henry Holt, 1995. *Gr. K-4*

Young, Ed. *Mouse Match: A Chinese Folktale.* Illus. by the author. Harcourt, 1997. *Gr. 1-6*

COLLECTIONS

Aardema, Verna. *Misoso: Once Upon a Time Tales from Africa.* Illus. by Reynold Ruffins. Knopf, 1994. *Gr. 2-6*

Bader, Barbara. *Aesop & Company: With Scenes from His Legendary Life.* Illus. by Arthur Geisert. Houghton Mifflin, 1991. *Gr. 3-6*

Baumgartner, Barbara. *Crocodile! Crocodile!: Stories Told Around the World.* Illus. by Judith Moffatt. DK, 1994. *Gr. PreK-2*

Bruchac, Joseph. *The Boy Who Lived with the Bears and Other Iroquois Stories.* Illus. by Murv Jacob. HarperCollins, 1995. *Gr. 1-6*

Brusca, María Cristina, and Tona Wilson. *When Jaguar Ate the Moon: And other Stories About Animals and Plants of the Americas.* Illus. by María Cristina Brusca. Henry Holt, 1995. *Gr. 2-6*

Calmenson, Stephanie. *The Children's Aesop: Selected Fables.* Illus. by Robert Byrd. Doubleday, 1988. *Gr. 2-5*

Campoy, F. Isabel, and Alma Flor Ada. *Tales Our Abuelitas Told: A Hispanic Folktale Collection.* Illus. by Felipe Dávalos, Viví Escrivá, Susan Guevara, and Leyla Torres. Atheneum, 2006. *Gr. 1-6*

Carle, Eric. *Twelve Tales from Aesop.* Illus. by the author. Philomel, 1980. *Gr. K-3*

Chase, Richard. *Grandfather Tales.* Illus. by Berkeley Williams, Jr. Houghton Mifflin, 1948. *Gr. K-6*

Chase, Richard. *Jack Tales.* Illus. by Berkeley Williams, Jr. Houghton Mifflin, 1943. *Gr. 4-6*

Chief Lelooska. *Echoes of the Elders: The Stories and Paintings of Chief Lelooska.* Illus. by the author. DK Ink, 1997. *Gr. 3-6*

Cohn, Amy L. *From Sea to Shining Sea: A Treasury of American Folklore and Folk Songs.* Illus. by 11 Caldecott Medal and 4 Caldecott Honor book artists. Scholastic, 1993. *Gr. 1-6*

Cole, Joanna. *Best Loved Folktales of the World.* Illus. by Jill Karla Schwarz. Doubleday, 1983. *Gr. 1-6*

Courlander, Harold, and George Herzog. *The Cow-Tail Switch and Other West African Stories.* Illus. by Madye Lee Chastain. Henry Holt, 1988. *Gr. 2-6*

Demi. *A Chinese Zoo: Fables and Proverbs.* Illus. by the author. Harcourt, 1987. *Gr. 2-6*

Emrich, Duncan. *The Nonsense Book.* Illus. by Ib Ohlsson. Four Winds, 1970. *Gr. 2-6*

Gag, Wanda. *Tales from Grimm.* Retold and illus. by Wanda Gag. Coward-McCann, 1936. *Gr. 2-6*

Gatti, Ann. *Aesop's Fables*. Illus. by Safaya Salter. Gulliver/Harcourt, 1992. *Gr. 1-6*

Grimm, Jacob. *The Juniper Tree and Other Tales from Grimm*. Selected by Lore Segal and Randall Jarrell. Illus. by Maurice Sendak. Farrar, 2003, c1973. *Gr. 3-6*

Gryski, Camilla. *Cat's Cradle, Owl's Eyes; A Book of String Games*. Illus. by Tom Sankey. Morrow, 1984. *Gr. 2-6*

Hamilton, Martha, and Mitch Weiss. *Scared Witless: Thirteen Eerie Tales to Tell*. Illus. by Kevin Pope. August House, 2006. *Gr. 3-6*

Hamilton, Virginia. *When Birds Could Talk & Bats Could Sing*. Illus. by Barry Moser. Scholastic, 1996. *Gr. 2-5*

Hausman, Gerald and Hausman, Loretta. *Dogs of Myth: Tales from Around the World*. Illus. by Barry Moser. Simon & Schuster, 1999. *Gr. 2-6*

Haviland, Virginia. *Favorite Fairy Tales Told Round the World*. Illus. by S. D. Schindler. Little, Brown, 1985. *Gr. 1-4*

Haviland, Virginia. *North American Legends*. Illus. by Ann Strugnell. Putnam, 1979. *Gr. 4-8*

Hicks, Ray. *The Jack Tales*. Illus. by Owen Smith. Callaway, 2000. *Gr. 2-5*

Johnson-Davies, Denys. *Goha the Wise Fool*. Illus. by Hany El Saed Ahmed from drawings by Hag Hamdy Mohamed Fattouh. Philomel, 2005. *Gr. 2-6*

Lang, Andrew. *The Blue Fairy Book*. Viking, 1978. *Gr. 2-6*

Leach, Maria. *The Thing at the Foot of the Bed and Other Scary Tales*. Illus. by Kert Werth. Putnam, 1987. *Gr. 2-6*

Lester, Julius. *The Knee-High Man and Other Tales*. Illus. by Ralph Pinto. Dial, 1972. *Gr. 2-5*

Lester, Julius. *The Tales of Uncle Remus: The Adventures of Brer Rabbit*. Illus. by Jerry Pinkney. Dial, 1990. *Gr. 2-5*

Lunge-Larsen, Lise, retel. *The Troll with No Heart in His Body: And Other Tales of Trolls from Norway*. Illus. by Betsy Bowen. Houghton Mifflin, 1999. *Gr. 2-5*

Lupton, Hugh, and Daniel Morden. *The Adventures of Odysseus*. Illus. by Christina Balit. Barefoot, 2006. *Gr. 3-7*

McCaughrean, Geraldine. *The Bonze Cauldron: Myths and Legends of the World*. Illus. by Bee Willey. McElderry, 1998. *Gr. 4-8*

McCaughrean, Geraldine. *Gilgamesh the Hero: The Epic of Gilgamesh*. Illus. by David Parkins. Eerdmans, 2003. *Gr. 6-8*

McClintock, Barbara. *Animal Fables from Aesop*. Illus. by the author. Godine, 1991. *Gr. 2-6*

McCormick, Dell J. *Paul Bunyan Swings His Axe*. Illus. by the author. Caxton, 1936. *Gr. 3-6*

McGill, Alice. *Sure as Sunrise: Stories of Bruh Rabbit & His Walkin' Talkin' Friends*. Illus. by Don Tate. Houghton Mifflin, 2004. *Gr. K-5*

McKissack, Patricia C. *Porch Lies: Tales of Slicksters, Tricksters, and Other Wily Characters*. Illus. by André Carrilho. Schwartz & Wade, 2006. *Gr. 4-8*

Minard, Rosemary. *Womenfolk and Fairy Tales*. Illus. by Suzanne Klein. Houghton Mifflin, 1975. *Gr. 3-6*

Morpurgo, Michael. *The McElderry Book of Aesop's Fables*. Illus. by Emma Chichester Clark. McElderry, 2005. *Gr. K-5*

Osborne, Mary Pope. *American Tall Tales*. Illus. by Michael McCurdy. Knopf, 1991. *Gr. 3-6*

Osborne, Mary Pope. *Mermaid Tales from Around the World*. Illus. by Troy Howell. Scholastic, 1993. *Gr. 3-6*

Parks, Van Dyke, and Malcolm Jones. *Jump!: The Adventures of Brer Rabbit*. Illus. by Barry Moser. Harcourt, 1986. *Gr. 2-5*

Paxton, Tom. *Aesop's Fables*. Illus. by Robert Rayevsky. Morrow, 1988. *Gr. 3-6*

Philip, Neil. *The Adventures of Odysseus*. Illus. by Peter Malone. Orchard, 1997. *Gr. 3-6*

Philip, Neil. *Odin's Family: Myths of the Vikings*. Illus. by Maryclare Foa. Orchard, 1996. *Gr. 3-6*

Pinkney, Jerry. *Aesop's Fables*. Illus. by the author. SeaStar, 2000. *Gr. 2-8*

Rounds, Glen. *Ol' Paul, the Mighty Logger*. Illus. by the author. Holiday House, 1976. *Gr. 4-6*

San Souci, Robert D. *Larger Than Life: The Adventures of American Legendary Heroes*. Illus. by Andrew Glass. Doubleday, 1991. *Gr. 3-6*

San Souci, Robert D. *Sister Tricksters: Rollicking Tales of Clever Females*. Illus. by Daniel San Souci. August House, 2006. *Gr. 3-6*

Schwartz, Alvin. *Scary Stories to Tell in the Dark*. Illus. by Stephen Gammell. HarperCollins, 1981. *Gr. 4-8*

Shannon, George. *Stories to Solve: Folktales from Around the World*. Illus. by Peter Sis. Greenwillow, 1985. *Gr. 2-6*

Shannon, George. *True Lies: 18 Tales for You to Judge*. Illus. by John O'Brien. Greenwillow, 1997. *Gr. 3-6*

Sierra, Judy. *Can You Guess My Name?: Traditional Tales Around the World*. Illus. by Stefano Vitale. Clarion, 2002. *Gr. PreK-2*

Sierra, Judy. *Nursery Tales Around the World*. Illus. by Stefano Vitale. Clarion, 1996. *Gr. PreK-2*

Singer, Isaac Bashevis. *When Shlemiel Went to Warsaw & Other Stories*. Illus. by Margot Zemach. Farrar, 1979. *Gr. 4-6*

Sutcliff, Rosemary. *Black Ships Before Troy!: The Story of the Iliad*. Illus. by Alan Lee. Delacorte, 1993. *Gr. 5-8*

Taback, Simms. *Kibitzers and Fools: Tales My Zayda (Grandfather) Told Me*. Illus. by the author. Viking, 2005. *Gr. 1-4*

Tashjian, Virginia A. *Juba This and Juba That: Story Hour Stretches for Large or Small Groups*. Illus. by Victoria de Larrea. Little, Brown, 1969. *Gr. PreK-4*

Untermeyer, Louis. *Aesop's Fables*. Illus. by Alice Provensen and Martin Provensen. Golden Press, 1965. *Gr. K-3*

Van Laan, Nancy. *In a Circle Long Ago: A Treasury of Native Lore from North America*. Illus. by Lisa Desimini. Knopf, 1995. *Gr. K-5*

Walker, Paul Robert. *Big Men, Big Country: A Collection of American Tall Tales*. Illus. by James Bernardin. Harcourt, 1993. *Gr. 4-6*

Washington, Donna L. *A Pride of African Tales*. Illus. by James Ransome. HarperCollins, 2004. *Gr. 4-8*

Wolkstein, Diane. *The Magic Orange Tree and Other Haitian Folktales*. Illus. by Elsa Henriquez. Knopf, 1978. *Gr. 2-6*

CUMULATIVE TALES

Aardema, Verna. *Traveling to Tondo: A Tale of the Nkundo of Zaire*. Illus. by Will Hillenbrand. Knopf, 1991. *Gr. 1-4*

Aardema, Verna. *Why Mosquitoes Buzz in People's Ears*. Illus. by Leo and Diane Dillon. Dial, 1975. *Gr. PreK-2*

Asbjørnsen, P. C. *The Three Billy Goats Gruff*. Illus. by Marcia Brown. Harcourt, 1957. *Gr. PreK-2*

Aylesworth, Jim. *Aunt Pitty Patty's Piggy*. Illus. by Barbara McClintock. Scholastic, 1999. *Gr. PreK-1*

Aylesworth, Jim. *The Gingerbread Man*. Illus. by Barbara McClintock. Scholastic, 1998. *Gr. PreK-1*

Aylesworth, Jim. *The Tale of Tricky Fox: A New England Trickster Tale*. Illus. by Barbara McClintock. Scholastic, 2001. *Gr. PreK-2*

Brown, Marcia. *Stone Soup*. Illus. by the author. Scribner, 1947. *Gr. 1-4*

Compestine, Ying Chang. *The Runaway Rice Cake*. Illus. by Tungwai Chau. Simon & Schuster, 2001. *Gr. PreK-2*

Diakité, Baba Wagué. *The Hatseller and the Monkeys*. Illus. by the author. Scholastic, 1999. *Gr. PreK-2*

Egielski, Richard. *The Gingerbread Boy*. Illus. by the author. HarperCollins, 1997. *Gr. PreK-1*

Galdone, Paul. *The Old Woman and Her Pig*. Illus. by the author. McGraw-Hill, 1960. *Gr. PreK-1*

Gilman, Phoebe. *Something from Nothing*. Illus. by the author. Scholastic, 1993. *Gr. PreK-2*

Ginsburg, Mirra. *Clay Boy: Adapted from a Russian Folk Tale*. Illus. by Jos. A. Smith. Greenwillow, 1997. *Gr. PreK-1*

Harper, Wilhelmina. *The Gunniwolf*. Illus. by William Wiesner. Dutton, 1978. *Gr. PreK-1*

Hogrogian, Nonny. *One Fine Day*. Illus. by the author. Macmillan, 1971. *Gr. PreK-2*

Kimmel, Eric A. *The Gingerbread Man*. Illus. by Megan Lloyd. Holiday House, 1993. *Gr. PreK-1*

Kurtz, Jane. *Trouble*. Illus. by Durga Bernhard. Gulliver/Harcourt, 1997. *Gr. K-2*

Lester, Julius. *Sam and the Tigers: A New Telling of Little Black Sambo.* Illus. by Jerry Pinkney. Dial, 1996. *Gr. PreK-3*

McGovern, Ann. *Too Much Noise.* Illus. by Simms Taback. Houghton Mifflin, 1967. *Gr. PreK-2*

Mosel, Arlene. *Tikki Tikki Tembo.* Illus. by Blair Lent. Henry Holt, 1968. *Gr. PreK-3*

Peck, Jan. *The Giant Carrot.* Illus. by Barry Root. Dial, 1998. *Gr. PreK-2*

Rosen, Michael. *We're Going on a Bear Hunt.* Illus. by Helen Oxenbury. Macmillan, 1989. *Gr. PreK-1*

Rounds, Glen. *The Three Billy Goats Gruff.* Illus. by the author. Holiday House, 1993. *Gr. PreK-2*

Simms, Laura. *The Squeaky Door.* Illus. by Sylvie Wickstrom. Crown, 1991. *Gr. PreK-2*

Sloat, Teri, retel. *Sody Sallyratus.* Illus. by the author. Dutton, 1997. *Gr. PreK-3*

So, Meilo. *Gobble, Gobble, Slip, Slop: The Tale of a Very Greedy Cat.* Illus. by the author. Knopf, 2004. *Gr. PreK-3*

Souhami, Jessica. *No Dinner!: The Story of the Old Woman and the Pumpkin.* Illus. by the author. Cavendish, 2000. *Gr. PreK-2*

Taback, Simms. *Joseph Had a Little Overcoat.* Illus. by the author. Viking, 1999. *Gr. PreK-1*

Taback, Simms. *There Was an Old Lady Who Swallowed a Fly.* Illus. by the author. Viking, 1997. *Gr. PreK-2*

Taback, Simms. *This Is the House That Jack Built.* Illus. by the author. Putnam, 2002. *Gr. PreK-1*

Thomson, Pat. *The Squeaky, Creaky Bed.* Illus. by Niki Daly. Doubleday, 2003. *Gr. PreK-1*

Wattenberg, Jane. *Henny-Penny.* Illus. by the author. Scholastic, 2000. *Gr. PreK-2*

Williams, Linda. *The Little Old Lady Who Was Not Afraid of Anything.* Illus. by Megan Lloyd. Crowell, 1986. Gr. PreK-2

Young, Ed. *Mouse Match: A Chinese Folktale.* Illus. by the author. Harcourt, 1997. *Gr. 1-6*

EASY FICTION/PICTURE BOOKS

Alexander, Lloyd. *How the Cat Swallowed Thunder.* Illus. by Judith Byron Schachner. Dutton, 2000. *Gr. PreK-3*

Andersen, Hans Christian. *The Nightingale.* Retold by Stephen Mitchell. Illus. by Bagram Ibatoulline. Candlewick, 2002. *Gr. 2-6*

Andersen, Hans Christian. *The Nightingale.* Retold and illus. by Jerry Pinkney. Putnam, 2002. *Gr. 2-6*

Andersen, Hans Christian. *The Tinderbox.* Adapted and illus. by Barry Moser. Little, Brown, 1990. *Gr. 4-6*

Anderson, Leone Castell. *The Wonderful Shrinking Shirt.* Illus. by Irene Trivas. Albert Whitman, 1983. *Gr. K-3*

Anholt, Catherine, and Laurence Anholt. *Chimp and Zee.* Illus. by the authors. Putnam, 2001. *Gr. PreK-1*

Auch, Mary Jane. *The Princess and the Pizza.* Illus. by Mary Jane Auch and Herm Auch. Holiday House, 2002. *Gr. K-5*

Bania, Michael. *Kumak's Fish: A Tall Tale from the Far North.* Illus. by the author. Alaska Northwest, 2004. *Gr. PreK-3*

Bateman, Teresa. *Farm Flu.* Illus. by Nadine Bernard Westcott. Albert Whitman, 2001. *Gr. PreK-2*

Beaumont, Karen. *I Ain't Gonna Paint No More.* Illus. by David Catrow. Harcourt, 2005. *Gr. PreK-2*

Bertrand, Lynne. *Granite Baby.* Illus. by Kevin Hawkes. Farrar, 2005. *Gr. 1-4*

Brett, Jan. *Honey . . . Honey . . . Lion!* Illus. by the author. Putnam, 2005. *Gr. PreK-2*

Briggs, Raymond. *Jim and the Beanstalk.* Illus. by the author. Coward-McCann, 1989. *Gr. 3-6*

Bruel, Nick. *Bad Kitty.* Illus. by the author. Roaring Brook, 2005. *Gr. PreK-2*

Buehner, Caralyn. *Fanny's Dream.* Illus. by Mark Buehner. Dial, 1996. *Gr. 1-6*

Calmenson, Stephanie. *The Frog Principal.* Illus. by Denise Brunkus. Scholastic, 2001. *Gr. K-4*

Child, Lauren. *Beware of the Storybook Wolves.* Illus. by the author. Scholastic, 2001. *Gr. PreK-2*

Child, Lauren. *Who's Afraid of the Big Bad Book?* Illus. by the author. Hyperion, 2003. *Gr. K-3*

Christelow, Eileen. *Five Little Monkeys Jumping on the Bed.* Illus. by the author. Clarion, 1989. *Gr. PreK-1*

Christelow, Eileen. *Where's the Big Bad Wolf?* Illus. by the author. Clarion, 2002. *Gr. PreK-2*

Compestine, Ying Chang. *The Story of Chopsticks.* Illus. by YongSheng Xuan. Holiday House, 2001. *Gr. K-4*

From *Once Upon a Time: Using Storytelling, Creative Drama, and Reader's Theater with Children in Grades PreK-6* by Judy Freeman. Westport, CT: Libraries Unlimited. Copyright © 2007.

Cronin, Doreen. *Click, Clack, Moo: Cows That Type.* Illus. by Betsy Lewin. Simon & Schuster, 2000. *Gr. K-6*

Davol, Marguerite W. *The Paper Dragon.* Illus. by Robert Sabuda. Atheneum, 1997. *Gr. K-3*

Edwards, Pamela Duncan. *The Leprechaun's Gold.* Illus. by Henry Cole. HarperCollins, 2004. *Gr. K-3*

Edwards, Pamela Duncan. *The Neat Line: Scribbling Through Mother Goose.* Illus. by Diann Cain Blumenthal. HarperCollins, 2005. *Gr. PreK-2*

Emberley, Michael. *Ruby.* Illus. by the author. Little, Brown, 1990. *Gr. K-3*

Emberley, Rebecca. *Three Cool Kids.* Illus. by the author. Little, Brown, 1995. *Gr. PreK-2*

Ernst, Lisa Campbell. *Little Red Riding Hood: A Newfangled Prairie Tale.* Illus. by the author. Simon & Schuster, 1995. *Gr. K-3*

Fleming, Denise. *The Cow Who Clucked.* Illus. by the author. Henry Holt, 2006. *Gr. PreK-1*

Gerstein, Mordicai. *Carolinda Clatter.* Illus. by the author. Roaring Brook, 2005. *Gr. PreK-2*

Grey, Mini. *The Adventures of the Dish and the Spoon.* Illus. by the author. Knopf, 2006. *Gr. PreK-2*

Hartman, Bob. *The Wolf Who Cried Boy.* Illus. by Tim Raglin. Putnam, 2002. *Gr. K-2*

Hawkins, Colin, and Jacqui Hawkins. *The Fairytale News.* Illus. by the authors. Candlewick, 2004. *Gr. PreK-3*

Henkes, Kevin. *Kitten's First Full Moon.* Illus. by the author. Greenwillow, 2004. *Gr. PreK-1*

Hicks, Barbara Jean. *Jitterbug Jam: A Monster Tale.* Illus. by Alexis Deacon. Farrar, 2005. *Gr. PreK-3*

Hindley, Judy. *Do Like a Duck Does!* Illus. by Ivan Bates. Candlewick, 2002. *Gr. PreK-1*

Isaacs, Anne. *Pancakes for Supper.* Illus. by Mark Teague. Scholastic, 2006. *Gr. PreK-2*

Jackson, Ellen. *Cinder Edna.* Illus. by Kevin O'Malley. Lothrop, 1994. *Gr. 1-6*

Johnson, Paul Brett. *Little Bunny Foo Foo.* Illus. by the author. Scholastic, 2004. *Gr. PreK-1*

Juster, Norton. *The Hello, Goodbye Window.* Illus. by Chris Raschka. Hyperion, 2005. *Gr. PreK-1*

Kesey, Ken. *Little Tricker the Squirrel Meets Big Double the Bear.* Illus. by Barry Moser. Viking, 1990. *Gr. 1-4*

Ketteman, Helen. *Armadilly Chili.* Illus. by Will Terry. Albert Whitman, 2004. *Gr. K-2*

Lester, Julius. *Sam and the Tigers: A New Telling of Little Black Sambo.* Illus. by Jerry Pinkney. Dial, 1996. *Gr. PreK-3*

Lewin, Ted. *The Storytellers.* Illus. by the author. Lothrop, 1998. *Gr. 1-3*

Little, Jean, and M. De Vries. *Once Upon a Golden Apple.* Illus. by Phoebe Gilman. Viking, 1991. *Gr. PreK-2*

Lobel, Arnold. *Fables.* Illus. by the author. HarperCollins, 1980. *Gr. 3-6*

Lum, Kate. *What! Cried Granny: An Almost Bedtime Story.* Illus. by Adrian Johnson. Dial, 1999. *Gr. PreK-1*

Manushkin, Fran. *The Shivers in the Fridge.* Illus. by Paul O. Zelinsky. Dutton, 2006. *Gr. PreK-2*

Mathews, Judith, and Fay Robinson. *Nathaniel Willy, Scared Silly.* Illus. by Alex Natchev. Bradbury, 1994. *Gr. PreK-2*

McClements, George. *Jake Gander, Storyville Detective.* Illus. by the author. Hyperion, 2002. *Gr. PreK-2*

McCully, Emily Arnold. *Beautiful Warrior: The Legend of the Nun's Kung Fu.* Illus. by the author. Scholastic, 1998. *Gr. 1-4*

McKissack, Patricia C. *Flossie & the Fox.* Illus. by Rachel Isadora. Dial, 1986. *Gr. K-3*

McKissack, Patricia, and Onawumi Jean Moss. *Precious and the Boo Hag.* Illus. by Kyrsten Brooker. Atheneum, 2005. *Gr. 1-4*

McMullan, Kate. *I Stink!* Illus. by Jim McMullan. HarperCollins, 2002. *Gr. PreK-1*

Meddaugh, Susan. *Hog-Eye.* Illus. by the author. Houghton Mifflin, 1995. *Gr. K-3*

Meddaugh, Susan. *The Witch's Walking Stick.* Illus. by the author. Houghton Mifflin, 2005. *Gr. PreK-3*

Medearis, Angela Shelf. *Seven Spools of Thread: A Kwanzaa Story.* Illus. by Daniel Minter. Albert Whitman, 2000. *Gr. K-4*

Mora, Pat. *Doña Flor: A Tall Tale About a Giant Woman with a Great Big Heart.* Illus. by Raúl Colón. Knopf, 2005. *Gr. PreK-3*

Moser, Barry. *Tucker Pfeffercorn: An Old Story Retold.* Illus. by the author. Little, Brown, 1994. *Gr. 3-6*

Muth, Jon J. *Zen Shorts.* Illus. by the author. Scholastic, 2005. *Gr. 1-6*

Myers, Tim. *Basho and the Fox.* Illus. by Oki Sittan. Marshall Cavendish, 2000. *Gr. 1-4*

Ogburn, Jacqueline K. *The Bake Shop Ghost.* Illus. by Marjorie Priceman. Houghton Mifflin, 2005. *Gr. K-3*

Palatini, Margie. *The Web Files.* Illus. by Richard Egielski. Hyperion, 2001. *Gr. K-3*

Pinkney, Andrea Davis. *Peggony-Po: A Whale of a Tale.* Illus. by Brian Pinkney. Hyperion, 2006. *Gr. 1-4*

Rodanas, Kristina. *The Blind Hunter.* Illus. by the author. Cavendish, 2003. *Gr. 1-4*

Root, Phyllis. *Rattletrap Car.* Illus. by Jill Barton. Candlewick, 2001. *Gr. PreK-1*

Rosen, Michael. *We're Going on a Bear Hunt.* Illus. by Helen Oxenbury. Macmillan, 1989. *Gr. PreK-1*

Rostoker-Gruber, Karen. *Rooster Can't Cock-a-Doodle-Doo.* Illus. by Paul Rátz de Tagyos. Dial, 2004. *Gr. PreK-1*

Rumford, James. *Dog-of-the-Sea-Waves.* Illus. by the author. Houghton Mifflin, 2004. *Gr. 2-5*

Ryan, Pam Muñoz. *Mice and Beans.* Illus. by Joe Cepeda. Scholastic, 2001. *Gr. PreK-2*

Sacre, Antonio. *The Barking Mouse.* Illus. by Alfredo Aguirre. Albert Whitman, 2003. *Gr. 1-4*

Say, Allen. *Kamishibai Man.* Illus. by the author. Houghton Mifflin, 2005. *Gr. 1-6*

Schaefer, Carole Lexa. *The Biggest Soap.* Illus. by Stacey Dressen-McQueen. Farrar, 2004. *Gr. PreK-2*

Schanzer, Rosalyn. *Davy Crockett Saves the World.* Illus. by the author. HarperCollins, 2001. *Gr. K-3*

Scieszka, Jon. *The Frog Prince, Continued.* Illus. by Steve Johnson. Viking, 1991. *Gr. 2-6*

Scieszka, Jon. *Squids Will Be Squids: Fresh Morals, Beastly Fables.* Illus. by Lane Smith. Viking, 1998. *Gr. 2-6*

Scieszka, Jon. *The Stinky Cheese Man and Other Fairly Stupid Tales.* Illus. by Lane Smith. Viking, 1992. *Gr. PreK-Adult*

Scieszka, Jon. *The True Story of the 3 Little Pigs.* Illus. by Lane Smith. Viking, 1989. *Gr. 2-Adult*

Seeger, Pete. *Abiyoyo.* Illus. by Michael Hays. Macmillan, 1986. *Gr. K-2*

Shulman, Lisa. *The Matzo Ball Boy.* Illus. by Rosanne Litzinger. Dutton, 2005. *Gr. PreK-2*

Shulman, Lisa. *Old MacDonald Had a Woodshop.* Illus. by Ashley Wolff. Putnam, 2002. *Gr. PreK-1*

Sierra, Judy. *Wild About Books.* Illus. by Marc Brown. Knopf, 2004. *Gr. PreK-2*

Silverman, Erica. *Big Pumpkin.* Illus. by S. D. Schindler. Macmillan, 1992. *Gr. PreK-2*

Stanley, Diane. *The Giant and the Beanstalk.* Illus. by the author. HarperCollins, 2004. *Gr. PreK-2*

Stanley, Diane. *Goldie and the Three Bears.* Illus. by the author. HarperCollins, 2003. *Gr. PreK-1*

Stanley, Diane. *Rumpelstiltskin's Daughter.* Illus. by the author. Morrow, 1997. *Gr. 2-5*

Stevens, Janet, and Susan Stevens Crummel. *And the Dish Ran Away with the Spoon.* Illus. by Janet Stevens. Harcourt, 2001. *Gr. K-3*

Stevens, Janet, and Susan Stevens Crummel. *Cook-a-Doodle-Doo!* Illus. by Janet Stevens. Harcourt, 1999. *Gr. PreK-2*

Sturges, Philemon. *The Little Red Hen (Makes a Pizza).* Illus. by Amy Walrod. Dutton, 1999. *Gr. PreK-1*

Sunami, Kitoba. *How the Fisherman Tricked the Genie: A Tale Within a Tale Within a Tale.* Illus. by Amiko Hirao. Atheneum, 2002. *Gr. 2-6*

Thiesing, Lisa. *The Viper.* Illus. by the author. Dutton, 2002. *Gr. K-2*

Thomas, Shelley Moore. *Get Well, Good Knight.* Illus. by Jennifer Plecas. Dutton, 2002. *Gr. PreK-1*

Thomson, Pat. *The Squeaky, Creaky Bed.* Illus. by Niki Daly. Doubleday, 2003. *Gr. PreK-1*

Wheeler, Lisa. *Old Cricket.* Illus. by Ponder Goembel. Atheneum, 2003. *Gr. PreK-1*

Wiesner, David. *The Three Pigs.* Illus. by the author. Clarion, 2001. *Gr. PreK-2*

Willems, Mo. *Knuffle Bunny: A Cautionary Tale.* Illus. by the author. Hyperion, 2004. *Gr. PreK-1*

Willems, Mo. *The Pigeon Finds a Hot Dog.* Illus. by the author. Hyperion, 2004. *Gr. PreK-2*

Williams, Linda. *The Little Old Lady Who Was Not Afraid of Anything.* Illus. by Megan Lloyd. Crowell, 1986. Gr. PreK-2

Wood, Audrey. *The Bunyans.* Illus. by David Shannon. Scholastic, 1996. *Gr. 1-4*

Yolen, Jane. *Pegasus, the Flying Horse.* Illus. by Li Ming. Dutton, 1998. *Gr. 2-8*

Yolen, Jane. *Wings.* Illus. by Dennis Nolan. Harcourt, 1991. *Gr. 4-6*

FABLES

Bader, Barbara. *Aesop & Company: With Scenes from His Legendary Life.* Illus. by Arthur Geisert. Houghton Mifflin, 1991. *Gr. 3-6*

Calmenson, Stephanie. *The Children's Aesop: Selected Fables.* Illus. by Robert Byrd. Doubleday, 1988. *Gr. 2-5*

Carle, Eric. *Twelve Tales from Aesop.* Illus. by the author. Philomel, 1980. *Gr. K-3*

Demi. *A Chinese Zoo: Fables and Proverbs.* Illus. by the author. Harcourt, 1987. *Gr. 2-6*

Gatti, Ann. *Aesop's Fables.* Illus. by Safaya Salter. Gulliver/Harcourt, 1992. *Gr. 1-6*

Lobel, Arnold. *Fables.* Illus. by the author. HarperCollins, 1980. *Gr. 3-6*

McClintock, Barbara. *Animal Fables from Aesop.* Illus. by the author. Godine, 1991. *Gr. 2-6*

Morpurgo, Michael. *The McElderry Book of Aesop's Fables.* Illus. by Emma Chichester Clark. McElderry, 2005. *Gr. K-5*

Paxton, Tom. *Aesop's Fables.* Illus. by Robert Rayevsky. Morrow, 1988. *Gr. 3-6*

Pinkney, Jerry. *Aesop's Fables.* Illus. by the author. SeaStar, 2000. *Gr. 2-8*

Scieszka, Jon. *Squids Will Be Squids: Fresh Morals, Beastly Fables.* Illus. by Lane Smith. Viking, 1998. *Gr. 2-6*

Untermeyer, Louis. *Aesop's Fables.* Illus. by Alice Provensen and Martin Provensen. Golden Press, 1965. *Gr. K-3*

Young, Ed. *Seven Blind Mice.* Illus. by the author. Philomel, 1992. *Gr. PreK-3*

FAIRY TALES

Babbitt, Natalie. *Ouch!: A Tale from Grimm.* Illus. by Fred Marcellino. HarperCollins, 1998. *Gr. 2-6*

Bang, Molly Garrett. *Wiley and the Hairy Man.* Illus. by the author. Macmillan, 1976. *Gr. K-3*

Bodkin, Odds. *The Crane Wife.* Illus. by Gennady Spirin. Harcourt, 1998. *Gr. 2-6*

Cheng, Hou-Tien. *The Six Chinese Brothers: An Ancient Tale.* Illus. by the author. Henry Holt, 1979. *Gr. PreK-2*

Choi, Yangsook. *The Sun Girl and the Moon Boy.* Illus. by the author. Knopf, 1997. *Gr. 1-4*

Climo, Shirley. *The Egyptian Cinderella.* Illus. by Ruth Heller. Crowell, 1989. *Gr. 2-6*

Cole, Joanna. *Bony-Legs.* Illus. by Dirk Zimmer. Four Winds, 1983. *Gr. K-2*

DePaola, Tomie. *Adelita: A Mexican Cinderella Story.* Illus. by the author. Putnam, 2002. *Gr. 1-6*

DePaola, Tomie. *Fin M'Coul, the Giant of Knockmany Hill.* Illus. by the author. Holiday House, 1981. *Gr. K-4*

DePaola, Tomie. *Jamie O'Rourke and the Big Potato: An Irish Folktale.* Illus. by the author. Putnam, 1992. *Gr. K-4*

DePaola, Tomie. *The Mysterious Giant of Barletta: An Italian Folktale.* Illus. by the author. Harcourt, 1984. *Gr. 1-4*

DePaola, Tomie. *Strega Nona.* Illus. by the author. Simon & Schuster, 1975. *Gr. K-4*

DeRegniers, Beatrice S. *Little Sister and the Month Brothers.* Illus. by Margot Tomes. Seabury, 1976. *Gr. K-3*

Gag, Wanda. *Tales from Grimm.* Retold and illus. by Wanda Gag. Coward-McCann, 1936. *Gr. 2-6*

Greene, Ellin. *Billy Beg and His Bull.* Illus. by Kimberley Bulcken Root. Holiday House, 1994. *Gr. 2-4*

Grimm, Jacob. *The Juniper Tree and Other Tales from Grimm.* Selected by Lore Segal and Randall Jarrell. Illus. by Maurice Sendak. Farrar, 2003, c1973. *Gr. 3-6*

Grimm, Jacob. *Rumpelstiltskin.* Retold and illus. by Paul O. Zelinsky. Dutton, 1986. *Gr. 1-4*

Grimm, Jacob. *The Sleeping Beauty.* Retold and illus. by Trina Schart Hyman. Little, Brown, 1977. *Gr. 2-5*

Hamilton, Virginia. *The Girl Who Spun Gold.* Illus. by Leo and Diane Dillon. Scholastic, 2000. *Gr. 2-6*

Hamilton, Virginia. *The People Could Fly: The Picture Book.* Illus. by Leo and Diane Dillon. Knopf, 2004. *Gr. 3-6*

Hancock, Sibyl. *Esteban and the Ghost.* Illus. by Dirk Zimmer. Dial, 1983. *Gr. 2-4*

Haviland, Virginia. *Favorite Fairy Tales Told Round the World.* Illus. by S. D. Schindler. Little, Brown, 1985. *Gr. 1-4*

Hoberman, Mary Ann. *You Read to Me, I'll Read to You: Very Short Fairy Tales to Read Together.* Illus. by Michael Emberley. Little, Brown, 2004. *Gr. K-3*

Hooks, William. *Moss Gown.* Illus. by Donald Carrick. Clarion, 1987. *Gr. 2-6*

Huck, Charlotte. *The Black Bull of Norroway.* Illus. by Anita Lobel. Greenwillow, 2001. *Gr. 2-5*

Huck, Charlotte. *Princess Furball.* Illus. by Anita Lobel. Greenwillow, 1989. *Gr. 1-4*

Hyman, Trina Schart. *Little Red Riding Hood.* Illus. by the author. Holiday House, 1983. *Gr. PreK-2*

Kimmel, Eric A. *Baba Yaga: A Russian Folktale.* Illus. by the author. Holiday House, 1991. *Gr. K-2*

Kimmel, Eric A. *Boots and His Brothers: A Norwegian Tale Retold.* Illus. by Kimberly Bulcken Root. Holiday House, 1992. *Gr. 2-6*

Kimmel, Eric A. *Count Silvernose: A Story from Italy.* Illus. by Omar Rayyan. Holiday House, 1996. *Gr. 3-6*

Kimmel, Eric A. *The Three Princes: A Tale from the Middle East.* Illus. by Leonard Everett Fisher. Holiday House, 1994. *Gr. 1-4*

Kimmel, Eric A. *Three Samurai Cats: A Story from Japan.* Illus. by Mordicai Gerstein. Holiday House, 2003. *Gr. K-4*

Kirstein, Lincoln. *Puss in Boots.* Illus. by Alain Vaïs. Little, Brown, 1992. *Gr. 1-4*

Louie, Ai-Ling. *Yeh-Shen: A Cinderella Story from China.* Illus. by Ed Young. Philomel, 1982. *Gr. 3-5*

Mahy, Margaret. *The Seven Chinese Brothers.* Illus. by Jean & Mou-sien Tseng. Scholastic, 1990. *Gr. K-4*

Marshall, James. *Red Riding Hood.* Illus. by the author. Dial, 1987. *Gr. PreK-2*

Martin, Rafe. *The Rough-Face Girl.* Illus. by David Shannon. Putnam, 1992. *Gr. 2-6*

Martin, Rafe. *The Shark God.* Illus. by David Shannon. Scholastic, 2001. *Gr. 1-6*

McClintock, Barbara. *Cinderella.* Illus. by the author. Scholastic, 2005. *Gr. K-4*

McVitty, Walter. *Ali Baba and the Forty Thieves.* Illus. by Margaret Early. Abrams, 1989. *Gr. 3-6*

Minard, Rosemary. *Womenfolk and Fairy Tales.* Illus. by Suzanne Klein. Houghton Mifflin, 1975. *Gr. 3-6*

Mosel, Arlene. *The Funny Little Woman.* Illus. by Blair Lent. Dutton, 1972. *Gr. Pre-K-3*

Onyefulu, Obi. *Chinye: A West African Folk Tale.* Illus. by Evie Safarewicz. Viking, 1994. *Gr. K-3*

Osborne, Mary Pope. *The Brave Little Seamstress.* Illus. by Giselle Potter. Atheneum, 2002. *Gr. 2-6*

Osborne, Mary Pope. *Kate and the Beanstalk.* Illus. by Giselle Potter. Atheneum, 2000. *Gr. K-5*

Osborne, Mary Pope. *Mermaid Tales from Around the World.* Illus. by Troy Howell. Scholastic, 1993. *Gr. 3-6*

Osborne, Will, and Mary Pope Osborne. *Sleeping Bobby.* Illus. by Giselle Potter. Atheneum, 2005. *Gr. K-6*

Paterson, Katherine. *The Tale of the Mandarin Ducks.* Illus. by Leo and Diane Dillon. Dutton/Lodestar, 1990. *Gr. 1-6*

Perrault, Charles. *Puss in Boots.* Illus. by Fred Marcellino. Farrar, 1990. *Gr. 1-4*

Pollock, Penny. *The Turkey Girl: A Zuni Cinderella Story.* Illus. by Ed Young. Little, Brown, 1996. *Gr. 2-5*

San Souci, Robert D. *Cendrillon: A Caribbean Cinderella.* Illus. by Brian Pinkney. Simon & Schuster, 1998. *Gr. 2-6*

San Souci, Robert D. *The Faithful Friend.* Illus. by Brian Pinkney. Simon & Schuster, 1995. *Gr. 3-6*

San Souci, Robert D. *Sukey and the Mermaid.* Illus. by Brian Pinkney. Four Winds, 1992. *Gr. 2-6*

San Souci, Robert D. *The Talking Eggs.* Illus. by Jerry Pinkney. Dial, 1989. *Gr. K-3*

Sawyer, Ruth. *The Remarkable Christmas of the Cobbler's Sons.* Illus. by Barbara Cooney. Viking, 1994. *Gr. K-3*

Shepard, Aaron. *The Princess Mouse: A Tale of Finland.* Illus. by Leonid Gore. Atheneum, 2003. *Gr. K-3*

Shute, Linda. *Momotaro, the Peach Boy: A Traditional Japanese Tale.* Illus. by the author. Lothrop, 1986. *Gr. K-4*

Sierra, Judy. *The Gift of the Crocodile: A Cinderella Story.* Illus. by Reynold Ruffins. Simon & Schuster, 2000. *Gr. K-4*

Sierra, Judy. *Tasty Baby Belly Buttons: A Japanese Folktale.* Illus. by Meilo So. Knopf, 1999. *Gr. K-3*

Souhami, Jessica. *Mrs. McCool and the Giant Cuhullin: An Irish Tale.* Illus. by the author. Henry Holt, 2002. *Gr. K-4*

Steptoe, John. *Mufaro's Beautiful Daughters: An African Tale.* Illus. by the author. Lothrop, 1987. *Gr. 1-4*

Tucker, Kathy. *The Seven Chinese Sisters.* Illus. by Grace Lin. Albert Whitman, 2003. *Gr. K-4*

White, Carolyn. *Whuppity Stoorie: A Scottish Folktale*. Illus. by S. D. Schindler. Putnam, 1997. *Gr. K-6*

Willey, Margaret. *Clever Beatrice: An Upper Peninsula Conte*. Illus. by Heather Solomon. Atheneum, 2001. *Gr. 1-4*

Yep, Laurence. *The Dragon Prince: A Chinese Beauty and the Beast Tale*. Illus. by Kam Mak. HarperCollins, 1997. *Gr. 2-6*

Young, Ed. *Lon Po Po: A Red-Riding Hood Story from China*. Illus. by the author. Philomel, 1989. *Gr. K-2*

Zelinsky, Paul O. *Rapunzel*. Illus. by the author. Dutton, 1997. *Gr. 3-6*

Zemach, Harve. *Duffy and the Devil*. Illus. by Margot Zemach. Farrar, 1973. *Gr. 2-5*

FICTION

Billingsley, Franny. *The Folk Keeper*. Simon & Schuster, 1999. *Gr. 5-8*

Black, Holly and Tony DiTerlizzi. *The Spiderwick Chronicles, Book 1: The Field Guide*. Illus. by Tony DiTerlizzi. Simon & Schuster, 2003. *Gr. 2-5*

Delaney, Joseph. *The Revenge of the Witch. (The Last Apprentice, Book One)*. Illus. by Patrick Arrasmith. Greenwillow, 2005. *Gr. 5-8*

DiCamillo, Kate. *The Tale of Despereaux: Being the Story of a Mouse, a Princess, Some Soup, and a Spool of Thread*. Illus. by Timothy Basil Ering. Candlewick, 2003. *Gr. 4-8*

Donaldson, Julia. *The Giants and the Joneses*. Illus. by Greg Swearington. Henry Holt, 2005. *Gr. 2-5*

Garcia, Laura Gallego. *The Legend of the Wandering King*. Translated by Dan Bellm. Scholastic, 2005. *Gr. 5-8*

Jenkins, Emily. *Toys Go Out: Being the Adventures of a Knowledgeable Stingray, a Toughy Little Buffalo, and Someone Called Plastic*. Illus. by Paul O. Zelinsky. Schwartz & Wade, 2006. *Gr. 1-4*

Langrish, Katherine. *Troll Fell*. HarperCollins, 2004. *Gr. 5-8*

Levine, Gail Carson. *Ella Enchanted*. HarperCollins, 1997. *Gr. 4-7*

Levine, Gail Carson. *The Fairy's Mistake*. Illus. by Mark Elliott. HarperCollins, 1999. *Gr. 4-7*

Lin, Grace. *The Year of the Dog*. Illus. by the author. Little, Brown, 2006. *Gr. 3-5*

Marcantonio, Patricia Santos. *Red Ridin' in the Hood: And Other Cuentos*. Illus. by Renato Alarcão. Farrar, 2005. *Gr. 4-8*

Napoli, Donna Jo. *The Prince of the Pond: Otherwise Known as De Fawg Pin*. Illus. by Judith Byron Schachner. Dutton, 1992. *Gr. 3-6*

Nodelman, Perry. *The Same Place But Different*. Simon & Schuster, 1995. *Gr. 5-8*

Pratchett, Terry. *The Wee Free Men*. HarperCollins, 2003. *Gr. 6-8*

Pullman, Philip. *I Was a Rat!* Illus. by Kevin Hawkes. Knopf, 2000. *Gr. 4-7*

Pullman, Philip. *The Scarecrow and His Servant*. Illus. by Peter Bailey. Knopf, 2005. *Gr. 4-7*

Riordan, Rick. *The Lightning Thief. (Percy Jackson & the Olympians, Book 1)* Miramax/Hyperion, 2005. *Gr. 5-8*

Rowling, J. K. *Harry Potter and the Sorcerer's Stone*. Illus. by Mary GrandPré. Scholastic, 1998. *Gr. 4-8*

Singh, Vandana. *Younguncle Comes to Town*. Illus. by B. M. Kamath. Viking, 2006. *Gr. 3-5*

Stanley, Diane. *Bella at Midnight*. HarperCollins, 2006. *Gr. 5-8*

Swope, Sam. *Jack and the Seven Deadly Giants*. Illus. by Carll Cneut. Farrar, 2004. *Gr. 3-5*

Wrede, Patricia. *Dealing with Dragons*. Harcourt, 1990. *Gr. 5-8*

Yolen, Jane, and Robert J. Harris. *Odysseus in the Serpent Maze*. HarperCollins, 2001. *Gr. 4-7*

Yolen, Jane. *Passager: The Young Merlin Trilogy, Book One*. Harcourt, 1996. *Gr. 4-7*

FOLKTALES

Aylesworth, Jim. *Aunt Pitty Patty's Piggy*. Illus. by Barbara McClintock. Scholastic, 1999. *Gr. PreK-1*

Aylesworth, Jim. *The Gingerbread Man*. Illus. by Barbara McClintock. Scholastic, 1998. *Gr. PreK-1*

Aylesworth, Jim. *Goldilocks and the Three Bears*. Illus. by Barbara McClintock. Scholastic, 2003. *Gr. PreK-1*

Aylesworth, Jim. *The Tale of Tricky Fox: A New England Trickster Tale*. Illus. by Barbara McClintock. Scholastic, 2001. *Gr. PreK-2*

Birdseye, Tom. *Soap! Soap! Don't Forget the Soap!: An Appalachian Folktale*. Illus. by Andrew Glass. Holiday House, 1993. *Gr. K-4*

Brown, Marcia. *Stone Soup*. Illus. by the author. Scribner, 1947. *Gr. 1-4*

Cole, Joanna. *Don't Tell the Whole World!* Illus. by Kate Duke. Crowell, 1990. *Gr. K-4*

Compestine, Ying Chang. *The Runaway Rice Cake*. Illus. by Tungwai Chau. Simon & Schuster, 2001. *Gr. PreK-2*

Compton, Patricia A. *The Terrible Eek*. Illus. by Sheila Hamanaka. Simon & Schuster, 1991. *Gr. K-3*

Day, Nancy Raines. *The Lion's Whiskers: An Ethiopian Folklore*. Illus. by Ann Grifalconi. Scholastic, 1995. *Gr. 2-5*

DeFelice, Cynthia C. *The Dancing Skeleton*. Illus. by Robert Andrew Parker. Macmillan, 1989. *Gr. 2-4*

Demi. *The Hungry Coat: A Tale from Turkey*. Illus. by the author. McElderry, 2004. *Gr. 1-6*

Demi. *One Grain of Rice: A Mathematical Folktale*. Illus. by the author. Scholastic, 1997. *Gr. 2-6*

Diakité, Baba Wagué. *The Hatseller and the Monkeys*. Illus. by the author. Scholastic, 1999. *Gr. PreK-2*

Diakité, Baba Wagué. *The Hunterman and the Crocodile*. Illus. by the author. Scholastic, 1997. *Gr. 1-5*

Diakité, Baba Wagué. *The Magic Gourd*. Illus. by the author. Scholastic, 2003. *Gr. 1-4*

Egielski, Richard. *The Gingerbread Boy*. Illus. by the author. HarperCollins, 1997. *Gr. PreK-1*

Farley, Carol. *Mr. Pak Buys a Story*. Illus. by Benrei Huang. Albert Whitman, 1997. *Gr. 1-4*

French, Vivian. *Lazy Jack*. Illus. by Russell Ayto. Candlewick, 1995. *Gr. K-4*

Gackenbach, Dick. *Arabella and Mr. Crack*. Illus. by the author. Macmillan, 1982. *Gr. K-3*

Galdone, Joanna. *The Tailypo: A Ghost Story*. Illus. by Paul Galdone. Seabury, 1977. *Gr. 2-4*

Galdone, Paul. *The Old Woman and Her Pig*. Illus. by the author. McGraw-Hill, 1960. *Gr. PreK-1*

Galdone, Paul. *The Three Sillies*. Illus. by the author. Clarion, 1982. *Gr. 1-4*

Garland, Sherry. *Why Ducks Sleep on One Leg*. Illus. by Leo and Diane Dillon. Scholastic, 1993. *Gr. 1-4*

Ginsburg, Mirra. *The Chinese Mirror*. Illus. by Margot Zemach. Harcourt, 1988. *Gr. 1-4*

Ginsburg, Mirra. *Clay Boy: Adapted from a Russian Folk Tale*. Illus. by Jos. A. Smith. Greenwillow, 1997. *Gr. PreK-1*

Harper, Wilhelmina. *The Gunniwolf*. Illus. by William Wiesner. Dutton, 1978. *Gr. PreK-1*

Hewitt, Kathryn. *The Three Sillies*. Illus. by the author. Harcourt, 1986. *Gr. 1-4*

Hong, Lily Toy. *Two of Everything: A Chinese Folktale*. Illus. by the author. Albert Whitman, 1993. *Gr. K-3*

Johnson, Paul Brett. *Fearless Jack*. Illus. by the author. McElderry, 2001. *Gr. K-5*

Johnson, Paul Brett. *Jack Outwits the Giants*. Illus. by the author. McElderry, 2002. *Gr. K-5*

Kajikawa, Kimiko. *Yoshi's Feast*. Illus. by Yumi Heo. DK Ink, 2000. *Gr. K-4*

Kimmel, Eric A. *Cactus Soup*. Illus. by Phil Huling. Marshall Cavendish, 2004. *Gr. K-4*

Kimmel, Eric A. *The Gingerbread Man*. Illus. by Megan Lloyd. Holiday House, 1993. *Gr. PreK-1*

Kurtz, Jane. *Pulling the Lion's Tail*. Illus. by Floyd Cooper. Simon & Schuster, 1995. *Gr. 2-6*

Kurtz, Jane. *Trouble*. Illus. by Durga Bernhard. Gulliver/Harcourt, 1997. *Gr. K-2*

Marshall, James. *Goldilocks and the Three Bears*. Illus. by the author. Dial, 1988. *Gr. PreK-1*

Mollel, Totolwa M. *Subira Subira*. Illus. by Linda Saport. Clarion, 2000. *Gr. 1-6*

Morimoto, Junko. *The Two Bullies*. Illus. by the author. Crown, 1999. *Gr. K-2*

Mosel, Arlene. *Tikki Tikki Tembo*. Illus. by Blair Lent. Henry Holt, 1968. *Gr. PreK-3*

Muth, Jon J. *Stone Soup*. Illus. by the author. Scholastic, 2003. *Gr. K-2*

Paye, Won-Ldy, and Margaret H. Lippert. *Head, Body, Legs: A Story from Liberia*. Illus. by Julie Paschkis. Henry Holt, 2002. *Gr. PreK-3*

Peck, Jan. *The Giant Carrot*. Illus. by Barry Root. Dial, 1998. *Gr. PreK-2*

Pitre, Felix. *Juan Bobo and the Pig: A Puerto Rican Folktale*. Illus. by Christy Hale. Dutton, 1993. *Gr. PreK-2*

San Souci, Robert D. *A Weave of Words: An Armenian Tale*. Illus. by Raúl Colón. Orchard, 1998. *Gr. 3-6*

Shepard, Aaron. *King o' the Cats*. Illus. by Kristin Sorra. Atheneum, 2004. *Gr. 2-5*

Simms, Laura. *The Squeaky Door*. Illus. by Sylvie Wickstrom. Crown, 1991. *Gr. PreK-2*

Sloat, Teri. *Sody Sallyratus*. Illus. by the author. Dutton, 1997. *Gr. PreK-3*

Snyder, Dianne. *The Boy of the Three Year Nap*. Illus. by Allen Say. Houghton Mifflin, 1988. *Gr. 2-5*

Souhami, Jessica. *No Dinner!: The Story of the Old Woman and the Pumpkin*. Illus. by the author. Cavendish, 2000. *Gr. PreK-2*

Thompson, Lauren. *One Riddle, One Answer*. Illus. by Linda S. Wingerter. Scholastic, 2001. *Gr. 2-6*

Wardlaw, Lee. *Punia and the King of Sharks: A Hawaii Folktale*. Illus. by Felipe Davalos. Dial, 1997. *Gr. K-3*

Withers, Carl. *Tale of a Black Cat*. Illus. by Alan E. Cober. Henry Holt, 1966. *Gr. PreK-2*

Wolkstein, Diane. *The Day Ocean Came to Visit*. Illus. by Steve Johnson and Lou Fancher. Harcourt, 2001. *Gr. PreK-3*

Yep, Laurence. *The Junior Thunder Lord*. Illus. by Robert Van Nutt. BridgeWater, 1994. *Gr. 1-4*

Yep, Laurence. *The Khan's Daughter: A Mongolian Folktale*. Illus. by Jean Tseng and Mou-Sien Tseng. Scholastic, 1997. *Gr. K-6*

LEGENDS

Climo, Shirley. *The Egyptian Cinderella*. Illus. by Ruth Heller. Crowell, 1989. *Gr. 2-6*

Early, Margaret. *William Tell*. Illus. by the author. Abrams, 1991. *Gr. 2-5*

Fisher, Leonard Everett. *William Tell*. Illus. by the author. Farrar, 1996. *Gr. 2-5*

Goldin, Barbara Diamond. *The Girl Who Lived with the Bears*. Illus. by Andrew Plewes. Harcourt, 1997. *Gr. 2-6*

Hastings, Selina. *Sir Gawain and the Loathly Lady*. Illus. by Juan Wijngaard. Lothrop, 1985. *Gr. 3-6*

Hayes, Sarah. *Robin Hood*. Illus. by Patrick Benson. Henry Holt, 1989. *Gr. 3-6*

Henderson, Kathy. *Lugalbanda: The Boy Who Got Caught Up in a War*. Illus. by Jane Ray. Candlewick, 2006. *Gr. 3-8*

Hodges, Margaret. *Saint George and the Dragon: A Golden Legend*. Illus. by Trina Schart Hyman. Little, Brown, 1984. *Gr. 3-6*

Hodges, Margaret. *Saint Patrick and the Peddler*. Illus. by Paul Brett Johnson. Orchard, 1993. *Gr. 1-4*

Kimmel, Eric A. *The Hero Beowulf*. Illus. by Leonard Everett Fisher. Farrar, 2005. *Gr. 4-8*

Larry, Charles. *Peboan and Seegwun*. Illus. by the author. Farrar, 1993. *Gr. 1-4*

McCaughrean, Geraldine. *Gilgamesh the Hero: The Epic of Gilgamesh*. Illus. by David Parkins. Eerdmans, 2003. *Gr. 6-8*

Sabuda, Robert. *Arthur and the Sword*. Illus. by the author. Atheneum, 1995. *Gr. 2-5*

San Souci, Robert D. *Young Arthur*. Illus. by Jamichael Henterly. Doubleday, 1997. *Gr. 2-5*

Yolen, Jane. Passager: *The Young Merlin Trilogy, Book One*. Harcourt, 1996. *Gr. 4-7*

MYTHS

Bernhard, Emery. *How Snowshoe Hare Rescued the Sun: A Tale from the Arctic*. Illus. by Durga Bernhard. Holiday House, 1993. *Gr. K-3*

Burleigh, Robert. *Pandora*. Illus. by Raúl Colón. Harcourt, 2002. *Gr. 3-6*

Chief Lelooska. *Echoes of the Elders: The Stories and Paintings of Chief Lelooska*. Illus. by the author. DK Ink, 1997. *Gr. 3-6*

Climo, Shirley. *Atalanta's Race: A Greek Myth*. Illus. by Alexander Koshkin. Clarion, 1995. *Gr. 3-5*

Climo, Shirley. *Stolen Thunder: A Norse Myth*. Illus. by Alexander Koshkin. Clarion, 1994. *Gr. 3-6*

Demi. *King Midas: The Golden Touch*. Illus. by the author. McElderry, 2002. *Gr. 2-5*

Esbensen, Barbara Juster. *The Star Maiden: An Ojibway Tale*. Illus. by Helen K. Davie. Little, Brown, 1988. *Gr. 2-5*

Fisher, Leonard Everett. *Cyclops*. Illus. by the author. Holiday House, 1991. *Gr. 4-6*

Gates, Frieda. *Owl Eyes*. Illus. by Yoshi Miyake. Lothrop, 1994. *Gr. K-4*

Gerson, Mary-Joan. *Why the Sky Is Far Away: A Nigerian Folktale*. Illus. by Carla Golembe. Little, Brown, 1992. *Gr. K-4*

Goble, Paul. *Iktomi and the Boulder: A Plains Indian Story*. Illus. by the author. Orchard, 1988. *Gr. K-3*

Goldin, Barbara Diamond. *The Girl Who Lived with the Bears*. Illus. by Andrew Plewes. Harcourt, 1997. *Gr. 2-6*

Grifalconi, Ann. *The Village of Round and Square Houses*. Illus. by the author. Little, Brown, 1986. *Gr. K-4*

Haley, Gail E. *A Story, a Story*. Illus. by the author. Atheneum, 1970. *Gr. K-3*

Haviland, Virginia. *North American Legends*. Illus. by Ann Strugnell. Putnam, 1979. *Gr. 4-8*

Hewitt, Kathryn. *King Midas and the Golden Touch*. Illus. by the author. Harcourt, 1987. *Gr. 1-4*

Hong, Lily Toy. *How the Ox Star Fell From Heaven*. Illus. by the author. Albert Whitman, 1991. *Gr. K-6*

Kimmel, Eric A. *Ten Suns: A Chinese Legend*. Illus. by Yongsheng Xuan. Holiday House, 1998. *Gr. 1-6*

Larry, Charles. *Peboan and Seegwun*. Illus. by the author. Farrar, 1993. *Gr. 1-4*

Lupton, Hugh, and Daniel Morden. *The Adventures of Odysseus*. Illus. by Christina Balit. Barefoot, 2006. *Gr. 3-7*

Maddern, Eric. *The Fire Children: A West African Creation Tale*. Illus. by Frané Lessac. Dial, 1993. *Gr. K-3*

McCaughrean, Geraldine. *The Bronze Cauldron: Myths and Legends of the World*. Illus. by Bee Willey. McElderry, 1998. *Gr. 4-8*

McDermott, Gerald. *Musicians of the Sun*. Illus. by the author. Simon & Schuster, 1997. *Gr. 2-5*

McDermott, Gerald. *Raven: A Trickster Tale from the Pacific Northwest*. Illus. by the author. Harcourt, 1993. *Gr. K-4*

McDermott, Gerald. *Zomo the Rabbit: A Trickster Tale from West Africa*. Illus. by the author. Harcourt, 1992. *Gr. PreK-1*

Mollel, Tololwa M. *The Orphan Boy: A Maasai Story*. Illus. by Paul Morin. Clarion, 1991. *Gr. 1-4*

Musgrove, Margaret. *The Spider Weaver: A Legend of Kente Cloth*. Illus. by Julia Cairns. Scholastic, 2001. *Gr. K-4*

Nolan, Dennis. *Androcles and the Lion*. Illus. by the author. Harcourt, 1997. *Gr. 1-6*

Philip, Neil. *The Adventures of Odysseus*. Illus. by Peter Malone. Orchard, 1997. *Gr. 3-6*

Philip, Neil. *Odin's Family: Myths of the Vikings*. Illus. by Maryclare Foa. Orchard, 1996. *Gr. 3-6*

Sutcliff, Rosemary. *Black Ships Before Troy!: The Story of the Iliad*. Illus. by Alan Lee. Delacorte, 1993. *Gr. 5-8*

Waldherr, Kris. *Persephone and the Pomegranate: A Myth from Greece*. Illus. by the author. Dial, 1993. *Gr. 2-6*

Yolen, Jane. *Pegasus, the Flying Horse*. Illus. by Li Ming. Dutton, 1998. *Gr. 2-8*

Yolen, Jane. *Wings*. Illus. by Dennis Nolan. Harcourt, 1991. *Gr. 4-6*

Young, Ed. *Cat and Rat: The Legend of the Chinese Zodiac*. Illus. by the author. Henry Holt, 1995. *Gr. K-4*

NOODLEHEAD STORIES

Birdseye, Tom. *Soap! Soap! Don't Forget the Soap!: An Appalachian Folktale*. Illus. by Andrew Glass. Holiday House, 1993. *Gr. K-4*

Cole, Joanna. *Don't Tell the Whole World!* Illus. by Kate Duke. Crowell, 1990. *Gr. K-4*

French, Vivian. *Lazy Jack*. Illus. by Russell Ayto. Candlewick, 1995. *Gr. K-4*

Galdone, Paul. *The Three Sillies*. Illus. by the author. Clarion, 1982. *Gr. 1-4*

Hewitt, Kathryn. *The Three Sillies*. Illus. by the author. Harcourt, 1986. *Gr. 1-4*

Hong, Lily Toy. *Two of Everything: A Chinese Folklore*. Illus. by the author. Albert Whitman, 1993. *Gr. K-3*

Johnson-Davies, Denys. *Goha the Wise Fool*. Illus. by Hany El Saed Ahmed from drawings by Hag Hamdy Mohamed Fattouh. Philomel, 2005. *Gr. 2-6*

Pitre, Felix. *Juan Bobo and the Pig: A Puerto Rican Folktale*. Illus. by Christy Hale. Dutton, 1993. *Gr. PreK-2*

Salley, Coleen. *Epossumondas*. Illus. by Janet Stevens. Harcourt, 2002. *Gr. PreK-2*

Salley, Coleen. *Why Epossumondas Has No Hair on His Tail*. Illus. by Janet Stevens. Harcourt, 2004. *Gr. PreK-2*

Schwartz, Alvin. *Tomfoolery: Trickery and Foolery with Words*. Illus. by Glen Rounds. Lippincott, 1973. *Gr. 1-6*

Singer, Isaac Bashevis. *When Shlemiel Went to Warsaw & Other Stories.* Illus. by Margot Zemach. Farrar, 1979. *Gr. 4-6*

Snyder, Dianne. *The Boy of the Three Year Nap.* Illus. by Allen Say. Houghton Mifflin, 1988. *Gr. 2-5*

Taback, Simms. *Kibitzers and Fools: Tales My Zayda (Grandfather) Told Me.* Illus. by the author. Viking, 2005. *Gr. 1-4*

PARODIES AND UPDATES

Auch, Mary Jane. *The Princess and the Pizza.* Illus. by Mary Jane Auch and Herm Auch. Holiday House, 2002. *Gr. K-5*

Briggs, Raymond. *Jim and the Beanstalk.* Illus. by the author. Coward-McCann, 1989. *Gr. 3-6*

Buehner, Caralyn. *Fanny's Dream.* Illus. by Mark Buehner. Dial, 1996. *Gr. 1-6*

Calmenson, Stephanie. *The Frog Principal.* Illus. by Denise Brunkus. Scholastic, 2001. *Gr. K-4*

Child, Lauren. *Beware of the Storybook Wolves.* Illus. by the author. Scholastic, 2001. *Gr. PreK-2*

Child, Lauren. *Who's Afraid of the Big Bad Book?* Illus. by the author. Hyperion, 2003. *Gr. K-3*

Christelow, Eileen. *Where's the Big Bad Wolf?* Illus. by the author. Clarion, 2002. *Gr. PreK-2*

Edwards, Pamela Duncan. *The Neat Line: Scribbling Through Mother Goose.* Illus. by Diann Cain Blumenthal. HarperCollins, 2005. *Gr. PreK-2*

Emberley, Michael. *Ruby.* Illus. by the author. Little, Brown, 1990. *Gr. K-3*

Emberley, Rebecca. *Three Cool Kids.* Illus. by the author. Little, Brown, 1995. *Gr. PreK-2*

Ernst, Lisa Campbell. *Little Red Riding Hood: A Newfangled Prairie Tale.* Illus. by the author. Simon & Schuster, 1995. *Gr. K-3*

Grey, Mini. *The Adventures of the Dish and the Spoon.* Illus. by the author. Knopf, 2006. *Gr. PreK-2*

Hartman, Bob. *The Wolf Who Cried Boy.* Illus. by Tim Raglin. Putnam, 2002. *Gr. K-2*

Hawkins, Colin, and Jacqui Hawkins. *The Fairytale News.* Illus. by the authors. Candlewick, 2004. *Gr. PreK-3*

Isaacs, Anne. *Pancakes for Supper.* Illus. by Mark Teague. Scholastic, 2006. *Gr. PreK-2*

Jackson, Ellen. *Cinder Edna.* Illus. by Kevin O'Malley. Lothrop, 1994. *Gr. 1-6*

Kesey, Ken. *Little Tricker the Squirrel Meets Big Double the Bear.* Illus. by Barry Moser. Viking, 1990. *Gr. 1-4*

Ketteman, Helen. *Armadilly Chili.* Illus. by Will Terry. Albert Whitman, 2004. *Gr. K-2*

Little, Jean, and M. De Vries. *Once Upon a Golden Apple.* Illus. by Phoebe Gilman. Viking, 1991. *Gr. PreK-2*

Lobel, Arnold. *Fables.* Illus. by the author. HarperCollins, 1980. *Gr. 3-6*

McClements, George. *Jake Gander, Storyville Detective.* Illus. by the author. Hyperion, 2002. *Gr. PreK-2*

Moser, Barry. *Tucker Pfeffercorn: An Old Story Retold.* Illus. by the author. Little, Brown, 1994. *Gr. 3-6*

Palatini, Margie. *The Web Files.* Illus. by Richard Egielski. Hyperion, 2001. *Gr. K-3*

Scieszka, Jon. *The Frog Prince, Continued.* Illus. by Steve Johnson. Viking, 1991. *Gr. 2-6*

Scieszka, Jon. *Squids Will Be Squids: Fresh Morals, Beastly Fables.* Illus. by Lane Smith. Viking, 1998. *Gr. 2-6*

Scieszka, Jon. *The Stinky Cheese Man and Other Fairly Stupid Tales.* Illus. by Lane Smith. Viking, 1992. *Gr. PreK-Adult*

Scieszka, Jon. *The True Story of the 3 Little Pigs.* Illus. by Lane Smith. Viking, 1989. *Gr. 2-Adult*

Shulman, Lisa. *The Matzo Ball Boy.* Illus. by Rosanne Litzinger. Dutton, 2005. *Gr. PreK-2*

Stanley, Diane. *The Giant and the Beanstalk.* Illus. by the author. HarperCollins, 2004. *Gr. PreK-2*

Stanley, Diane. *Goldie and the Three Bears.* Illus. by the author. HarperCollins, 2003. *Gr. PreK-1*

Stanley, Diane. *Rumpelstiltskin's Daughter.* Illus. by the author. Morrow, 1997. *Gr. 2-5*

Stevens, Janet, and Susan Stevens Crummel. *And the Dish Ran Away with the Spoon.* Illus. by Janet Stevens. Harcourt, 2001. *Gr. K-3*

Stevens, Janet, and Susan Stevens Crummel. *Cook-a-Doodle-Doo!* Illus. by Janet Stevens. Harcourt, 1999. *Gr. PreK-2*

Sturges, Philemon. *The Little Red Hen (Makes a Pizza).* Illus. by Amy Walrod. Dutton, 1999. *Gr. PreK-1*

Wiesner, David. *The Three Pigs.* Illus. by the author. Clarion, 2001. *Gr. PreK-2*

Wood, Audrey. *The Bunyans.* Illus. by David Shannon. Scholastic, 1996. *Gr. 1-4*

POETRY AND NURSERY RHYMES

Booth, David, comp. *Doctor Knickerbocker and Other Rhymes.* Illus. by Maryann Kovalski. Ticknor & Fields, 1993. *Gr. 2-5*

Cousins, Lucy, comp. *The Little Dog Laughed and Other Nursery Rhymes.* Illus. by the author. Dutton, 1990. *Gr. PreK-1*

Crews, Nina. *The Neighborhood Mother Goose.* Illus. by the author. Greenwillow, 2004. *Gr. PreK-1*

DePaola, Tomie. *The Comic Adventures of Old Mother Hubbard and Her Dog.* Illus. by the author. Harcourt, 1981. *Gr. PreK-2*

DePaola, Tomie. *Tomie dePaola's Mother Goose.* Illus. by Tomie dePaola. Putnam, 1985. *Gr. PreK-2*

Hoberman, Mary Ann. *You Read to Me, I'll Read to You: Very Short Fairy Tales to Read Together.* Illus. by Michael Emberley. Little, Brown, 2004. *Gr. K-3*

Hoberman, Mary Ann. *You Read to Me, I'll Read to You: Very Short Stories to Read Together.* Illus. by Michael Emberley. Little, Brown, 2001. *Gr. K-2*

Lobel, Arnold. *The Random House Book of Mother Goose.* Illus. by Arnold Lobel. Random House, 1986. *Gr. PreK-2*

Long, Sylvia, comp. *Sylvia Long's Mother Goose.* Illus. by Sylvia Long. Chronicle, 1999. *Gr. PreK-1*

Marshall, James. *Old Mother Hubbard and Her Wonderful Dog.* Illus. by the author. Farrar, 1991. *Gr. PreK-1*

Moses, Will. *Mother Goose.* Illus. by Will Moses. Philomel, 2003. *Gr. PreK-K*

Opie, Iona, ed. *Here Comes Mother Goose.* Illus. by Rosemary Wells. Candlewick Press, 1999. *Gr. PreK-1*

Opie, Iona, ed. *My Very First Mother Goose.* Illus. by Rosemary Wells. Candlewick, 1996. *Gr. PreK-1*

Opie, Iona and Opie, Peter, eds. *I Saw Esau: The Schoolchild's Pocket Book.* Illus. by Maurice Sendak. Candlewick, 1992. *Gr. 1-5*

Prelutsky, Jack, comp. *Poems of A. Nonny Mouse.* Illus. by Henrik Drescher. Knopf, 1989. *Gr. K-4*

Rex, Adam. *Frankenstein Makes a Sandwich: And Other Stories You're Sure to Like, Because They're All About Monsters, and Some of Them Are Also About Food. You Like Food, Don't You? Well, All Right Then.* Illus. by the author. Harcourt, 2006. *Gr. 2-6*

Schwartz, Alvin. *And the Green Grass Grew All Around: Folk Poetry from Everyone.* Illus. by Sue Truesdale. HarperCollins, 1992. *Gr. 2-6*

Schwartz, Alvin. *Busy Buzzing Bumblebees and Other Tongue Twisters.* Illus. by Kathie Abrams. HarperCollins, 1982. *Gr. PreK-2*

Schwartz, Alvin. *I Saw You in the Bathtub and Other Folk Rhymes.* Illus. by Syd Hoff. HarperCollins, 1989. *Gr. K-3*

Sierra, Judy. *Schoolyard Rhymes: Kids' Own Rhymes for Rope Skipping, Hand Clapping, Ball Bouncing, and Just Plain Fun.* Illus. by Melissa Sweet. Knopf, 2005. *Gr. 1-5*

Sutherland, Zena. *The Orchard Book of Nursery Rhymes.* Illus. by Faith Jaques. Orchard, 1990. *Gr. PreK-1*

Taback, Simms. *There Was an Old Lady Who Swallowed a Fly.* Illus. by the author. Viking, 1997. *Gr. PreK-2*

Taback, Simms. *This Is the House That Jack Built.* Illus. by the author. Putnam, 2002. *Gr. PreK-1*

Tripp, Wallace, comp. *A Great Big Ugly Man Came Up and Tied His Horse to Me; A Book of Nonsense Verse.* Illus. by the author. Little, Brown, 1973. *Gr. PreK-4*

Westcott, Nadine Bernard. *Peanut Butter and Jelly; a Play-Rhyme.* Illus. by the author. Dutton, 1987. *Gr. PreK-2*

Whipple, Laura. *If the Shoe Fits: Voices from Cinderella.* Illus. by Laura Beingessner. McElderry, 2002. *Gr. 4-8*

Withers, Carl, comp. *A Rocket in My Pocket: The Rhymes and Chants of Young Americans.* Illus. by Susanne Suba. Henry Holt, 1948. *Gr. K-4*

POURQUOI TALES

Aardema, Verna. *Why Mosquitoes Buzz in People's Ears.* Illus. by Leo and Diane Dillon. Dial, 1975. *Gr. PreK-2*

Auch, Mary Jane. *The Princess and the Pizza.* Illus. by Mary Jane Auch and Herm Auch. Holiday House, 2002. *Gr. K-5*

Bernhard, Emery. *How Snowshoe Hare Rescued the Sun: A Tale from the Arctic.* Illus. by Durga Bernhard. Holiday House, 1993. *Gr. K-3*

Bruchac, Joseph, and James Bruchac. *How Chipmunk Got His Stripes: A Tale of Bragging and Teasing.* Illus. by Jose Aruego and Ariane Dewey. Dial, 2001. *Gr. K-2*

Bruchac, Joseph, and James Bruchac. *Raccoon's Last Race: A Traditional Abenaki Story.* Illus. by Jose Aruego and Ariane Dewey. Dial, 2004. *Gr. PreK-2*

Choi, Yangsook. *The Sun Girl and the Moon Boy.* Illus. by the author. Knopf, 1997. *Gr. 1-4*

Doucet, Sharon Arms. *Why Lapin's Ears Are Long and Other Tales from the Louisiana Bayou.* Illus. by David Catrow. Orchard, 1997. *Gr. 1-4*

Ehlert, Lois. *Cuckoo: A Mexican Folktale/Cucú: Un Cuento Folklórico Mexicano.* Illus. by the author. Harcourt, 1997. *Gr. PreK-3*

Esbensen, Barbara Juster. *The Star Maiden: An Ojibway Tale.* Illus. by Helen K. Davie. Little, Brown, 1988. *Gr. 2-5*

Garland, Sherry. *Why Ducks Sleep on One Leg.* Illus. by Leo and Diane Dillon. Scholastic, 1993. *Gr. 1-4*

Gates, Frieda. *Owl Eyes.* Illus. by Yoshi Miyake. Lothrop, 1994. *Gr. K-4*

Gerson, Mary-Joan. *Why the Sky Is Far Away: A Nigerian Folktale.* Illus. by Carla Golembe. Little, Brown, 1992. *Gr. K-4*

Goble, Paul. *Her Seven Brothers.* Illus. by the author. Bradbury, 1988. *Gr. 3-6*

Goble, Paul. *Iktomi and the Boulder: A Plains Indian Story.* Illus. by the author. Orchard, 1988. *Gr. K-3*

Grifalconi, Ann. *The Village of Round and Square Houses.* Illus. by the author. Little, Brown, 1986. *Gr. K-4*

Haley, Gail E. *A Story, a Story.* Illus. by the author. Atheneum, 1970. *Gr. K-3*

Hamilton, Virginia. *When Birds Could Talk & Bats Could Sing.* Illus. by Barry Moser. Scholastic, 1996. *Gr. 2-5*

Hong, Lily Toy. *How the Ox Star Fell From Heaven.* Illus. by the author. Albert Whitman, 1991. *Gr. K-6*

Johnston, Tony. *The Tale of Rabbit and Coyote.* Illus. by Tomie dePaola. Putnam, 1994. *Gr. PreK-2*

Maddern, Eric. *The Fire Children: A West African Creation Tale.* Illus. by Frané Lessac. Dial, 1993. *Gr. K-3*

McDermott, Gerald. *Jabutí the Tortoise: A Trickster Tale from the Amazon.* Illus. by the author. Harcourt, 2001. *Gr. K-2*

McDermott, Gerald. *Musicians of the Sun.* Illus. by the author. Simon & Schuster, 1997. *Gr. 2-5*

McDermott, Gerald. *Raven: A Trickster Tale from the Pacific Northwest.* Illus. by the author. Harcourt, 1993. *Gr. K-4*

McDermott, Gerald. *Zomo the Rabbit: A Trickster Tale from West Africa.* Illus. by the author. Harcourt, 1992. *Gr. PreK-1*

Mollel, Tololwa M. *The Orphan Boy: A Maasai Story.* Illus. by Paul Morin. Clarion, 1991. *Gr. 1-4*

Morimoto, Junko. *The Two Bullies.* Illus. by the author. Crown, 1999. *Gr. K-2*

Musgrove, Margaret. *The Spider Weaver: A Legend of Kente Cloth.* Illus. by Julia Cairns. Scholastic, 2001. *Gr. K-4*

Paye, Won-Ldy, and Margaret H. Lippert. *Head, Body, Legs: A Story from Liberia.* Illus. by Julie Paschkis. Henry Holt, 2002. *Gr. PreK-3*

Ross, Gayle. *How Turtle's Back Was Cracked: A Traditional Cherokee Tale.* Illus. by Murv Jacob. Dial, 1995. *Gr. 1-4*

Salley, Coleen. *Why Epossumondas Has No Hair on His Tail.* Illus. by Janet Stevens. Harcourt, 2004. *Gr. PreK-2*

Shepard, Aaron. *Master Man: A Tall Tale of Nigeria.* Illus. by David Wisniewski. HarperCollins, 2001. *Gr. K-5*

Stevens, Janet. *Coyote Steals the Blanket: A Ute Tale.* Illus. by the author. Holiday House, 1993. *Gr. PreK-3*

Van Laan, Nancy. *In a Circle Long Ago: A Treasury of Native Lore from North America.* Illus. by Lisa Desimini. Knopf, 1995. *Gr. K-5*

Wolkstein, Diane. *The Day Ocean Came to Visit.* Illus. by Steve Johnson and Lou Fancher. Harcourt, 2001. *Gr. PreK-3*

Yep, Laurence. *The Junior Thunder Lord.* Illus. by Robert Van Nutt. BridgeWater, 1994. *Gr. 1-4*

Young, Ed. *Cat and Rat: The Legend of the Chinese Zodiac.* Illus. by the author. Henry Holt, 1995. *Gr. K-4*

SCARY STORIES

Bang, Molly Garrett. *Wiley and the Hairy Man.* Illus. by the author. Macmillan, 1976. *Gr. K-3*

Cole, Joanna. *Bony-Legs.* Illus. by Dirk Zimmer. Four Winds, 1983. *Gr. K-2*

DeFelice, Cynthia C. *The Dancing Skeleton.* Illus. by Robert Andrew Parker. Macmillan, 1989. *Gr. 2-4*

Galdone, Joanna. *The Tailypo: A Ghost Story.* Illus. by Paul Galdone. Seabury, 1977. *Gr. 2-4*

Hamilton, Martha, and Mitch Weiss. *Scared Witless: Thirteen Eerie Tales to Tell.* Illus. by Kevin Pope. August House, 2006. *Gr. 3-6*

Hancock, Sibyl. *Esteban and the Ghost.* Illus. by Dirk Zimmer. Dial, 1983. *Gr. 2-4*

Kimmel, Eric A. *Baba Yaga: A Russian Folktale.* Illus. by the author. Holiday House, 1991. *Gr. K-2*

Leach, Maria. *The Thing at the Foot of the Bed and Other Scary Tales.* Illus. by Kert Werth. Putnam, 1987. *Gr. 2-6*

Schwartz, Alvin. *Scary Stories to Tell in the Dark.* Illus. by Stephen Gammell. HarperCollins, 1981. *Gr. 4-8*

Shepard, Aaron. *King o' the Cats.* Illus. by Kristin Sorra. Atheneum, 2004. *Gr. 2-5*

TALL TALES

Isaacs, Anne. *Swamp Angel.* Illus. by Paul O. Zelinsky. Dutton, 1994. *Gr. 1-6*

Keats, Ezra Jack. *John Henry: An American Legend.* Illus. by the author. Knopf, 1987. *Gr. 1-4*

Kellogg, Steven. *Johnny Appleseed.* Illus. by the author. Morrow, 1988. *Gr. 1-4*

Kellogg, Steven. *Sally Ann Thunder Ann Whirlwind Crockett: A Tall Tale.* Illus. by the author. Morrow, 1995. *Gr. 1-4*

Lester, Julius. *John Henry.* Illus. by Jerry Pinkney. Dial, 1994. *Gr. 1-4*

McCormick, Dell J. *Paul Bunyan Swings His Axe.* Illus. by the author. Caxton, 1936. *Gr. 3-6*

Osborne, Mary Pope. *American Tall Tales.* Illus. by Michael McCurdy. Knopf, 1991. *Gr. 3-6*

Osborne, Mary Pope. *New York's Bravest.* Illus. by Steve Johnson and Lou Fancher. Knopf, 2002. *Gr. PreK-6*

Rounds, Glen. *Ol' Paul, the Mighty Logger.* Illus. by the author. Holiday House, 1976. *Gr. 4-6*

San Souci, Robert D. *Larger Than Life: The Adventures of American Legendary Heroes.* Illus. by Andrew Glass. Doubleday, 1991. *Gr. 3-6*

Schanzer, Rosalyn. *Davy Crockett Saves the World.* Illus. by the author. HarperCollins, 2001. *Gr. K-3*

Shepard, Aaron. *Master Man: A Tall Tale of Nigeria.* Illus. by David Wisniewski. HarperCollins, 2001. *Gr. K-5*

Stamm, Claus. *Three Strong Women: A Tall Tale from Japan.* Illus. by Jean Tseng and Mou-Sien Tseng. Viking, 1990. *Gr. 1-4*

Walker, Paul Robert. *Big Men, Big Country: A Collection of American Tall Tales.* Illus. by James Bernardin. Harcourt, 1993. *Gr. 4-6*

TRICKSTER TALES

Arkhurst, Joyce Cooper. *The Adventures of Spider: West African Folk Tales.* Illus. by Jerry Pinkney. Little, Brown, 1992, c1964. *Gr. 1-4*

Aylesworth, Jim. *The Tale of Tricky Fox: A New England Trickster Tale.* Scholastic, 2001. *Gr. PreK-2*

Chase, Richard. *The Jack Tales.* Illus. by Berkeley Williams, Jr. Houghton Mifflin, 1943. *Gr. 4-6*

Cheng, Hou-Tien. *The Six Chinese Brothers: An Ancient Tale.* Illus. by the author. Henry Holt, 1979. *Gr. PreK-2*

DePaola, Tomie. *Fin M'Coul, the Giant of Knockmany Hill.* Illus. by the author. Holiday House, 1981. *Gr. K-4*

DePaola, Tomie. *Jamie O'Rourke and the Big Potato: An Irish Folktale.* Illus. by the author. Putnam, 1992. *Gr. K-4*

DePaola, Tomie. *The Mysterious Giant of Barletta: An Italian Folktale.* Illus. by the author. Harcourt, 1984. *Gr. 1-4*

DePaola, Tomie. *Strega Nona.* Illus. by the author. Simon & Schuster, 1975. *Gr. K-4*

Diakité, Baba Wagué. *The Hunterman and the Crocodile.* Illus. by the author. Scholastic, 1997. *Gr. 1-5*

Doucet, Sharon Arms. *Why Lapin's Ears Are Long and Other Tales from the Louisiana Bayou.* Illus. by David Catrow. Orchard, 1997. *Gr. 1-4*

Goble, Paul. *Iktomi and the Boulder: A Plains Indian Story.* Illus. by the author. Orchard, 1988. *Gr. K-3*

Haley, Gail E. *A Story, a Story.* Illus. by the author. Atheneum, 1970. *Gr. K-3*

Hamilton, Virginia. *Bruh Rabbit and the Tar Baby Girl.* Illus. by James E. Ransome. Blue Sky/Scholastic, 2003. *Gr. PreK-4*

Han, Suzanne Crowder. *The Rabbit's Escape.* Illus. by Yumi Heo. Henry Holt, 1995. *Gr. 1-5*

Hicks, Ray. *The Jack Tales.* Illus. by Owen Smith. Callaway, 2000. *Gr. 2-5*

Ho, Minfong, and Saphan Ros. *Brother Rabbit: A Cambodian Tale.* Illus. by Jennifer Hewitson. Lothrop, 1997. *Gr. K-3*

Johnson, Paul Brett. *Fearless Jack.* Illus. by the author. McElderry, 2001. *Gr. K-5*

Johnson, Paul Brett. *Jack Outwits the Giants.* Illus. by the author. McElderry, 2002. *Gr. K-5*

Johnston, Tony. *The Tale of Rabbit and Coyote.* Illus. by Tomie dePaola. Putnam, 1994. *Gr. PreK-2*

Kimmel, Eric A. *Anansi and the Magic Stick.* Illus. by Janet Stevens. Holiday House, 2001. *Gr. PreK-2*

Kimmel, Eric A. *Anansi and the Moss-Covered Rock.* Illus. by Janet Stevens. Holiday House, 1990. *Gr. PreK-2*

Kimmel, Eric A. *Anansi and the Talking Melon.* Illus. by Janet Stevens. Holiday House, 1994. *Gr. PreK-2*

Kimmel, Eric A. *Anansi Goes Fishing.* Illus. by Janet Stevens. Holiday House, 1992. *Gr. PreK-2*

Knutson, Barbara. *Love and Roast Chicken: A Trickster Tale from the Andes Mountains.* Illus. by the author. Carolrhoda, 2004. *Gr. K-3*

Lester, Julius. *The Tales of Uncle Remus: The Adventures of Brer Rabbit.* Dial, 1990. *Gr. 2-5*

MacDonald, Margaret Read. *Mabela the Clever.* Illus. by Tim Coffey. Albert Whitman, 2001. *Gr. PreK-2*

McDermott, Gerald. *Coyote: A Trickster Tale from the American Southwest.* Illus. by the author. Harcourt, 1994. *Gr. PreK-2*

McDermott, Gerald. *Jabutí the Tortoise: A Trickster Tale from the Amazon.* Illus. by the author. Harcourt, 2001. *Gr. K-2*

McDermott, Gerald. *Raven: A Trickster Tale from the Pacific Northwest.* Illus. by the author. Harcourt, 1993. *Gr. K-4*

McDermott, Gerald. *Zomo the Rabbit: A Trickster Tale from West Africa.* Illus. by the author. Harcourt, 1992. *Gr. PreK-1*

McGill, Alice. *Sure as Sunrise: Stories of Bruh Rabbit & His Walkin' Talkin' Friends.* Houghton Mifflin, 2004. *Gr. K-5*

Mollel, Tololwa M. *Ananse's Feast: An Ashanti Tale.* Illus. by Andrew Glass. Clarion, 1997. *Gr. K-3*

Parks, Van Dyke, and Malcolm Jones. *Jump!: The Adventures of Brer Rabbit.* Illus. by Barry Moser. Harcourt, 1986. *Gr. 2-5*

Paye, Won-Ldy and Margaret H. Lippert. *Mrs. Chicken and the Hungry Crocodile.* Illus. by Julie Paschkis. Henry Holt, 2003. *Gr. PreK-1*

San Souci, Robert D. *Sister Tricksters: Rollicking Tales of Clever Females.* Illus. by Daniel San Souci. August House, 2006. *Gr. 3-6*

Sierra, Judy. *Tasty Baby Belly Buttons: A Japanese Folktale.* Illus. by Meilo So. Knopf, 1999. *Gr. K-3*

Souhami, Jessica. *The Leopard's Drum: An Asante Tale from West Africa.* Illus. by the author. Frances Lincoln, 2005. Gr. PreK-2

Souhami, Jessica. *Mrs. McCool and the Giant Cuhullin: An Irish Tale.* Illus. by the author. Henry Holt, 2002. *Gr. K-4*

Stevens, Janet. *Coyote Steals the Blanket: A Ute Tale.* Illus. by the author. Holiday House, 1993. *Gr. PreK-3*

Stevens, Janet. *Tops & Bottoms.* Illus. by the author. Harcourt, 1995. *Gr. PreK-3*

Van Laan, Nancy. *In a Circle Long Ago: A Treasury of Native Lore from North America.* Illus. by Lisa Desimini. Knopf, 1995. *Gr. K-5*

Wardlaw, Lee. *Punia and the King of Sharks: A Hawaii Folktale.* Illus. by Felipe Davalos. Dial, 1997. *Gr. K-3*

Willey, Margaret. *Clever Beatrice: An Upper Peninsula Conte.* Illus. by Heather Solomon. Atheneum, 2001. *Gr. 1-4*

Bibliography of Professional Books about Storytelling

Baltuck, Naomi. *Crazy Gibberish and Other Story Hour Stretches (From a Storyteller's Bag of Tricks).* **Illus. by Doug Cushman. Linnett Books, 1993. ISBN 978-0-208-02336-0**

Irresistible chants, audience participation stories, songs and musical games, and jokes that will ensure story hour success, and if you order the accompanying toe-tapping tape, you can learn it all in the car on your way to work.

Bauer, Caroline Feller. *Handbook for Storytellers.* **American Library Association, 1977. ISBN 978-0-8389-0225-7**

From planning to delivery, a gold mine of ideas.

Bauer, Caroline Feller. *Leading Kids to Books Through Magic.* **Illus. by Richard Laurent. American Library Association, 1996. ISBN 978-0-8389-0684-2**

Spice up your book presentations and lessons with this amiable collection of easy-to-perform magic tricks, each accompanied with an annotated bibliography of tie-in children's books.

Bauer, Caroline Feller. *New Handbook for Storytellers: With Stories, Poems, Magic, and More.* **Illus. by Lynn Gates Bredeson. American Library Association, 1993. ISBN 978-0-8389-0664-4**

A compendium of techniques, story sources, activities and programs that will make you dizzy with the sheer numbers of doable and kid-pleasing ideas.

Bettelheim, Bruno. *The Uses of Enchantment: The Meaning and Importance of Fairy Tales.* **Knopf, 1976. ISBN 978-0-679-72393-6**

Fascinating interpretations by the famous child psychologist. Little Red Riding Hood will never be the same.

Brady, Martha, and Patsy T. Gleason. *Artstarts: Drama, Music, Movement, Puppetry, and Storytelling Activities.* **Teacher Ideas Press, 1994. ISBN 978-1-56308-148-4**

A lesson plan guide to using drama and the arts with children, with scads of ideas and pragmatic instructions.

Bruchac, Joseph. *Tell Me a Tale: A Book about Storytelling.* **Harcourt, 1997. ISBN 978-0-15-201221-2**

An autobiographical look at storytelling by the well-known Native American children's book writer, with ideas and activities for listening, observing, remembering, and sharing tales, and 14 stories to tell.

Champlin, Connie, and Nancy Renfro. *Storytelling with Puppets.* **American Library Association, 1998. ISBN 978-0-8389-0709-2**

A useful overview, including puppet patterns, techniques for storytelling and puppet manipulation, participatory activities, story bibliographies, and plenty of sensible advice.

Dailey, Sheila. *Putting the World in a Nutshell: The Art of the Formula Tale.* **H. W. Wilson, 1994. ISBN 978-0-8242-0860-8**

A collection of 38 easy-to-learn stories to tell, with examples of each of nine types of stories: chain, cumulative, circle, endless, catch, compound triad, question, "air castles," and good/bad. Story notes, a story formula outline for telling, and an annotated bibliography of other versions and variants accompany each tale.

De Las Casas, Dianne. *Kamishibai Story Theater: The Art of Picture Telling.* **Libraries Unlimited, 2006. ISBN 978-1-59158-404-9**

How to begin a Kamishibai program of making and using illustrated story cards to tell stories with children in grades 2 to 6; plus 25 Asian folktales to get you started.

De Vos, Gail. *Storytelling for Young Adults: A Guide to Tales for Teens, 2nd edition.* **Libraries Unlimited, 2003. ISBN 978-1-56308-903-9**

Describes benefits, basic techniques, and classroom extension activities; gives plot summaries and sources for 200 fairy tales, myths and legends, ghost stories, urban belief legends, love and romance stories, trickster, tall, and literary tales; and includes a selection of retellings of stories that will wake up and involve even a jaded teenage audience.

De Wit, Dorothy. *Children's Faces Looking Up: Program Building for the Storyteller.* **American Library Association, 1979. ISBN 978-0-8389-0272-1**

Develops storytelling programs on a multitude of themes, with suggestions for tales that tie in.

Freeman, Judy. *Books Kids Will Sit Still For 3: The Complete Read-Aloud Guide.* **Libraries Unlimited, 1990. ISBN 978-1-5915-8164-2**

This kid-tested, comprehensive bibliography of 1,700 children's read-aloud books for grades PreK-6 is indispensable for teachers and librarians looking to develop a literature-based curriculum. Part of a series which also includes *Books Kids Will Sit Still For* (1990) and *More Books Kids Will Sit Still For* (1995), with practical ideas for storytelling, creative drama, Reader's Theater, booktalking, and ways to celebrate reading across the curriculum.

Freeman, Judy. *Hi Ho Librario!: Songs, Chants, and Stories to Keep Kids Humming.* **Rock Hill, 1997. ISBN 978-1-89060-401-1 (includes book & CD)**

Filled with plenty of story hour fodder, this useful book with its accompanying tape and CD is a fitting resource for librarians, teachers, parents, and silly song lovers.

Fujita, Hiroko. *Stories to Play With: Kids' Tales Told with Puppets, Paper, Toys, and Imagination.* **August House, 1999. ISBN 978-0-87483-553-3**

More than 25 easy-to-construct props and stories to use with them, most from Japan or the U.S, from a Japanese storyteller.

Geisler, Harlynne. *Storytelling Professionally: The Nuts and Bolts of a Working Performer.* **Libraries Unlimited, 1997. ISBN 978-1-56308-370-9**

Issues a professional storyteller faces and how to handle them, from publicity to performance.

Goforth, Frances S., and Carolyn V. Spillman. *Using Folk Literature in the Classroom: Encouraging Children to Read and Write.* **Oryx, 1994. ISBN 978-0-89774-747-9**

In setting up instructional units on changes and challenges, overcoming odds, animals, transformations, enchantment, and heroes and heroines, each of the 54 folktale lessons includes a story summary and activities designed to connect children to prior knowledge of the story, construct personal meaning, and create a verbal, artistic, or written response.

Gordh, Bill. *Stories in Action: Interactive Tales and Learning Activities to Promote Early Literacy.* **Libraries Unlimited, 2006. ISBN 978-1-59158-338-7**

Forty tales from around the world to use with children ages 4 to 8 and related activities including acting out, retelling, writing, and discussions; the three sections include Exploring Structures of Stories, Exploring Themes and Characters through Stories, and Exploring Cultures through Stories.

Greene, Ellin. *Storytelling: Art and Technique.* **3rd. ed. Libraries Unlimited, 1996. ISBN 978-0-8352-3458-0**

A sensible manual for beginning and experienced storytellers alike.

Hamilton, Martha, and Mitch Weiss. *Children Tell Stories: A Teaching Guide.* **Richard C. Owen, 1990. ISBN 978-1-57274-663-3**

The authors, aka Beauty & the Beast Storytellers, describe ways to integrate kids as storytellers into the school curriculum.

Haven, Kendall. *Story Proof: The Science Behind the Startling Power of Story.* **Libraries Unlimited, 2007. ISBN 978-1-59158-546-6**

Haven's research shows how reading and telling stories contribute to brain development and the effectiveness of educational achievement.

Haven, Kendall. *Super Simple Storytelling: A Can-Do Guide for Every Classroom, Every Day.* **Teacher Ideas Press, 2000. ISBN 978-1-56308-681-6**

Contains 40 storytelling exercises to use with children, plus Haven's own Step-by-Step Super Simple System for learning stories.

Holt, David, and Bill Mooney, eds. *Ready-to-Tell Tales: Sure-fire Stories from America's Favorite Storytellers.* **August House, 1994. ISBN 978-0-87483-380-5**

A collection of 42 international tales selected by an impressive roster of storytelling greats, along with notes from the tellers. Follow up with 45 additional stories in the companion volume, *More Ready-to-Tell Tales from Around the World* (2000).

Irving, Jan. *Stories Neverending: A Program Guide for Schools and Libraries.* **Illus. by by Joni Giarratono. Libraries Unlimited, 2004. ISBN 978-1-56308-997-8**

Programs based on 10 general themes—such as Red Hot Readers, Art Smarts, The Poetry Place, and Storytelling Sampler—include scripts, stories, reproducible patterns, writing ideas, and annotated bibliographies of children's books. Also look for the companion book, *Stories, Time and Again: A Program Guide for Schools and Libraries* (2005).

Irving, Jan, and Robin Currie. *Straw into Gold: Books and Activities About Folktales.* **Libraries Unlimited, 1993. ISBN 978-1-56308-074-6**

Songs, poems, chants, retellings, and ideas for projects for eight traditional folktales to use with grades K-4.

Keifer, Barbara, Janet Hickman, and Susan Hepler. *Charlotte Huck's Children's Literature.* **6th ed. McGraw-Hill, 2006. ISBN 978-0-07325-769-3**

A thorough study of the field, encompassing every aspect of developing a successful literature program. No professional collection is complete without this invaluable text, which used to be called *Children's Literature in the Elementary School.*

Kinghorn, Harriet R., and Mary Helen Pelton. *Every Child a Storyteller: A Handbook of Ideas.* **Illus. by Myke Knutson. Teacher Ideas Press, 1991. ISBN 978-0-87287-868-6**

Includes stories, bibliographies, reproducibles, and a slew of ideas for teaching children to tell stories.

Kraus, Anne Marie. *Folktale Themes and Activities for Children, Volume 1: Pourquoi Tales.* **Illus. by Susan K. Bins. Teacher Ideas Press, 1998. ISBN 978-1-56308-521-5**

Includes background on and curriculum connections for pourquoi tales, with a variety of stories, ideas, and activities. You'll also want the companion book, *Folktale Themes and Activities for Children, Volume 2: Trickster and Transformation Tales* (1999).

Lehrman, Betty, ed. *Telling Stories to Children: A National Storytelling Guide.* **National Storytelling Press, 2005. ISBN 978-1-879991-34-7**

Chapters from well-known experts in the field cover choosing, learning, and performing stories. Order this book from the National Storytelling Network at **www.storynet.org**.

Lipman, Doug. *Improving Your Storytelling: Beyond the Basics for All Who Tell Stories in Work or Play.* **August House, 1999. ISBN 978-0-87483-530-4**

A thoughtful analysis of more than how to tell a story, including how to find its MIT (Most Important Thing) and how to connect with the story in different ways, transferring imagery from the teller to the audience.

Lipman, Doug. *Storytelling Games: Creative Activities for Language, Communication, and Composition Across the Curriculum.* **Oryx, 1994. ISBN 978-0-89774-848-3**

Descriptions of and step-by-step instructions on how to play more than 40 games for children in kindergarten to high school, along with a Game-finder index and a subject index.

Livo, Norma J. *Bringing Out Their Best: Values Education and Character Development Through Traditional Tales.* **Libraries Unlimited, 2003. ISBN 978-1-56308-934-3**

More than 60 tales from around the globe, sorted by values characteristics into 12 sections including love, perseverance, fairness, and cooperation, plus suggestions for activities and discussions

Livo, Norma J., and Sandra A. Rietz. *Storytelling Folklore Sourcebook.* **Libraries Unlimited, 2001. ISBN 978-0-87287-601-9**

A compendium of world folktales, poetry, aphorisms, songs, dances, games, riddles, proverbs, superstitions, customs, and legends, and ideas for using them with upper elementary and secondary students

Livo, Norma J., and Sandra A. Rietz. *Storytelling: Process and Practice.* **Libraries Unlimited, 1986. ISBN 978-0-87287-443-5**

Practical and comprehensive guidance through every aspect of the art.

MacDonald, Margaret Read. *Celebrate the World: Twenty Tellable Folktales for Multicultural Festivals.* **Illus. by Roxane Murphy Smith. H. W. Wilson, 1994. ISBN 978-0-8242-0862-2**

A treasure trove of easy-to-learn stories set in ethnopoetic format, to go along with less well known holidays such as Chinese New Year and Diwali in India. Each tale includes notes describing its background and tips for delivery, comparative notes of similar stories, and suggestions for celebrating each holiday.

MacDonald, Margaret Read. *Look Back and See: Twenty Lively Tales for Gentle Tellers.* **Illus. by Roxane Murphy. H. W. Wilson, 1991. ISBN 978-0-8242-0810-3**

Participation stories from around the globe, many with songs or chantable refrains, with the text laid out in free verse to ensure easy mastery of each tale's natural phrasing, appropriate rhythm, and emphasis.

MacDonald, Margaret Read. *A Parent's Guide to Storytelling: How to Make Up New Stories and Retell Old Favorites.* **HarperCollins, 1995. ISBN 978-0-06-446180-1**

Lots of tips for parents, and lots of stories for them to try, categorized as favorite nursery tales, fingerplay stories, bedtime stories, expandable stories, endless tales, participation folktales, scary stories, and family stories.

MacDonald, Margaret Read. *Shake-It-Up Tales!: Stories to Sing, Dance, Drum, and Act Out.* **August House, 2000. ISBN 978-0-87483-590-8**

Twenty multicultural audience participation tales with tips and source notes.

MacDonald, Margaret Read. *The Storyteller's Start-Up Book: Finding, Learning, Performing and Using Folktales.* **August House, 1993. ISBN 978-0-87483-305-8**

What you need to know to jump into storytelling, along with 12 tales, performance tips, and source notes.

MacDonald, Margaret Read. *Tell the World: Storytelling Across Language Barriers.* **Libraries Unlimited, 2007. ISBN 978-1-59158-314-1**

How to tell stories to listeners who speak little or no English, with and without translation, covering techniques for bilingual storytelling including summarizing, line-by-line translation, and tandem telling.

MacDonald, Margaret Read. *Three-Minute Tales: Stories from Around the World to Tell or Read When Time Is Short.* **August House, 2004. ISBN 978-0-87483-728-5**

More than 70 quick stories to learn and tell, sorted by types—scary, humorous, chants, riddles—and including source notes and tips for telling.

MacDonald, Margaret Read. *Twenty Tellable Tales: Audience Participation Folktales for the Beginning Storyteller.* **Illus. by Roxane Murphy. H. W. Wilson, 1986. ISBN 978-0-8242-0719-9**

Step-by-step, for people who are afraid to tell stories.

MacDonald, Margaret Read. *When the Lights Go Out: Twenty Scary Stories to Tell.* **Illus. by Roxane Murphy. H. W. Wilson, 1988. ISBN 978-0-8242-0770-0**

Includes extensive notes on how to tell, sources, and variants for each tale.

MacDonald, Margaret Read, and Brian W. Sturm. *The Storyteller's Sourcebook: A Subject, Title, and Motif Index to Folklore Collections for Children, 1983-1999.* **Gale, 2001. ISBN 978-0-8103-5485-2**

An index to 210 folktale collections and 790 picture books, published between 1983 and 1999, by subject, tale title, geographic/ethnic origin, and tale motif. For each story, there's also a plot description. You'll also want, for your reference shelf, the first edition of this essential resource, published in 1982.

Mooney, Bill, and David Holt. *The Storyteller's Guide: Storytellers Share Advice for the Classroom, Boardroom, Showroom, Podium, Pulpit and Center Stage.* **August House, 1996. ISBN 978-0-87483-482-6**

Utterly practical guidance from top professional storytellers.

Norfolk, Sherry, Jane Stenson, and Diane Williams. *The Storytelling Classroom: Applications Across the Curriculum.* **Libraries Unlimited, 2006. ISBN 978-1-59158-305-9**

Essays by storytellers and teachers about using storytelling to teach language arts, social studies, math, and science, plus lesson plans linked to National Standards.

Pellowski, Anne. *Drawing Stories from Around the World and a Sampling of European Handkerchief Stories.* **Libraries Unlimited, 2005. ISBN 978-1-59158-222-9**

Get your children drawing along with you with 40 ingenious and easy-to-tell stories from Japan, China, Alaska, and more.

Pellowski, Anne. *The Family Storytelling Handbook: How to Use Stories, Anecdotes, Rhymes, Handkerchiefs, Paper and Other Objects to Enrich Your Family Traditions.* **Illus. by Lynn Sweat. Macmillan, 1987. ISBN 978-0-02-770610-9**

A gem that parents and all other storytellers will treasure.

Pellowski, Anne. *The Storytelling Vine: A Source Book of Unusual and Easy-to-Tell Stories from Around the World.* **Illus. by Lynn Sweat. Macmillan, 1984. ISBN 978-0-02-770590-4**

Indispensable "gimmicks," with instructions for string, picture-drawing, sand, doll, fingerplay, and musical instrument stories.

Rubright, Lynn. *Beyond the Beanstalk: Interdisciplinary Learning Through Storytelling.* **Heinemann Drama, 1996. ISBN 978-0-43-507028-1**

Practical ideas, activities, stories, and drama games to use across the curriculum with children in grades K-8.

Rydell, Katy, ed. *A Beginner's Guide to Storytelling.* **National Storytelling Press, 2003. ISBN 978-1-879991-32-3**

A pocket guide to everything you need to know, with advice from some of the leaders in the field.

Sawyer, Ruth. *The Way of the Storyteller.* **Rev. ed. Viking Penguin, 1977. ISBN 978-0-14-004436-2**

Engrossing commentary on the art by a famous American storyteller, with a sampling of her favorite tales.

Schimmel, Nancy. *Just Enough to Make a Story: A Sourcebook for Telling.* **2nd. ed. Sisters Choice Press, 1992. ISBN 978-0-932164-03-2**

Practical, down-to-earth advice, and an assortment of good stories to tell.

Sierra, Judy. *Oryx Multicultural Folktale Series: Cinderella.* **Illus. by Joanne Caroselli. Oryx, 1992. ISBN 0-89774-727-5**

Examines and compares the texts of 25 more versions of the same basic Cinderella story from many different cultures. Others in series include *A Knock at the Door* by George Shannon (1992), *Tom Thumb* by Margaret Read MacDonald (1993), and *Beauties & Beasts* by Betsy Hearne (1993).

Sierra, Judy, and Robert Kaminski. *Multicultural Folktales: Stories to Tell Young Children.* **Oryx, 1991. ISBN 978-0-89774-688-5**

25 easy-to-tell tales from around the globe for children ages 2 to 7, including tips for tellers, suggestions of other story tie-ins, and patterns for making simple flannel board figures or puppets.

Sierra, Judy, and Robert Kaminski. *Twice Upon a Time: Stories to Tell, Retell, Act Out, and Write About.* **H. W. Wilson, 1989. ISBN 978-0-8242-0775-5**

In addition to the texts of 21 easy-to-learn folktales are tips for telling and suggestions for related creative drama and writing activities.

Sima, Judy, and Kevin Cordi. *Raising Voices: Creating Youth Storytelling Groups and Troupes.* **Libraries Unlimited, 2003. ISBN 978-1-56308-919-0**

Practical techniques for children as storytellers.

Strauss, Kevin. *Tales with Tails: Storytelling the Wonders of the Natural World.* **Libraries Unlimited, 2006. ISBN 978-1-59158-269-4**

Along with activities and information about environmental concepts, integrate storytelling into your elementary or middle school science curriculum with the more than 60 tellable international tales about animals and the natural world.

Wolf, Joan M. *The Beanstalk and Beyond: Developing Critical Thinking Through Fairy Tales.* **Teacher Ideas Press, 1997. ISBN 978-1-56308-482-9**

Provides creative and useful activities and motivators to analyze characterization, perspective, and point of view using well-known fairy tales, and strategies for writing new ones.

Yolen, Jane. *Favorite Folktales from Around the World.* **Pantheon, 1986. ISBN 978-0-394-75188-7**

An intelligent assortment of tellable stories, grouped by types of tales and characters.

Yolen, Jane. *Touch Magic: Fantasy, Faerie and Folklore in the Literature of Childhood.* **Philomel, 1981. ISBN 978-0-399-20830-0**

Lyrical essays on the art and artistry of storytelling.

Ziskind, Sylvia. *Telling Stories to Children.* **H. W. Wilson, 1976. ISBN 978-0-8242-0588-1**

The chapter on "Mastering Technique" should be required reading for beginning storytellers.

Folklore and Storytelling Websites

New Jersey storyteller, Carol Titus, who provided some of the links on this list, says, "These sites shift and change like the sands and this is in no way a definitive list. Put 'storytelling' in as a subject on your favorite search engine and the sea of story will wash over you. Surfing them will turn up lots of shiny pebbles, interesting shells and some buried treasure. Happy hunting and when you find a good story, catch it and cast it adrift again for others to hear and ponder."

AARON SHEPARD.COM (http://aaronshep.com/rt/)

Check out author Aaron Shepard's amazing website, download one of his many fine Reader's Theater scripts, or get in touch with him to book him for a workshop at your school.

AESOP'S FABLES (www.aesopsfables.com)

Contains all 655 of Aesop's fables,—indexed in table format—with morals listed, illustrations, lesson plan links, and Real Audio narrations.

ANDREW LANG'S FAIRY BOOKS (www.mythfolklore.net/andrewlang/)

A fabulous resource! Find the full text of every story in Andrew Lang's 13 *Fairy Books*, first published in the late-19th century. Access the stories by book, title, or place of origin.

DRAWANDTELL.COM (www.drawandtell.com)

Richard Thompson, writer and storyteller from Canada, has posted more than a dozen of his own original draw-and-tell stories, wordplay, and general fun and resources for, as he says, "parents, grandparents, teachers, storytellers and other grown-ups to use with children."

FOLKLORE AND MYTHOLOGY ELECTRONIC TEXTS
(www.pitt.edu/~dash/folktexts.html)

Texts and commentary on thousands of stories, arranged by themes, motifs, and, story titles; compiled by D. L. Ashliman, a retired professor from the University of Pittsburgh.

INTERNATIONAL STORYTELLING CENTER (www.storytellingfoundation.net)

Website of the International Storytelling Center in Jonesboro, TN, "dedicated to building a better world through the power of storytelling," and a sponsor of the National Storytelling Festival in Jonesboro every October.

KIDIDDLES (www.kididdles.com)

Find the lyrics to thousands of children's songs, and playable music for lots of them.

LEGENDS (www.bestoflegends.org)

A comprehensive site providing "guided access to primary source material and up-to-date scholarship; personal essays and extended reviews." Includes texts of *King Arthur*, *Robin Hood*, and Andrew Lang's *Fairy Books* series.

MIMI'S MOTIFS (www.mimismotifs.com)

Fabulous source for storytelling dolls and puppets that tie into children's books and stories.

STORYARTS (www.storyarts.org)

Useful site from Heather Forest, the well-known storyteller and writer, with loads of stories to download, as well as telling techniques, ideas, lesson plans, and activities.

STORY-LOVERS.COM (www.story-lovers.com)

Comprehensive free archival library for finding thousands of stories, sources, and advice from professional storytellers.

STORYNET (www.storynet.org)

Website of the National Storytelling Association (NSA); provides a U.S. calendar of events and links to resources for storytelling.

STORYTELL (www.twu.edu/cope/slis/storytell.htm)

A forum for discussion about storytelling sponsored by the School of Library and Information Studies at Texas Woman's University in Denton, Texas; home page contains all info on how to subscribe to the listserv STORYTELL.

STORYTELLING ARTS OF INDIANA (www.storytellingarts.org)

Teaching guides, games, activities, and resources.

SURLALUNE FAIRY TALE PAGES (www.surlalunefairytales.com)

Annotated texts of 35 well-known fairy tales, with detailed analysis of illustrations, history, variants, and modern interpretations of each.

TALES OF WONDER (www.darsie.net/talesofwonder)

An archive of more than 100 folktales from Africa, Asia, and Europe, plus a selection of Native American stories.

TURNER LEARNING NETWORK (www.turnerlearning.com/turnersouth/storytelling/index.html)

An "Educator's Guide to Learning Through Storytelling" includes resources, a how-to list for beginners, and practical lesson plans for teaching children how to be storytellers.

Getting Started With Creative Drama and Reader's Theater

Revised, expanded, rewritten, and adapted in part from chapters in Judy Freeman's *Books Kids will Sit Still For* (Libraries Unlimited, 1990), *More Books Kids will Sit Still For* (1995), and *Books Kids will Sit Still For 3* (2006) and from the NoveList article, "Book Performance Art: Using Reader's Theater and Creative Drama with Young Readers" by Judy Freeman. Reprinted with permission, NoveList/EBSCO, copyright 2007. (The original version appeared in NoveList in February, 2007.)

Teachers and librarians are always searching for new and innovative ways to get children reading with comprehension, expression, confidence, and fluency. Like Ponce de Leon in his fruitless search for the Fountain of Youth, we're always on the prowl for that magic bullet that will erase all of our children's reading problems. After you've been in the business a while, you realize there isn't any one-shot solution. Teaching is an art, with some elements of science, and there's no one way to do it "right." There are great tools we can add to our arsenals, however, and drama is one of them.

When children read, they make pictures in their heads and connect personally to the text. When we read aloud or tell stories to children, our voices resonate in their heads as the story's dialogue comes to life. But when children act out a story themselves, they hear it, they see it, and they live it. They become the story. They know how a character feels from the inside out, since they've been in that character's skin for a little while. Children love to act out stories. Often even the shyest children will shine when they get a chance to play another character.

What's so welcome about using the dramatic arts is you don't need expensive equipment—or any equipment at all. When you read or tell a good story to your eager listeners and then announce, "Now let's act it out," they'll cheer. Perhaps they think they're sidestepping real work for a while and pulling one over on you. In reality, they're working hard through play, putting their public speaking skills into practice, overcoming shyness, interpreting the thoughts and motivations of characters, mastering challenging vocabulary, and using language in a fluid and interesting way. And, most important of all, they're discovering how much joy there is in reading.

For a fictional but believable example of the transformative effects of drama and theater, share Aliki's picture book, *A Play's the Thing* (HarperCollins, 2005). Enthusiastic teacher Miss Brilliant celebrates the end of testing by having her class write, practice, and perform an original play based on the nursery rhyme, "Mary Had a Little Lamb." Even José, whose constant disruptive behavior annoys everyone in class, gets into the swing of it when he reluctantly accepts the part of the teacher in the play

189

and discovers himself enjoying his new role. The cheerful, bordered, watercolor pictures, arranged in panels, are filled with the students' balloon dialogue as they rehearse, create scenery, and finally perform for an enthusiastic audience of family members and friends.

With creative drama, you act out a story by recalling its plot and dialogue. Creative drama is wonderful for retelling the sequence of a story, interacting with other story characters, and bringing a story to life through creativity, imagination, and improvisation. Reader's Theater incorporates elements of creative drama, but adds a proscribed play script to follow, and helps children develop as readers. Both are adored by children of all ages, and both foster a love and appreciation of language and literature. Both should have a regular presence in all classroom, school library, and public library programs.

USING CREATIVE DRAMA

All the comprehension skills booklets in the world won't help students fathom cause and effect the way acting out a story will. Using creative drama to extend a story allows children to develop new criteria for interpreting characters and understanding their actions, and gain intuitive knowledge of story structure and plot. As a group activity, creative drama provides children with the freedom to try out ideas without fear of ridicule.

Narrative Pantomime

Narrative pantomime—where you narrate the events from a story, either word-for-word or self-edited to fit the situation, while the actors put it into motion—is the easiest technique to direct and perform. Look for a story or episode with scads of action, a simple plot, and little or no dialogue.

Narrative pantomime can mean acting out images as basic as eating an apple or a drippy ice cream cone, preening your feathers and fanning out your tail as peacocks, or playing a short piece on an invisible piano. Impromptu mini-pantomimes like these keep listeners alert and involved, and can be a nice way to stretch and relax after a test or a tough morning.

With young children, nursery rhymes and fingerplays are natural choices for drama. Mother Goose is bursting with possibilities. As Little Jack Horner, we hold onto our Christmas pies, stick in our thumbs, pull out our plums and chomp them right down. As Jack-Be-Nimble, we jump over our invisible candlesticks. "Humpty Dumpty" can be done as a group, with half comprising the giant tottering egg and the other half the soldiers who gamely try to piece the shell together. For "Little Miss Muffet," break into pairs: Miss Muffet versus the spider. Each time the spider sits beside her and scares her away, change roles so the spider now becomes Miss Muffet, spooning up her mush.

While you may feel self-conscious and unsure the first time you lead your crew in a narrative pantomime, these feelings will soon flee when you note the actors' ecstatic faces and hear them exclaim, "Let's do it again."

After reading a story aloud, you can usually complete a narrative pantomime tour de force in less than ten minutes. More complex productions take longer, but if you start out simply, you will find the activities easy to complete successfully.

KITTEN'S FIRST FULL MOON

Some books are tailor made for narrative pantomime and can be read aloud with few changes, like Kevin Henkes's Caldecott Medal winner, *Kitten's First Full Moon* (HarperCollins, 2005). Kitten sees a little bowl of milk in the sky, and she races after it, climbs a tree, and even jumps into the pond where the moon is reflected. After reading the book aloud, children can act out the kitten's saga as you narrate it. You can hold up the book so actors can keep an eye on the pictures as you recite the story. What's nice about this one is the quiet ending where the kitten drinks her milk and settles down to sleep.

BAD KITTY

But not every kitten is so placid. I read Nick Bruel's alphabet book *Bad Kitty* (Roaring Brook, 2005) to several kindergarten classes at Adamsville School in Bridgewater, New Jersey. Afterwards, we jumped into action with a bit of narrative pantomime. The kindergartners were eager to play the part of that black kitty who comes unglued because there's no good food left in the house. There are four alliterative alphabets in this innovative picture book, and two of them—of the kitty being bad, and then the kitty being good—are custom made for creative drama.

When I ask grown-ups to stand up and act out a scene like this during one of my children's literature workshops, some of them look like they'd rather clean latrines. It's so public, acting out stories. Everyone can see how silly you look. As we get older and crankier, it's harder for us to act silly. It's not that I want teachers to feel uncomfortable, but to put themselves in their children's places and try something a bit different to bring literature alive. Lucky for us, we work with children who help keep us young. When you tell them it's time to act something out, they're on their feet, ready to go.

I said to the kindergartners, "OK, everyone, you are now going to be the Bad Kitty. Find yourself a space where no one is in your way, and let's do everything the kitty did."

Usually, when you act out a story like this in unison, with all of the children playing the same character, you have them do it without talking, like a silent movie. This is partly so they'll focus on the action and listen for clues as you reread the story aloud, and partly to save your sanity. If you'd like them to chant along or include sound effects, let them know. You are the director, and as such, must set the sights for each presentation. In this case, I wickedly encouraged them to add feline sound effects, and they didn't let me down.

The bad kitty . . . "ate my homework, bit grandma, clawed the curtains, damaged the dishes, hurled hairballs at our heads . . ." As I read aloud each scenario in the alphabet, the bad kitties leaped and yowled and hacked (hairballs, that is). You don't have to own a cat to play one in class.

Yes, you can read that story aloud to children and they will love it, but if you really want it to stick, try a little bit of drama. Based on my own observations, I believe children have better recall and understanding of the stories they act out.

"Now," I said, "let's see how much of the kitty's behavior you can recall." Remember, we had read the book only once and then acted it out once. And yet, they were able to recite, from memory, most of the actions in sequence. Because they had acted out the whole alphabet, their bodies had internalized each scene; as they recalled each letter, you could see them assuming their different poses as they came up with each phrase.

Afterwards the children in Miss Tricarico's kindergarten collaborated on, wrote, and illustrated a fabulous new book, inspired by Nick Bruel's. They called it "Bad Kiddies," about how they used to be good kiddies, and what went wrong, and then right, alphabetically speaking, in their classroom.

Behavior Guidelines

What about that story *Bad Kitty*? Does acting out a story like that rile children up and make them wild? Not if you set some parameters. Go over the rules, such as not touching anyone else, and ask them to think how they might pantomime the parts where the cat is "Violent with the vet." Ask for two volunteers to demonstrate their solutions, so all can see the difference between doing and acting or pretending to do so. By working out potential problems in advance, you minimize the chances of children becoming overzealous or attempting a headstand.

If a child touches or pokes or annoys another child while acting, let him know he is acting inappropriately, and lead him to a time out chair until he's ready to rejoin the group. Enforce this in a kind, non-threatening way, without letting yourself appear annoyed or upset, by calmly leading the child over to the designated chair and saying quietly, "Josh, when you do that it spoils the magic for the rest of us.

Take some time to think about what you should be doing, and when you're ready to join in again, come back to the group."

Children want to do this activity; they don't want to sit and watch, which gives them good incentive to act instead of act out. They usually simmer down fast after being spectators for a spell.

Set up behavior guidelines for your students; when you clap your hands, bang a drum, or say "Freeze," all children are to stop instantly and listen for directions. Practice that with them so they know what to expect. Go over any other rules, such as not interfering with anyone else or not crawling under tables or chairs. Before you begin, have students space themselves so they are not within touching distance of other children.

Editing is essential in narrative pantomime to speed up the action so children are not standing around pondering their next moves. You will find that most children will be unself-conscious once they get involved and realize that no one is scrutinizing their actions for mistakes or to criticize. Each person becomes too wrapped up in the story to take notice of anyone else. When editing a story—which you do as you are reading it aloud for the pantomime—omit or paraphrase the talky sections, condense the time span if necessary, and cut or add description to make the action flow logically and sequentially.

If the children are enthusiastic after you've acted out a story, run through it again. It's a good idea to offer them positive suggestions for improvement—no personal comments, just some new ideas on which to focus. For example, "This time, when we get to the final alphabet, imagine that you are very, very, sorry for your bad behavior and you want to make up for it." After your encouragement, the next time you act out the scene, the students will take their roles more seriously. Usually, little character development occurs in simple narrative pantomime; it's only a literal interpretation of a story. Yet after you finish, you will find that your children have a sharper sense of setting and sequence, and can imbue main characters with personality.

While most children are raring to go whenever you undertake a new dramatic scene, sometimes a child or two will balk and be reluctant to take part. They may be scared, shy, cynical, or looking for extra attention. Again, keep your response low-key. Allow them to watch, but suggest that they feel free to join in at any time. If a child chooses to stay seated, encourage him or her to pantomime along with the group. A child in a wheelchair will be able to participate in this way, too, as one can be just as expressive with the hands and head as with the entire body.

KNUFFLE BUNNY

You can act out whole books, of course, but also keep a lookout for simple scenes. You can be in the middle of a story and say, "This part is just so perfect. Let's stop and act it out."

Reading aloud *Knuffle Bunny* by Mo Willems (Hyperion, 2004)? When you get to the scene where toddler Trixie knows her stuffed bunny is in the washing machine at the laundromat but Daddy doesn't understand her anguished babble, you can have your listeners act it out. "She went boneless," the text says, as Trixie goes into meltdown mode. Your listeners can stand up and go boneless, too. That's a 10-second example of doing creative drama in the middle of a story, and it can be quite effective in involving listeners. Then sit down and resume the story

TOOTH-GNASHER SUPERFLASH

Sometimes a simple follow-up drama activity extends the story. Daniel Pinkwater's inspired picture book *Tooth-Gnasher Superflash* (Macmillan, 1990) is a longtime favorite of mine. Accompanied by nervous car salesman Mr. Sandy, Mrs. Popsnorkle, and the five little Popsnorkles, Mr. Popsnorkle test-drives the flashy new car and finds, to his great satisfaction, that every time he pushes a different button on the dashboard, the car turns into a dinosaur, an elephant, a turtle, or a giant flying chicken.

After you finish reading the story aloud, rev up your engines and take your listeners on a test drive. Remind your drivers to be very careful not to touch anyone else's car. Practice stopping at red lights, using turn signals and beeping the horn.

Then you can say, "Oh, look at this nice blue button. Let's push it. Oh, my! The car is turning into an ELEPHANT!" Children will lumber about, until you have them push another button. Each time you discover a new color button on the dashboard, push it and announce what the vehicle will become. Start out with the animals in the story, then throw in a few exotic ones like a snake or a kangaroo, or a whale. Ending up with the flying chicken, swoop back to the car dealer, park, and turn off your engines. This is great fun for everyone and you will laugh and laugh.

STRAIGHT TO THE POLE

Be dramatic with your choices of books. Look for great emotion and tension, even for the youngest actors. Kevin O'Malley's *Straight to the Pole* (Walker, 2003) fills the bill, even though it's the simplest of picture books. A child, so overdressed in cold weather gear only his (or her; you can't really tell) eyes are showing, presses on alone through the raging snow, slipping, falling, trudging upward. The storm is getting worse.

"I told Mom this would happen," he moans. Just then, up bounds a WOLF! "Won't somebody save me," the child cries piteously. Well, okay, it's really his little brown dog, tail wagging.

"But wait, in the distance, A RESCUE." It's the boy's friends who tell him that school has been closed for the day. Leaving his backpack at the bus stop, he runs off to go sledding. Whew. Crisis over.

The story starts and ends on the endpapers, and the blue, purple and white watercolors will make you feel cold. Sure, you can have your listeners describe what was really happening in the story, but how much more fun and evocative it is when you have them act out the child's perceived adventure in narrative pantomime. Afterwards, they can talk or write about or act out a time they were really cold. Or hot. Or wet.

WALK ON!

I read Marla Frazee's *Walk On!: A Guide for Babies of All Ages* (Harcourt, 2006) to Maren Vitali's second grade class at Van Holten School in Bridgewater, New Jersey. It starts with the omniscient narrator asking, "Is sitting there on your bottom getting boring? Has lying around all the time become entirely unacceptable? It is time to learn how to walk!"

On the page, the bald, round-headed pre-toddler in blue diaper-cover and yellow booties is taking in every word. With the narrator's careful coaching, the baby stands, holds on, sways, falls, cries, and tries again until, "Baby, you are walking! Beautiful."

"OK, babies," I said to the class after we finished, "let's see how hard it is to learn how to walk."

With that, we launched back into the story, and they became the babies. How fun it is to act like a baby when you aren't one anymore. After you do this, ask your children what they remember about being really little. The floodgates will open. Ask them what difficult skill they would like to master this year and how they plan to do it. *Walk On!* is a metaphor for all of the challenges we meet in our lives, and as such is certainly a book for all ages.

THE MONSTER'S RING

When you read aloud fiction books or booktalk fiction to older children, keep your eyes peeled for descriptive scenes that your students can act out. This provides an interesting interlude in your reading, and helps them visualize a graphic scene.

Monster-loving middle graders will appreciate Russell's plight when his magic ring causes him to become a heinous fang-filled monster one full-mooned Halloween. In chapter two of Bruce Coville's *The Monster's Ring* (Harcourt, 2002), read aloud the description of Russell's transformation while your listeners act it out. First, horns break through his forehead, then hair sprouts on his face and hands, and his fingernails become sharp claws. Children would enjoy drawing a double self-portrait of before and after.

Pairs Pantomime

Narrative pantomime need not always be a solo venture, with all children playing the same part. Children can also work in pairs or groups, depending on the story to be performed. Pairs pantomime is especially satisfying since actors can switch roles the second go-round and experience two characters for the price of one.

For pairs pantomime, look for stories with dynamic duos: James Marshall's "George and Martha" or Arnold Lobel's "Frog and Toad" tales are ideal candidates.

Mirror Exercises

Most children love to to do mirror exercises. Remember how Pooh Bear did his stretching exercises before the mirror each morning in A. A. Milne's *Winnie-the-Pooh*? One child can be Pooh, and the other, the mirrored image. If you can get copies to show, both the Marx Brothers' movie *Duck Soup* and the *I Love Lucy* episode with Lucy and Harpo have hilarious scenes where two identically-costumed characters meet unexpectedly, and mirror each other's actions.

First, demonstrate the activity by having the whole group mirror you. Next, ask partners to face each other; as one child begins to move, the partner must attempt to mirror each action. Start out slowly, then have everyone speed up a bit. Now switch so the follower becomes the leader. When the children get the hang of it, announce that neither one is to be the leader, but they must mirror each other and keep moving regardless. The role of leader thus passes back and forth between each twosome in an unspoken exchange of power. Try it yourself—it's trickier than it looks.

THE GUNNIWOLF

One of my favorites has always been Wilhelmina Harper's "Little Red Riding Hood" variant, *The Gunniwolf* (Dutton, 2003), a story I like to tell and act out with kindergarten and first grade. Little Girl promises her mother she won't go near the jungle, but, of course, there wouldn't be much of a story if she didn't disobey. She sets off, picking flowers and singing, until she's deep in the jungle. Up rises the *Gunniwolf*! What is a gunniwolf, exactly? Children figure he's a wolf with a gun, though there's no gun in the story. It's a reasonable assumption, though.

"Little girl, why for you move?" the Gunniwolf asks the terrified child.

"I no move," she says, trembling.

"Then you sing that guten sweeten song again," he orders, and she sings until he falls asleep. Then she makes a run for it ("Pit pat, pit pat."), but he comes after her ("Hunker-cha, hunker-cha.").

Don't worry—she ultimately makes it home safely, but she's surely learned her lesson about disobeying her mother. Children love to assist in the refrains of this cautionary tale as you tell or read it.

When you finish, pair up your group. One child will be the little girl (or little boy); the other the Gunniwolf. Have them act out the scenes in the jungle, adding the singing and the snoring and the chasing. Then pairs can switch parts and do it again.

Group Pantomime

Once you've tried solo and pairs pantomime, the next logical step is group pantomime, where the class works together to act out a story with a large cast. This is the simplest sort of group story to act out because children do not need to add dialogue, and you provide the sequence in your narration.

"THE TURNIP"

If you're telling the folktale "The Turnip," or any of those "they pulled and they pulled but they could not pull it up" types of stories, such as Michael Bania's *Kumak's Fish: A Tall Tale from the Far North* (Alaska Northwest, 2004), Jan Peck's *The Giant Carrot* (Dial, 1998), or Erica Silverman's *Big Pumpkin* (Macmillan, 1992), ask for volunteers to play the root vegetable, the old man, the old woman, their granddaughter, the dog, the cat and the mouse. Cast more than one child for each role if necessary, so that everyone has a part. Warm up by having all the children pretend they are turnips, sown from seeds, leaves peeking above the earth, and slowly growing toward the sun. Pretend to pull on their leaves so they lean precariously but stay embedded in the soil. Then, have them assume their places and begin the whole story for the group to act out.

Adding Sound

Sometimes a segment of a story or novel is appropriate for a sound effects interlude. Incorporate noises into your stories by asking the audience to join in. Narrative pantomime is usually silent because children must listen carefully for the various clues to their next actions. In many stories, though, children need to use their voices as well to mimic the sounds that enrich the telling. Children who are read to regularly know just when to join in, and are eager to do so. Think of the scene in Robert McCloskey's *Make Way for Ducklings* (Viking, 1941) where the ducklings, on their way into the Public Garden, tie up Boston street traffic. Cars honk, ducks quack.

For a sound exercise all ages enjoy, try the "Rainstorm" activity on page 56.

I STINK

Your group can also work together to form a unit, as in the picture book *I Stink* by Kate McMullan (HarperCollins, 2002), a personal narrative from the point of view of a New York City garbage truck. Jim McMullan's thick black-outlined watercolors are evocative of the eau de garbage. That truck's got quite an expressive mug, by turns grinning, scowling, and looking tough. And the monologue is crammed with actable moments—BUUURP!

Have students perform the pick up and roll and all the different functions of a garbage truck. With you in charge of the "controls," have your "machines" speed up or slow down, and request accompanying sound effects for each function.

Afterwards, your kids can list all the machines and vehicles they know and love, draw pictures of them with faces, and act out a monologue, telling the rest of the crew what they do. Think of it: airplanes, toasters, canoes—the possibilities are uproarious. For older kids, this is a sublime look at personification and personal narrative that demonstrates how voice can drive a story.

PEACE AT LAST

A slapstick story like Jill Murphy's *Peace at Last* (Dial, 1980) would fall flat if the listeners didn't join in on all the snoring, ticking, dripping and tweeting noises that keep Mr. Bear from getting his forty winks. After I read the story to one first grade class, we recorded a cassette tape of the sound effects in sequence. We all love/hate to hear ourselves on tape because our voices come out so different from the way we hear them ourselves. Children are fascinated with identifying their own recorded voices, and the actors listened very carefully to directions so their output would be a success.

First we discussed the sequence of the noises and practiced how a dripping faucet or ticking clock might sound. I purposely did not add my own interpretations so the children would feel free to devise their own sounds. After a short rehearsal, we taped in sequence, pushing the "pause" button after each noise. When we finished taping, we acted out the complete story in pantomime, with each child playing the part of Mr. Bear who goes from place to place inside and outside his house, trying desperately to find a quiet spot to sleep. As each noise came up in the story, I switched on our tape so we could hear it, after which the multitude of bears exclaimed Mr. Bear's repeated refrain of, "Oh, NO! I can't stand THIS."

Repetitive Dialogue

"Peanut butter, peanut butter,
Jelly, Jelly"

That's the repeated refrain from Nadine Bernard Westcott's elephant-filled version of the chant, *Peanut Butter and Jelly; a Play-Rhyme* (Dutton, 1987), a kitchen-bound cousin to the myriad tellings of "I'm Going on a Bear Hunt," where the audience copycats your every word and movement. (Find another version of the Peanut Butter and Jelly chant to try with your kids in the songbook section on page 44 and "We're Going on a Lion Hunt" on page 65.)

Children thrive on helping out with a story when there is a refrain to chant. Acting out a tale with much repetitive dialogue is an icebreaker for shy children as they don't need to worry about what to say. Lines are repeated often and are easy to recall. While reading aloud or telling stories such as Jim Aylesworth's *Aunt Pitty Patty's Piggy* (Scholastic, 1999) or Linda Williams's *The Little Old Lady Who Was Not Afraid of Anything* (Crowell, 1986), children will be eager to join in on all the chantable refrains, sound effects and body motions.

Cumulative sequence stories are a good choice to use with younger children who enjoy the linear structure of cause and effect. *Aunt Pitty Patty's Piggy*, with its appealing pen and ink and watercolors, is set in New England, but it is based on an old English folktale. Paul Galdone's picture book version of the original tale, The *Old Woman and Her Pig* (McGraw-Hill, 1960), is one I have always loved to tell.

"Pig, pig, jump over the stile, or I shan't get home tonight," the Old Woman implores, but the stubborn pig says, "I WON'T!" Telling the story is interactive in and of itself. I have found that kindergartners have no trouble remembering and reciting the entire final sequence in which the cat begins to kill the mouse who starts to gnaw the rope that attempts to tie the butcher who starts to kill the ox who commences drinking the water that tries to quench the fire that begins to burn the stick that beats the dog who bites the pig who finally jumps over the stile so the old woman can get home that night.

Children also love chanting the rhythmic refrain in Aylesworth's humorous retelling, "Dog won't bite Aunt Pitty Patty's Piggy. It's gettin' late and piggy's by the gate sayin', 'No no no, I will not go.' "

Whichever version you choose, first have your children retell it. Then act out the whole story. To make sure everyone has a part, you can have more than one of each character. ("Who wants to be the pig? Okay, you three can all be the pigs. The old woman? Very good. We have two old women." And so on.) As they act out the story in sequence, with you narrating as needed, each new character says, "I *won't*" and joins the line beside the stubborn pig until it stretches across your room. At the end of the story, when the cat begins to bite the rat, they will understand the concept of cause and effect firsthand.

These tales also work great as flannelboard stories, or with easy props and puppets the kids can use to act it out. Ask them to draw that final sequence of the story on long line strips of white paper, maybe 8" x 24" or 36". You'll be astonished to see how well they can recall all of the characters in action.

Here's an interesting aside, as we contemplate the folk process. "Chad Gadya" which in Aramaic means "one goat," is a folk song sung at the end of the Passover seder. The song can be traced back to fifteenth century Germany. The last verse will certainly seem familiar now:

Then came the Holy One, Blessed be He

And killed the angel of death

That killed the slaughterer

That killed the ox

That drank the water

That quenched the fire

That burned the stick

That beat the dog

That bit the cat

That ate the kid

That my father bought for two coins

One kid, one kid!

Character Dialogues

In many stories, two conflicting characters must solve a problem, and children can pair up to hammer out the solution. The purpose of this exercise is to argue out a problem where each person must listen and respond to the other partner.

DON'T LET THE PIGEON DRIVE THE BUS

When you read aloud Mo Willems's picture book, *Don't Let the Pigeon Drive the Bus* (Hyperion, 2003), something amazing happens. The children talk back to the book. The pigeon really wants to drive the bus, even though the bus driver has warned you not to let him do this. He looks out of the page at you and pleads, cajoles, demands, and whines. Each time, listeners respond, usually with a loud, "NO!" I've read this to preschoolers through fifth graders, and they all talk back to the book.

Teachers are always looking for a good book to use with persuasive writing assignments, and this one's my favorite. Not only can students write a persuasive letter to or from the Pigeon, they can also act out his whole argument. One child plays the Pigeon; the other plays him or herself. For children of all ages, a heated discussion will ensue as the Pigeon tries to persuade his partner to let him drive that bus. Will the Pigeon triumph? Will his opponent cave or stay strong?

After the children choose partners, allow them five minutes to conduct their arguments and settlements. Remind both sides to employ good reasons for their cases, and to listen to each other without screaming. The partner must respond to Pigeon one way or the other. ("No, you can't drive because you're not old enough.") So you don't truly know what the outcome will be. Once they begin, walk around the room and eavesdrop a bit. If you like, you can have them switch roles and do it again.

Afterwards, call the group back together and discuss how each pair's discussion went and what each outcome was.

Improvised Drama

Improvised drama depends on the talents of the actors to make the unscripted production smooth and believable. With Reader's Theater, a more structured drama variation, children are given or are asked to write their own scripts to act out a scene or a story. With pre-readers, of course, scripts are not an option. But even with older children, sometimes you read a story and decide it would be fun to act out the whole thing right then and there.

Of course, children do this on their own all the time. If given the chance for free play in the preschool classroom, children will spontaneously act out a story they've heard and liked. "You be the little girl and I'll be the frog!" they'll say, and then off they go.

To reap the benefits of more formal improvised drama activities, allow time for the discussion and planning that come before any actual acting. Have them retell the story so they have a good sense of the plot. Children will not respond well if you thrust them into an improvised drama without any prior experience to warm them up. Unlike narrative pantomime which is basically intuitive, improvising dialogue to reconstruct a story or scene is more complex. Actors must use reasoning skills, cooperate and interact intimately with their peers, respond to cues, recall a specific sequence, and make the scene become real using their ingenuity. Improvised dialogue is looser and less structured than a scripted play which stays the same each time. You can easily replay scenes as needed to work out rough spots, and develop characterization.

Children won't necessarily recall every line of dialogue in a story, nor do they need to. They'll make it up as they go along, based on what they recall from the story you just read or told them. Discuss the importance of listening so everyone does not talk at the same time and the necessity of staying in character so the play does not turn into a free-for-all.

BARK, GEORGE

Jules Feiffer's *Bark, George* (HarperCollins, 1999) is one of the most perfect interactive picture books. A little brown dog named George tries to obey his mother but every time he tries to bark on her command, he meows, quacks, oinks, or moos instead. George's dismayed mother takes him to the vet.

"The vet reached deep down inside of George . . . And pulled out a cat." And then, in succession, the vet extracts a duck, a pig, and, finally—after reaching deep, deep, deep, deep, deep, deep, deep, deep, deep, deep, deep down—a cow.

Your littlest listeners will adore this book and join in with gusto, but you can also read it to older children, grades three to eight, to explore story structure—beginning, rising action, climax, falling action, conclusion—and to demonstrate the effects of a surprise or unexpected ending in a story.

There are seven roles in this story. To act this out with a large class, you could assign two to four children for each part. Or you could have a new George and a new mom and a new vet for each little scene. Or you could just perform the play two or three times, each time with a new cast. That way, children would get to be actors and audience. It's not a long story, so doing it three times is not unreasonable nor any less pleasurable.

"TRAVELS OF A FOX"

For primary grade children, cumulative folktales are a splendid source for creative drama. Folktales such as "The Gingerbread Boy" or "The Three Little Pigs" include whole sections that children know by heart. (Look on page 163 for a list of cumulative tales.) If they can tell the story with you, why not stage a simple production?

I have always loved telling kindergarten classes Joseph Jacobs's English folktale, "The Travels of a Fox."

It starts:

Once a fox was digging behind a stump when he unearthed a bumblebee. He put the bee in his sack, which he always carried with him, and traveled. At the first house he came to, he knocked on the door. The woman of the house answered it. "Yes?" she said.

"May I leave my bag here while I go to Squintums?" the fox asked.

198

"You may," she said. So the fox placed his bag in a corner. But before he left, he said, "Be careful not to open the bag."

And off he went. Well, as soon as that fellow left, the woman of the house got curious. "I wonder what that fellow has in his bag that he's so careful about. I shall have a look and see. It can't do any harm, for I shall tie it right back up again."

She unloosed the string, just to take a little peep. But as soon as she did, the bumblebee flew out of the bag, and the woman's rooster caught the bumblebee and ate it.

A little while later, the fox came back. He could see at once the bumblebee was not in the bag.

"Where's my bumblebee?" he asked.

"Oh," said the woman of the house. "I unloosed the string, just to take a little peep, but as soon as I did, the bumblebee flew out and my rooster caught the bumblebee and ate it."

"Very well," said the fox, "I shall have to take the rooster, then."

He stuffed the rooster into his sack, tied it back up, slung it over his shoulder, and traveled.

At each house the fox visits, the woman gets curious. The fox ends up taking the pig that ate the rooster, the ox that gored the pig with its horns and killed it, and finally, the little boy that chased the ox across the meadow and clear out of sight.

Whenever I tell this story, and get to the line, "Very well. I shall have to take the LITTLE BOY, then." The children shiver and squeal. Luckily, that little boy escapes unscathed, thanks to the woman at the next house, who is baking a cake for her own children and who puts her fierce house dog in the sack. The fox thinks the little boy is still in the bag and sets off. He starts to feel hungry. He wonders how the little boy in the bag will taste.

And if the little boy had been in the bag, things would have gone badly with him. But the little boy was at the house of the woman who made the cake.

The original ending goes like this: "When the fox untied the bag the house-dog jumped out and killed him." Okay, that's a tad abrupt. Justified, perhaps, since the fox *was* planning to eat the little boy. But still, too quick. I always add this line: "And that was the last time *that* fox . . . ever . . . went to Squintums." It gives the story closure

I love the wonderfully evocative refrain, "May I leave my bag here while I go to Squintums?" What or where is Squintums, exactly? Perhaps you could tell me, because I haven't a clue. Each time I tell that story, however, I ask my listeners what or where they think it is. They've been living the story in their mind's eye while I told it, and many of them are quite definite in their responses. "It's his house." "It's a town." "It's a restaurant." "It's in the forest where all the other foxes live." And I love the response from one pragmatic child who said, "I don't think he really went anywhere. He was just waiting outside in the bushes for the lady to open his sack so he could take something else in his bag."

"The Travels of a Fox" is a satisfying story to tell, with lots of repeated refrains the children will chime in on as you go. Other retellings of the same tale, though long out of print, include Paul Galdone's *What's in Fox's Sack* (Clarion, 1982) and Jennifer Westwood's *Going to Squintum's: A Foxy Folktale* (Dial, 1985). You can find the story in collections of English folktales and even online. Jim Aylesworth's rollicking picture book version, *The Tale of Tricky Fox: A New England Trickster Tale* (Scholastic, 2001), harks back to a late-19th century version from Massachusetts.

What makes this a good candidate for improvised drama? The sequence is easy to recall, there are enough characters for everyone to have a part, and the dialogue is simple enough to either remember or invent.

How do you act out a longer story like this? The cast consists of one fox, five women (or men), one little boy (or girl), and five animals. The rest of the children can play the children waiting for cake. As you give out parts ("Who wants to be the bumblebee?") have the cast sit in one long row on the floor, or in a long semicircle of chairs, in the order of each character's appearance. Students move in and out of each scene as needed and sit back down in their given seats when their scenes are over.

Sometimes the use of a simple prop makes the story more immediate. Give the child playing the fox a long knitted scarf. The fox can tie it loosely around the necks of each successive creature he appropriates. Each animal can the walk closely behind the fox, then crouch in the corner, and leap out of the "bag" when the woman of the house unlooses the scarf. Though these parts are not speaking ones, children can certainly add dialogue for the bumblebee and the other animals.

The house dog is going to kill the fox at the end. You may want to have two children to demonstrate how to do this as acting, and not for real. Children know the difference; you just need to make sure they don't forget it and get carried away. Biting in the classroom or library is not something you care to encourage, even if it is in the story.

You may want to do some side-coaching, or narrating the story line, in between the dialogue. Side-coaching helps you keep the action flowing smoothly. Or you may want to have several children act as the narrators to announce what happens next.

Other good cumulative tales to act out include "Sody Sallyraytus" from Richard Chase's *Grandfather Tales* (Houghton Mifflin, 1948), Mirra Ginsburg's *The Clay Boy* (Greenwillow, 1997) and Meilo So's *Gobble, Gobble, Slip, Slop: The Tale of a Very Greedy Cat* (Knopf, 2004). Since all three are swallowing stories it would be interesting to compare and contrast them.

Since not every story has enough characters to go around, don't be afraid to assign two or more children to the same part or to have some children as spectators. Another alternative is to divide the class into groups so that each group can work on a different scene from one or more stories. Aesop's fables work wonderfully for all ages. Stellar collections like Michael Morpurgo's *The McElderry Book of Aesop's Fables* (McElderry, 2005) and Jerry Pinkney's *Aesop's Fables* (SeaStar, 2000) are perfect to use with small groups since they're complete stories with a beginning, middle, and end. They're also short, easy to recall, and entertaining. Arnold Lobel's original collection, *Fables* (HarperCollins, 1980), is also just right. Read a variety of the stories aloud, and then hand out a different story, photocopied, to each group. Each group can decide who will play each part and whether they want to use improvised dialogue to act it out, or rely on the text as a quasi-script. Walk around the room, dispensing advice and encouragement. Groups can rehearse for 10 minutes or so, and then act out their skits for the rest of the class.

PROBUDITI!

Chris Van Allsburg's *Probuditi!* (Houghton Mifflin, 2006) is a tale of sibling revenge, and as such, it would be satisfying for children in grades two to five to act out scenes between older brother Calvin and his wily little sister Trudy. For his birthday, Calvin and his best friend Rodney attend a performance by magician and hypnotist Lomax the Magnificent, where the great man hypnotizes a woman into thinking she's a chicken. He snaps her out of her clucking prance with the word "PROBUDITI!" (How do you pronounce that? It rhymes with "nudity.")

Back home, Calvin and his friend Rodney construct their own hypnotizing machine. "Want to be in an experiment?" they ask Trudy. She stares at the spinning disk. "You are a dog," Calvin proclaims. Lo and behold, she starts acting like one. It works! The trouble is, they can't snap her out of it. In pairs or trios (if you include Rodney), children can act out the second half of the book where the boys try to remember the word to turn Trudy back into herself again.

As with many of Van Allsburg's tales, this has a very funny twist ending, where Calvin discovers that his little sister is nobody's fool. The final scene where Trudy gives Calvin his well-deserved comeuppance is also satisfying to act out in pairs.

With some tinkering, you could write this up as a script for Reader's Theater. You could also do some improv with you as Lomax hypnotizing your group into thinking they are other animals. Have them think up and write down situations which you can read aloud and have them act out, on the order of: "You take a bite of chocolate ice cream. It is delicious. But wait! What's this? It's not chocolate ice cream at all! It's LIVER!"

GREGOR THE OVERLANDER

Look for scenes with dialogue and action, such as in the first two chapters of Suzanne Gregory's exciting underworld fantasy for grades four to seven, *Gregor the Overlander* (Scholastic, 2003) where Gregor's two-year-old sister, Boots, is somehow sucked into the air duct of the laundry room of their New York City apartment. He dives after her and the two fall down, down, down into in the Underland, a dark, underground world where people ride on giant bats for transportation, monstrous rats threaten Gregor's life, and there seems to be no way home. You can have children work in trios to dramatize the scenes at their own pace, and then come back together in one group to discuss how they brought the book to life, how it felt, and what they learned about the characters.

Third through sixth graders can dramatize a trio of scenes such as Billy's encounter with the first worm in Thomas Rockwell's *How to Eat Fried Worms* (Yearling, 2006); the classroom chapter in Daniel Pinkwater's *Fat Men from Space* (Yearling, 1980), when teacher Mr. Wendell can't figure out who has the hidden radio; and the argument the three Jones siblings have in their front yard and their subsequent abduction by Jumbeelia, the girl giant in Julia Donaldson's *The Giants and the Joneses* (Henry Holt, 2005). Each group will need to ponder—with your help, of course—how to set up each scene and what to say, a good experience in cooperation for everyone.

Interviews and Trials

When you're reading a book aloud to children or using it for Guided Reading, Literature Circles, Book Clubs, or whatever you call your book groups, there are many strategies, activities, and discussion points you can employ to insure that the children respond to what they are reading or hearing. The Live Interview, complete with microphone, is one powerful drama technique you can use to elicit a heightened awareness and general discussion of the whys and wherefores of protagonists and antagonists. You don't even need to have the mike attached to anything. Just holding it in front of a student's face and asking questions brings out the most wonderful responses, though you may want to tape record the exchange.

Any memorable story with diverse and potentially complex main characters is fair game for the interviewing technique. Fairy tales are a good source; although little detail is given about each character, children will make remarkable inferences about them.

BUD, NOT BUDDY

Let's say you are using Christopher Paul Curtis's Newbery Medal winner *Bud, Not Buddy* (Delacorte, 1999) as a class read-aloud or book discussion title with your students, grades four to seven. Take on the David Letterman/Jay Leno/news reporter role with your "studio audience." Say to your students, "Today, folks, we have as our guests the cast of *Bud, Not Buddy*. We're hoping to get to know our characters a little better. Our first guest is in the audience right now. Now, let's see. I know Todd is here somewhere."

As you peer at your audience, either wait for someone to volunteer, or say, "Oh yes, there he is. Todd, we're so glad you could make it today," and point to one of your more verbal students. You need as your first "guest" that person who will be willing to transform himself instantly into the character without being self-conscious or tongue-tied.

"Come on up here, Todd, and tell us about Bud Caldwell, that foster child your parents took in."

Once "Todd" is sitting in a chair next to you, facing the audience, say, "Well, Todd, you and Bud Caldwell certainly didn't hit it off the one night he spent in your house. Can you tell us your side of the story?"

And you're off and running, with bully "Todd" explaining his side of the story of why he stuck that Ticonderoga pencil up Bud's nose while he was sleeping. Next, interview other major and minor characters in the story. Even Bud's late mother can come back from the grave and describe what he was like when he was little. This allows children to get far deeper into a character than when you ask, "What kind of boy was Bud?" and wait for the six usual kids, the real verbal ones, to raise their hands. It's the quietest children who often surprise us the most with this activity.

After you start the interview, open the floor to questions from the audience as well. Once the ice is broken, many children will want to volunteer to be interviewed in character. Several students, one after another, can be interviewed as the same character, answering different questions. If a child is reticent and only offers one-word answers, begin with literal questions requiring simple responses. Change characters frequently to allow more children a chance to be in the limelight.

The interview technique enables children to develop oral language and creative thinking skills. They must incorporate knowledge of plot structure, story sequence, setting, and character personalities into their questions and responses. As students will both sympathize and identify with major and minor characters, here is the chance to measure affective or emotional response to a work of literature, in addition to the more straightforward cognitive or factual response.

Students can also break into small interview groups, write a list of questions that they would ask each character, and then conduct further interviews with one child as a Moderator and the other as Guests.

THE TALE OF DESPEREAUX

"Such the disappointment," says the mouse mother, Antoinette, upon learning that all of her latest litter of babies except one has died. He's a small mouse—ridiculously small, born within the walls of the castle. Despereaux, his mother names him, for all the sadness and despairs in the castle.

No mouse is ever born with its eyes open. Despereaux's eyes are open. "He'll be dead soon," says his practical father. "He can't live. Not with his eyes wide open like that."

"But, reader, he did live. This is his story." Despereaux is sickly. He faints at loud noises. He can not learn to scurry. And the day his sister, Merlot, brings him to the castle library to chew on the books, something remarkable happens. He can read the squiggles on an open page. It says, "Once upon a time."

Despereaux breaks one of the most basic and elemental mouse rules: Do not ever, under any circumstances, reveal yourself to humans. He lets a human, the Princess Pea, see him.

"Is it ridiculous for a very small, sickly, big-eared mouse to fall in love with a beautiful princess named Pea?... The answer is yes. Of course it's ridiculous. But also wonderful. And powerful."

Unfortunately, his older brother Furlough sees him. "Cripes! Oh, cripes! He's nuts! He's a goner." He runs off to tell his father the terrible, unbelievable news of what he has seen.

And having broken that first rule, Despereaux breaks another. He lets the Princess Pea lift him up. In her hand. And then he breaks the last of the great ancient rules of mice. He speaks. To a human. To her. "My name is Despereaux. I honor you." And that, dear reader, leads to his downfall.

Despereaux is sentenced by the mouse council—to death. Down to the dungeon, with a red thread tied around his neck. Down to the dark, fearsome dungeon to be eaten by the rats.

Will he die? Oh, dear reader, our hero can not die. The subtitle says it all: *Being the Story of a Mouse, a Princess, Some Soup, and a Spool of Thread.*

Kate DiCamillo's Newbery Award book works on so many levels and is such a satisfying book, whether you are booktalking it, reading it aloud, or reading it with your fourth through seventh graders. You'll discover many wonderful scenes to be acted out and discussed and unforgettable characters to get to know.

The following list covers some of the literal, interpretive, critical, and creative questions that you might pose during a class interview of the characters from *The Tale of Despereaux*, with an eye to all six levels of Bloom's Taxonomy: knowledge, comprehension, application, analysis, synthesis, and evaluation

A FEW QUESTIONS TO GET YOU STARTED

Despereaux's Mother:
In what ways was Despereaux different from the other mice in your family?

Despereaux's Father:
Why did you banish your own son to the dungeon?

Merlot, Despereaux's Sister:
How did your brother learn to read?

Furlough, Despereaux's Brother:
Why did you tell your father about what you saw between your brother and the Princess Pea?

Roscuro, the Rat:
How did you end up in the Queen's soup?
What are the problems with being a rat?
What did you have against the Princess Pea?

Despereaux:
Why did you break the most basic of all mouse rules?
Why did you refuse to repent to the Mouse Council?
Was it worth losing your tail to save the princess?

Princess Pea:
Why don't you like rats?
What are your feelings towards Despereaux?

Miggery Sow:
Why did you go along with Roscuro's plan?
If you had become a princess, what would your life be like?

Mock Trial

Another way to get your students pondering the intricacies of a character's personality is to hold a mock trial. Third grade teacher Lindsay Bezak at Van Holten School in Bridgewater, New Jersey does this every year with her students. They've used folk and fairy tales for their cases. Applying their knowledge of the judicial process, they've brought to trial the wolf in "Little Red Riding Hood" who allegedly ate two humans; Goldilocks, who was accused of breaking and entering; and that unrepentant wolf who blew down a bunch of houses in "The Three Little Pigs.

After a discussion of how your court will operate, appoint both a prosecutor and counsel for the defense and permit each side to discuss the case and develop questions. Lawyers may call main and minor characters as witnesses. Questions should require a range of responses from simple one-word answers to those that entail thought and ingenuity.

As the judge, your role is to supervise the proceedings and ask questions when clarification is necessary. You may want to select jurors and run your courtroom according to protocol, which means offering your group a crash course in the judicial process. Upper grades studying the judicial system will want to go into more detail, though all will thrive on knowing how to throw around terms like "Your witness," or "I object, your honor!"

The thundering headmistress Miss Trunchbull in Roald Dahl's *Matilda* (Viking, 1988), and the Grand High Witch in Dahl's *The Witches* (Farrar, 1983) would make fascinating defendants. And, of course, Despereaux is brought before the Mouse Council and sentenced to death for talking to the Princess Pea in *The Tale of Despereaux by* Kate DiCamillo. You could stage that trial, or give the mouse a retrial.

After dramatizing a story with a fifth grade class one day, I made a startling discovery. The fifth grade teacher, upon entering the library and observing her children in full actor mode, shook her head, rolled her eyes and said, semi-seriously, "Thanks a heap, Judy. I'll never get them down to earth now, after all this excitement." And yet, after we finished, the children were noticeably relaxed and content with themselves as they browsed for books, and not in the least bit rowdy or wound up. After noting the same result with most other classes that undertook improvised dramas, I've concluded that these activities actually have a calming effect on children, leaving them exhilarated and feeling very positive about themselves.

Let yourself go crazy once in a while. Back in my school librarian days, a first grade teacher implored me to read aloud Harry Allard's then-new *Miss Nelson Has a Field Day* (Houghton Mifflin, 1985) to her class. I was momentarily dismayed, as I already had plans for her class, of course, but she was so insistent, I said sure. Don't ask me why I didn't suspect anything. How was I to know she was in cahoots with the nefarious Mrs. Balunis, a fourth grade teacher who had already spent a day in character as Amelia Bedelia and as Strega Nona. Evelyn Balunis really got into the characters of the stories she loved, sometimes literally, and so did her class.

I read the book. The children laughed a lot. The library door flew open. In marched Coach Swamp, in her black sweat shirt, which said "COACH SWAMP AND DON'T YOU FORGET IT."

"Attention," she screeched, and blew her silver whistle. The first graders and I shrank back against the bookshelves in shock. In marched the Smedley Tornadoes football team, in full regalia. They ran through their paces. "Forty-three, sixty-two, HUT!"

Next came the uniformed cheerleaders, pom poms flying, for a few peppy chants, along with several spectators waving banners. Then they all came to attention, turned around, and marched out. "WOW," my first graders sighed. "Was that really Miss Swamp?"

Now *that's* creative drama.

USING READER'S THEATER

Improvised drama depends on the talents of the actors to make its unscripted production smooth and believable. With Reader's Theater, a more structured drama variation, children are given or write their own scripts to act out a scene. Reader's Theater stresses reading aloud, and as such, is a boon to the children who are less confidant about extemporaneous speaking.

When my very first edition of *Books Kids Will Sit Still For* was published back in 1984, I recall one reviewer who was disappointed because I didn't include any information on or mention of Reader's Theater. "What on earth is Reader's Theater?" I said as I looked it up. I found it means you hand out copies of a script derived from a book or story, and have readers act it out. "Wait, I do that!" I said.

The inspiration for what we now call Reader's Theater had to be old time radio. Before television, people listened to weekly radio shows like *The Lone Ranger* and *Fibber McGee and Molly*. In the radio studio, actors would stand in front of their microphones, scripts in hand, and read their parts.

You can find some of these great old scripts online, including Abbott and Costello's famous bit, "Who's On First?" (**www.louandbud.com/WOF.htm**), and act them out. There are scripts for 117 different vintage radio series from 1930-1960 at **www.genericradio.com**.

Here's how I got started with Reader's Theater. It was the week before Christmas vacation and I was gearing up to do a week of storytelling for the students in the elementary school where I was the librarian. Then laryngitis struck.

I got to school that morning, and headed straight for the books of plays on the library shelf—the 812s. Finding several cute holiday-related plays with lots of parts, I ran off scripts for each class, rearranged the chairs into a big semicircle, and crossed my fingers. I wrote instructions on the board. Something like: "Can't talk. It's up to you today. Let's put on a play." It was a huge hit. Necessity was the mother of invention, though I had no idea there was a name for what we were doing and that it was an educationally sound and wise process. We were just having fun with drama. A lot of fun. And I've been doing it ever since.

Reader's Theater is not to be confused with round robin reading where one child after another reads paragraphs aloud from a story. Round robin reading can be deadening.

When I was a child in elementary school, my classmates and I spent a fair amount of time reading aloud from our basal readers, round robin–style, up and down the rows. I remember, when it was my turn, trying to read aloud with lots of expression. I never could recall any details from the passage I was assigned, focused, as I was, on the written text in lieu of comprehending its meaning. If I made a mistake, I felt humiliated. Kids would laugh at stumblers, stammerers, and mispronouncers, unless they were too busy nervously surveying the upcoming text for their own turns. That type of round robin reading has fallen out of fashion.

So how do we help sharpen children's oral reading skills and encourage their response to literature? How do you get them to think deeper, beyond the usual glib happy-sad-mad-glad-bad responses when you read aloud a picture book like *The Trial of Cardigan Jones* by Tim Egan (Houghton Mifflin, 2004). Cardigan, a moose, is accused of stealing Mrs. Brown's freshly baked apple pie. He says he didn't do it.

Write up a script of the story for your children to act out. After your class has acted it out two or three times, you can ask, "How did Cardigan Jones feel when the jury finally declared him not guilty?"

Your actors will not just have seen the book and heard the story and read the story. They will have lived the story. They'll know that story from the inside out. Maybe you'll even bring out an apple pie for the cast party. What a fine way to get children invested in literature.

We all know there are no quick fixes in turning children into readers, don't we? Well, there are a few. And Reader's Theater is one of them.

If you're searching for a painless, effective way to get your children reading aloud with comprehension, expression, fluency, volume, and, most important, joy, Reader's Theater is a miracle. It allows children to get invested in the plot of a story, to see it unfold and come together.

What is Reader's Theater (or Readers Theatre, another of its many spellings)? It's nothing fancy. And you can do it yourself. After you read a book aloud to your children, you hand out a photocopied play script of the story with a part for each child, and they simply read the script aloud and act it out. You don't need props, costumes, or scenery, unless you want them. Children don't need to memorize their lines, though they will often do so just because they want to. (They have more brain cells than we do. Memorizing lines is child's play to them.) You don't need to perform your play in front of an audience, though actors may decide they want to do that, too. That's it? Pretty much. It's the process that's important here, not a finished product. And then magic happens.

Students have a script to hold and follow, but they also interact with the other readers as the group acts out its playlet. They bond with their fellow actors and respond to them in character, walking, for a short time, in their characters' shoes. By participating in an activity they love, they become more proficient and self-confident as readers and as performers.

If you are looking for a way to enhance presentation and public speaking skills, to get your children working together in harmony, to enunciate when they speak, to listen to what others have to say, to get to the heart of a story, to boost self esteem, and to hone every reading skill, Reader's Theater is your free ticket to change lives and raise contented, fulfilled, and motivated children. Watch your reading scores soar while children think they're just having a great time.

In my many years as a school librarian, I had each class put on at least one Reader's Theater play each year, starting with first grade (spring is best, when their reading skills are coming along so well), based on books I read aloud to them. Children thrive, even the quiet ones, on the thrill of being a star for a little while.

Sources of Reader's Theater Plays

How do you get going with Reader's Theater? First off, choose a good book and read it aloud to your group. They need to hear your expressive voice in their heads and have a sense of the characters, plot, setting, and sequence. They will be making an important connection between a book and the play that emerges from the book's text.

When you finish reading aloud or sharing a book, tell children you will then be acting out the story as a Reader's Theater play. They will probably cheer.

Where can you get plays? Look in the 812s on your library shelves for books of plays. Check out *Plays: The Drama Magazine for Young People* (and its website at **www.playsmag.com**), an indispensable magazine that comes out monthly, and is filled with good, royalty-free plays for elementary through high school. These are not always connected with children's books, but they're still good plays to read.

Look for scripts, instructions, and good advice in the books listed in the Bibliography of Professional Books on page 253. There you'll find wonderful books containing Reader's Theater scripts by Suzanne Barchers, Caroline Feller Bauer, Toni Buzzeo, Anthony Fredericks, Aaron Shepard, and Judy Sierra.

Authors are starting to write Reader's Theater scripts for their own books and putting them on their websites. See Margie Palatini's site, **www.margiepalatini.com**, and Toni Buzzeo's site, **www.tonibuzzeo.com**, for instance.

Another excellent online source is Rick Swallow's Reader's Theater/Language Arts Home Page for Teachers at **www.timelessteacherstuff.com**, with more than 80 scripts, many from well-known children's picture books.

My favorite source for Reader's Theater scripts is the amazing website of author Aaron Shepard, who has retold and published many wonderful folktales, most of which he has also adapted into Reader's Theater Scripts. Go to **http://aaronshep.com/rt**, where you can easily download his scripts, buy his books, or get in touch with him to have him visit your school to give a workshop.

YOU READ TO ME, I'LL READ TO YOU

Poet Mary Ann Hoberman calls the poems in her You Read to Me, I'll Read to You series of books as being "like a little play for two voices." *You Read to Me, I'll Read to You: Very Short Stories to Read Together* (Little, Brown, 2001) contains 14 stories in rhyme, all charmingly illustrated with pen and ink and watercolors, about cats and puppies, bears and mice, snakes, telephones, snowmen, birthdays, and friendships. Each of the two-page, two-person poems ends the same way—with the characters hunkering down with a good book, and repeating the book's title refrain, "You read to me, I'll read to you." *You Read to Me, I'll Read to You: Very Short Fairy Tales to Read Together* (Little, Brown, 2004) takes eight well-known fairy tales and retells them in gentle and genial dialogues between Goldilocks and Baby Bear, the Princess and the Pea, and Jack and the Giant.

This is Poetry Reader's Theater, also called choral reading, done either by the whole class in two groups, or by quartets or pairs, working together. Children can then compare and contrast the poems with the original folk and fairy tales. Older children can use this as a kickoff to scripting other familiar tales into dialogues between the characters.

PAUL FLEISCHMAN

For older readers, grades five to eight, Paul Fleischman's *Bull Run* (HarperCollins, 1993) and *Seedfolks* (HarperCollins, 1997) are both written from varying characters' points of view, and are meant to be brought to life in Reader's Theater productions, according to instructions by the author, as was his Newbery Medal book of poetry, *Joyful Noise: Poems for Two Voices* (HarperCollins, 1988).

LOVE THAT DOG

Another outstanding book is Sharon Creech's book *Love That Dog* (Joanna Cotler/HarperCollins, 2001), a collection of free verse poems from the pen of Jack, written in his journal as a response to the poems his perceptive teacher, Miss Stretchberry, is reading aloud to the class.

At first Jack is resentful about having to write poems, which he's sure he can't do well. By the end of January, though, Jack is writing about a dog he had, a yellow dog, and he doesn't mind so much when Miss Stretchberry types up his poems. He falls hard for a poem by Mr. Walter Dean Myers and writes his own poem about that yellow dog, Sky, patterned after Myers's poem. Jack is elated when Mr. Walter Dean Myers agrees to visit his school for an author visit, after Jack has written him a fan letter asking him to come.

It'll take you very little time to read this book aloud, but keep your handkerchief ready for a surprise tear and a story that'll stay with you and give you hope. The poems Miss Stretchberry reads, by William Carlos Williams, Robert Frost, Valerie Worth, William Blake, and of course, that lovely New Jersey guy, children's book author and poet, Walter Dean Myers, are appended so you can read them aloud, too.

First off, make transparencies of the poems so your listeners can read them and fully understand the context for the poems Jack writes in response. Then have them read the whole book aloud as a Reader's Theater, dividing up Jack's 47 poems, among your students, giving them time to practice their parts, and then performing them in sequence. You, as Miss Stretchberry, can intersperse the readings with the teacher-read poems. As Jack says, "Wow! Wow wow wow wow wow!"

Writing Your Own Reader's Theater Scripts

You can, of course, write up your own scripts, just like Aaron Shepard does, which is far easier than you might think. I write up at least one new Reader's Theater script a year. If you type up just one script each year, pretty soon you'll have a drawerful of interesting plays to use with your kids.

Many books you read aloud or booktalk have scenes or chapters with multiple characters and an emphasis on dialogue. Picture books are a logical starting place, but controlled vocabulary Easy Readers, dialogue-rich scenes or chapters in fiction books, folktales, narrative poems like "Casey at the Bat," picture book biographies, and even science and history books can lend themselves to being turned into plays. Keep an open mind when considering possibilities for drama.

When deciding on a book or excerpt to transform into a play, I consider my own "Freeman's Five Essential Ingredients". For the elementary school audience, a story should have:

1. Peppy dialogue

2. A little action

3. Laugh out loud parts

4. Lively narration

5. Enough roles for all

It takes me about an hour to do a good first draft of a picture book, even when typing with my usual two fingers and a thumb. Some more of my favorite picture books I've adapted include Matt Novak's *Mouse TV* (Orchard, 1994), Helen Bannerman's *The Story of Little Babaji* (HarperCollins, 1996), Susan Meddaugh's *Martha Walks the Dog* (Houghton Mifflin, 1998), Diane Stanley's *Raising Sweetness* (Putnam, 1999), Doreen Cronin's *Click, Clack, Moo: Cows That Type* (Simon & Schuster, 2000), Shelley Moore Thomas's *Get Well, Good Knight* (Dutton, 2002), Antonio Sacre's *The Barking Mouse* (Albert Whitman, 2003; see full RT script on page 230 below), Tim Egan's *The Trial of Cardigan Jones* (Houghton Mifflin, 2004), Kate DiCamillo's *Mercy Watson to the Rescue* (Candlewick, 2005), and Lane Smith's *John, Paul, George & Ben* (Hyperion, 2006; see excerpt below on page 210).

Scriptwriting Tips

If you've ever seen a real script for a play or movie, you'll note that the formatting of a Reader's Theater script is simpler. It needs to be easy for children to read so they can scan down and find their lines, and follow along as the play progresses. Here are some of my script tips:

1. At the top of your script, include a list of all the acting roles, in order of appearance, plus the narrators.

2. Use a good-sized font for your scripts, so students can see and read their lines clearly. I like 14- or 18-point Helvetica or Times, both of which are easy on the eyes.

3. Justify your right margin to give the script a clean look.

4. Add page numbers at the bottom.

5. Always photocopy your scripts single-sided. It's very confusing to try to follow a double-sided script, especially for children. "I can't find the page," they'll wail.

6. Character names, including narrators, are on the left, in caps and in bold. Set up tabs for the dialogue, so actors can scan down the left side of each page to find their names and look on the right for their lines.

7. Single-space each character's lines, but add a double space between lines.

8. Put your stage directions in italics and in parenthesis. *(Explain to children that they don't read these out loud as lines, but that they should follow the stage directions so they know what to do.)*

9. Bold and / or capitalize those lines, phrases, or words you want an actor to say with more **force** or VOLUME or **EXPRESSION**.

10. In writing a script, try to incorporate verbatim as much of the story's actual dialogue and narration as possible, but don't be afraid to change, rearrange, edit, or add, if it will make the play flow better. You don't have to be a word-for-word slave to the book, though you do want to stay true to the author's words.

11. You can condense scenes, or even leave them out, especially if you're doing a long, involved chapter or scene from a fiction book.

12. Try to ensure that everyone will get a good speaking part, both actors and narrators. This means you may need to add lines. You might turn some dialogue into narration, and vice versa

13. Even if you proofread and run your spellcheck, you won't catch all of the typos you made until you run off a script and hand it out. Then they will jump out at you.

14. As for problems with the script itself, make notes as you watch your group perform their first reading. Did one character get too many lines? Not enough? Are the stage directions clear? Afterwards go back to your computer and fix everything that wasn't perfect, and run off a second draft.

15. If you like, you can start with the characters introducing themselves. ("I'm Josh, and I play the Lawyer.") This makes sure the audience knows who's who, and also gives each character an extra line. This isn't necessary, and you don't have to write it in the script if you want your players to do it.

As an example of how to format and adapt text into a script, below is an excerpt from a typical Reader's Theater script that I wrote from Lane Smith's *John, Paul, George & Ben* (Hyperion, 2006). You can use this as a model for when you write your own scripts or have your students write them.

In this fabulous picture book about the fictional youths of our founding fathers, we see how the annoying personality traits each had as a boy—bold John Hancock, noisy Paul Revere, honest George Washington, clever Ben Franklin, and that independent lad, Tom Jefferson—stood them in good stead when they grew up and starred in the Revolutionary War.

You can find both my complete Reader's Theater script of the whole story and the comprehensive teacher's guide at **www.hyperionbooksforchildren.com**. (Type the book's title in the search bar, and when you get to the book's home page, you'll see, on the left hand side, information about downloading them.)

AN EXCERPT FROM JUDY FREEMAN'S READER'S THEATER SCRIPT OF *JOHN, PAUL, GEORGE & BEN*

(Reprinted with permission of Hyperion Books for Children.)

NARRATOR 1:	Paul was a noisy lad.
NARRATOR 2:	Before fun was invented, people joined bell-ringing clubs.
NARRATOR 3:	As a member of Boston's Old North Church, Paul spent hours practicing in the belfry tower.
NARRATORS 1-4:	(*loudly*) **BING! BONG! BING! BONG!**
PAUL:	(*pantomimes ringing bells and pulling on ropes*)
NARRATOR 4:	Over time, that bell-ringing took a toll on young Paul. All day his head was filled with . . .
NARRATORS 1-4:	(*loudly*) **BING! BONG! BING! BONG!**
PAUL:	(*walks all discombobulated, head and eyes rolling*)
NARRATOR 1:	He had to practically scream just to hear himself talk. Now that's fine around the belfry, but not at work.
LADY CUSTOMER:	(*softly*) Young man, do you have some, uh, well, some extra large underwear?
PAUL:	(*yells loudly*) **EXTRA LARGE UNDERWEAR? SURE WE HAVE SOME! LET'S SEE, LARGE . . . LARGE . . . EXTRA LARGE! HERE THEY ARE! GREAT, BIG, EXTRA-LARGE UNDERWEAR!**
LADY CUSTOMER:	Oh, my!
NARRATOR 2:	Paul was like a bullhorn in a china shop.

 From *Once Upon a Time: Using Storytelling, Creative Drama, and Reader's Theater with Children in Grades PreK-6* by Judy Freeman. Westport, CT: Libraries Unlimited. Copyright © 2007.

MAN CUSTOMER:	(*softly*) Young man, have you received the package I ordered?
PAUL:	(*yells loudly*) **YOUR WIG? YES, IT'S COMING!**
MAN CUSTOMER:	GRRR!
PAUL:	(*yelling*) **AND YOUR POLKA-DOT SHIRTS ARE COMING! AND THE PINK BREECHES ARE COMING!**
NARRATOR 3:	It took many years and a midnight ride for people to finally appreciate his special talent.
PAUL:	(*galloping on a horse*) **THE REDCOATS ARE COMING! THE REDCOATS ARE COMING!**
NARRATOR 3:	Everyone except that big-underwear lady.
NARRATOR 4:	She was still mad.
LADY CUSTOMER:	**Harrrrumph!**

If you compare the script above with the original text of the picture book, you'll see I've made some changes. First of all, I added new lines for both the big underwear lady and the man who ordered the wig. This provides more speaking parts for the actors. I gave the narrators the "*bings* and *bongs*" to do as sound effects together. Most of the time, narrators each read their own lines, but it's also enjoyable and effective to have them read some lines in unison, like a Greek chorus.

About props, costumes, and scenery. You don't have to have them for a simple Reader's Theater in-house production. But they're fun to use. For *John, Paul, George & Ben*, I gathered together a simple prop for each of the five principal characters to use. John Hancock had a piece of chalk; Paul Revere, a tricorn hat, which I made from a brown paper grocery bag. (Cut a huge oval from the unprinted back of the bag. Cut a large cross down the middle of the oval so it will fit on a child's head. Fold up the side edges in between each of the cuts. Voilà! A tricorn.) George Washington used a little toy hatchet to pretend to chop down trees; Ben Franklin held up a little kite, and Thomas Jefferson got a scroll and a quill pen to write and draw with.

Kids Write Scripts

As a writing exercise, scripting a scene is challenging and fun for children, once you have demonstrated the format and construction. Students in grades two and up can learn to write scripts, adapting published books or their own original stories. Get them started by giving each person a copy of a sample play for reference.

From *Once Upon a Time: Using Storytelling, Creative Drama, and Reader's Theater with Children in Grades PreK-6* by Judy Freeman. Westport, CT: Libraries Unlimited. Copyright © 2007.

Do your first script together as a class. First hand out copies of a brief story for all to read. With their input, outline the story on the board, chart, or overhead. Model how to turn dialogue from a story into play dialogue and how to turn narration into lines for narrators to read. Show them how to write stage directions in italics.

When students are adapting print into a script, photocopy the original story. Have them mark up the copy with highlighters, using a different color for each part. This will make it easier for them to transcribe and keep track of who says what.

The tedious part is copying down or typing the dialogue and narration. Think of it as a good way to practice handwriting or keyboarding.

One excellent source for younger readers is the "I Can Read" genre, those easy-to-read early chapter books like the *Frog and Toad* series by Arnold Lobel or the *Henry and Mudge* and *Poppleton* books by Cynthia Rylant. Short, self-contained chapters contain both narration and short, snappy dialogues and are ideal for small group productions. Break children into small groups to work on their scripts and then act them out.

Students in all grades can also write new chapters about the characters. Just because these stories are easy to read, doesn't mean they're that easy to write. Third through sixth graders can write new chapters about the characters for younger kids to read. If your students create a couple of new scripts each year, in no time, your will have a lifetime supply of scripts to use.

Reader's Theater Logistics

How do you give everyone a part? You'll need to do a bit of juggling to make everything come out even. With Reader's Theater scripts, you can expand the number of parts by adding narrators, doubling up on characters, or even splitting a character's part into two or more. When you type up a new script, estimate how many acting parts you have and how many students, and add narrators to make up the difference. If you have 12 narrators and 10 to 12 actors, this usually works fine. If you have more parts than actors, double the lines of the narrators. Have Narrator 11 also read Narrator 10's part as well, for instance.

What about an existing script that has 11 parts when you have 23 kids? You can easily add more parts by doubling or tripling the number of narrators. Tell one child, for example, "You are Narrator 1, pages one to three," and the next one, "And you are Narrator 1, pages four to six." And so on. If necessary, divide the roles of your main characters in the same way.

You can also break the script into three or four smaller scenes, with a separate cast for each. Each group can practice its small scenes several times and then put it on for the others.

Or you could have two separate casts, rehearsing on separate sides of the room. They can then do the play for each other, giving everyone a chance to be both actors and audience members. You also can have simultaneous rehearsals for two or three separate plays, and then have the casts perform for each other. As long as everyone gets a part, you can make it work.

It's Showtime!

In a classroom, where there is not usually a lot of space, children can act out the story at the front of the room so all can see. If you're planning on doing creative drama on a regular basis, you'll most likely want to have children rearrange the desks to make space for a makeshift stage. By introducing a standard procedure for doing this and practicing it once or twice, it will be easy enough for children to clear the floor quickly and effectively with little disruption.

In a library, you'll need to move tables, which could be trickier, but certainly not impossible. I like to arrange 24 chairs in a big semicircle or arc so actors can see each other, with open space in the front of the chairs for interaction—a chase scene, for instance—so they can get up and move around. Set up a chair for yourself, facing the actors, so you can be the director, prompter, and appreciative audience all in one.

Once the children are sitting in the chairs, hand out the scripts in order. About half of your group will be narrators. I designate the children who sit on the left side as narrators, and the right side, actors. I hand out the parts sequentially, with Narrator 1 on the left, and then 2, 3, 4, and so on, sitting next to each other. Don't get fancy here. You always want to be able to figure out whose line is next. Someone will always say, "I can't remember which narrator I am." Count over and say, "You're Narrator 5." Easy.

Unless you have a few parts that are particularly difficult to read, don't worry about who gets what role. Some of your shyest kids will shine doing this activity. I do try to make sure the boys get boy parts, as there's usually an outcry if they don't. The girls tend to be a bit more flexible and don't mind as much if they get a boy part.

Give the children a few minutes to go over their lines and practice a bit. When they can't figure out a word or phrase, instruct them to turn to the actors on their left or right for help.

Give a little pep talk as follows:

"This is a first reading, just like real actors do on Broadway or on TV when they start to rehearse a new play or episode. Nobody expects it to be perfect and nobody should care if someone misses a line or stumbles on a word. Never laugh at a fellow actor who makes a mistake. We're all in this together.

"Keep an eye out for your neighbors on either side of you during the play. If you see the person next to you has lost his place, don't say a thing. Just lean over and put your finger on his script to show him where we are.

"I am the prompter for this play. When an actor gets stuck, the prompter helps by giving the correct line or word. Even actors on Broadway look to the prompter if they forget their lines. If you get confused and your neighbors can't help you, then look at me."

Then it's showtime. Each time a child has a line, he or she must stand up to deliver it in a loud, clear, and expressive voice. Prompt them as needed, and laugh with them. That first reading, while exhilarating, can be choppy, but who cares?

Once is not enough with Reader's Theater; try for two or even three readings for it to be truly effective. Even though your group will have heard you read the story aloud, the first time they undertake to plow through the script for themselves, they will stumble and stammer and lose their places. They'll struggle with decoding unfamiliar words, getting a sense of how their parts might sound, and making sense of the plot.

During the second reading, your actors will start to listen to the others' lines, to relax and watch the story unfold, and they'll read with more understanding and expression. If you have time to do it a third time, it will seem like a revelation. Readers will be able to focus on enjoying the performance and their parts in it.

You might want to change parts the third time you run through the script, giving the actors a chance to be narrators, and vice versa. Challenge your actors in a constructive way. Say to them, "How can you make this next reading better? What will you do this time that you didn't do the first time?"

Now when you ask all those lovely interpretive questions to foster higher level thinking and reasoning skills, your children will be brilliantly prepared to discuss a story they have heard, then read, then lived.

Make sure you have extra copies of the script. You want your actors to mark up their parts—they love to use highlighter marks—and get comfortable with their scripts. If they take them home to read and practice, that's ideal. So don't chew them out for leaving their scripts home. Just hand out extra copies.

If you expect your students to do well, they probably will. I used my Reader's Theater script of Matt Novak's picture book *Mouse TV* (Orchard 1994) with several classes of first graders in my school library one year. It was the first time these children had ever done Reader's Theater and I was excited about it. We had read the story the week before.

When the first class entered the library, I had them sit in the chairs I had arranged in a long arc across the room. We talked about the story. I handed out parts and let them find their lines and practice them for a few minutes. Then we started acting. I had written the song "Three Blind Mice" into the script for the whole cast to sing, and when we got to that part in the script, they sang it with great exuberance. They read with great expression. They had a ball. Their teacher was amazed. "Wow! I didn't know they could do that!"

The next class came in and I explained what we were going to do. The teacher said, sharply, "They won't be able to read that! This is *much* too hard for first grade!"

Well, guess what. Those children found it much too hard. They whined and said, "I don't know what to do!" and "I can't read this."

Talk about your self-fulfilling prophecy. If I hadn't seen the first class, I would have believed that teacher. Yeah, this is too hard for first grade, I guess. Maybe next year. But I knew they could do it and they did. You will have children and teachers who tell you it's too hard. Don't give up on them. They feel so proud of themselves when they realize they can do it.

In 2002, when Aaron Shepard's book of the West African pourquoi tale, *Master Man: A Tall Tale of Nigeria* (HarperCollins, 2001), was published, I couldn't wait to try out his new script with two classes of third graders at Van Holten School.

In the first production, the boy who played Shadusa, the cocksure man who considers himself the strongest man in the world, was himself a self-assured, brash kid, well-liked for his comic take on the world. He was very funny and brazen in the part.

Then in came the second class for their chance to act. I handed out the scripts, giving the lead part of Shadusa to the boy who sat at the end of the semicircle of chairs, on the right. His teacher pulled me aside. "Maybe he's not such a good person to play the main character," she whispered. "He's so shy, he barely talks. We haven't heard him say Boo all year."

"That's OK," I told her. "It doesn't matter if he's not fabulous. The play will still be fun."

And then the miracle happened. The boy playing Shadusa got into his role. And while he wasn't as flamboyant as the first boy had been, he was still plenty expressive and blustery, fitting the part just fine. The other children in the class looked at him in amazement when he started to speak, hearing that quiet boy become a whole new person.

When children finish reading a script, they usually feel pretty good about it. Reinforce that by teaching them how to do their bows, just like on Broadway. I have them face front, join hands, hold their arms up high, and then bow in unison on the count of three. They come up on the count of three, and repeat it three times. They have to watch each other out of the corners of their eyes so they go down and come up together. It looks pretty cool. You keep the count and applaud and cheer like crazy, especially if you are their only audience member.

PERFORMANCE TIPS FOR ACTORS

1. Read over your lines so you know where they are in the script and how to pronounce all the words.

2. Hold your script still. If you rattle the paper, the other actors will be distracted. When you need to turn the page of your script, do it quickly and as quietly as you can.

      [*NOTE FOR TEACHERS:* You can circumvent the problem by putting the pages of each script in plastic sleeves and in a notebook binder. Children can either hold their binders or place them on music stands in front of them. For everyday RT, this is more work than necessary, but if you're putting on a performance for parents or an audience, it's a nice professional touch.]

3. If the cast is sitting in chairs, stand up when you have a line. Sit down when you finish.

4. When you stand up to deliver a line, hold your script down by your belly button. (I call this, "Belly It Up.") Make sure it stays there so everyone can see and hear you. Don't let your script creep up to cover your face.

5. If you can't see the audience, they can't see you either. In Reader's Theater, you act with your face. Make sure it's visible at all times.

6. Never turn your back on the audience. People need to be able to see your face, not your fanny.

7. Read your lines slowly and clearly so everyone can understand you.

8. Use your playground voice. Imagine your voice bouncing off the back wall like a rubber ball. You may think you are speaking loudly, but chances are no one can hear you.

9. Always read with expression. Concentrate. Think about how your lines should sound or how you can do them better next time.

10. If your line is funny, don't laugh unless the script calls for it. Let the audience will figure out the funny parts.

11. If you're acting for an audience and they laugh, freeze until they stop laughing. If you say your next line while they are still laughing, they won't hear it.

12. Stay in character. When you act out a play, you become someone else. Try to act like that person would.

13. Follow along in your script so you don't lose your place.

14. If you do lose your place, catch the eye of the actor sitting next to you. Point to his or her script, and shrug your shoulders. That person will know you're lost and will put a finger on the correct line of your script. Return the favor when needed.

15. If you mess up a line, don't worry about it. Just keep going.

16. Be considerate of the other actors. If you fool around while they're delivering their lines, they might do the same to you.

17. Take your script home and practice reading it aloud with someone—a friend, your parents, or a brother or sister. If there's no one around, read it to the mirror.

Some Good Books to Dramatize

INSPECTOR HOPPER

The controlled vocabulary, easy-to-read chapter book, *Inspector Hopper* by Doug Cushman (HarperCollins, 2000), one of HarperCollins's I Can Read series, is an example of great script material. In the three chapters, dedicated detective, Inspector Hopper, and his faithful but always hungry sidekick, McBugg: find a missing ladybug (the one from the "Ladybug, Ladybug, fly away home" nursery rhyme); catch a rat stealing seeds; and solve the mystery of Skeet, the mosquito's, missing leaf boat. (Conrad the Caterpillar ate it.) Dialogue is sparky, sprightly, and tongue-in-cheek; characters are well rounded.

Each chapter is a little short story in brief, with a problem, rising action, conflict, a climax, and a satisfying ending. You could break a class into three casts of three to eight readers, depending on the number of characters and possible narrators in each chapter. If you simply photocopy the chapters, children could use them as their scripts and highlight their own parts with highlighter markers, just like real actors do. Have each group practice a few times, and then perform its skit for the others.

THE SHIVERS IN THE FRIDGE

Fran Manushkin's *The Shivers in the Fridge* (Dutton, 2006) will make a great Reader's Theater script for your actors to perform. The humor is subtle; acting out the story will help listeners understand the wordplay and sheer cleverness of the plot.

"Brrr! It's cold today," Papa Shivers groans.

Sonny, the youngest, says, "It's been c-c-cold ever since we got here—and dark."

The Shivers family lives in a cardboard box in a most unusual location. They have to watch out for the earthquakes and the blazing light and the monsters who invade every day, taking things away and sometimes putting them back. Sonny says, "Look! Cheesy square is gone."

Grandma says, "Cold we are and cold we'll *always* be." When Papa sets off to find a warmer place, he trips on Buttery Cliff, and is taken away by a monster, which children will see is a big human hand. One by one, the Shivers are carried off until only young Sonny is left. Zelinsky's deliciously busy pastels show a whole other side of the refrigerator—the inside. You'll never look at refrigerator magnets the same way again.

Listeners will delight in reciting the bedtime story Mama tries to tell to Sonny each night, ending with an "OUCH!"; making the "PHOOMPH" noise of the refrigerator door closing; and identifying all the geographical areas and foods in the fridge.

TOYS GO OUT

In Emily Jenkin's *Toys Go Out* (Schwartz & Wade, 2006), StingRay, Lumphy the buffalo, and Plastic are buh-bumping in the damp and smelly backpack of the Little Girl with the blue barrette. Where is she taking them? Feeling nervous, Plastic hums. Lumphy feels sick. StingRay is sure they're heading to the vet or the zoo or the dump. But, no. The Little Girl takes them out of her backpack and introduces them at show-and-tell as her best friends in the world.

In six delectable chapters filled with dialogue, the omniscient narrator looks closely and compassionately at each toy's new misadventure. Plastic suffers an identity crisis until TukTuk the towel helps her figure out what she is. (Spoiler Alert: a ball.) Lumphy gets peanut butter on himself but is afraid of the washing machine. And StingRay, whose tag says "dry clean only" tries to prove she can float in the tub.

Each of these chapters can be abridged and written in script form for small groups to act out. Children who talk to their own toys will not doubt for a minute the rich interior lives and the conversations between the personified trio. If you're talking about the importance of point of view in stories, break into pairs or small groups to write or improvise dialogues or scenes between two or more of their own toys and perform them for each other.

MATILDA

Matilda by Roald Dahl (Viking, 1988) is one of those books you either adore or find hideously offensive. Brilliant five-year-old Matilda, daughter of a crooked car salesman father and a TV soap opera–addicted mother, gets revenge on her family and on the outrageous headmistress at her school, the dreaded Miss Trunchbull. In a chapter entitled "The Ghost," Matilda borrows a friend's talking parrot for the evening and plays along when it talks, convincing her parents there are robbers in the house. The simple scene is practically all dialogue and would be a cinch to work into a five or six-person script. Other possibilities abound in the chapters "Bruce Bogtrotter and the Cake" and "The Weekly Test."

KATE DICAMILLO

Back on page 202, we looked at Kate DiCamillo's *The Tale of Despereaux* in terms of acting out scenes. There are so many gripping dialogues in this book that would make fine short Reader's Theater scripts. Photocopy some of them to hand out to students to adapt and read aloud. The same holds true with her book *The Miraculous Journey of Edward Tulane*. You can find a Reader's Theater script of a climactic scene (a serious one), online at **www.edwardtulane.com**. DiCamillo's books employ rich language and introduce unforgettable characters.

THE LIGHTNING THIEF

Try this for a booktalk:

You think you get in trouble in school? Meet Percy Jackson, a dyslexic ADHD kid at Yancy Academy, a private boarding school for troubled kids in upstate New York. The chapter headings in Rick Riordan's *The Lightning Thief* (Miramax, 2005) are most instructive and, actually, accurate, as in Chapter 1: "I Accidentally Vaporize My Pre-Algebra Teacher."

On his sixth grade class field trip to the Metropolitan Museum of Art in New York City, Percy tries to stay out of trouble. The school's headmaster has threatened him with death-by-in-school-suspension if anything bad, embarrassing, or even mildly entertaining happens to him on this trip. Mr. Brunner, his Latin teacher, a middle-aged but very cool guy who uses a motorized wheelchair, and the only teacher who doesn't put Percy to sleep, is leading the tour, which is good.

But redheaded kleptomaniac classmate, Nancy Bobofit, won't leave Percy's best friend, Grover, alone. She throws chunks of her peanut butter and ketchup sandwich at his head when they're on the bus, and then, when they're outside eating lunch by the museum fountain, she dumps her half-eaten lunch in Grover's lap. Percy never has been able to control his temper. The next thing he knows, Nancy is sitting on her butt in the fountain, screaming, "Percy pushed me!"

Mrs. Dodds, Percy's inhumanly mean math teacher, looks triumphant. "Come with me," she orders. She sends him into the museum and meets up with him in the Greek and Roman gallery. She's standing there, in her black leather jacket, making a weird growling noise.

"You've been giving us problems, honey."

"Yes, ma'am," Percy says. "I'll—I'll try harder, ma'am." The look in her eyes is beyond mad. It's evil. Percy thinks, "She's a teacher. It's not like she's going to hurt me."

"Your time is up," she hisses, her eyes glowing like barbecue coals. Then her fingers stretch into talons. Her leather jacket melts into large, leathery bat wings, and Mrs. Dodds turns into a shriveled hag with a mouth full of yellow fangs and a murderous look in her eyes. She is about to slice Percy to ribbons when his Latin teacher, Mr. Brunner, wheels his chair into the gallery.

"What ho, Percy," he shouts, and tosses his pen in the air. Percy catches it, but when he does, it isn't a pen anymore. It's a bronze sword.

"Die, honey," Mrs. Dodds snarls, and lunges for him. Lucky for Percy, he has that sword.

What's going on here? Who is Mrs. Dodds and why does she want him dead? It seems that Percy is about to find out the truth about his lineage: his mother is from New York City. He's never met his father. "Lost at sea" is all his mother has ever told him. Well, Percy's father is a god. A Greek god. A real one. And that makes Percy a demigod, a half-blood. He's also in mortal danger. There are lots of creatures out there who want him dead. Welcome to Book 1 of the series <u>Percy Jackson and the Olympians</u>, *The Lightning Thief*.

Wow! Now *that's* a book crammed full of scenes for you and your students to transform into mini-scripts.

THE BARKING MOUSE

The Barking Mouse by Antonio Sacre, is based on an old Cuban folktale about a family of four mice—Mamá Ratón, Papá Ratón, and their two children, Hermana and Hermano—who go on a picnic and encounter a gato—a cat! "Hola, gato flaco," those two bold mouse children taunt. "Hello, skinny cat!"

This is a charmer of a story Antonio Sacre learned from his Cuban grandmother about his experiences speaking Spanish in an English-only culture that you'll find inspirational to read and discuss with your listeners. Be sure to read the Author's Note.

When children act out this tale, they'll learn new Spanish language phrases, and see the humor of the ending. Talk over the final line and message: "Es muy importante hablar otra idioma! It pays to speak another language!"

Here's something memorable that happened one day during a Reader's Theater production of *The Barking Mouse* during one of my children's literature seminars for BER (Bureau of Education and Research). There were several men in the audience that day, which in an otherwise female-dominated group of elementary school teachers and librarians, is always a pleasure. When I called for ten volunteers to be in the play, two men joined the line across the front of the room, along with eight women. I handed out parts—giving one of the guys the part of Papá Raton, and the other the brother mouse.

They began reading their scripts aloud with great feeling and humor. Mamá Raton says, "Children, you go play by yourselves. Me and Papá, we're going to stay here and smooch." The two mice children say, "Eewwww" and run off to play. When they come back to the picnic blanket, Mamá and Papá are still smooching.

"Smoooch." The guy playing Papá grabbed the woman playing Mamá, dipped her back in a swoon, and planted a huge and passionate kiss on her lips—like the sailor in Times Square in the famous photo at the end of World War II. It wasn't a fake kiss. This was a *very* real kiss, and we couldn't believe what we were watching. It was theater verité. I gasped. The audience gasped.

From the middle of the audience, a little voice called out, "They're *married*!" And everyone just fell over laughing. The rest of us had no idea the two playing Mamá and Papá were actually husband and wife until that moment. It was hilarious, and I still crack up every time I read the book, remembering that day. It sure was great theater!

For the complete Reader's Theater script for *The Barking Mouse*, go to page 230.

READER'S THEATER: 9 PERFECT PICTURE BOOKS

Dooby Dooby Moo. Cronin, Doreen. Illus. by Betsy Lewin. Atheneum, 2006. Gr. 1-6 (easy fiction)

Farmer Brown's farm animals have already gone on strike in *Click Clack Moo: Cows That Type*, they've ordered in pizza in *Giggle, Giggle, Quack*, and Duck was even elected to the highest office in the land in *Duck for President*. What are they up to this time? Scanning Farmer Brown's newspaper, Duck notes that there's a talent show scheduled for this Saturday's County Fair. First prize is a trampoline; second prize, a box of chalk. Duck directs rehearsals in the barn for the cows, sheep, and pigs. (As Eric N., second grader at Van Holten School in Bridgewater, New Jersey, said, "He's the conDUCKtor." Exactly!) Farmer Brown knows the animals are up to something, so he loads them in the back of his pickup truck so he can keep an eye on them and takes them to the fair. Big mistake.

ACT IT OUT:

There's a lot of soulful singing in this book that your children can join in on: the cows sing "Twinkle, Twinkle Little Star" ("Dooby, dooby, dooby moo"); the sheep sing "Home on the Range" (Fa, la, la, la baa); and at the show, Duck gets a standing O for his rendition of "Born to Be Wild" (Quack, quack, quack, quuuaaaaaack!). Children can act out each group's performances, but you can also write up the whole story as a Reader's Theater script, adding some extra dialogue for Farmer Brown and the judges at the contest.

Duck & Goose. Hills, Tad. Illus. by the author. Schwartz & Wade, 2006. Gr. PreK-1 (easy fiction)

"I saw it first," Duck says of the enormous white egg with orange, red, and yellow spots, lying on the grass in the middle of the meadow. "I touched it first," Goose counters. After fussing and fighting, the two conclude that they will need to sit on the remarkable egg together so it will hatch. Full bleed oils in bucolic sky blues and spring greens introduce the two endearing big-billed little fellows who can't wait for that baby bird to emerge. See if your listeners buy into Duck and Goose's egg dilemma, or if someone says, "Wait a minute! That's not an egg. It's just a big ball!" Which it is, as a little blue bird tells them, although the way the two egg-sitters come to terms with that embarrassing revelation is told just right.

ACT IT OUT:

For pre-readers, you can have them act out the confrontation scenes between Duck and Goose. For first-graders, you can script up the dialogue between Duck and Goose (and, at the end, the little blue bird) and hand them out to trios of children for private little performances they can do together as a threesome. Write your script entirely in dialogue; you don't really need the narration. Have each little group find an unoccupied space in the room to act out the story. They can then switch parts and try it again.

The Great Fuzz Frenzy. **Stevens, Janet, and Susan Stevens Crummel. Illus. by Janet Stevens. Harcourt, 2005. Gr. 1-3 (easy fiction)**

When Violet, a golden retriever, drops a neon green tennis ball into a prairie dog hole, the prairie dogs are scared of the big round thing. "It's fuzzy," says little Pip Squeak, pulling off a piece and putting it on his head. Soon, everyone wants a piece of fuzz, and when the ball is stripped clean, they fight over the fuzz, a now precious commodity, with "friend against friend, cousin against cousin, dog against dog." They fall asleep, exhausted from their confrontations, all "fuzzled out," but awake to find the fuzz is gone. Who stole it? Big Bark, the big-mouthed leader of the group is proud to show everyone that he is the culprit, but all that fuzz attracts the eye of a swooping eagle. Plucky Pip Squeak rallies the prairie dogs to save Big Bark, and everything is happy-ever-after, until the final endpaper, where we see Violet the dog dropping a new orange tennis ball into the hole. Listeners can predict what might happen this time.

ACT IT OUT:

For your script, you'll find such funny dialogue both in the text and incorporated into the illustrations, but also a thoughtful examination of how greed, jealousy, and self-interest can overcome even the most laid-back community. For a simple prop, use pieces of green fuzzy yarn and maybe a big beach ball, which you can put in the middle of the acting space. Your script may be challenging for second graders, and probably too hard for first. Don't forget to consider stories like this for older readers, who can perform their readings for younger ones.

Leonardo the Terrible Monster. **Willems, Mo. Illus. by the author. Hyperion, 2005. Gr. PreK-2 (easy fiction)**

"Leonardo was a terrible monster . . . He couldn't scare anyone." The little horned monster does some research to find the most scaredy-cat kid in the whole world so he can scare the tuna salad out of him. Who is that poor unsuspecting victim? A forlorn little boy named Sam. When Leonardo lets loose, giving it all he's got (including my personal favorite noise, "blaggle blaggle"), Sam is so terrified that he cries. "Yes! I did it!" Leonardo crows, but Sam has a whole other list of reasons why he came to tears. Go to the website, **www. hyperionbooksforchildren.com**, type "Leonardo the Terrible Monster" in the search bar, and you'll find my extensive teacher's guide to the book which you can download as a PDF file.

ACT IT OUT:

Act out the scaring scene in pairs, with script or without, with one child being the not-so-scary monster, and the other the tearful Sam. Then switch parts. With younger children, you can have them improvise the dialogue between Leonardo and Sam. Reenact another perfect pairing of two boys' dialogue that ends with a similar friendship in *Yo! Yes?* by Chris Raschka (Orchard, 1993). You don't need a printed script—just hold up the book so children can read aloud the large printed words on each page. Divide the group in two: one side can assume the stance and body language of the vivacious and friendly boy on each left page, and the other side the shy, sad-sack boy on the right.

Mercy Watson to the Rescue. **DiCamillo, Kate. Illus. by Chris Van Dusen. Candlewick, 2005. Gr. K-3 (easy fiction)**

Mercy Watson, beloved pig of Mr. and Mrs. Watson, loves nothing more than hot buttered toast. On the night the rotund pig climbs into bed with them, the bed creaks, the floor moans, and a hole opens up in the floor below, leaving them all hanging on for dear life. Mercy escapes. Mr. Watson exclaims, "She is going to alert the fire department." But, no, actually, Mercy is going to the kitchen to look for . . . some toast. In the course of this slapstick tale, written like an easy reader from the Dick and Jane era, but with glossier illustrations, Mercy scares the daylights out of the two elderly Lincoln sisters next door, and they call . . . the fire department!

ACT IT OUT:

The wry and wacky text has everything a good Reader's Theater production needs and more. It even has a chase scene. Bring out the toaster when you finish your play and make some hot, buttered toast.

The Neat Line: Scribbling Through Mother Goose. **Edwards, Pamela Duncan. Illus. by Diann Cain Blumenthal. HarperCollins, 2005. Gr. PreK-2 (easy fiction)**

"Once upon a time there was a scribble. The scribble was only a baby." That baby scribble practices and practices, and, when it grows up to be a Neat Line, heads off into the first page of a real book of Mother Goose's Nursery Rhymes. It helps Little Boy Blue gather up his missing cows and sheep by redrawing itself into the shape of a horn for the sleepy shepherd boy to blow. It comes to the rescue of Jack and Jill by becoming a pathway up the hill. For Mary, Mary, Quite Contrary's parched flowers, it transforms itself into a big rain cloud; and lends aid to Little Miss Muffet who wants nothing to do with that awful pesky spider. "All in a day's work," says the Neat Line.

ACT IT OUT:

You can expand the dialogue for each set of characters the Neat Line meets, or even add more scenes from other nursery rhymes. Grab the chance to do some interactive and collaborative writing with your students. They can dictate each line as you (or they) write it down.

Nouns and Verbs Have a Field Day. **Pulver, Robin. Illus. by Lynn Rowe Reed. Holiday House, 2006. Gr. K-3 (easy fiction)**

When Mr. Wright's class rushes outside for Field Day, the nouns and verbs left behind in the classroom organize their own field day, with the nouns on one team and the verbs on the other. They quickly discover that they need each other, so they form new teams to have the time of their lives playing tug-of-words, hide-and-seek, Simon Says, and a compound word three-legged race. Filled with puns, clever wordplay, and lots of adorable little noun and verb characters, the graphically bright and busy acrylics will certainly pep up your grammar lessons.

ACT IT OUT:

You'll need to fiddle around with this story to turn it into a script, but there's lots of balloon dialogue and plenty of parts for a large group. You might even want to stage a noun and verb field day with outside games and activities. Share the author's companion story, *Punctuation Takes a Vacation* (Holiday House, 2003), which would also make a great theater production.

Oink? **Palatini, Margie. Illus. by Henry Cole. Simon & Schuster, 2006. Gr. PreK-3 (easy fiction)**

Thomas and Joseph are sloppy, lazy, dirty . . . and happy pigs. Their neighbors, two hens, a rabbit, and a duck, are disgusted with their slovenly ways and come up with an improvement plan involving fresh paint, a diet of fresh vegetables, and a bath. "Oink?" the two say before making a hash of painting the fence, picking vegetables from the garden, and digging a nice, refreshing waterhole. Exasperated, the neighbors take over each chore, which might remind you of an old book by Mark Twain where a boy gets his friends to whitewash that fence. Comical watercolor, colored pencil, and ink illustrations show two huge hogs who turn out to be nobody's fools.

ACT IT OUT:

This would be a blast to act out in creative drama or to write up in script form. Sure, Thomas and Joseph's lines consist of the word "oink," but a good actor can get a lot of expression from even a single word. Go to **www.margiepalatini.com** for Reader's Theater scripts for the author's books *Bad Boys*, *Earthquack*, *Piggie Pie*, and *The Web Files*.

Pancakes for Supper. **Isaacs, Anne. Illus. by Mark Teague. Scholastic, 2006. Gr. PreK-2 (easy fiction)**

Riding through the woods on the back of her parents' wagon on the way to Whisker Creek, Toby, a plucky young girl wearing a colorful set of brand new clothes, is sent airborne when the wagon hits a big bump. Landing in a patch of snow, she encounters a hungry wolf. "Please don't eat me . . . and I will make you the grandest animal in the forest," Toby cries, offering up her beautiful blue coat in exchange. Encountering a cougar, a skunk, a porcupine, and a bear, she soon divests herself of everything save her red union suit, but gets them all back and a bucket of pancake syrup to boot when the animals set to arguing amongst themselves. This is, of course, a remake of Helen Bannerman's "Little Black Sambo" story, which has been liberated and reclaimed from its controversial past by illustrator Fred Marcellino in *The Story of Little Babaji* (HarperCollins, 1996) and by Julius Lester in *Sam and the Tigers* (Dial, 1996). Compare and contrast each retelling to see how a story can be reworked.

ACT IT OUT:

Teague's huge and exuberant full-bleed oil paintings and the repeated refrains of the story will make this spirited pourquoi and tall tale a storytime hit. There are wonderful scenes to act out in pairs, with one child playing Toby and the other child one of the animals who want to eat her. It would also make a fine puppet show. Bring in some maple syrup, and maybe even cook up a mess of pancakes for a cast party.

Precious and the Boo Hag. **McKissack, Patricia, and Onawumi Jean Moss. Illus. by Kyrsten Brooker. Atheneum, 2005. Gr. 1-4 (easy fiction)**

Recovering from a stomach ache, Precious stays home while Mama and Brother go out to plant the corn on the prairie, and she promises Mama she won't let anyone in the house. Before he leaves, Brother warns her not to disobey, and scares her good with his description of Pruella the Boo Hag, who, he claims, might try to get inside. Pruella is "tricky and she's scary, and she tries to make you disobey yo' mama." Of course, Pruella shows up, but don't worry about young

Precious. Even though Pruella tries her best to trick her way inside, Precious sees though her shenanigans and false words every time.

ACT IT OUT:

Third graders at Van Holten School in Bridgewater, New Jersey, wrote up scenes into Reader's Theater scripts, and they made wonderful oversized stick puppets of each of the characters so they could act it out. If you are working with a whole class, have each group write up one scene and stage it with puppets or people.

READER'S THEATER: 8 TOP CHOICES FOR OLDER READERS

Aliens Are Coming!: The True Account Of The 1938 War Of The Worlds Radio Broadcast. **McCarthy, Meghan. Illus. by the author. Knopf, 2006. Gr. 2-6 (nonfiction)**

While the cover of the picture book, featuring two green tentacled aliens foaming at the mouth, makes you think it's going to be a science fiction romp, you quickly realize this tale is true. It's a lively, humorous, but factual account of that memorable CBS evening radio broadcast of October 30, 1938, when Orson Wells and his Mercury Theater company put on a Halloween production of H. G. Wells's classic novel, *The War of the Worlds,* and scared everyone silly. Incorporated into the text are quotes from the actual broadcast about marauders from Mars taking over first Grovers Mill, New Jersey, and then the whole country, events which gullible folks believed to be happening.

ACT IT OUT:

At Meghan McCarthy's website, **www.aliensarecoming.com**, where she provides guidance in drawing your own alien, you'll find photos of Grovers Mill, and links to related sites. Best of all, she's included a transcript of the actual radio show, which older readers can read aloud in tribute to radio days of old, when folks sure knew how to appreciate a good script.

Babymouse: Our Hero. **Holm, Jennifer L., and Matthew Holm. Illus. by Matthew Holm. Random House, 2005. Gr. 2-5 (fiction)**

The *Babymouse* series is a wildly popular set of graphic novels about a sassy and effervescent daydreaming mouse whose creative fantasies help her get through the indignities of everyday life. The cartoon panels and characters are drawn with heavy black lines and accented with Babymouse's signature color, hot pink. In this episode, Babymouse misses the school bus and has to walk to school; contends with her homework-eating locker ("BURP!"); puts up with her sneering feline nemesis, Felicia Furrypaws; lives through fractions in math; and, worst of all, has to play the dreaded dodgeball in gym. While her escapades mirror the life of a middle-school girl, readers of all ages find Babymouse a memorable character.

ACT IT OUT:

Graphic novels are, by their very nature, not exactly suitable as read-alouds, since they are an intricate combination of balloon dialogue, narration, and cartoon illustrations. Babymouse books have loads of dialogues to act out, though, and the mouse even converses with the omniscient narrator. Students can take scenes and type up their own scripts. Give each small group one or two pages to turn into and act out as skits, and then have them put it all together for an all-class collection of Babymouse vignettes. They'll love the animated website, **www.babymouse.com**, where there are even illustrated pages for fans to try out their graphic writing skills.

Blood on the River: James Town 1607. **Carbone, Elisa. Viking, 2006. Gr. 5-8 (easy fiction)**

In his clear-eyed, harrowing account of the first year of the Jamestown Settlement, eleven-year-old orphan Samuel Collier becomes a page to Captain John Smith and sails to Virginia. Commoner Smith has his own problems with the gentlemen in the group, who resent him for presuming to rise above his station, and clap him in irons. The settlers live through a deadly attack face starvation; construct a fort and watch it destroyed by fire; and bury too many men dead of sickness. Samuel soon comes to understand the lionhearted Captain Smith's insistence on cooperating with others, including the inscrutable Chief Powhatan. In her extensive Author's Note, Carbone suggests several websites for planning a virtual or real-time visit to Jamestown. Students can find a plethora of primary sources, including John Smith's own writings, maps, portraits, and documents at **www.virtualjamestown.org**. The author's website, **www.elisacarbone.com** provides a teacher's study guide to the book.

ACT IT OUT:

Historical fiction gives children an authentic and personal feel for a bygone era. There are many scenes and dialogues from this novel that are ripe for dramatizing, including an unforgettable encounter on page 55 between Samuel and a frustrated Captain Smith after the sullen boy has once again been fighting with the other boys. "Stand on one foot," Smith orders, and the boy tries unsuccessfully to keep his balance while the ship pitches and rolls in a storm. Students can write it up as a two-person dialogue and act it out.

Clementine. **Pennypacker, Sara. Illus. by Marla Frazee. Hyperion, 2006. Gr. 1-4 (fiction)**

"Pay attention!" teachers tell third-grader Clementine all the time, though she insists she is excellent at noticing things. For instance, she notices that her friend Margaret has been in the bathroom for a really long time, even for Margaret "who washes her hands one finger at a time." She finds Margaret in dire straits, with a big chunk of her halfway-down-her-waist straight brown hair missing because she got glue in it in the art room and tried to cut it out herself. So Clementine offers to help Margaret even it up a little, and when the art teacher finds them, Clementine once again gets sent to the principal's office, even though she thinks Margaret's new haircut makes her look beautiful, like a dandelion.

ACT IT OUT:

The dialogue between Clementine and Margaret in that outrageously funny first chapter makes a perfect short scene to act out. You could even photocopy those pages and have children act it out in pairs, highlighting their lines with markers. Look for funny scenes like these in fiction books. You don't always have to act out a complete story.

Journey to the Blue Moon: In Which Time Is Lost and Then Found Again. **Rupp, Rebecca. Candlewick, 2006. Gr. 3-6 (fiction)**

Alex has just gotten a report card of mostly D's because school just doesn't seem worth his time. In fact, he can't see the point in doing much of anything anymore, since, as he says, "Our time just keeps running out and then everything's over." He's even lost his pocket watch, a family heirloom inscribed with the words "Chose time or lose time." At the library to return an overdue book, he tells his troubles to an eccentric elderly woman named Lulu. She insists his lost watch is on the Moon, which is about to turn Blue, and she even gives him a ticket to get there. On the night of the blue moon, Alex and his dog Zeke hitch a ride on a rickety spaceship with five three-foot Moon Rats, and land on a Blue Moon where everyone has lost something.

ACT IT OUT:

This is an inventive and action-filled fantasy, a *Wizard of Oz* or *The Phantom Tollbooth*-like quest that incorporates many aspects of lost time. Alex meets a number of unusual and eccentric characters, and you'll find many dialogues and scenes for students to stage. Photocopy various scenes, one per group of writers, and have them transform the pages into dialogue and narration to act out.

Out from Boneville (Bone #1). Smith, Jeff. Illus. by the author. Graphix/Scholastic, 2005. Gr. 4-8 (fiction)

Originally published in the early 1990s as the first in a series of nine black-and-white comic books, this start to the epic, a compelling graphic novel now in gorgeous color, will unleash a love-fest amongst your readers. The three Bone cousins have just been chased out of their hometown of Boneville. There's responsible and sensible Fone Bone; Phoney Bone, the larcenous and scheming ex-richest guy in town; and lackadaisical, cigar-chomping Smiley Bone. They look like a combination of Casper the Friendly Ghost, the Pillsbury Dough Boy and something out of Walt Kelley's comic strip, Pogo. When they become separated, Fone Bone lands in a mountain valley where he encounters a mostly invisible dragon, a leaf-like talking bug named Ted, two evil rat creatures, and a beautiful human girl named Thorn. The Bone cousins spend the rest of the book in outrageous adventures trying to get back together.

ACT IT OUT:

Here's another great source of scenes for scripting. If this book gets your students into graphic novels, have them check out the graphic novel reviewing website, run by librarian Robin Brenner, **www.noflyingnotights.com/sidekicks**. There you'll find core lists, including all the Bone books. If your school or public library has access to NoveList, the online fiction site, show your students how to use it to find more graphic novels like their favorites (through the Find Similar Books search) or to get full lists of series in reading order.

Red Ridin' in the Hood: And Other Cuentos by Patricia Santos Marcantonio, illustrated by Renato Alarcão. Farrar, 2005. Gr. 4-8 (fiction)

This is an original take on 11 well-known fairy tales. Marcantonio has reset all of the stories in the barrios of the United States and rethought them, integrating Spanish vocabulary into her retellings and giving them contemporary plot twists. In the title story, for example, Roja's mother instructs her to take the bus to her ailing abuelita's house, and to stay away from dangerous Forest Street. Wanting to save the bus fare, the girl disobeys her mamá. Sure enough, Lobo Chavez, a real wolf, pulls up in his glossy brown low-rider Chevy and asks her where she's headed. Don't worry about Roja, though. The wolf doesn't stand a chance when Roja takes out of her basket a hunk of goat cheese that smells just like her Uncle José's feet. Not all of the stories are funny like that one, but all are fascinating to compare with the original tales on which they are based, including "Snow White," "Jack and the Beanstalk," and "Hansel and Gretel."

ACT IT OUT:

There's a glossary of Spanish words at the back (though no pronunciation guide). These stories are ideal for groups of children to script up for Reader's Theater presentations. As a follow-up, they can select another traditional fairy tale and rewrite it with details from their own modern lives.

Replay. Creech, Sharon. HarperCollins, 2005. Gr. 4-7 (fiction)

"Earth to Fog Boy," Leo's sister calls to him, and it's true, Leo has a rich interior life and an imagination that leads him to daydreams where he is a hero, a rescuer, a winner, and a star. In real life, he's just gotten the part of the old Crone in drama teacher Mr. Beeber's new play, "Rumpopo's Porch." It could be worse. His good friend Ruby was cast as the donkey, but at least it's the front half. At home with his loving, quarreling, large, Italian family, Leo uncovers a secret. His father once had a sister named Rosario. Where is Aunt Rosario now, and why won't anyone in the family say her name?

ACT IT OUT:

Snippets of the story are written in play format, ready for readers to act out. And the script for the play the drama class stages is appended at the back. Have your students write up scripts based on a scene from their own lives and dramatize them.

I CAN'T PAY THE RENT!

Reprinted from *Books Kids Will Sit Still For 3: A Read-Aloud Guide* by Judy Freeman
(Libraries Unlimited, 2006).

Remember those silent movies with a villain, a damsel in distress, and an upstanding hero who saves the day? (The old Bullwinkle cartoons used to parody them with the characters Snidely Whiplash, sweet Nell, and Dudley Do-Right of the Mounties.)

Surely you've heard or done the melodrama below, with its little problem about paying the rent. It's a humorous way to review these stock character types in literature—the poor little damsel (you might want to talk briefly about damsels not being so distressed these days, or so dependent on the big strong guys to save them), the hero, and the villain—and to act them out in character.

For the following short sketch, give everyone napkins to use. Twist the napkins in the center to become an all-purpose prop. For the damsel's lines, hold the napkin to your temple; for the villain, use it as a mustache; and for the hero, hold the bow under your chin as a bow tie. The fun of it is in using different voices: the desperate damsel in distress, the dastardly villain, and the stalwart hero. If you prefer, hand out a copy of script (see page 229) for children to read, but listeners will pick this up orally just as easily.

Once children get the hang of it and know the lines, they should do the whole skit a final time as fast as they can. They will be eager to take their napkins home to perform the skit for their parents. Also use the script as a template for young playwrights to extend the scene or write new scenes employing the same characters and act them out.

I CAN'T PAY THE RENT

DAMSEL: I CAN'T pay the rent!

VILLAIN: You MUST pay the rent!

DAMSEL: But I CAN'T pay the rent!

VILLAIN: But you MUST pay the rent!

DAMSEL: But I CAN'T pay the rent!

VILLAIN: But you MUST pay the rent!

HERO: *I'll* pay the rent!

DAMSEL: My hero!

VILLAIN: Curses! Foiled again!

The Barking Mouse

Adapted from the book *The Barking Mouse* by Antonio Sacre, illustrated by Alfredo Aguirre, Albert Whitman, 2003. (For grades 1-4.)

Reader's Theater adaptation by Judy Freeman; reprinted with permission of the publisher, Albert Whitman.

ROLES

Narrator 1	**Mamá Ratón**
Narrator 2	**Papá Ratón**
Narrator 3	**Sister**
Narrator 4	**Brother**
Narrator 5	**Cat**

NARRATOR 1: Once upon a time there was a family of mice.

NARRATOR 2: There was Mamá Ratón, Papá Ratón, and Brother and Sister Ratón.

NARRATOR 3: They all went on a picnic on a beautiful day.

NARRATOR 4: Mamá had a beautiful voice and sang as she walked.

MAMÁ: *(sings)* Three blind mice, three blind mice.

NARRATOR 5: Papá had big muscles, or so he thought. He carried a huge picnic basket.

PAPÁ: *(flexes his biceps)*

NARRATOR 1: Sister was older than brother and was very brave.

SISTER: *(jumps at Brother)* **BOO!**

NARRATOR 2: Brother had big muscles like his dad, or so he thought, and was almost as brave as his sister.

BROTHER: *(jumps back in alarm)* **YIKES!**

NARRATOR 3: As they searched for a place to eat, they passed a tall fence.

BROTHER: Psst! Hermana! I hear a cat lives behind this fence!

Reader's Theater adaption of *The Barking Mouse* by Antonio Sacre, illus. by Alfredo Aguirre (Albert Whitman, 2003) written by Judy Freeman for *Once Upon a Time: Using Storytelling, Creative Drama, and Reader's Theater with Children in Grades PreK-6* (Libraries Unlimited, 2007). Reprinted with permission.

SISTER:	I'm not scared of any cat!
BROTHER:	Me, neither.
NARRATOR 4:	Mamá sang a pretty song while Brother and Sister helped Papá unload the food.
PAPÁ:	Here are the medianoches, and the pollo frito, and the congrí, and the bread, and the lemonade. What are *you* all going to eat?
MAMÁ:	Papá, you are so bad!
PAPÁ:	I have to eat a lot to keep these muscles so huge! (*flexes his muscles*)
NARRATOR 5:	He was just kidding, of course. Then they ate their picnic lunch.
SISTER & BROTHER:	Mamá, Papá! Vamos a jugar. We want to go play.
MAMÁ:	Children, you go play by yourselves. Me and Papá, we're going to stay here and smooch.
PAPÁ:	Yippee!
SISTER & BROTHER:	EEEWWWW!!!
NARRATOR 1:	So they went to play by themselves.
NARRATOR 2:	They played Hide-and-Go-Seek.
BROTHER:	You're it.
NARRATOR 3:	They played fútbal.
SISTER:	I scored again!
NARRATOR 4:	They played "close your eyes and spin till you fall down."
SISTER & BROTHER:	We both win! It's a tie! (*they jump up and down*)
NARRATOR 5:	They had a great time.

Reader's Theater adaption of *The Barking Mouse* by Antonio Sacre, illus. by Alfredo Aguirre (Albert Whitman, 2003) written by Judy Freeman for *Once Upon a Time: Using Storytelling, Creative Drama, and Reader's Theater with Children in Grades PreK-6* (Libraries Unlimited, 2007). Reprinted with permission.

231

NARRATOR 1:	They went to check on Mamá and Papá. They were still smooching.
MAMÁ & PAPÁ:	**SMMOOOCCH.**
SISTER & BROTHER:	**EEEWWWW!!!**
NARRATOR 2:	So Brother and Sister went and played some more.
SISTER:	Race you to that fence, Hermano.
BROTHER:	That's where that cat lives!
SISTER:	Chicken!
BROTHER:	I'm no chicken. Look at these muscles! *(flexes his muscles)*
SISTER:	**BOO!** *(jumps at Brother)*
BROTHER:	**YIKES!!** *(jumps back in alarm)*
NARRATOR 3:	Then they raced to the fence. Sister touched it first. But Brother was not too far behind.
BROTHER:	Do you think the cat is there?
SISTER:	Let's look.
NARRATOR 4:	They looked through the fence. Sure enough, there was the cat.
SISTER:	Hola, Gato!
BROTHER:	Hola, Gato!
NARRATOR 5:	The cat didn't say a word.
SISTER:	Hola, Gato!
BROTHER:	Hola, Gato!
NARRATOR 5:	The cat didn't move a whisker.
BROTHER:	*(flexes his muscles)* Hola, Gato flaco! You're no match for these. Hee hee hee!

Reader's Theater adaption of *The Barking Mouse* by Antonio Sacre, illus. by Alfredo Aguirre (Albert Whitman, 2003) written by Judy Freeman for *Once Upon a Time: Using Storytelling, Creative Drama, and Reader's Theater with Children in Grades PreK-6* (Libraries Unlimited, 2007). Reprinted with permission.

SISTER:	Hola, Gato flaco! Hee hee hee! *(holds her sides with laughter)*
NARRATOR 1:	They laughed so hard that they didn't see the cat's bright green eyes get a little smaller.
NARRATOR 2:	Sister stuck out her tongue and gave the cat a great big raspberry.
SISTER:	Pplllllllllhhhhhhhhhhhhhhh!
BROTHER:	Pplllllllllhhhhhhhhhhhhhhh!
NARRATOR 3:	They fell over laughing, tears coming out of their eyes.
NARRATOR 4:	They laughed so hard they didn't see the cat's tail stop moving.
NARRATOR 5:	They laughed so hard they didn't see his claws digging into the earth.
NARRATOR 1:	They were laughing so hard they didn't see that cat jump to the top of that fence and look down at them.
NARRATOR 2:	Brother and sister looked up. They stopped laughing.
SISTER & BROTHER:	**Uhhh! Adiós, Gato!**
NARRATOR 3:	Then they turned around and started running as fast as they could.
SISTER & BROTHER:	**Mamá! Papá!**
NARRATORS 1-5:	**WHOOSH. They could hear the cat running behind them!**
NARRATORS 1-5:	**WHOOSH.**
NARRATORS 4-5:	**It was getting closer!**
NARRATORS 1-3:	**And closer!**
NARRATOR 4:	Finally, they reached the picnic blanket.

Reader's Theater adaption of *The Barking Mouse* by Antonio Sacre, illus. by Alfredo Aguirre (Albert Whitman, 2003) written by Judy Freeman for *Once Upon a Time: Using Storytelling, Creative Drama, and Reader's Theater with Children in Grades PreK-6* (Libraries Unlimited, 2007). Reprinted with permission.

MAMÁ & PAPÁ:	**SMMOOOCCH**
SISTER & BROTHER:	**Mamá! Papá! Stop smooching!**
PAPÁ:	What?
SISTER & BROTHER:	El gato! The cat is going to eat us!
PAPÁ:	*(flexes his muscles)* Yo no tengo miedo del gato! I'm not scared of that cat! If that cat comes, I'm going to tell him, "Yo soy Papá Ratón! Yo voy a darle *pow!* I am going to give him *pow! Pow! Pow! Pow!*"
NARRATOR 5:	And just then Papá saw the cat.
PAPÁ:	**Mamá!** *(jumps behind Mamá)*
NARRATOR 1:	He jumped behind Mamá.
NARRATOR 2:	Then Brother and Sister jumped behind Mamá.
NARRATOR 3:	The only thing that stood between that mean cat and her familia was Mamá.
NARRATOR 4:	Her heart pounded.
NARRATOR 5:	She didn't know what to do.
NARRATOR 1:	With the courage a mother feels when her family is threatened, she stood on her hind paws, looked right into the great green eyes of that cat, and from somewhere deep inside her, she said . . .
MAMÁ:	**WOOF! WOOF! WOOF! WOOF! WOOF! WOOF!**
NARRATOR 2:	The cat stopped.
CAT:	This is WEIRD! A barking mouse? No vale la pena! It's not worth it!
NARRATOR 3:	He turned around, jumped over the fence, and was gone.
BROTHER:	Whoa!

234 Reader's Theater adaption of *The Barking Mouse* by Antonio Sacre, illus. by Alfredo Aguirre (Albert Whitman, 2003) written by Judy Freeman for *Once Upon a Time: Using Storytelling, Creative Drama, and Reader's Theater with Children in Grades PreK-6* (Libraries Unlimited, 2007). Reprinted with permission.

SISTER:	Cool!
PAPÁ:	I *knew* I married the right woman!
NARRATORS 1-5:	And when they all got home, nice and safe, Mamá said . . .
MAMÁ:	**You see, kids? Es muy importante hablar otro idioma! It pays to speak another language!**

Reader's Theater adaption of *The Barking Mouse* by Antonio Sacre, illus. by Alfredo Aguirre (Albert Whitman, 2003) written by Judy Freeman for *Once Upon a Time: Using Storytelling, Creative Drama, and Reader's Theater with Children in Grades PreK-6* (Libraries Unlimited, 2007). Reprinted with permission.

Glossary of Spanish Words from
The Barking Mouse
by Antonio Sacre (Albert Whitman, 2003)

adiós:	goodbye
congrí:	rice and black beans
familia:	family
flaco:	skinny, thin
fútbol:	soccer
gato:	cat
hermana:	sister
hermano:	brother
hola:	hello
medianoches:	"midnight" sandwiches of ham and cheese
No vale la pena.:	It's not worth it.
pollo frito:	fried chicken
ratón:	mouse
Vamos a jugar.:	Go play.
Yo soy:	I am
Yo voy a darle . . . :	I am going to give him . . .

100+ Children's Books Just Right for Creative Drama and / or Reader's Theater

Adapted in part from entries in *Books Kids will Sit Still For* (Libraries Unlimited, 1990), *More Books Kids will Sit Still For* (1995), and *Books Kids will Sit Still For 3* (2006).

(NOTE: See also "Reader's Theater: 9 Perfect Picture Books" on page 219 and Reader's Theater: 8 Top Choices for Older Readers" on page 224)

Here are a few more of my favorite candidates to dramatize with children. Though we encourage our audiences to interact with stories as we read—joining in on repeated refrains and animal noises, for instance—most of the time it's best to read aloud and finish a story before launching into full-scale drama activities.

Note that the majority of the creative drama titles on the list below are picture books. Be on the lookout as well for good, actable scenes in the fiction books you're reading aloud, booktalking, or using for book discussion groups with your older students. And remember that many folk and fairy tales are splendid candidates for acting out. See the annotated bibliography "400+ Children's Books Every Storyteller Should Know" on page 111 for more options.

KEY TO CATEGORIES:

EASY FICTION: easy fiction picture books

FICTION: chapter books, most of them fantasies dealing with folklore themes

FOLKTALE: folk or fairy tales from 398.2 section of library

NONFICTION: informational books, or books from the nonfiction section of the library)

POETRY: Mother Goose and other nursery rhymes or poetry

Andreae, Giles. *K Is for Kissing a Cool Kangaroo.* **Illus. by Guy Parker-Rees. Orchard, 2003. Gr. PreK-K (easy fiction)**

"A is for apple that grows on the tree/B is for busy and big bumblebee." This big, bright, bouncy, rhyming and alliterative alphabet book is full of active animals whose actions you can act out in narrative pantomime.

Arnold, Tedd. *Hi! Fly Guy.* **Illus. by the author. Scholastic/Cartwheel, 2005. Gr. PreK-2 (easy fiction)**

A boy named Buzz catches the smartest pet in the world, a fly, and enters Fly Guy in The Amazing Pet Show. This simple-to-read chapter book makes a perfect candidate for Reader's Theater for first graders. Also write up the script for *Super Fly Guy* (2006), so you can have two casts.

Asch, Frank. *Mr. Maxwell's Mouse.* **Illus. by the author. Kids Can, 2004. Gr. 2-5 (easy fiction)**

Celebrating his new job promotion, Mr. Howard Maxwell, a dignified gray cat, decides to have a raw mouse for lunch, but the loquacious mouse will not be easy to eat. It would be satisfying to write a Reader's Theater script and have children act out the story in small groups—one cat, one mouse, and one or two narrators.

Ashman, Linda. *Rub-a-Dub Sub.* **Illus. by Jeff Mack. Harcourt, 2003. Gr. PreK-1 (easy fiction)**

Sinking in his orange submarine, a little boy dives through the colorful underwater oceanscape and emerges safe in his own bathtub. Make up motions and undersea sound effects for each set of rhymes and vivid action verbs and act it all out.

Aylesworth, Jim. *Aunt Pitty Patty's Piggy.* **Illus. by Barbara McClintock. Scholastic, 1999. Gr. PreK-1 (easy fiction)**

Aunt Pitty Patty's niece enlists the help of everyone and everything she meets—the dog, stick, fire, water, ox, butcher, rope, rat, cat, and farmer—in order to make that stubborn new piggy enter her gate, but they all refuse. Form a long line of children to act this out using dialogue.

Aylesworth, Jim. *The Tale of Tricky Fox: A New England Trickster Tale.* **Illus. by Barbara McClintock. Scholastic, 2001. Gr. PreK-2 (folktale)**

Tricky Fox boasts to Brother Fox that he can fool a human into putting a fat pig into his sack. Children can pair up to act out the scenes between the fox and ladies he tricks.

Bania, Michael. *Kumak's Fish: A Tall Tale from the Far North.* **Illus. by the author. Alaska Northwest, 2004. Gr. PreK-3 (easy fiction)**

Using his Uncle Aglu's amazing hooking stick, Kumak catches a huge fish that everyone in the family and the village tries to help pull up. This Alaskan version of "The Enormous Turnip," is great fun to act out in a long line.

Bannerman, Helen. *The Story of Little Babaji.* **Illus. by Fred Marcellino. HarperCollins, 1996. Gr. PreK-2 (easy fiction)**

Little Babaji gives up his fine and colorful new clothes to five vain and growly tigers, and then, through his own bravery and cleverness, outwits the tigers and reclaims his wardrobe. This newly updated version of the old "Little Black Sambo" story makes a splendid Reader's Theater.

Barton, Byron. *My Car.* **Illus. by the author. Greenwillow, 2001. Gr. PreK-K (easy fiction)**

Sam describes how he keeps his car in shape and drives safely. Act this one out, with children becoming both Sam and his car, driving around the room and obeying all the traffic signs.

Beaumont, Karen. *Move Over, Rover!* **Illus. by Jane Dyer. Harcourt, 2006. Gr. PreK-1 (easy fiction)**

When the rain begins, Cat, Raccoon, Squirrel, Blue Jay, and Snake all come in Rover's doghouse to stay dry. A building chantable refrain makes the story just right to act out and recite. Write up an easy-to-read Reader's theater with a part for everyone. You could have several children playing each animal.

Black, Holly, and Tony DiTerlizzi. *The Spiderwick Chronicles, Book 1: The Field Guide.* **Illus. by Tony DiTerlizzi. Simon & Schuster, 2003. Gr. 2-5 (fiction)**

Nine-year-old Jared, his twin, Simon, and their 13-year-old sister, Mallory, have just moved with their mother to Great-Aunt Lucinda's creepy old Victorian mansion where unexplainable mischief occurs. There are several wonderful scenes in this fiction book that you or your readers can script out and dramatize for Reader's Theater.

Browne, Anthony. *Willy the Dreamer.* **Illus. by the author. Candlewick, 1998. Gr. PreK-2 (easy fiction)**

Willy, a gentle, amiable chimp, dreams of being a painter or an explorer, a beggar or a king. Children can act out Willy's dreams in narrative pantomime as you reread it aloud.

Bruel, Nick. *Bad Kitty.* **Illus. by the author. Roaring Brook, 2005. Gr. PreK-2 (easy fiction)**

The black kitty used to be good until the day her people ran out of kitty food and tried to offer her an unappetizing and alphabetical array of vegetables, which led her to become a very BAD kitty. Act out the kitten's antics, both bad and good, in narrative pantomime.

Buzzeo, Toni. *Dawdle Duckling.* **Illus. by Margaret Spengler. Dial, 2003. Gr. PreK-K (easy fiction)**

Mama Duck's fourth little duckling dawdles and dreams, preens and plays, and refuses to stay with the others. Line your little ducklings up and act this out, with you as Mama Duck wearing your favorite straw hat. At **www.mimismotifs.com**, you can buy a set of six adorable crocheted finger puppets of the book's characters just right for little ones to use to reenact the story together.

Byars, Betsy. *My Brother, Ant.* **Illus. by Marc Simont. Viking, 1996. Gr. 1-3 (easy fiction)**

This amiable, easy-to-read first chapter book is narrated by an unnamed older brother who describes life with his younger brother, Anthony, who sometimes drives him crazy. Chapters are just the right length for small-group Reader's Theater activities.

Carle, Eric. *From Head To Toe.* **Illus. by the author. HarperCollins, 1997. Gr. PreK-K (easy fiction)**

Bright and expressive animals, from penguin to monkey to crocodile, ask children if they can turn their heads, wave their arms, or wiggle their hips. Act out each animal's motion.

Cazet, Denys. *Elvis the Rooster Almost Goes to Heaven.* **Illus. by the author. HarperCollins, 2003. Gr. PreK-2 (easy fiction)**

In an easy reader that makes an uproarious read-aloud, Elvis the rooster chokes on a bug at crowing time, and when the sun still comes up without him, he faints at the shock. The dialogue is so jocular, it would be a shame not to write this up as a Reader's Theater.

Chaconas, Dori. *Cork & Fuzz: Short and Tall.* **Illus. by Lisa McCue. Viking, 2006. Gr. PreK-2 (easy fiction)**

Cork, a short muskrat, feels that since he is older than his best friend, Fuzz, a possum, he should be taller as well. The three chapters in this easy reader are mostly dialogue, just waiting to be acted out by pairs of readers. Simply photocopy the stories and assign each pair of children one chapter to read together. To distinguish between characters' dialogue and actions, children can highlight their characters' dialogue with one highlighter marker and their characters' actions with another. Have them switch parts and act it out again.

Clark, Emma Chichester. *Follow the Leader!* **Illus. by the author. Simon & Schuster, 2003. Gr. PreK-2 (easy fiction)**

A little boy leads an ever-growing line of animals into the woods, where they encounter a menacing tiger who wants to join their follow-the-leader game. Act the whole thing out in a nice long line.

Collins, Suzanne. *Gregor the Overlander.* **Scholastic, 2003. Gr. 4-7 (fiction)**

Twelve-year-old Gregor and his two-year-old sister, Boots, fall through an airduct in their New York City apartment house laundry room, and land far below in the Underland, populated by pale humans, giant cockroaches, bats, and vicious, warring rats. Have students work in groups to turn dramatic scenes into Reader's Theater scripts.

Coville, Bruce. *The Monster's Ring.* **Illus. by Katherine Coville. Harcourt, 2002. Gr. 3-6 (fiction)**

Russell obtains and uses a magic ring that turns him into a monster and scares the meanness out of bully Eddy Tacker. Students can act out Russell's horrifying transformations in narrative pantomime.

Creech, Sharon. *Love That Dog.* **Joanna Cotler/HarperCollins, 2001. Gr. 4-8 (fiction)**

In a series of spare, free-verse journal entries, Jack ponders the poems his teacher reads aloud and tries to relate them to his own life and what happened to his beloved yellow dog, Sky. Children can read aloud Jack's poems, stage a poetry reading of favorite poets, or hold a poetry slam featuring their own work.

Cronin, Doreen. *Click, Clack, Moo: Cows That Type.* **Illus. by Betsy Lewin. Simon & Schuster, 2000. Gr. PreK-1 (easy fiction)**

Farmer Brown can't believe his eyes when his cows find an old typewriter in the barn and post a typed demand for electric blankets on the barn door. Type up a Reader's Theater script and have your students read it aloud as they act it out.

Crummel, Susan Stevens. *All in One Hour.* **Illus. by Dorothy Donohue. Marshall Cavendish, 2003. Gr. PreK-2 (easy fiction)**

At 6:00 a.m., when the cat follows a mouse out the window, a madcap chase ensues involving a dog, a dogcatcher, a robber, a policeman, and a grocer, all described in rhyme. Recall the sequence of the chase and act it out.

Crummell, Susan Stevens. *Ten-Gallon Bart.* **Illus. by Dorothy Donohue. Marshall Cavendish, 2006. Gr. PreK-2 (easy fiction)**

Tired of being brave, courageous, and bold, Ten-Gallon Bart, sheriff of Dog City plans to retire until Billy the Kid, the "roughest, toughest, leanest, meanest goat in the country," comes to town. With lots of good characters, dialogue, action, narration, and humor, this parody of old TV Westerns like *Gunsmoke* is just the ticket for a Reader's Theater play.

Cushman, Doug. *Inspector Hopper.* Illus. by the author. HarperCollins, 2000. Gr. PreK-2 (easy fiction)

In three sprightly dialogue-filled chapters, grasshopper detective Inspector Hopper and his assistant McBugg solve two mysteries and stop a crime. Write Reader's Theater scripts for all three chapters and have small groups act them out.

Davis, Katie. *Who Hops?* Illus. by the author. Harcourt, 1998. Gr. PreK-K (easy fiction)

"Frogs hop. Rabbits hop. Kangaroos hop. Cows hop . . . NO THEY DON'T!" Act out each animal's actions and create some new scenarios: who runs or purrs or barks or dives?

Diakité, Baba Wagué. *The Hunterman and the Crocodile: A West African Folktale.* Illus. by the author. Scholastic, 1997. Gr. 1-5 (folktale)

Donso the Hunterman helps Bamba the crocodile across the river and then looks for a way out when the croc plans to eat him. Act this story out in creative drama or script as a Reader's Theater.

DiCamillo, Kate. *The Miraculous Journey of Edward Tulane.* Illus. by Bagram Ibatoulline. Candlewick, 2006. Gr. 3-7 (fiction)

Three-foot china rabbit Edward Tulane begins a difficult odyssey and learns about love. For far more ideas and related titles, see Judy Freeman's teacher's guide online at **www. edwardtulane.com** which includes a Reader's Theater script of a climactic scene.

Dillon, Leo, and Diane Dillon. *To Everything There Is a Season.* Illus. by the authors. Scholastic, 1998. Gr. 1-6 (nonfiction)

The well-known verses from The Book of Ecclesiastes in the Bible are depicted in 16 breathtaking single and double page paintings drawn from a wide variety of world cultures. Follow up with a class choral reading or an exercise in creative drama where you read the verses aloud while the children act them out in pantomime.

Dodds, Dayle Ann. *Where's Pup?* Illus. by Pierre Pratt. Dial, 2003. Gr. PreK-1 (easy fiction)

A bespectacled little clown searches the circus grounds for his dog, Pup. The rhyming text would be such fun to act out as a Reader's Theater for emergent readers.

Donaldson, Julia. *The Gruffalo.* Illus. by Axel Scheffler. Dial, 1999. Gr. PreK-1 (easy fiction)

A mouse talks a fox, an owl, and a snake out of eating him by describing the Gruffalo, a fierce made-up monster he is pretending to meet for lunch. All of the repetition, humor, and just a touch of danger make this story a good candidate for Reader's Theater for first grade, or to act out for pre-readers.

Dooling, Michael. *The Great Horse-less Carriage Race.* Illus. by the author. Holiday House, 2002. Gr. 2-6 (nonfiction)

On November 28, 1895, a Chicago newspaper sponsored a 52-mile horse-less carriage race through the city to show the superiority of the "newfangled" machines to the horse and buggy. With your students, write up the action-packed true story into a Reader's Theater script for them to act out.

Dunrea, Olivier. *Ollie.* **Illus. by the author. Houghton Mifflin, 2003. Gr. PreK-1 (easy fiction)**

Geese friends, Gossie and Gertie, have been waiting for weeks for Ollie to hatch out of his egg, but he refuses to come out. Use hard-boiled eggs for Ollie, and make popsicle stick puppets for Gossie and Gertie, so everyone can act this one out. Also act out *Gossie* (2002), having children pretend to be the little goose walking about in her bright red boots.

Egan, Tim. *Serious Farm.* **Illus. by the author. Houghton Mifflin, 2003. Gr. K-2 (easy fiction)**

Nothing makes Farmer Fred laugh or even smile, not even when the animals don mustaches, climb trees, and do tricks, until they all decide to pack up and leave the farm. This would make a hilarious Reader's Theater. Play the laugh game. Working in pairs, each person has 30 silent seconds to make the other laugh out loud. Then switch.

Egan, Tim. *The Trial of Cardigan Jones.* **Illus. by the author. Houghton Mifflin, 2004. Gr. K-3 (easy fiction)**

Cardigan, the new moose in town, is arrested and put on trial for pie theft, and the jury's convinced he's guilty! You and your students can write this up into a Reader's Theater script to act out for other classes.

Emberley, Michael. *Ruby and the Sniffs.* **Illus. by the author. Little, Brown, 2004. Gr. K-2 (easy fiction)**

Mouse Ruby thinks she hears burglars in Mrs. Mastiff's apartment building, but really, it's just the new neighbors—three enormous pigs. The action, vivacious dialogue, and wild humor make this a prime candidate for turning into a Reader's Theater for good readers to perform.

Emberley, Rebecca. *Three Cool Kids.* **Illus. by the author. Little, Brown, 1995. Gr. PreK-2 (easy fiction)**

In a big-city version of "The Three Billy Goats Gruff," three kid goats are challenged by a potbellied sewer rat who threatens to eat them for dinner. Increase the numbers of goats and rats so everyone gets a part when you reenact the whole story.

Ernst, Lisa Campbell. *Stella Louella's Runaway Book.* **Illus. by the author. Simon & Schuster, 1998. Gr. PreK-2 (easy fiction)**

Book-lover Stella is distraught when her now-due library book disappears on Saturday morning, and she spends a frantic day trying to track it down. This delightful circular story will be fun to act out in Reader's Theater (if you write up a script) or creative drama

Feiffer, Jules. *Bark, George.* **Illus. by the author. HarperCollins, 1999. Gr. PreK-1 (easy fiction)**

George's mother says, "Bark, George," but every time the floppy brown dog tries to bark, he meows, quacks, oinks, or moos instead. Act out the entire swallowing story in creative drama with lots of animal noises and that great surprise ending.

Feiffer, Jules. *I Lost My Bear.* **Illus. by the author. Morrow, 1998. Gr. PreK-6 (easy fiction)**

A blonde ponytailed little girl is distraught when she can't find her stuffed bear. Listeners can act out each scene, especially the last one when she finds Bearsie under her covers.

Feiffer, Jules. *Meanwhile . . .* **Illus. by the author. HarperCollins, 1997. Gr. K-3 (easy fiction)**

Raymond duels with the pirate captain, gets chased by a posse out West, and dodges Martians in his rocket ship. Children can act out each of his wild encounters in creative drama, or work in pairs to come up with more "Meanwhile . . ." situations to act out.

Fleischman, Paul. *Joyful Noise: Poems for Two Voices*. **Illus. by Eric Beddows. HarperCollins, 1988. Gr. 4-8 (poetry)**

In pairs or quartets, students can read aloud the 14 insect poems in this joyful Newbery Award winner. Or make transparencies of the poems, divide your group into two, and perform as larger scale choral readings.

Fleischman, Paul. *Seedfolks*. **Illus. by Judy Pedersen. HarperCollins, 1997. Gr. 5-8 (fiction)**

After Kim plants lima bean seeds in a vacant junk-filled lot in her Cleveland neighborhood, the whole neighborhood gets involved in cleaning up and planting the plot of ground. As with Fleischman's similarly formatted Civil War book, *Bull Run* (1993), you can hand out a chapter per student and have them read their character's story aloud to the rest of the class, Reader's Theater style.

Fleming, Denise. *Alphabet Under Construction*. **Illus. by the author. Henry Holt, 2002. Gr. PreK-1 (easy fiction)**

"Mouse airbrushes the A; buttons the B; carves the C; dyes the D . . ." and continues on through all 26 letters. Act out the whole alphabet in narrative pantomime

Frazee, Marla. *Walk On!: A Guide for Babies of All Ages*. **Illus. by the author. Harcourt, 2006. All Ages (easy fiction)**

Following the narrator's careful coaching, a bald, round-headed pre-toddler stands, holds on, sways, falls, cries, and tries again until, "Baby, you are walking! Beautiful." Your post-babies can act this out, based on baby behavior they've witnessed or can recall firsthand.

Gaiman, Neil. *The Day I Swapped My Dad for Two Goldfish.* **Illus. by Dave McKean. HarperCollins, 2004. Gr. 1-4 (easy fiction)**

After a boy trades his newspaper-reading dad for his friend Nathan's two goldfish, he must do a lot more swapping before he can get his dad back. This bizarrely absurd picture book will be fun to retell and act out in sequence.

George, Lindsay Barrett. *Inside Mouse, Outside Mouse*. **Illus. by the author. HarperCollins, 2004. Gr. PreK-1 (easy fiction)**

Inspecting each large pair of pages, we see how a gray mouse inside a house and a brown mouse outside are the same and different. Each page highlights a different preposition, which makes the story a great candidate for acting out in pairs as you read it aloud.

Gray, Libba Moore. *Is There Room on the Feather Bed?* **Illus. by Nadine Bernard Westcott. Orchard, 1997. Gr. PreK-1 (easy fiction)**

In the midst of a downpour, a host of farm animals entreat the wee fat man and woman to let them in the house, but flee when the skunk arrives. Act out the whole story with dialogue.

Grimes, Nikki. *Talkin' about Bessie: The Story of Aviator Elizabeth Coleman*. **Illus. by E. B. Lewis. Orchard, 2002. Gr. 3-6 (nonfiction)**

The life of the first African-American woman pilot is described in free verse poems through the eyes of 21 observers—family, friends, sponsors, and admirers. Your class can easily stage a Reader's Theater reading of the whole book.

Harper, Wilhelmina. *The Gunniwolf*. **Illus. by Barbara Upton. Dutton, 2003. Gr. K-2 (folktale)**

Little Girl disobeys her mother and wanders off into the jungle to pick flowers, meeting up with the Gunniwolf, a wolf who makes her sing to him until he falls asleep. Have your children pair off, one as the little child, and the other as the Gunniwolf, and act out the singing and chasing scenes; then switch roles and run through it again.

Harter, Debbie. *Walking Through the Jungle.* **Illus. by the author. Orchard, 1997. Gr. PreK-1 (easy fiction)**

In this colorful and jaunty call-and-response story with lots of animal noises for children to make, a young girl is chased by a lion, a whale, a wolf, a crocodile, a snake, and a polar bear as she makes her way through jungle, ocean, mountain, river, desert, and ice.

Hartman, Bob. *The Wolf Who Cried Boy.* **Illus. by Tim Raglin. Putnam, 2002. Gr. K-2 (easy fiction)**

Detesting the lamburgers and Sloppy Does his mom makes for dinner, Little Wolf sets out to catch a nice boy so he can have a decent meal for once. This witty Aesop's fable turnaround will make wonderful Reader's Theaters to act out with a class and compare with the original story.

Hausman, Bonnie. *A to Z: Do You Ever Feel Like Me?* **Photos by Sandi Fellman. Dutton, 1999. Gr. PreK-2 (easy fiction)**

In an alphabet of emotions, each double page spread contains a large color photo of an expressive child acting out one emotion for children to identify and mimic.

Henkes, Kevin. *Kitten's First Full Moon.* **Illus. by the author. Greenwillow, 2004. Gr. PreK-1 (easy fiction)**

When she sees her first full moon, Kitten thinks it's a little bowl of milk, and she wants it. Act out the story in narrative pantomime with your children playing the kitten.

Hoberman, Mary Ann. *It's Simple, Said Simon.* **Illus. by Meilo So. Knopf, 2001. Gr. PreK-1 (easy fiction)**

Simon demonstrates his growl for a dog, a stretch for a cat, and a jump for a horse, but then he meets a tiger who plans to have boy for supper. Act out, in small groups or pairs, each boy-animal encounter.

Hoberman, Mary Ann. *You Read to Me, I'll Read to You: Very Short Fairy Tales to Read Together.* **Illus. by Michael Emberley. Little, Brown, 2004. Gr. K-3 (poetry)**

Eight well-known fairy tales have been adapted into witty, easy to read, rhyming poems for two voices. Duplicate each story and hand out the scripts to actors who can then bring it to life, Reader's Theater style. *You Read to Me, I'll Read to You: Very Short Stories to Read Together* (2001) is another of several companion books using the same format.

Howard, Arthur. *The Hubbub Above.* **Illus. by the author. Harcourt, 2005. Gr. PreK-1 (easy fiction)**

Sydney loves her quiet apartment until the noisy Kabooms move in upstairs. Close the book when you get to where Sydney rides the elevator to confront the Kabooms and ask children to break into trios and act out what they think will happen next.

Katz, Alan. *I'm Still Here in the Bathtub: Brand New Silly Dilly Songs.* **Illus. by David Catrow. Simon & Schuster, 2003. Gr. PreK-3 (easy fiction)**

Here is a collection of 14 seriously silly songs, each one a parody of a well known song, that is perfect for Singers Theater; hand out the words and sing up a storm.

Kimmel, Eric A. *Anansi and the Talking Melon.* **Illus. by Janet Stevens. Holiday House, 1994. Gr. Pre-2 (folktale)**

Anansi the Spider eats so much of the inside of a ripe cantaloupe, he's too fat to squeeze back out. To pass the time, he insults Elephant, Hippo, Warthog, and even the king, all of whom believe the melon can talk. All of Kimmel's Anansi books are rich sources for Reader's Theater, including *Anansi and the Moss-Covered Rock* (1988) and *Anansi Goes Fishing* (1992) and *Anansi and the Magic Stick* (2001).

Kimmel, Eric A. *Cactus Soup.* **Illus. by Phil Huling. Marshall Cavendish, 2004. Gr. K-4 (folktale)**

In this lively retelling of "Stone Soup" set in early-20th century Mexico, a troop of soldiers arrive at a town where the townsfolk hide their food and pretend to be poor. A natural for recreating the story or adapting as a Reader's Theater script.

Kindl, Patrice. *Goose Chase.* **Houghton Mifflin, 2001. Gr. 5-8 (fiction)**

Shut up in a tower for the past six months, a poor orphan Goose Girl must figure out a way to avoid marriage with King Claudio the Cruel or vacuous Prince Edmund. Photocopy some of the Goose Girl's many caustic dialogues in this novel, a tribute to fairy tales, including her encounters with three ravenous, human-eating ogresses, and have pairs of readers perform them aloud as Reader's Theater.

Lester, Julius. *Sam and the Tigers: A New Telling of Little Black Sambo.* **Illus. by Jerry Pinkney. Dial, 1996. Gr. PreK-3 (easy fiction)**

Meeting five tigers on his way to school, Sam appeases each with an item of his new and colorful wardrobe. Act out the scenes with Sam and the menacing tigers.

Lobel, Arnold. *Mouse Tales.* **Illus. by the author. HarperCollins, 1972. Gr. PreK-2 (easy fiction)**

Papa Mouse tells his seven mouse children stories, one for each. An easy reader, these vignettes are great for acting out or writing up as mini Reader's Theater scripts.

Lum, Kate. *What! Cried Granny: An Almost Bedtime Story.* **Illus. by Adrian Johnson. Dial, 1999. Gr. PreK-1 (easy fiction)**

For Patricks first sleepover at Granny's, she chops down a tree to make him a bed, plucks chickens for his pillow, shears sheep to weave him a blanket, and sews him a huge teddy. Children can act out the wild story in pairs, with one half as Granny and the other half as Patrick.

MacDonald, Margaret Read. *Pickin' Peas.* **Illus. by Pat Cummings. HarperCollins, 1998. Gr. PreK-2 (folktale)**

While Little Girl picks the peas in her garden and sings a picking song, a pesky and brazen rabbit jumps in the row behind her and starts picking and eating up all the peas she's left behind. Cast your listeners as gardeners and rabbits and act it out; it's also simple enough to do as an easy-to-read Reader's Theater for emergent readers.

Mayo, Margaret. *Tortoise's Flying Lesson: Animal Stories.* **Illus. by Emily Bolam. Harcourt, 1995. Gr. PreK-2 (folktale)**

Eight cheerful animal folktales introduce us to a mischievous monkey, a bossy lion, a shy tabby cat, and a protective mother hare, in stories that are fun to tell, act out, or turn into Reader's Theater scripts for all to read.

McCarthy, Meghan. *Steal Back the Mona Lisa.* Illus. by the author. Harcourt, 2006. Gr. PreK-2 (easy fiction)

When crooks steal the Mona Lisa, young Jack rappels out his bedroom window, speeds away in a roadster, flies to France, and gets it back. Condense the narrative and act out Jack's saga.

McCloskey, Robert. *Homer Price.* Illus. by the author. Viking, 1943. Gr. 3-6 (easy fiction)

The famed "Doughnut Machine" chapter in this classic fiction book was once made into a short film and would make a dandy Reader's Theater script.

McFarland, Lyn Rossiter. *Widget.* Illus. by Jim McFarland. Farrar, 2001. Gr. PreK-1 (easy fiction)

Sad and lonely, cold and hungry, the little white dog, Widget, pretends he's a cat to join the six cats in Mrs. Diggs's cozy little house. Dramatize the scene when Widget acts like the cats by puffing up, hissing, and growling.

McMullan, Kate. *I Stink!* Illus. by Jim McMullan. HarperCollins, 2002. Gr. PreK-2 (easy fiction)

A no-nonsense, tough-talking New York City garbage truck explains how he scarfs down your bags of trash each night while you sleep. Children can create a composite vehicle, with some being the wheels, doors, engine, and compacter, all working together and making lots of noise.

Medearis, Angela Shelf. *Too Much Talk.* Illus. by Stefano Vitale. Candlewick, 1995. Gr. PreK-2 (folktale)

First, a farmer's yam talks to him, and then his dog talks, and even the water in the riverbed has something to say. You'll find the script of the West African folktale "Talk" in Aaron Shepard's *Stories on Stage: Scripts for Reader's Theater.*

Montes, Marisa. *Los Gatos Black on Halloween.* Illus. by Yuyi Morales. Henry Holt, 2006. Gr. 1-4 (easy fiction)

In a spooky graveyard on Halloween night, los gatos (cats) slink, las calabazas (pumpkins) burn bright, and las brujas (witches) glide on their escobas (broomsticks) to a haunted house for a party. Try this as a choral reading or Reader's Theater.

Morpurgo, Michael. *The McElderry Book of Aesop's Fables.* Illus. by Emma Chichester Clark. McElderry, 2005. Gr. K-5 (folktale)

Twenty-one fables, some familiar, along with large, full-bleed, soft, sweet watercolors, introduce the usual assortment of misbehaving and misguided rats, dogs, foxes, crows, and other animal friends and enemies, all of whom learn their lessons. Act these out in small groups as skits or have each group write up one of the stories in script form.

Murphy, Jill. *Peace at Last.* Illus. by the author. Dial, 1980. Gr. PreK-1 (easy fiction)

Mr. Bear can't sleep. One of the greats for acting out in narrative pantomime.

Murray, Marjorie Dennis. *Don't Wake Up the Bear!* Illus. by Patricia Wittmann. Marshall Cavendish, 2003. Gr. PreK-1 (easy fiction)

One by one, on a cold winter's eve, a hare, a badger, a fox, and a squirrel snuggle against a sleeping bear to get warm, cautioning each new arrival, "Don't wake up the bear." The repeated refrain and rousing climax make it a natural for story times and creative drama.

Muth, Jon J. *Stone Soup.* Illus. by the author. Scholastic, 2003. Gr. K-2 (folktale)

Three Chinese monks arrive in an inhospitable village and help show the people the way to happiness by making soup from a stone. Write up a Reader's Theater production or act it out with invented dialogue.

Novak, Matt. *Mouse TV.* Illus. by the author. Orchard, 1994. Gr. PreK-2 (easy fiction)

When the TV goes on the fritz, the whole Mouse family gets involved in doing instead of watching. Write this up as a dandy Reader's Theater play and act it out for No TV Week.

Numeroff, Laura Joffe. *If You Take a Mouse to School.* Illus. by Felicia Bond. HarperCollins, 2003. Gr. PreK-2 (easy fiction)

A pink-eared brown mouse visits his human friend's classroom, doing a little math, conducting a science experiment, writing his own book, and playing sports. Lots of action makes this a good candidate for creative drama as well. You can narrate, and the kids can be the mouse.

O'Malley, Kevin. *Straight to the Pole.* Illus. by the author. Walker, 2003. Gr. PreK-2 (easy fiction)

Swathed in winter gear and a backpack, a solitary child trudges stoically through a fierce snowstorm, braving the elements to get to the school bus stop. Just right for acting out and feeling the cold.

Palatini, Margie. *Bad Boys.* Illus. by Henry Cole. HarperCollins, 2003. Gr. K-3 (easy fiction)

On the run again, Willy and Wally Wolf disguise themselves in lady sheep's clothing, and set off to fleece an unsuspecting flock of sheep. You'll find the Reader's Theater script on the author's website at **www.margiepalatini.com**.

Palatini, Margie. *Earthquack!* Illus. by Barry Moser. Simon & Schuster, 2002. Gr. PreK-1 (easy fiction)

Little Chucky Ducky feels the ground rumble and concludes, Henny-Penny style, that the earth is crumbling. Palatini's already written the script for you; download it from her gorgeous website at **www.margiepalatini.com**.

Palatini, Margie. *Moo Who?* Illus. by Keith Graves. HarperCollins, 2004. Gr. PreK-1 (easy fiction)

After being knocked out by a hard and high-flying cow pie, Hilda Mae Heifer can't remember who she is. This will make an adorable Reader's Theater script for grade 1, with lots of lovely animal noises. For a creative drama exercise, have your children pair up. The child playing the other animal character needs to explain to Hilda why she is not, say, a cat or a rooster, and to engage her in a question and answer session, modeled on the dialogue in the original story.

Palatini, Margie. *Piggie Pie.* Illus. by Howard Fine. Clarion, 1995. Gr. PreK-2 (easy fiction)

Gritch the Witch needs to find eight plump piggies so she can prepare her secret recipe for Piggie Pie. Find the author's Reader's Theater script for the book on the author's website, **www.margiepalatini.com**.

Palatini, Margie. *The Web Files.* **Illus. by Richard Egielski. Hyperion, 2001. Gr. K-3 (easy fiction)**

Ducktective Web and his partner, Bill, are hot on the trail of some missing, about-to-be-pickled, purple peppers in this deadpan barnyard takeoff on the old *Dragnet* TV show. The Reader's Theater script can be found at **www.margiepalatini.com**.

Palatini, Margie. *Zoom Broom.* **Illus. by Howard Fine. Hyperion, 1998. Gr. PreK-2 (easy fiction)**

Gritch the Witch, of *Piggie Pie* fame, visits fast-talking salesman Foxy's showroom in her search for the perfect broom. There's a hilarious takeoff on Abbott & Costello's "Who's on First" routine, where Gritch asks Foxy, "Which one is the one I want?" Your actors can stage it in pairs as a Reader's Theater scene.

Paul, Ann Whitford. *Mañana, Iguana.* **Illus. by Ethan Long. Holiday House, 2004. Gr. PreK-2 (easy fiction)**

Iguana is planning a fiesta on sábado (Saturday), and Conejo (rabbit), Tortuga (turtle), and Culebra (snake) keep making excuses instead of helping. This would make a droll Reader's Theater script, with its amusing dialogue, Spanish words, and repeated phrases.

Paye, Won-Ldy, and Margaret H. Lippert. *Head, Body, Legs: A Story from Liberia.* **Illus. by Julie Paschkis. Henry Holt, 2002. Gr. PreK-3 (folktale)**

Head joins forces with Arms, Body, and Legs so they can work together to reach up high and pick mangoes. An amusing pourquoi tale for acting out or Reader's Theater.

Pearson, Tracey Campbell. *Bob.* **Illus. by the author. Farrar, 2002. Gr. PreK-1 (easy fiction)**

Bob, a rooster who clucks, finds that his newly learned meowing, barking, ribbeting, and mooing work just fine to scare off a hungry fox. Act out the story with invented dialogue, having several actors play the parts of each animal Bob encounters.

Peck, Jan. *The Giant Carrot.* **Illus. by Barry Root. Dial, 1998. Gr. PreK-2 (easy fiction)**

Papa Joe and Mama Bess plant a carrot seed, Brother Abel waters it, but sweet Little Isabelle, who sings and dances around it, gets it growing. Actors will need to pull together to get that big carrot out of the ground.

Pinkney, Jerry. *Aesop's Fables.* **Retold and illus. by Jerry Pinkney. SeaStar, 2000. Gr. 2-8 (folktale)**

These 60 well-told Aesop's fables, some beloved and others lesser known, make wonderful short skits for creative drama, Reader's Theater, puppet shows, and flannel board stories.

Pinkwater, Daniel. *Tooth-Gnasher Superflash.* **Illus. by the author. Macmillan, 1990. Gr. PreK-2 (easy fiction)**

Mr. and Mrs. Popsnorkle and the five little Popsnorkles trade in their old car for a nice new one that turns into a dinosaur, an elephant, a turtle, and a flying chicken. A must for narrative pantomime, where the children drive around the room and turn into creatures.

Polacco, Patricia. *Oh, Look!* **Illus. by the author. Philomel, 2004. Gr. PreK-1 (easy fiction)**

Two young shepherd girls chase three frisky goats across the countryside. You'll recognize the old call-and-response story, "I'm Going on a Bear Hunt," joyously revamped here; children will be eager to act out the sounds and motions, as narrated by those naughty goats.

Raschka, Chris *Yo! Yes?* **Illus. by the author. Orchard, 1993. Gr. PreK-6 (easy fiction)**

Two boys, one confidant and the other friendless, become friends. Act this out in pairs or divide the class to act out the boys' brief but effective dialogue and body language.

Rathmann, Peggy. *Good Night, Gorilla.* **Illus. by the author. Putnam, 1994. Gr. PreK-1 (easy fiction)**

After stealing the zookeeper's ring of keys, Gorilla lets all the other animals out of their cages, and they follow the zookeeper home to bed. This is a treat to act out in narrative pantomime.

Rathmann, Peggy. *Officer Buckle and Gloria.* **Illus. by the author. Putnam, 1995. Gr. K-2 (easy fiction)**

When well-meaning but dull Officer Buckle brings obedient new police dog, Gloria, to his safety tip assembly at Napville School, the children sit up and take notice. Act out the scene where Officer Buckle gives his rules and Martha mimes behind his back. You can play Officer Buckle; the children can be Gloria. Pat them on the head and say, "Good dog."

Riordan, Rick. *The Lightning Thief.* **Miramax/Hyperion, 2005. Gr. 5-8 (fiction)**

In Book 1 of a crackling new series, *Percy Jackson and the Olympians*, meet Percy, troubled dyslexic ADHD kid, who is about to find out who his real father is: a Greek god. Chapter 1: "I Accidentally Vaporize My Pre-Algebra Teacher," will make a brilliant Reader's Theater script.

Root, Phyllis. *Rattletrap Car.* **Illus. by Jill Barton. Candlewick, 2001. Gr. PreK-K (easy fiction)**

Poppa doesn't know if he and the kids—Junie, Jakie, and the baby—can make it all the way to the lake in his old jalopy. Children can join in on all the jaunty chantable refrains and will love acting this out. Arrange chairs so kids feel like they're sitting in the car. Get an old record or the lid to a large round container to use as the steering wheel.

Rostoker-Gruber, Karen. *Rooster Can't Cock-a-Doodle-Doo.* **Illus. by Paul Rátz de Tagyos. Dial, 2004. Gr. PreK-1 (easy fiction)**

Rooster wakes with a terrible sore throat and enlists the help of the other animals to figure out how to wake up Farmer Ted without cock-a-doodle-doing. Act this out or write a Reader's Theater script for your first graders to read.

Rotner, Shelley. *Action Alphabet.* **Illus. by the author. Atheneum, 1996. Gr. PreK-1 (easy fiction)**

One color photo per page displays children in action—giggling, kicking, napping—with a one word caption for each letter of the alphabet. Listeners can then act out each verb.

Ryder, Joanne. *Earthdance.* **Illus. by Norman Gorbaty. Henry Holt, 1996. Gr. K-3 (easy fiction)**

This stirring free verse poem celebrating our own planet, Earth, works as a narrative pantomime or a dramatic Reader's Theater piece for Earth Day, with each child or pair of children reading aloud a sentence.

Sachar, Louis. *Holes.* **Farrar, 1998. Gr. 5-8 (fiction)**

For stealing a famous basketball player's sneakers, overweight, unlucky, but innocent Stanley Yelnats, is sentenced to hot, desolate Camp Green Lake in Texas, a detention center for bad boys. Given photocopies of key scenes, children can reenact them as Reader's Theater. You can discuss, compare, contrast, and evaluate the book versus the movie version. Go to

http://content.scholastic.com/browse/lessonplan.jsp?id=532 for a detailed lesson plan called "Write Your Own Screen Play," using *Holes*.

Salley, Coleen. *Epossumondas*. Illus. by Janet Stevens. Harcourt, 2002. Gr. PreK-2 (folklore)

Sweet little patootie, Epossumondas, can't get anything right and his Mama tells him, "Epossumondas, you don't have the sense you were born with." This uproarious noodlehead story, which will have your listeners chiming in on every refrain, is a natural to act out in creative drama or script as a Reader's Theater.

San Souci, Robert D. *Cinderella Skeleton*. Illus. by David Catrow. Harcourt, 2000. Gr. 1-5 (easy fiction)

Cinderella Skeleton is scorned by her ghoulish stepsisters and Stepmother Skreech, who won't let her go to Prince Charnel's frightfully infamous Halloween Ball. Wonderfully icky for Halloween, this is a tale your older kids will love reading aloud as a Reader's Theater.

Scieszka, Jon. *Squids Will Be Squids: Fresh Morals, Beastly Fables*. Illus. by Lane Smith. Viking, 1998. Gr. 2-6 (easy fiction)

The 18 hip, off-the-wall fables are just the ticket for small groups to perform, Reader's Theater-style.

Slobodkina, Esphyr. *Caps for Sale*. Illus. by the author. HarperCollins, 1947. Gr. PreK-1 (easy fiction)

"You monkeys you. Give me back my caps!" demands the frustrated peddler. Divide your group in half—monkeys versus peddlers—to act out this classic tale; then switch parts.

Smith, Jeff. *Bone #1: Out from Boneville*. Illus. by the author. Graphix/Scholastic, 2005. Gr. 4-8 (fiction)

When the three Bone cousins become separated, Fone Bone lands in a mountain valley where he encounters a mostly invisible dragon, a leaf-like talking bug named Ted, two evil rat creatures, and a beautiful human girl named Thorn. Scenes from this brilliant graphic novel will be a blast to script up as Reader's Theater.

Smith, Lane. *The Happy Hocky Family Moves to the Country*. Illus. by the author. Viking, 2003. Gr. 1-3 (easy fiction)

In this takeoff of old-fashioned easy readers of "Dick and Jane" vintage, Mr. and Mrs. Hocky and their three kids encounter smelly animals, poison ivy, and the county fair. As in *The Happy Hocky Family* (Viking, 1993), the short chapters or vignettes are wildly funny examples of understatement, all of which would be great fun for pairs or trios of children to read and act out as simple skits.

Smith, Lane. *John, Paul, George & Ben*. Illus. by the author. Hyperion, 2006. Gr. 1-8 (easy fiction)

What were our Founding Fathers like as boys? Follow the colonial childhoods of five of our most august patriots—bold John Hancock, noisy Paul Revere, honest George Washington, clever Ben Franklin, and that independent lad, Tom Jefferson—as they never were but could have been. Download Judy Freeman's teacher's guide and Reader's Theater script for this book at **www.hyperionbooksforchildren.com/board/displayBook.asp?id=1598.**

Soto, Gary. *Chato and the Party Animals.* **Illus. by Susan Guevara. Putnam, 2000. Gr. PreK-2 (easy fiction)**

Cool cat Chato plans a surprise bash for his best barrio buddy, stray cat Novio Boy but forgets to invite the guest of honor. Try a bit of creative drama with the party games the cats play, such as Shake-Paws, Jiggle-the-Mice, Toss-the-Cat-in-the-Blanket, and my personal favorite: Going to the Vet, where you have to scream your head off.

Souhami, Jessica. *No Dinner!: The Story of the Old Woman and the Pumpkin.* **Illus. by the author. Marshall Cavendish, 2000. Gr. PreK-2 (folktale)**

On her way to visit her granddaughter on the other side of the forest, an old woman meets and outwits the wolf, tiger, and bear who would like to eat her. Filled with humor and repeated refrains, this sly folktale is a storyteller's dream for acting out, telling and retelling, Reader's Theater, making flannelboard or puppet characters, comparing with similar stories, and predicting outcomes.

Stanley, Diane. *Raising Sweetness.* **Illus. by G. Brian Karas. Putnam, 1999. Gr. K-3 (easy fiction)**

When the sheriff, newly adoptive pa to eight orphans, receives a mysterious letter which no one, can read, Sweetness, the teeniest child, volunteers to stand outside of the schoolhouse to learn her letters. Great dialogue from Pa and his kids will fuel a comical Reader's Theater script.

Steen, Sandra, and Susan Steen. *Car Wash.* **Illus. by G. Brian Karas. Putnam, 2001. Gr. PreK-2 (easy fiction)**

Sitting in the back seat of their dirty car, two giggling siblings head into the deep dark space of the car wash in an undersea adventure where their imaginations run wild. As you share the simple text aloud, encourage your children to act out all the action and sound effects. Afterwards, you can simulate all the components of a car wash with your group. Have each team act out a different set of motions and noises: the rolling brush, the slapping felt arms, the drying machine, while other children can be the cars driving through.

Stevens, Janet, and Susan Stevens Crummel. *And the Dish Ran Away with the Spoon.* **Illus. by Janet Stevens. Harcourt, 2001. Gr. K-3 (easy fiction)**

After their performance of "Hey Diddle Diddle," Dish and Spoon don't come back so Cat, Dog, and Cow set off to find them. You may want to put this on as a formal play.

Stojic, Manya. *Rain.* **Illus. by the author. Crown, 2000. Gr. PreK-1 (easy fiction)**

The animals of the African savanna—the porcupine, zebras, baboons, rhino, and lion—smell, see, hear, feel, and taste the rain coming to the hot, cracked, red-soiled plain. Children can act out the story, using all their senses.

Teague, Mark. *Dear Mrs. LaRue: Letters from Obedience School.* **Illus. by the author. Scholastic, 2002. Gr. K-3 (easy fiction)**

Is that hypochondriac, serial exaggerator, and kvetcher, Ike the dog, in prison or at dog obedience school? Photocopy Ike's letters home, hand out one per student to practice, and stage a reading.

Thiesing, Lisa. *The Viper.* **Illus. by the author. Dutton, 2002. Gr. K-2 (easy fiction)**

Peggy the pig gets more and more frightened each time she gets a call from "zee Viper" who says he is coming to her house in one year, month, week, and minute. Act this one out in trios: Peggy, the Viper, and a narrator. See Judy Freeman's version on page 91.

Thomas, Shelley Moore. *Get Well, Good Knight.* **Illus. by Jennifer Plecas. Dutton, 2002. Gr. PreK-1 (easy fiction)**

When the Good Knight's three little dragon friends come down with colds, he seeks a cure from the old wizard. This easy reader is a lively candidate for acting out or Reader's Theater along with the others in the series, including *Good Night, Good Knight* (2000) and *Take Care, Good Knight* (2006)..

Vagin, Vladimir. *The Enormous Carrot.* **Illus. by the author. Scholastic, 1998. Gr. PreK-1 (easy fiction)**

After rabbits Daisy and Floyd plant seeds in their garden, they discover an enormous carrot growing there, and though they enlist their animal friends to help, the carrot won't come out. Act this out with your children, using their own names as the characters.

Van Allsburg, Chris. *Probuditi!* **Illus. by the author. Houghton Mifflin, 2006. (Gr. K-3 (easy fiction)**

After seeing a performance by magician and hypnotist Lomax the Magnificent, Calvin and his best friend Rodney hypnotize Calvin's little sister, Trudy, into thinking she's a dog. Act out the second half of the story where Calvin tries to snap Trudy out of it, or write it up as a Reader's Theater scene.

Waber, Bernard. *Bearsie Bear and the Surprise Sleepover Party.* **Illus. by the author. Houghton Mifflin, 1997. Gr. PreK-1 (easy fiction)**

On a cold snowy night, as Bearsie Bear is just dozing off in his big warm bed, his friends show up at the door wanting to spend the night. Listeners will quickly join in on the repeated dialogue. Afterwards, act out the whole story, using a long woolen scarf as Bearsie Bear's blanket.

Wattenberg, Jane. *Henny-Penny.* **Illus. by the author. Scholastic, 2000. Gr. PreK-2 (folktale)**

"CHICKABUNGA!" Henny-Penny squawks when an acorn smacks her on top of her fine red comb. "The sky is falling!" Listeners can chime in on all the repeated refrains. Do it as a play, encouraging actors to paraphrase any dialogue they can't remember.

Willems, Mo. *Don't Let the Pigeon Drive the Bus.* **Illus. by the author. Hyperion, 2003. Gr. PreK-6 (easy fiction)**

Even though the bus driver warns us not to let the pigeon drive the bus, the big-eyed persistent pigeon tries everything from whining to temper spells to get his way. In this interactive story, your listeners will talk back to the pigeon for sure.

Williams, Linda. *The Little Old Lady Who Was Not Afraid of Anything.* **Illus. by Megan Lloyd. Crowell, 1986. Gr. PreK-1 (easy fiction)**

On her way home one spooky night, a little old lady encounters shoes, pants, a shirt, gloves, a top hat, and a pumpkin head. Repeated sound effects and motions make this an inspired choice for group dramatics.

Young, Ed. *The Sons of the Dragon King: A Chinese Legend.* **Illus. by the author. Atheneum, 2004. Gr. 2-6 (folktale)**

Pondering the singular talents of his nine immortal sons, the Dragon King finds a new job or role for which each son is best suited. With your students' help, write the story as a Reader's Theater production they can put on for Chinese New Year.

Bibliography of Professional Books About Creative Drama and Reader's Theater

Barchers, Suzanne I. *Multicultural Folktales: Readers Theatre for Elementary Students.* **Teacher Ideas Press, 2000. ISBN 978-1-563-08760-8**

Take a tour of world folklore for grades 1 to 5 with 40 scripts and more than 30 countries. Check the Libraries Unlimited website, **www.lu.com**, for additional collections of scripts by Barchers.

Barchers, Suzanne I., and Charla R. Pfeffinger. *Getting Ready to Read with Readers Theatre.* **Teacher Ideas Press, 2007. ISBN 978-1-591-58501-5**

For your youngest readers, in kindergarten and first grade, here are 50 two-page scripts based on nursery rhymes and across-the-curriculum topics.

Barchers, Suzanne I., and Charla R. Pfeffinger. *More Readers Theatre for Beginning Readers.* **Teacher Ideas Press, 2006. ISBN 978-1-591-58363-9**

Animal tales and folktale retellings with 30 stories for grades 1 to 3. Also look for the first book, *Readers Theatre for Beginning Readers* (1993) and *Fifty Fabulous Fables: Beginning Readers Theatre* (1997).

Bauer, Caroline Feller. *Presenting Reader's Theater: Plays and Poems to Read Aloud.* **Illus. by Lynn Gates Bredeson. H. W. Wilson, 1987. ISBN 978-0-8242-0748-9**

More than 50 read-aloud scripts based on children's literature and folklore will get you started with Reader's Theater.

Buzzeo, Toni. *Read! Perform! Learn!: 10 Reader's Theater Programs for Literary Enhancement.* **Upstart, 2006. ISBN 978-1-932146-59-2**

For each of the 10 scripts included, you'll find an introduction to the children's picture book on which it is based, an author interview, and corresponding activities that connect to content standards. Look for the second volume coming out in 2007.

Cohen, Arlene. *Stories on the Move: Integrating Literature and Movement with Children, from Infants to Age 14.* Illus. by Andrea Fitcha McAllister. Libraries Unlimited, 2007. ISBN 978-1-59158-418-6

Literature and story ideas for infants to teens, incorporating movement, vocal improvisation, and creative dramatics.

Fontichiaro, Kristin. *Active Learning through Drama, Podcasting and Puppetry.* Libraries Unlimited, 2007. ISBN 978-1-59158-402-5

How to use dramatic arts in a school library as tools to meet curriculum objectives in the K-8 media center; includes sample lessons.

Fredericks, Anthony D. *Mother Goose Readers Theatre for Beginning Readers.* Libraries Unlimited, 2007. ISBN 978-1-591-58500-8

Easy-to-read scripts for grades 1 to 2, including several with Spanish translations, based on traditional Mother Goose rhymes.

Fredericks, Anthony D. *Nonfiction Readers Theatre for Beginning Readers.* Libraries Unlimited, 2007. ISBN 978-1-591-58499-5

30 short, factual, and fun scripts for grades 1 to 3 on topics in science, social studies, and across the primary school curriculum.

Fredericks, Anthony D. *Silly Salamanders and Other Slightly Stupid Stuff for Readers Theatre.* Libraries Unlimited, 2000. ISBN 978-1-563-08825-4

24 humorous scripts of fractured fairy tales for grades 3 to 6. Also look for the companion volumes, *Frantic Frogs and Other Frankly Fractured Folktales for Readers Theatre* (Teacher Ideas Press, 1993) and, for younger readers in grades 1 to 4, *Tadpole Tales and Totally Terrific Treats for Readers Theatre* (Libraries Unlimited, 1997), with more than 25 scripts based on Mother Goose rhymes and fairy tales. Check the Libraries Unlimited website (**www.lu.com**) or catalog for additional titles by Fredericks.

Giff, Patricia Reilly. *Show Time at the Polk Street School: Plays You Can Do Yourself or in the Classroom.* Delacorte, 1992. ISBN 978-0-385-30794-9

For use with grades 1 to 4, based on chapters in the Polk Street School books.

Heinig, Ruth Beall and Stillwell, Lydia. *Creative Drama for the Classroom Teacher.* 4th ed. Prentice-Hall, 1988. ISBN 978-0-13-189415-0

An exhaustive guide that relates children's literature to drama activities.

Heinig, Ruth Beall. *Improvisation with Favorite Tales: Integrating Drama into the Reading/Writing Classroom.* Heinemann, 1992. ISBN 978-0-435-08609-1

Ways to use creative drama in the classroom to extend 19 mostly well-known folk and fairy tales, including an annotated bibliography of related children's book titles, various types of pantomime and verbal exercises, and related writing and art activities for each tale.

Kelner, Lenore Blank. *Creative Classroom: A Guide for Using Creative Drama in the Classroom, PreK-6.* Heinemann, 1993. ISBN 978-0-435-08628-2

Each of the more than 50 creative drama activities described is written up in a comprehensive lesson plan, encompassing grammar and spelling, classifying and sequencing techniques, comprehension and writing skills, language and thinking skills, and literature enrichment.

Kline, Suzy. *The Herbie Jones Reader's Theater: Funny Scenes to Read Aloud.* **Putnam, 1992. ISBN 978-0-399-22120-0**

For use with grades 1 to 4, based on chapters in the Herbie Jones books.

Larrick, Nancy. *Let's Do a Poem!: Introducing Poetry to Children Through Listening, Singing, Chanting, Impromptu Choral Reading, Body Movement, Dance, and Dramatization.* **Delacorte, 1991. ISBN 978-0-385-30292-0**

This competent hands-on guide provides more than five dozen verse examples and demonstrates how to use poetry to stimulate children's imaginations.

Shepard, Aaron. *Folktales on Stage: Children's Plays for Reader's Theater (or Readers Theatre), with 16 Scripts from World Folk and Fairy Tales and Legends, Including Asian, African, Middle Eastern, European, and Native American.* **Shepard, 2003. ISBN 978-0-938497-20-2**

Scripts to accompany Shepard's many wonderful fairy tale picture books you'll find in your library; first read one of his titles then print out his script of it to act out with your children, grades 3 to 8. Aaron Shepard is the King of Reader's Theater for children. His books and scripts on his amazing website, **http://aaronshep.com/rt/**, have inspired thousands of teachers and librarians.

Shepard, Aaron. *Readers on Stage: Resources for Reader's Theater (or Readers Theatre), With Tips, Play Scripts, and Worksheets, or How to Do Children's Plays Anywhere, Anytime, Without Scenery, Costumes, or Memorizing.* **Shepard, 2004. ISBN 978-0-938497-21-9**

Plenty of practical suggestions, tips and techniques from the master of Reader's Theater.

Shepard, Aaron. *Stories on Stage: Children's Plays for Reader's Theater (or Readers Theatre), With 15 Play Scripts From 15 Authors, Including Roald Dahl's The Twits and Louis Sachar's Sideways Stories from Wayside School.* **Shepard Publications, 2005. ISBN 978-0-938-49722-6**

See how Shepard has adapted well-known children's books into scripts for children to act out, but also to compare and contrast with the original titles.

Sierra, Judy. *Fantastic Theater: Puppets and Plays for Young Performers and Young Audiences.* **H. W. Wilson, 1991. ISBN 978-0-89774-727-1**

Contains 30 short puppet plays taken from folklore, plus production notes, follow-up activities, and instructions and traceable patterns for making puppets, props, and scenery.

Sierra, Judy. *Multicultural Folktales for Feltboard and Reader's Theater.* **Oryx Press, 1996. ISBN 978-1-573-56003-0**

20 short tales from around the globe, written in two formats—prose and Reader's Theater script; includes patterns for feltboard figures and rod puppets.

Sloyer, Shirlee. *From the Page to the Stage: The Educator's Complete Guide to Readers Theatre.* **Teacher Ideas Press, 2003. ISBN 978-1-56308-897-1**

Part 1 includes electing, adapting, and performing Reader's Theater; Part 2 provides sample scripts and production notes.

Wisniewski, David, and Donna Wisniewski. *Worlds of Shadow: Teaching with Shadow Puppetry.* **Teacher Idea Press, 1997. ISBN 978-1-56308-450-8**

A step-by-step guide with suggestions for stage directions, puppet patterns, scripts, scenery, and special effects from professional master puppeteers.

Worthy, Jo. *Readers Theater for Building Fluency: Strategies and Scripts for Making the Most of This Highly Effective, Motivating, and Research-Based Approach to Oral Reading.* **Scholastic Professional Books, 2005. ISBN 978-0-439-52223-6**

Instructions on how to find, write, and perform scripts, plus an appendix with 12 Reader's Theater scripts for grades 3 to 6.

Creative Drama and Reader's Theater Websites

Look online and find ideas, techniques, lesson plans, scripts, and guidelines for writing, acting, and staging. Try these for starters.

AARON SHEPARD.COM (http://aaronshep.com/rt)
Check out author Aaron Shepard's amazing website, download one of his many fine Reader's Theater scripts, or get in touch with him to book him for a workshop at your school.

AUTHORS' WEBSITES
Several children's book authors are providing Reader's Theater scripts for their books on their websites, which is a wonderful service for all of us.

Toni Buzzeo: www.tonibuzzeo.com

Katie Davis: www.katiedavis.com

Suzy Kline: www.suzykline.com

Margie Palatini: www.margiepalatini.com

BAD WOLF PRESS (www.badwolfpress.com)
More than 30 clever, melodious, and entertaining shows for children to perform, all available at very reasonable prices. The Bad Wolf folks advertise their scripts as "Musical plays for musically timid teachers." Each play comes with a spiral bound script and practical guide for the teacher, with permission to make copies of the script for the whole class, and a CD with a recording of each song.

CREATIVE DRAMA AND THEATRE EDUCATION RESOURCE SITE
(www.creatived rama.com)
Information and concrete ideas, sectioned into Reader's Theater, classroom ideas, theater games, and an extensive booklist.

CHILDDRAMA (www.childdrama.com)
Matt Buchanan, playwright and drama teacher, has packed his website with resources for drama teachers, including his original plays, lesson plans, detailed curriculum outlines, and a bibliography of professional books.

FICTIONTEACHERS.COM (www.fictionteachers.com)
Bruce Lansky and Meadowbrook Press's wonderful website contains Classroom Theater scripts based on stories from books in the Girls to the Rescue series, featuring clever, courageous girls, and Newfangled Fairy Tales, featuring fairy tales with humorous twists. You'll also find links to Poetry Theater poems from **www.gigglepoetry. com.**

LITERACY CONNECTIONS (www.literacyconnections.com/ReadersTheater.php)
"Promoting literacy and a love of reading" is the banner for this useful site which has many annotated links to other Reader's Theater sites.

LOIS WALKER (www.loiswalker.com/catalog/teach.html)
Canadian Reader's Theater maven, Lois Walker, provides a step-by-step teacher's guide to get you started using scripts in the classroom. This site links to her website, **www. scriptsforschools.com**, where you'll find more than 250 of her scripts for sale and a few free ones, too.

PLAYS MAGAZINE (www.playsmag.com)
Plays: The Drama Magazine for Young People is an indispensable magazine which comes out monthly, and is filled with good, royalty-free plays for elementary through high school. Find subscription information and a few sample plays you can download for free on their website.

TIMELESS TEACHER STUFF (www.timelessteacherstuff.com)
Teacher Rick Swallow offers extensive language arts materials and Reader's Theater activities, and many scripts you can download.

WEB ENGLISH TEACHER (www.webenglishteacher.com/rt.html)
"Web English Teacher presents the best of K-12 English/Language Arts teaching resources: lesson plans, WebQuests, videos, biography, e-texts, criticism, jokes, puzzles, and classroom activities," including Reader's Theater.

AUTHOR / TITLE INDEX

A to Z: Do You Ever Feel Like Me? (Hausman, Bonnie), 244

Aardema, Verna
  Misoso: Once Upon a Time Tales from Africa, 112
  Traveling to Tondo, 112
  Why Mosquitoes Buzz in People's Ears, 15, 112

Abiyoyo (Seeger, Pete), 149

Action Alphabet (Rotner, Shelley), 249

Active Learning through Drama, Podcasting and Puppetry (Fontichiaro, Kristin), 254

Actual Size (Jenkins, Steve), 52

Ada, Alma Flor. *Tales Our Abuelitas Told,* 116

Adelita (DePaola, Tomie), 120

The Adventures of Odysseus (Lupton, Hugh, and Daniel Morden), 135

The Adventures of Odysseus (Philip, Neil), 143

The Adventures of Spider (Arkhurst, Joyce Cooper), 113

The Adventures of the Dish and the Spoon (Grey, Mini), 125

Aesop & Company (Bader, Barbara), 114

Aesop's Fables (Gatti, Ann), 124

Aesop's Fables (Paxton, Tom), 143

Aesop's Fables (Pinkney, Jerry), 144, 200, 248

Aesop's Fables (Untermeyer, Louis), 154

Alexander, Lloyd. *How the Cat Swallowed Thunder,* 112

Ali Baba and the Forty Thieves (McVitty, Walter), 139

Aliens Are Coming!: The True Account Of The 1938 War Of The Worlds Radio Broadcast (McCarthy, Meghan), 224

Allard, Harry. *Miss Nelson Has a Field Day,* 204

All in One Hour (Crummel, Susan Stevens), 240

Alphabet Under Construction (Fleming, Denise), 243

American Tall Tales (Osborne, Mary Pope), 142

Ananse's Feast: An Ashanti Tale (Mollel, Tololwa M.), 139

Anansi and the Magic Stick (Kimmel, Eric A.), 131

Anansi and the Moss-Covered Rock (Kimmel, Eric A.), 131

Anansi and the Talking Melon (Kimmel, Eric A.), 132, 245

Anansi Goes Fishing (Kimmel, Eric A.), 132

Andersen, Hans Christian
  The Nightingale (Retold and illus. by Jerry Pinkney), 113
  The Nightingale (Retold by Stephen Mitchell; illus. by Bagram Ibatoulline), 112
  The Tinderbox (Adapted and illus. by Barry Moser), 113

Anderson, Leone Castell. *The Wonderful Shrinking Shirt,* 113

Andreae, Giles. *K Is for Kissing a Cool Kangaroo,* 238

Androcles and the Lion (Nolan, Dennis), 141

And the Dish Ran Away with the Spoon (Stevens, Janet, and Susan Stevens Crummel), 152, 251

And the Green Grass Grew All Around: Folk Poetry from Everyone (Schwartz, Alvin), 148

Anholt, Catherine. *Chimp and Zee,* 113

Anholt, Laurence. *Chimp and Zee,* 113

Animal Fables from Aesop (McClintock, Barbara), 137

Arabella and Mr. Crack (Gackenbach, Dick), 123

Arkhurst, Joyce Cooper. *The Adventures of Spider,* 113

Armadilly Chili (Ketteman, Helen), 131

Arnold, Tedd. *Hi! Fly Guy,* 238

Arthur and the Sword (Sabuda, Robert), 146

Artstarts: Drama, Music, Movement, Puppetry, and Storytelling Activities (Brady, Martha, and Patsy T. Gleason), 179

Asbjørnsen, P. C. *The Three Billy Goats Gruff,* 113

Asch, Frank. *Mr. Maxwell's Mouse,* 238

Ashman, Linda. *Rub-a-Dub Sub,* 238

Atalanta's Race (Climo, Shirley), 117

Auch, Mary Jane. *The Princess and the Pizza,* 113

Aunt Pitty Patty's Piggy (Aylesworth, Jim), 113, 196, 238

Aylesworth, Jim
  Aunt Pitty Patty's Piggy, 113, 196, 238
  The Gingerbread Man, 113
  Goldilocks and the Three Bears, 67, 113
  The Tale of Tricky Fox, 114, 199, 238

Baba Yaga (Kimmel, Eric A.), 132

Babbitt, Natalie. *Ouch!,* 114

"Baby Jaws" (song), 49-50

Babymouse: Our Hero (Holm, Jennifer L., and Matthew Holm), 224

Bad Boys (Palatini, Margie), 222, 247

Bader, Barbara. *Aesop & Company: With Scenes from His Legendary Life,* 114

Bad Kitty (Bruel, Nick), 87, 191, 239

The Bake Shop Ghost (Ogburn, Jacqueline K.), 141

Baltuck, Naomi. *Crazy Gibberish and Other Story Hour Stretches (From a Storyteller's Bag of Tricks),* 179

Bang, Molly Garrett. *Wiley and the Hairy Man,* 114

Bania, Michael. *Kumak's Fish,* 114, 195, 238

Bannerman, Helen. *The Story of Little Babaji,* 208, 222, 238

Barchers, Suzanne I.
  Getting Ready to Read with Readers Theatre, 253
  More Readers Theatre for Beginning Readers, 253
  Multicultural Folktales: Readers Theatre for Elementary Students, 253

Bark, George (Feiffer, Jules), 198, 242

The Barking Mouse (Sacre, Antonio), 87, 146, 208, 218, 230-236

Barton, Byron. *My Car,* 238

Basho and the Fox (Myers, Tim), 141

Bateman, Teresa. *Farm Flu*, 114

Bauer, Caroline Feller
  Handbook for Storytellers, 179
  Leading Kids to Books Through Magic, 179
  New Handbook for Storytellers: With Stories, Poems, Magic, and More, 179
  Presenting Reader's Theater: Plays and Poems to Read Aloud, 253

Baumgartner, Barbara. *Crocodile! Crocodile!: Stories Told Around the World*, 114

The Beanstalk and Beyond: Developing Critical Thinking Through Fairy Tales (Wolf, Joan M.), 185

Bearsie Bear and the Surprise Sleepover Party (Waber, Bernard), 252

Beaumont, Karen
  I Ain't Gonna Paint No More, 114
  Move Over, Rover!, 239

Beautiful Warrior: The Legend of the Nun's Kung Fu (McCully, Emily Arnold), 137

A Beginner's Guide to Storytelling (Rydell, Katy), 185

Bella at Midnight (Stanley, Diane), 152

Bernhard, Emery. *How Snowshoe Hare Rescued the Sun*, 114

Bertrand, Lynne. *Granite Baby*, 115

Best Loved Folktales of the World (Cole, Joanna), 118

Bettelheim, Bruno. *The Uses of Enchantment: The Meaning and Importance of Fairy Tales*, 179

Beware of the Storybook Wolves (Child, Lauren), 117

Beyond the Beanstalk: Interdisciplinary Learning Through Storytelling (Rubright, Lynn), 184

The Biggest Soap (Schaefer, Carole Lexa), 148

Big Men, Big Country (Walker, Paul Robert), 155

Big Pumpkin (Silverman, Erica), 90, 150, 195

Billingsley, Franny. *The Folk Keeper*, 115

Billy Beg and His Bull (Greene, Ellin), 125

Birdseye, Tom. *Soap! Soap! Don't Forget the Soap!*, 115

Black, Holly. *The Spiderwick Chronicles, Book 1: The Field Guide*, 115, 239

The Black Bull of Norroway (Huck, Charlotte), 129

Black Ships Before Troy!: The Story of the Iliad (Sutcliff, Rosemary), 153

The Blind Hunter (Rodanas, Kristina), 145

Blood on the River: James Town 1607 (Carbone, Elisa), 225

The Blue Fairy Book (Lang, Andrew), 133

Bob (Pearson, Tracey Campbell), 248

Bodkin, Odds. *The Crane Wife*, 115

Bone #1: Out from Boneville (Smith, Jeff), 226, 250

Bony-Legs (Cole, Joanna), 118

Books Kids Will Sit Still For 3: The Complete Read-Aloud Guide (Freeman, Judy), 180

Booth, David. *Doctor Knickerbocker and Other Rhymes*, 115

Boots and His Brothers (Kimmel, Eric A.), 132

The Boy of the Three Year Nap (Snyder, Dianne), 151

The Boy Who Lived with the Bears and Other Iroquois Stories (Bruchac, Joseph), 115

Brady, Martha. *Artstarts: Drama, Music, Movement, Puppetry, and Storytelling Activities*, 179

The Brave Little Seamstress (Osborne, Mary Pope), 142

Brett, Jan. *Honey . . . Honey . . . Lion!*, 115

Briggs, Raymond. *Jim and the Beanstalk*, 115

Bringing Out Their Best: Values Education and Character Development Through Traditional Tales (Livo, Norma J.), 182

The Bronze Cauldron (McCaughrean, Geraldine), 137

Brother Rabbit (Ho, Minfong, and Saphan Ros), 128

Brown, Marcia. *Stone Soup*, 115

Browne, Anthony. *Willy the Dreamer*, 239

Bruchac, James
  How Chipmunk Got His Stripes, 67, 116
  Raccoon's Last Race, 116

Bruchac, Joseph
  The Boy Who Lived with the Bears and Other Iroquois Stories, 115
  How Chipmunk Got His Stripes, 67, 116
  Raccoon's Last Race, 116
  Tell Me a Tale: A Book about Storytelling, 180

Bruel, Nick. *Bad Kitty*, 87, 191, 239

Bruh Rabbit and the Tar Baby Girl (Hamilton, Virginia), 126

Brusca, María Cristina. *When Jaguar Ate the Moon*, 116

Bud, Not Buddy (Curtis, Christopher Paul), 201-202

Buehner, Caralyn. *Fanny's Dream*, 116

Bull Run (Fleischman, Paul), 207

The Bunyans (Wood, Audrey), 157

Burleigh, Robert. *Pandora*, 116

Busy Buzzing Bumblebees and Other Tongue Twisters (Schwartz, Alvin), 148

Buzzeo, Toni
  Dawdle Duckling, 239
  Read! Perform! Learn!: 10 Reader's Theater Programs for Literary Enhancement, 253

Byars, Betsy. *My Brother, Ant*, 239

Cactus Soup (Kimmel, Eric A.), 132, 245

Calmenson, Stephanie
  The Children's Aesop, 116
  The Frog Principal, 116

Campoy, F. Isabel. *Tales Our Abuelitas Told*, 116

Can You Guess My Name?: Traditional Tales Around the World (Sierra, Judy), 150

Caps for Sale (Slobodkina, Esphyr), 250

Carbone, Elisa. *Blood on the River: James Town 1607*, 225

Carle, Eric
  From Head To Toe, 239
  Twelve Tales from Aesop, 116

Carolinda Clatter (Gerstein, Mordicai), 124

Carter, David A. *In a Dark, Dark Wood*, 55

Car Wash (Steen, Sandra, and Susan Steen), 251

Cat and Rat: The Legend of the Chinese Zodiac (Young, Ed), 158

Cat's Cradle, Owl's Eyes; A Book of String Games (Gryski, Camilla), 125

Cazet, Denys. *Elvis the Rooster Almost Goes to Heaven*, 239

Celebrate the World: Twenty Tellable Folktales for Multicultural Festivals (MacDonald, Margaret Read), 183

Cendrillon: A Caribbean Cinderella (San Souci, Robert D.), 146

Chaconas, Dori. *Cork & Fuzz: Short and Tall*, 240

Champlin, Connie. *Storytelling with Puppets*, 180

Charlotte Huck's Children's Literature (Keifer, Barbara, Janet Hickman, and Susan Hepler), 182

Chase, Richard
    Grandfather Tales, 116, 200
    Jack Tales, 117

Chato and the Party Animals (Soto, Gary), 251

Cheng, Hou-Tien. *Six Chinese Brothers*, 117

Chief Lelooska. *Echoes of the Elders*, 117

Child, Lauren
    Beware of the Storybook Wolves, 117
    Who's Afraid of the Big Bad Book?, 117

The Children's Aesop (Calmenson, Stephanie), 116

Children's Faces Looking Up: Program Building for the Storyteller (De Wit, Dorothy), 180

Children Tell Stories: A Teaching Guide (Hamilton, Martha, and Mitch Weiss), 80, 181

Chimp and Zee (Anholt, Catherine, and Laurence Anholt), 113

The Chinese Mirror (Ginsburg, Mirra), 124

A Chinese Zoo: Fables and Proverbs (Demi), 120

Chinye (Onyefulu, Obi), 141

Choi, Yangsook. *The Sun Girl and the Moon Boy*, 117

Christelow, Eileen
    Five Little Monkeys Jumping on the Bed, 117
    Where's the Big Bad Wolf?, 117

Cinder Edna (Jackson, Ellen), 130

"Cinderella", 27-30

Cinderella (McClintock, Barbara), 137

Cinderella Skeleton (San Souci, Robert D.), 250

Clark, Emma Chichester. *Follow the Leader!*, 240

Clay Boy (Ginsburg, Mirra), 23, 74, 125, 200

Clementine (Pennypacker, Sara), 225

Clever Beatrice (Willey, Margaret), 156

Click, Clack, Moo: Cows That Type (Cronin, Doreen), 119, 208, 240

Climo, Shirley
    Atalanta's Race, 117
    The Egyptian Cinderella, 118
    Stolen Thunder, 118

Cohen, Arlene. *Stories on the Move: Integrating Literature and Movement with Children, from Infants to Age 14*, 254

Cohn, Amy L. *From Sea to Shining Sea*, 118

Cole, Joanna
    Best Loved Folktales of the World, 118
    Bony-Legs, 118
    Don't Tell the Whole World!, 118

Collins, Suzanne. *Gregor the Overlander*, 201, 240

The Comic Adventures of Old Mother Hubbard and Her Dog (DePaola, Tomie), 120

Compestine, Ying Chang
    The Runaway Rice Cake, 118
    The Story of Chopsticks, 118

Compton, Patricia A. *The Terrible Eek*, 119

Cook-a-Doodle-Doo! (Stevens, Janet, and Susan Stevens Crummel), 152

Cookies: Bite-Size Life Lessons (Rosenthal, Amy Krouse), 46

Cordi, Kevin. *Raising Voices: Creating Youth Storytelling Groups and Troupes*, 185

Cork & Fuzz: Short and Tall (Chaconas, Dori), 240

Count Silvernose: A Story from Italy (Kimmel, Eric A.), 132

Courlander, Harold. *The Cow-Tail Switch and Other West African Stories*, 119

Cousins, Lucy. *The Little Dog Laughed and Other Nursery Rhymes*, 119

Coville, Bruce. *The Monster's Ring*, 193, 240

The Cow-Tail Switch and Other West African Stories (Courlander, Harold, and Herzog, George), 119

The Cow Who Clucked (Fleming, Denise), 123

Coyote (McDermott, Gerald), 137

Coyote Steals the Blanket: A Ute Tale (Stevens, Janet), 152

The Crane Wife (Bodkin, Odds), 115

Crazy Gibberish and Other Story Hour Stretches (From a Storyteller's Bag of Tricks) (Baltuck, Naomi), 179

Creative Classroom: A Guide for Using Creative Drama in the Classroom, PreK-6 (Kelner, Lenore Blank), 254

Creative Drama for the Classroom Teacher (Heinig, Ruth Beall, and Lydia Stillwell), 254

Creech, Sharon
    Love That Dog, 207, 240
    Replay, 227

"Creeping, Creeping" (song), 54

Crews, Nina. *The Neighborhood Mother Goose*, 119

Crocodile! Crocodile!: Stories Told Around the World (Baumgartner, Barbara), 114

Cronin, Doreen
    Click, Clack, Moo: Cows That Type, 119, 208, 240
    Dooby Dooby Moo, 219

Crummel, Susan Stevens
    All in One Hour, 240
    And the Dish Ran Away with the Spoon, 152, 251
    Cook-a-Doodle-Doo!, 152
    The Great Fuzz Frenzy, 220
    Ten-Gallon Bart, 240

Cuckoo (Ehlert, Lois), 122

Currie, Robin. *Straw into Gold: Books and Activities About Folktales*, 182

Curtis, Christopher Paul. *Bud, Not Buddy*, 201-202

Cushman, Doug. *Inspector Hopper*, 216, 241

Cyclops (Fisher, Leonard Everett), 123

Dahl, Roald
    Matilda, 204, 217
    The Witches, 204

Dailey, Sheila. *Putting the World in a Nutshell: The Art of the Formula Tale*, 180

The Dancing Skeleton (DeFelice, Cynthia C.), 119

Davis, Katie. *Who Hops?*, 241

Davol, Marguerite W. *The Paper Dragon*, 119

Davy Crockett Saves the World (Schanzer, Rosalyn), 148

Dawdle Duckling (Buzzeo, Toni), 239

Day, Nancy Raines. *The Lion's Whiskers*, 119

The Day I Swapped My Dad for Two Goldfish (Gaiman, Neil), 243

The Day Ocean Came to Visit (Wolkstein, Diane), 156

Dealing with Dragons (Wrede, Patricia), 157

Dear Mrs. LaRue: Letters from Obedience School (Teague, Mark), 251

Dee, Ruby. *Two Ways to Count to Ten*, 119

DeFelice, Cynthia C. *The Dancing Skeleton*, 119

Delaney, Joseph. *The Revenge of the Witch*, 120

De Las Casas, Dianne. *Kamishibai Story Theater: The Art of Picture Telling*, 180

Demi
    A Chinese Zoo, 120
    The Hungry Coat, 120
    King Midas: The Golden Touch, 120
    One Grain of Rice, 120

DePaola, Tomie
    Adelita, 120
    The Comic Adventures of Old Mother Hubbard and Her Dog, 120
    Fin M'Coul, the Giant of Knockmany Hill, 120
    Jamie O'Rourke and the Big Potato: An Irish Folktale, 120
    The Mysterious Giant of Barletta: An Italian Folktale, 120
    Strega Nona, 121
    Tomie dePaola's Mother Goose, 121
    26 Fairmount Avenue, 1

DeRegniers, Beatrice S. *Little Sister and the Month Brothers*, 121

De Vos, Gail. *Storytelling for Young Adults: A Guide to Tales for Teens*, 180

De Vries, Maggie. *Once Upon a Golden Apple*, 134

De Wit, Dorothy. *Children's Faces Looking Up: Program Building for the Storyteller*, 180

Diakité, Baba Wagué
    The Hatseller and the Monkeys, 121
    The Hunterman and the Crocodile, 121, 241
    The Magic Gourd, 121

DiCamillo, Kate
    Mercy Watson to the Rescue, 208, 221
    The Miraculous Journey of Edward Tulane, 217, 241
    The Tale of Despereaux, 121, 202, 204, 217

Dillon, Diane. *To Everything There Is a Season*, 241

Dillon, Leo. *To Everything There Is a Season*, 241

DiTerlizzi, Tony. *The Spiderwick Chronicles, Book 1: The Field Guide*, 115, 239

Doctor Knickerbocker and Other Rhymes (Booth, David), 115

Dodds, Dayle Ann. *Where's Pup?*, 241

Dog-of-the-Sea-Waves (Rumford, James), 146

Dogs of Myth: Tales from Around the World (Hausman, Gerald, and Hausman, Loretta), 127

Do Like a Duck Does! (Hindley, Judy), 128

Doña Flor (Mora, Pat), 140

Donaldson, Julia
    The Giants and the Joneses, 121, 201
    The Gruffalo, 241

Don't Let the Pigeon Drive the Bus (Willems, Mo), 197, 252

Don't Tell the Whole World! (Cole, Joanna), 118

Don't Wake Up the Bear! (Murray, Marjorie Dennis), 246

Dooby Dooby Moo (Cronin, Doreen), 219

Dooling, Michael. *The Great Horse-less Carriage Race*, 241

Doucet, Sharon Arms. *Why Lapin's Ears Are Long and Other Tales from the Louisiana Bayou*, 121

The Dragon Prince (Yep, Laurence), 157

Drawing Stories from Around the World and a Sampling of European Handkerchief Stories (Pellowski, Anne), 184

Duck & Goose (Hills, Tad), 219

Duffy and the Devil (Zemach, Harve), 158

Dunrea, Olivier. *Ollie*, 242

Early, Margaret. *William Tell*, 122

Earthdance (Ryder, Joanne), 249

Earthquack! (Palatini, Margie), 222, 247

Echoes of the Elders (Chief Lelooska), 117

Edwards, Pamela Duncan
    The Leprechaun's Gold, 122
    Livingstone Mouse, 43
    The Neat Line: Scribbling Through Mother Goose, 122, 221

Egan, Tim
    Serious Farm, 242
    The Trial of Cardigan Jones, 205, 208, 242

Egielski, Richard. *The Gingerbread Boy*, 23 , 122

The Egyptian Cinderella (Climo, Shirley), 118

Ehlert, Lois. *Cuckoo*, 122

Ella Enchanted (Levine, Gail Carson), 134

Ellis, Elizabeth, 63-64

Elvis the Rooster Almost Goes to Heaven (Cazet, Denys), 239

Emberley, Michael
    Ruby, 122
    Ruby and the Sniffs, 242

Emberley, Rebecca. *Three Cool Kids*, 122, 242

Emrich, Duncan. *The Nonsense Book*, 122

The Enormous Carrot (Vagin, Vladimir), 252

Epossumondas (Salley, Coleen), 31, 146, 250

Ernst, Lisa Campbell
    Little Red Riding Hood: A Newfangled Prairie Tale, 122
    Stella Louella's Runaway Book, 242

Esbensen, Barbara Juster. *The Star Maiden*, 123

Esteban and the Ghost (Hancock, Sibyl), 126

Every Child a Storyteller: A Handbook of Ideas (Kinghorn, Harriet R., and Mary Helen Pelton), 182

Fables (Lobel, Arnold), 134, 200
The Fairy's Mistake (Levine, Gail Carson), 134
The Fairytale News (Hawkins, Colin, and Jacqui Hawkins), 18, 127
The Faithful Friend (San Souci, Robert D.), 147
The Family Storytelling Handbook (Pellowski, Anne), 184
Fanny's Dream (Buehner, Caralyn), 116
Fantastic Theater: Puppets and Plays for Young Performers and Young Audiences (Sierra, Judy), 255
Farley, Carol. *Mr. Pak Buys a Story*, 123
Farm Flu (Bateman, Teresa), 114
Fat Men from Space (Pinkwater, Daniel), 201
Faulkner, Keith. *The Wide-Mouthed Frog: A Pop-Up Book*, 80
Favorite Fairy Tales Told in Italy (Haviland, Virginia), 13
Favorite Fairy Tales Told Round the World (Haviland, Virginia), 127
Favorite Folktales from Around the World (Yolen, Jane), 185
Fearless Jack (Johnson, Paul Brett), 130
Feiffer, Jules
    Bark, George, 198, 242
    I Lost My Bear, 242
    Meanwhile . . , 242
Fin M'Coul, the Giant of Knockmany Hill (DePaola, Tomie), 120
The Fire Children: A West African Creation Tale (Maddern, Eric), 135
Fisher, Leonard Everett
    Cyclops, 123
    William Tell, 123
Five Little Monkeys Jumping on the Bed (Christelow, Eileen), 117
Fleischman, Paul
    Bull Run, 207
    Joyful Noise: Poems for Two Voices, 207, 243
    Seedfolks, 207, 243
Fleming, Denise
    Alphabet Under Construction, 243
    The Cow Who Clucked, 123
Flossie & the Fox (McKissack, Patricia C.), 138
The Folk Keeper (Billingsley, Franny), 115
Folktales on Stage (Shepard, Aaron), 255
Folktale Themes and Activities for Children, Volume 1: Pourquoi Tales (Kraus, Anne Marie), 182
Follow the Leader! (Clark, Emma Chichester), 240
Fontichiaro, Kristin. *Active Learning through Drama, Podcasting and Puppetry*, 254
Foolish Rabbit's Big Mistake (Martin, Rafe), 136
Frankenstein Makes a Sandwich (Rex, Adam), 145
Frazee, Marla. *Walk On!: A Guide for Babies of All Ages*, 193, 243
Fredericks, Anthony D.

Mother Goose Readers Theatre for Beginning Readers, 254
Nonfiction Readers Theatre for Beginning Readers, 254
Silly Salamanders and Other Slightly Stupid Stuff for Readers Theatre, 254
Freeman, Judy
    Books Kids Will Sit Still For 3: The Complete Read-Aloud Guide, 180
    Hi Ho Librario!: Songs, Chants, and Stories to Keep Kids Humming, 180
French, Vivian. *Lazy Jack*, 123
The Frog Prince, Continued (Scieszka, Jon), 148
The Frog Principal (Calmenson, Stephanie), 116
From Head To Toe (Carle, Eric), 239
From Sea to Shining Sea: A Treasury of American Folklore and Folk Songs (Cohn, Amy L.), 118
From the Page to the Stage: The Educator's Complete Guide to Readers Theatre (Sloyer, Shirlee), 255
Fujita, Hiroko. *Stories to Play With: Kids' Tales Told with Puppets, Paper, Toys, and Imagination*, 80, 181
The Funny Little Woman (Mosel, Arlene), 140

Gackenbach, Dick. *Arabella and Mr. Crack*, 123
Gag, Wanda. *Tales from Grimm*, 123
Gaiman, Neil. *The Day I Swapped My Dad for Two Goldfish*, 243
Galdone, Joanna. *The Tailypo*, 123
Galdone, Paul
    The Old Woman and Her Pig, 123, 196
    The Three Sillies, 124
Garcia, Laura Gallego. *The Legend of the Wandering King*, 124
Garland, Sherry. *Why Ducks Sleep on One Leg*, 124
Gates, Frieda. *Owl Eyes*, 124
Gatti, Ann. *Aesop's Fables*, 124
Geisler, Harlynne. *Storytelling Professionally: The Nuts and Bolts of a Working Performer*, 181
George, Lindsay Barrett. *Inside Mouse, Outside Mouse*, 243
"George Washington Bridge" (song), 48
Gerson, Mary-Joan. *Why the Sky Is Far Away*, 124
Gerstein, Mordicai. *Carolinda Clatter*, 124
Getting Ready to Read with Readers Theatre (Barchers, Suzanne I., and Charla R. Pfeffinger), 253
Get Well, Good Knight (Thomas, Shelley Moore), 154, 208, 252
The Giant and the Beanstalk (Stanley, Diane), 152
The Giant Carrot (Peck, Jan), 143, 195, 248
The Giants and the Joneses (Donaldson, Julia), 121, 201
Giff, Patricia Reilly. *Show Time at the Polk Street School: Plays You Can Do Yourself or in the Classroom*, 254
The Gift of the Crocodile (Sierra, Judy), 150
Gilgamesh the Hero: The Epic of Gilgamesh (McCaughrean, Geraldine), 137
Gilman, Phoebe. *Something from Nothing*, 124
The Gingerbread Boy (Egielski, Richard), 23 , 122
The Gingerbread Man (Aylesworth, Jim), 113

The Gingerbread Man (Kimmel, Eric A.), 132
Ginsburg, Mirra
    The Chinese Mirror, 124
    Clay Boy, 23, 74, 125, 200
The Girl Who Lived with the Bears (Goldin, Barbara
    Diamond), 125
The Girl Who Spun Gold (Hamilton, Virginia), 126
Gleason, Patsy T. *Artstarts: Drama, Music, Movement,*
    Puppetry, and Storytelling Activities, 179
Gobble, Gobble, Slip, Slop (So, Meilo), 74, 151, 200
Goble, Paul
    Her Seven Brothers, 125
    Iktomi and the Boulder, 125
Goforth, Frances S. *Using Folk Literature in the*
    Classroom: Encouraging Children to Read and
    Write, 181
Goha the Wise Fool (Johnson-Davies, Denys), 130
Goldie and the Three Bears (Stanley, Diane), 152
Goldilocks and the Three Bears (Aylesworth, Jim), 67, 113
Goldilocks and the Three Bears (Marshall, James), 67, 136
Goldin, Barbara Diamond. *The Girl Who Lived with the*
    Bears, 125
Good Night, Gorilla (Rathmann, Peggy), 249
Goose Chase (Kindl, Patrice), 245
Gordh, Bill. *Stories in Action: Interactive Tales and*
    Learning Activities to Promote Early Literacy, 181
Grandfather Tales (Chase, Richard), 116, 200
Granite Baby (Bertrand, Lynne), 115
Gray, Libba Moore. *Is There Room on the Feather Bed?*,
    243
A Great Big Ugly Man Came Up and Tied His Horse to Me
    (Tripp, Wallace), 154
The Great Fuzz Frenzy (Stevens, Janet, and Susan Stevens
    Crummel), 220
The Great Horse-less Carriage Race (Dooling, Michael),
    241
Greene, Ellin
    Billy Beg and His Bull, 125
    Storytelling: Art and Technique, 181
Gregor the Overlander (Collins, Suzanne), 201, 240
Grey, Mini. *The Adventures of the Dish and the Spoon*, 125
Grifalconi, Ann. *The Village of Round and Square Houses*,
    125
Grimes, Nikki. *Talkin' about Bessie: The Story of Aviator*
    Elizabeth Coleman, 243
Grimm, Jacob. *The Juniper Tree and Other Tales from*
    Grimm, 125
The Gruffalo (Donaldson, Julia), 241
Gryski, Camilla. *Cat's Cradle, Owl's Eyes; A Book of*
    String Games, 125
The Gunniwolf (Harper, Wilhelmina), 126, 194, 243

Haley, Gail E. *A Story, a Story*, 126
Hamilton, Martha
    Children Tell Stories: A Teaching Guide, 80, 181
    Scared Witless: Thirteen Eerie Tales to Tell, 126
Hamilton, Virginia

Bruh Rabbit and the Tar Baby Girl, 126
The Girl Who Spun Gold, 126
The People Could Fly: The Picture Book, 126
When Birds Could Talk & Bats Could Sing, 126
Han, Suzanne Crowder. *The Rabbit's Escape*, 126
Hancock, Sibyl. *Esteban and the Ghost*, 126
Handbook for Storytellers (Bauer, Caroline Feller), 179
The Happy Hocky Family Moves to the Country (Smith,
    Lane), 250
Harper, Wilhelmina. *The Gunniwolf*, 126, 194, 243
Harris, Robert J. *Odysseus in the Serpent Maze*, 157
Harry Potter and the Sorcerer's Stone (Rowling, J. K.), 146
Harter, Debbie. *Walking Through the Jungle*, 244
Hartman, Bob. *The Wolf Who Cried Boy*, 127, 244
The Hatseller and the Monkeys (Diakité, Baba Wagué), 121
Hausman, Bonnie. *A to Z: Do You Ever Feel Like Me?*, 244
Hausman, Gerald. *Dogs of Myth: Tales from Around the*
    World, 127
Hausman, Loretta. *Dogs of Myth: Tales from Around the*
    World, 127
Haven, Kendall
    Story Proof: The Science Behind the Startling Power of
    Story, 181
    Super Simple Storytelling: A Can-Do Guide for Every
    Classroom, Every Day, 181
Haviland, Virginia
    Favorite Fairy Tales Told in Italy, 13
    Favorite Fairy Tales Told Round the World, 127
    North American Legends, 127
Hawkins, Colin. *The Fairytale News*, 18, 127
Hawkins, Jacqui. *The Fairytale News*, 18, 127
Hayes, Sarah. *Robin Hood*, 127
Head, Body, Legs: A Story from Liberia (Paye, Won-Ldy,
    and Margaret H. Lippert), 143, 248
Heinig, Ruth Beall
    Creative Drama for the Classroom Teacher, 254
    Improvisation with Favorite Tales: Integrating Drama
    into the Reading/Writing Classroom, 254
The Hello, Goodbye Window (Juster, Norton), 131
Henderson, Kathy. *Lugalbanda: The Boy Who Got Caught*
    Up in a War, 127
Henkes, Kevin. *Kitten's First Full Moon*, 127, 190, 244
Henny-Penny (Wattenberg, Jane), 155, 252
Hepler, Susan. *Charlotte Huck's Children's Literature*, 182
The Herbie Jones Reader's Theater: Funny Scenes to Read
    Aloud (Kline, Suzy), 255
Here Comes Mother Goose (Opie, Iona), 141
The Hero Beowulf (Kimmel, Eric A.), 132
Her Seven Brothers (Goble, Paul), 125
Herzog, George. *The Cow-Tail Switch and Other West*
    African Stories, 119
Hest, Amy. *In the Rain with Baby Duck*, 39
Hewitt, Kathryn
    King Midas and the Golden Touch, 128
    The Three Sillies, 128
Hi! Fly Guy (Arnold, Tedd), 238

Hi Ho Librario!: Songs, Chants, and Stories to Keep Kids Humming (Freeman, Judy), 180

Hickman, Janet. *Charlotte Huck's Children's Literature*, 182

Hicks, Barbara Jean. *Jitterbug Jam*, 128

Hicks, Ray. *The Jack Tales*, 128

Hills, Tad. *Duck & Goose*, 219

Hindley, Judy. *Do Like a Duck Does!*, 128

Ho, Minfong. *Brother Rabbit*, 128

Hoberman, Mary Ann
  It's Simple, Said Simon, 244
  You Read to Me, I'll Read to You: Very Short Fairy Tales to Read Together, 128, 207, 244
  You Read to Me, I'll Read to You: Very Short Stories to Read Together, 128, 207

Hodges, Margaret
  Saint George and the Dragon, 128
  Saint Patrick and the Peddler, 129

Hog-Eye (Meddaugh, Susan), 139

Hogrogian, Nonny. *One Fine Day*, 129

"Hoimie the Woim" (story), 73-74

Holes (Sachar, Louis), 249

Holm, Jennifer L. *Babymouse: Our Hero*, 224

Holm, Matthew. *Babymouse: Our Hero*, 224

Holt, David
  Ready-to-Tell Tales: Sure-fire Stories from America's Favorite Storytellers, 181
  The Storyteller's Guide: Storytellers Share Advice for the Classroom, Boardroom, Showroom, Podium, Pulpit and Center Stage, 63, 184

Homer Price (McCloskey, Robert), 246

Honey . . . Honey . . . Lion! (Brett, Jan), 115

Hong, Lily Toy
  How the Ox Star Fell From Heaven, 15, 129
  Two of Everything, 129

Hooks, William H.
  Moss Gown, 129
  The Three Little Pigs and the Fox, 129

How Chipmunk Got His Stripes: A Tale of Bragging and Teasing (Bruchac, Joseph, and James Bruchac), 67, 116

How Snowshoe Hare Rescued the Sun: A Tale from the Arctic (Bernhard, Emery), 114

How the Cat Swallowed Thunder (Alexander, Lloyd), 112

How the Fisherman Tricked the Genie: A Tale Within a Tale Within a Tale (Sunami, Kitoba), 153

How the Ox Star Fell From Heaven (Hong, Lily Toy), 15, 129

How to Eat Fried Worms (Rockwell, Thomas), 201

How Turtle's Back Was Cracked (Ross, Gayle), 145

Howard, Arthur. *The Hubbub Above*, 244

The Hubbub Above (Howard, Arthur), 244

Huck, Charlotte
  The Black Bull of Norroway, 129
  Princess Furball, 129

The Hungry Coat: A Tale from Turkey, (Demi), 120

The Hunterman and the Crocodile (Diakité, Baba Wagué), 121, 241

Hyman, Trina Schart
  Little Red Riding Hood, 24, 129
  The Sleeping Beauty, 129

I Ain't Gonna Paint No More (Beaumont, Karen), 114

"I Can't Pay the Rent", 230

If the Shoe Fits: Voices from Cinderella (Whipple, Laura), 28, 155

"If You Ask Your Mother to Tell You a Story" (story), 108-109

If You Take a Mouse to School (Numeroff, Laura Joffe), 247

Iktomi and the Boulder (Goble, Paul), 125

I Lost My Bear (Feiffer, Jules), 242

"I'm a Little Teapot (Alternate Version)" (song), 42-43

"I'm Bringing Home a Baby Bumblebee" (song), 51

Improving Your Storytelling: Beyond the Basics for All Who Tell Stories in Work or Play (Lipman, Doug), 182

Improvisation with Favorite Tales: Integrating Drama into the Reading/Writing Classroom (Heinig, Ruth Beall), 254

The Impudent Rooster (Rascol, Sabina I.), 144

I'm Still Here in the Bathtub: Brand New Silly Dilly Songs (Katz, Alan), 244

In a Circle Long Ago (Van Laan, Nancy), 154

In a Dark, Dark Wood (Carter, David A.), 55

"In a Dark, Dark Woods" (chant), 55

Inside Mouse, Outside Mouse (George, Lindsay Barrett), 243

Inspector Hopper (Cushman, Doug), 216, 241

In the Land of Small Dragon (Kha, Dang Manh), 13

In the Rain with Baby Duck (Hest, Amy), 39

Irving, Jan
  Straw into Gold: Books and Activities About Folktales, 182
  Stories Neverending: A Program Guide for Schools and Libraries, 182

Isaacs, Anne
  Pancakes for Supper, 67, 130, 222
  Swamp Angel, 67, 130

I Saw Esau: The Schoolchild's Pocket Book (Opie, Iona, and Peter Opie), 141

I Saw You in the Bathtub and Other Folk Rhymes (Schwartz, Alvin), 148

I Stink! (McMullan, Kate), 139, 195, 246

Is There Room on the Feather Bed? (Gray, Libba Moore), 243

Itching and Twiching (McKissack, Patricia C., and Robert L. McKissack), 138

"It's Halloween" (poem), 88-90

"It's Raining, It's Pouring" (song), 39

It's Simple, Said Simon (Hoberman, Mary Ann), 244

I Was a Rat! (Pullman, Philip), 144

Jabutí the Tortoise (McDermott, Gerald), 138

Jack and the Seven Deadly Giants (Swope, Sam), 153

Jack Outwits the Giants (Johnson, Paul Brett), 130

Jack Tales (Chase, Richard), 117
The Jack Tales (Hicks, Ray), 128
Jackson, Ellen. *Cinder Edna*, 130
Jake Gander, Storyville Detective (McClements, George), 137
Jamie O'Rourke and the Big Potato (DePaola, Tomie), 120
Jenkins, Emily. *Toys Go Out*, 130, 216
Jenkins, Steve. *Actual Size*, 52
Jim and the Beanstalk (Briggs, Raymond), 115
Jitterbug Jam (Hicks, Barbara Jean), 128
John, Paul, George & Ben (Smith, Lane), 208, 209-211, 250
John Henry (Lester, Julius), 134
John Henry (Keats, Ezra Jack), 131
Johnny Appleseed (Kellogg, Steven), 72, 131
Johnson, Paul Brett
    Fearless Jack, 130
    Jack Outwits the Giants, 130
    Little Bunny Foo Foo, 130
Johnson-Davies, Denys. *Goha the Wise Fool*, 130
Johnston, Tony. *The Tale of Rabbit and Coyote*, 130
Jones, Malcolm. *Jump!: The Adventures of Brer Rabbit*, 142
Joseph Had a Little Overcoat (Taback, Simms), 153
Journey to the Blue Moon (Rupp, Rebecca), 225
Joyful Noise: Poems for Two Voices (Fleischman, Paul), 207, 243
Juan Bobo and the Pig (Pitre, Felix), 144
Juba This and Juba That: Story Hour Stretches for Large or Small Groups (Tashjian, Virginia A.), 154
Jump!: The Adventures of Brer Rabbit (Parks, Van Dyke, and Malcolm Jones), 142
The Junior Thunder Lord (Yep, Laurence), 157
The Juniper Tree and Other Tales from Grimm (Grimm, Jacob), 125
Just Enough to Make a Story: A Sourcebook for Telling (Schimmel, Nancy), 98, 185
Juster, Norton. *The Hello, Goodbye Window*, 131

Kajikawa, Kimiko. *Yoshi's Feast*, 131
Kaminski, Robert
    Multicultural Folktales: Stories to Tell Young Children, 185
    Twice Upon a Time: Stories to Tell, Retell, Act Out, and Write About, 185
Kamishibai Man (Say, Allen), 147
Kamishibai Story Theater: The Art of Picture Telling (De Las Casas, Dianne), 180
Kate and the Beanstalk (Osborne, Mary Pope), 142
Katz, Alan. *I'm Still Here in the Bathtub*, 244
Keats, Ezra Jack. *John Henry*, 131
Keifer, Barbara. *Charlotte Huck's Children's Literature*, 182
Kellogg, Steven
    Johnny Appleseed, 72, 131
    Sally Ann Thunder Ann Whirlwind Crockett, 131

Kelner, Lenore Blank. *Creative Classroom: A Guide for Using Creative Drama in the Classroom, PreK-6*, 254
Kesey, Ken. *Little Tricker the Squirrel Meets Big Double the Bear*, 131
Ketteman, Helen. *Armadilly Chili*, 131
Kha, Dang Manh. *In the Land of Small Dragon*, 13
The Khan's Daughter (Yep, Laurence), 157
Kibitzers and Fools: Tales My Zayda (Grandfather) Told Me (Taback, Simms), 153
Kimmel, Eric A.
    Anansi and the Magic Stick, 131
    Anansi and the Moss-Covered Rock, 131
    Anansi and the Talking Melon, 132, 245
    Anansi Goes Fishing, 132
    Baba Yaga, 132
    Boots and His Brothers, 132
    Cactus Soup, 132, 245
    Count Silvernose, 132
    The Gingerbread Man, 132
    The Hero Beowulf, 132
    Ten Suns: A Chinese Legend, 132
    The Three Princes, 133
    Three Samurai Cats, 133
Kindl, Patrice. *Goose Chase*, 245
Kinghorn, Harriet R. *Every Child a Storyteller: A Handbook of Ideas*, 182
King Midas and the Golden Touch (Hewitt, Kathryn), 128
King Midas: The Golden Touch (Demi), 120
King o' the Cats (Shepard, Aaron), 149
Kirstein, Lincoln. *Puss in Boots*, 133
K Is for Kissing a Cool Kangaroo (Andreae, Giles), 238
Kitten's First Full Moon (Henkes, Kevin), 127, 190, 244
Kline, Suzy. *The Herbie Jones Reader's Theater: Funny Scenes to Read Aloud*, 255
The Knee-High Man and Other Tales (Lester, Julius), 13, 134
Knudsen, Michelle. *Library Lion*, 67
Knuffle Bunny (Willems, Mo), 156, 192
Knutson, Barbara. *Love and Roast Chicken*, 133
Kraus, Anne Marie. *Folktale Themes and Activities for Children, Volume 1: Pourquoi Tales*, 182
Kumak's Fish (Bania, Michael), 114, 195, 238
Kurtz, Jane
    Pulling the Lion's Tail, 133
    Trouble, 133

Lambert, Jonathan. *The Wide-Mouthed Frog*, 80
Lang, Andrew. *The Blue Fairy Book*, 133
Langrish, Katherine. *Troll Fell*, 133
Larger Than Life (San Souci, Robert D.), 147
Larrick, Nancy. *Let's Do a Poem!: Introducing Poetry to Children Through Listening, Singing, Chanting, Impromptu Choral Reading, Body Movement, Dance, and Dramatization*, 255
Larry, Charles. *Peboan and Seegwun*, 133
Lazy Jack (French, Vivian), 123

Leach, Maria. *The Thing at the Foot of the Bed and Other Scary Tales*, 133

Leading Kids to Books Through Magic (Bauer, Caroline Feller), 179

The Legend of the Wandering King (Garcia, Laura Gallego), 124

Lehrman, Betty. *Telling Stories to Children: A National Storytelling Guide*, 182

Leonardo the Terrible Monster (Willems, Mo), 220

The Leopard's Drum (Souhami, Jessica), 151

The Leprechaun's Gold (Edwards, Pamela Duncan), 122

Lester, Julius
    John Henry, 134
    The Knee-High Man and Other Tales, 13, 134
    Sam and the Tigers, 134, 222, 245
    The Tales of Uncle Remus: The Adventures of Brer Rabbit, 134

Let's Do a Poem!: Introducing Poetry to Children Through Listening, Singing, Chanting, Impromptu Choral Reading, Body Movement, Dance, and Dramatization (Larrick, Nancy), 255

Levine, Gail Carson
    Ella Enchanted, 134
    The Fairy's Mistake, 134

Lewin, Ted. *The Storytellers*, 134

Library Lion (Knudsen, Michelle), 67

The Lightning Thief (Riordan, Rick), 145, 217, 249

"The Limerick Song" (song), 59-60

Lin, Grace. *The Year of the Dog*, 134

The Lion's Whiskers (Day, Nancy Raines), 119

Lipman, Doug
    Improving Your Storytelling: Beyond the Basics for All Who Tell Stories in Work or Play, 182
    Storytelling Games: Creative Activities for Language, Communication, and Composition Across the Curriculum, 182

Lippert, Margaret H. *Head, Body, Legs: A Story from Liberia*, 143, 248

Little, Jean. *Once Upon a Golden Apple*, 134

Little Bunny Foo Foo (Johnson, Paul Brett), 130

The Little Dog Laughed and Other Nursery Rhymes (Cousins, Lucy), 119

The Little Old Lady Who Was Not Afraid of Anything (Williams, Linda), 90, 156, 196, 252

The Little Red Hen (Makes a Pizza) (Sturges, Philemon), 153

The Little Red Hen (Pinkney, Jerry), 144

Little Red Riding Hood (Hyman, Trina Schart), 24, 129

Little Red Riding Hood: A Newfangled Prairie Tale (Ernst, Lisa Campbell), 122

"The Little Round Red House" (story), 68-72

Little Sister and the Month Brothers (DeRegniers, Beatrice S.), 121

Little Tricker the Squirrel Meets Big Double the Bear (Kesey, Ken), 131

Livingstone Mouse (Edwards, Pamela Duncan), 43

Livo, Norma J.

Bringing Out Their Best: Values Education and Character Development Through Traditional Tales, 182
    Storytelling Folklore Sourcebook, 184
    Storytelling: Process and Practice, 183

Lobel, Arnold
    Fables, 134, 200
    Mouse Tales, 245
    The Random House Book of Mother Goose, 135

Long, Sylvia. *Sylvia Long's Mother Goose*, 135

Lon Po Po; A Red-Riding Hood Story from China (Young, Ed), 158

Look Back and See: Twenty Lively Tales for Gentle Tellers (MacDonald, Margaret Read), 183

"Look for 398.2" (chant), 37

Los Gatos Black on Halloween (Montes, Marisa), 246

Louie, Ai-Ling. *Yeh-Shen: A Cinderella Story from China*, 13, 135

Love and Roast Chicken: A Trickster Tale from the Andes Mountains (Knutson, Barbara), 133

Love That Dog (Creech, Sharon), 207, 240

Lugalbanda: The Boy Who Got Caught Up in a War (Henderson, Kathy), 127

Lum, Kate. *What! Cried Granny: An Almost Bedtime Story*, 135, 245

Lunge-Larsen, Lise. *The Troll with No Heart in His Body: And Other Tales of Trolls from Norway*, 135

Lupton, Hugh. *The Adventures of Odysseus*, 135

Mabela the Clever (MacDonald, Margaret Read), 135

MacDonald, Margaret Read
    Celebrate the World: Twenty Tellable Folktales for Multicultural Festivals, 183
    Look Back and See: Twenty Lively Tales for Gentle Tellers, 183
    Mabela the Clever, 135
    A Parent's Guide to Storytelling: How to Make Up New Stories and Retell Old Favorites, 183
    Pickin' Peas, 245
    Shake-It-Up Tales!: Stories to Sing, Dance, Drum, and Act Out, 183
    The Storyteller's Sourcebook: A Subject, Title, and Motif Index to Folklore Collections for Children, 1983-1999, 184
    The Storyteller's Start-Up Book: Finding, Learning, Performing and Using Folktales, 183
    Tell the World: Storytelling Across Language Barriers, 183
    Three-Minute Tales: Stories from Around the World to Tell or Read When Time Is Short, 183
    Twenty Tellable Tales: Audience Participation Folktales for the Beginning Storyteller, 184
    When the Lights Go Out: Twenty Scary Stories to Tell, 184

Maddern, Eric. *The Fire Children: A West African Creation Tale*, 135

The Magic Gourd (Diakité, Baba Wagué), 121

The Magic Orange Tree and Other Haitian Folktales (Wolkstein, Diane), 7, 156

Mahy, Margaret. *The Seven Chinese Brothers*, 135

The Maid and the Mouse and the Odd-Shaped House (Zelinsky, Paul O.), 87

Make Way for Ducklings (McCloskey, Robert), 195

Mañana, Iguana (Paul, Ann Whitford), 248

Manushkin, Fran. *The Shivers in the Fridge*, 136, 216

Marcantonio, Patricia Santos. *Red Ridin' in the Hood: And Other Cuentos*, 18, 136, 226

Marshall, James
   Goldilocks and the Three Bears, 67, 136
   Old Mother Hubbard and Her Wonderful Dog, 136
   Red Riding Hood, 136
   The Three Little Pigs, 136

Martha Walks the Dog (Meddaugh, Susan), 208

Martin, Rafe
   Foolish Rabbit's Big Mistake, 136
   The Rough-Face Girl, 136
   The Shark God, 50, 136

Master Man: A Tall Tale of Nigeria (Shepard, Aaron), 57, 149, 214

Mathews, Judith. *Nathaniel Willy, Scared Silly*, 137

Matilda (Dahl, Roald), 204, 217

The Matzo Ball Boy (Shulman, Lisa), 149

Mayo, Margaret. *Tortoise's Flying Lesson*, 245

McCarthy, Meghan
   Aliens Are Coming!: The True Account Of The 1938 War Of The Worlds Radio Broadcast, 224
   Steal Back the Mona Lisa, 246

McCaughrean, Geraldine
   The Bronze Cauldron, 137
   Gilgamesh the Hero: The Epic of Gilgamesh, 137

McClements, George. *Jake Gander, Storyville Detective*, 137

McClintock, Barbara
   Animal Fables from Aesop, 137
   Cinderella, 137

McCloskey, Robert
   Homer Price, 246
   Make Way for Ducklings, 195

McCormick, Dell J. *Paul Bunyan Swings His Axe*, 137

McCully, Emily Arnold. *Beautiful Warrior: The Legend of the Nun's Kung Fu*, 137

McDermott, Gerald
   Coyote, 137
   Jabutí the Tortoise, 138
   Musicians of the Sun, 138
   Raven, 138
   Zomo the Rabbit, 138

The McElderry Book of Aesop's Fables (Morpurgo, Michael), 140, 200, 246

McFarland, Lyn Rossiter. *Widget*, 246

McGill, Alice. *Sure as Sunrise: Stories of Bruh Rabbit & His Walkin' Talkin' Friends*, 138

McGovern, Ann. *Too Much Noise*, 138

McKissack, Patricia C.
   Flossie & the Fox, 138

Itching and Twiching, 138

Porch Lies: Tales of Slicksters, Tricksters, and Other Wily Characters, 138

Precious and the Boo Hag, 139, 222

McKissack, Robert L. *Itching and Twiching*, 138

McMullan, Kate. *I Stink!*, 139, 195, 246

"McTavish" (song), 61

McVitty, Walter. *Ali Baba and the Forty Thieves*, 139

Meanwhile . . . (Feiffer, Jules), 242

Meddaugh, Susan
   Hog-Eye, 139
   Martha Walks the Dog, 208
   The Witch's Walking Stick, 139

Medearis, Angela Shelf
   Seven Spools of Thread, 139
   Too Much Talk, 246

Mercy Watson to the Rescue (DiCamillo, Kate), 208, 221

Mermaid Tales from Around the World (Osborne, Mary Pope), 142

Mice and Beans (Ryan, Pam Muñoz), 146

Milne, A. A. *Winnie-the-Pooh*, 194

Minard, Rosemary. *Womenfolk and Fairy Tales*, 139

The Miraculous Journey of Edward Tulane (DiCamillo, Kate), 217, 241

Misoso: Once Upon a Time Tales from Africa (Aardema, Verna), 112

Miss Nelson Has a Field Day (Allard, Harry), 204

Mollel, Tololwa M.
   Ananse's Feast, 139
   The Orphan Boy, 139
   Subira Subira, 140

Momotaro, the Peach Boy (Shute, Linda), 150

The Monster's Ring (Coville, Bruce), 193, 240

Montes, Marisa. *Los Gatos Black on Halloween*, 246

Mooney, Bill
   Ready-to-Tell Tales: Sure-fire Stories from America's Favorite Storytellers, 181
   The Storyteller's Guide: Storytellers Share Advice for the Classroom, Boardroom, Showroom, Podium, Pulpit and Center Stage, 63, 184

Moo Who? (Palatini, Margie), 247

Mora, Pat. *Doña Flor*, 140

Morden, Daniel. *The Adventures of Odysseus*, 135

More Readers Theatre for Beginning Readers (Barchers, Suzanne I., and Charla R. Pfeffinger), 253

Morimoto, Junko. *The Two Bullies*, 140

Morpurgo, Michael. *The McElderry Book of Aesop's Fables*, 140, 200, 246

Mosel, Arlene
   The Funny Little Woman, 140
   Tikki Tikki Tembo, 140

Moser, Barry
   The Three Little Pigs, 140
   Tucker Pfeffercorn, 140

Moses, Will. *Mother Goose*, 140

Moss, Onawumi Jean. *Precious and the Boo Hag*, 139, 222

Moss Gown (Hooks, William H.), 129

Mother Goose (Moses, Will), 140

Mother Goose Readers Theatre for Beginning Readers (Fredericks, Anthony D.), 254

Mouse Match (Young, Ed), 24, 158

Mouse Tales (Lobel, Arnold), 245

Mouse TV (Novak, Matt), 213, 247

Move Over, Rover! (Beaumont, Karen), 239

Mr. Maxwell's Mouse (Asch, Frank), 238

Mr. Pak Buys a Story (Farley, Carol), 123

Mrs. Chicken and the Hungry Crocodile (Paye, Won-Ldy, and Margaret H. Lippert), 143

Mrs. McCool and the Giant Cuhullin (Souhami, Jessica), 151

Mufaro's Beautiful Daughters (Steptoe, John), 152

Multicultural Folktales for Feltboard and Reader's Theater (Sierra, Judy), 255

Multicultural Folktales: Readers Theatre for Elementary Students (Barchers, Suzanne I.), 253

Multicultural Folktales: Stories to Tell Young Children (Sierra, Judy, and Robert Kaminski), 185

Murphy, Jill. *Peace at Last*, 195, 246

Murray, Marjorie Dennis. *Don't Wake Up the Bear!*, 246

Musgrove, Margaret. *The Spider Weaver*, 140

Musicians of the Sun (McDermott, Gerald), 138

Muth, Jon J.
 Stone Soup, 141, 247
 Zen Shorts, 141

My Brother, Ant (Byars, Betsy), 239

My Car (Barton, Byron), 238

Myers, Bernice. *Sidney Rella and the Glass Sneaker*, 14

Myers, Tim. *Basho and the Fox*, 141

My Very First Mother Goose (Opie, Iona), 142

The Mysterious Giant of Barletta (DePaola, Tomie), 120

Napoli, Donna Jo. *The Prince of the Pond*, 141

Nathaniel Willy, Scared Silly (Mathews, Judith, and Fay Robinson), 137

The Neat Line: Scribbling Through Mother Goose (Edwards, Pamela Duncan), 122, 221

The Neighborhood Mother Goose (Crews, Nina), 119

New Handbook for Storytellers: With Stories, Poems, Magic, and More (Bauer, Caroline Feller), 179

New York's Bravest (Osborne, Mary Pope), 142

The Nightingale (Andersen, Hans Christian, illus. by Jerry Pinkney), 113

The Nightingale (Andersen, Hans Christian, retold by Stephen Mitchell, illus. by Bagram Ibatoulline), 112

Nodelman, Perry. *The Same Place But Different*, 141

No Dinner!: The Story of the Old Woman and the Pumpkin (Souhami, Jessica), 151, 251

Nolan, Dennis. *Androcles and the Lion*, 141

Nonfiction Readers Theatre for Beginning Readers (Fredericks, Anthony D.), 254

The Nonsense Book (Emrich, Duncan), 122

Norfolk, Sherry. *The Storytelling Classroom: Applications Across the Curriculum, 184*

North American Legends (Haviland, Virginia), 127

Nouns and Verbs Have a Field Day (Pulver, Robin), 221

Novak, Matt. *Mouse TV*, 213, 247

Numeroff, Laura Joffe. *If You Take a Mouse to School*, 247

Nursery Tales Around the World (Sierra, Judy), 150

Odin's Family: Myths of the Vikings (Philip, Neil), 143

Odysseus in the Serpent Maze (Yolen, Jane, and Robert J. Harris), 157

Officer Buckle and Gloria (Rathmann, Peggy), 249

Oh, Look! (Polacco, Patricia), 248

"Oh, My Aunt Came Back" (song), 47

Oink? (Palatini, Margie), 222

Old Cricket (Wheeler, Lisa), 155

Old MacDonald Had a Woodshop (Shulman, Lisa), 150

Old Mother Hubbard and Her Wonderful Dog (Marshall, James), 136

The Old Woman and Her Pig (Galdone, Paul), 123, 196

Ollie (Dunrea, Olivier), 242

Ol' Paul, the Mighty Logger (Rounds, Glen), 145

O'Malley, Kevin. *Straight to the Pole*, 193, 247

Once Upon a Golden Apple (Little, Jean, and Maggie de Vries), 134

One Fine Day (Hogrogian, Nonny), 129

One Grain of Rice: A Mathematical Folktale (Demi), 120

One Riddle, One Answer (Thompson, Lauren), 154

Onyefulu, Obi. *Chinye*, 141

Opie, Iona
 Here Comes Mother Goose, 141
 I Saw Esau, 141
 My Very First Mother Goose, 142

Opie, Peter
 I Saw Esau, 141

The Orchard Book of Nursery Rhymes (Sutherland, Zena), 153

The Orphan Boy: A Maasai Story (Mollel, Tololwa M.), 139

Oryx Multicultural Folktale Series: Cinderella (Sierra, Judy), 185

Osborne, Mary Pope
 American Tall Tales, 142
 The Brave Little Seamstress, 142
 Kate and the Beanstalk, 142
 Mermaid Tales from Around the World, 142
 New York's Bravest, 142
 Sleeping Bobby, 142

Osborne, Will. *Sleeping Bobby*, 142

Ouch!: A Tale from Grimm (Babbitt, Natalie), 114

Owl Eyes (Gates, Frieda), 124

Palatini, Margie
 Bad Boys, 222, 247
 Earthquack!, 222, 247
 Moo Who?, 247
 Oink?, 222
 Piggie Pie, 222, 247
 The Web Files, 142, 222, 248
 Zoom Broom, 248

Pancakes for Supper (Isaacs, Anne), 67, 130, 222

Pandora (Burleigh, Robert), 116

The Paper Dragon (Davol, Marguerite W.), 119

A Parent's Guide to Storytelling: How to Make Up New Stories and Retell Old Favorites (MacDonald, Margaret Read), 183

Parks, Van Dyke. Jump!: The Adventures of Brer Rabbit, 142

Passager (Yolen, Jane), 157

Paterson, Katherine. *The Tale of the Mandarin Ducks,* 143

Paul, Ann Whitford. *Mañana, Iguana,* 248

Paul Bunyan Swings His Axe (McCormick, Dell J.), 137

Paxton, Tom. *Aesop's Fables,* 143

Paye, Won-Ldy. *Head, Body, Legs,* 143, 248

Paye, Won-Ldy, and Margaret H. Lippert. *Mrs. Chicken and the Hungry Crocodile,* 143

Peace at Last (Murphy, Jill), 195, 246

"Peanut Butter and Jelly" (chant), 44-45

Peanut Butter and Jelly: A Play-Rhyme (Westcott, Nadine Bernard), 45, 155, 196

Pearson, Tracey Campbell. *Bob,* 248

Peboan and Seegwun (Larry, Charles), 133

Peck, Jan. *The Giant Carrot,* 143, 195, 248

Pegasus, the Flying Horse (Yolen, Jane), 157

Peggony-Po: A Whale of a Tale (Pinkney, Andrea Davis), 143

Pellowski, Anne
   Drawing Stories from Around the World and a Sampling of European Handkerchief Stories, 184
   The Family Storytelling Handbook: How to Use Stories, Anecdotes, Rhymes, Handkerchiefs, Paper and Other Objects to Enrich Your Family Traditions, 184
   The Storytelling Vine: A Source Book of Unusual and Easy-to-Tell Stories from Around the World, 184

Pelton, Mary Helen. *Every Child a Storyteller: A Handbook of Ideas,* 182

Pennypacker, Sara. *Clementine,* 225

The People Could Fly: The Picture Book (Hamilton, Virginia), 126

Perrault, Charles. *Puss in Boots.* (Illus. by Fred Marcellino), 143

Persephone and the Pomegranate (Waldherr, Kris), 155

Pfeffinger, Charla R.
   Getting Ready to Read with Readers Theatre, 253
   More Readers Theatre for Beginning Readers, 253

Philip, Neil
   The Adventures of Odysseus, 143
   Odin's Family, 143

Pickin' Peas (MacDonald, Margaret Read), 245

The Pigeon Finds a Hot Dog (Willems, Mo), 156

Piggie Pie (Palatini, Margie), 222, 247

Pinkney, Andrea Davis. *Peggony-Po: A Whale of a Tale,* 143

Pinkney, Jerry
   Aesop's Fables, 144, 200, 248
   The Little Red Hen, 144

Pinkwater, Daniel
   Fat Men from Space, 201
   Tooth-Gnasher Superflash, 192, 248

Pitre, Felix. *Juan Bobo and the Pig,* 144

Poems of A. Nonny Mouse (Prelutsky, Jack), 144

Polacco, Patricia. *Oh, Look!,* 248

Pollock, Penny. *The Turkey Girl,* 144

Porch Lies: Tales of Slicksters, Tricksters, and Other Wily Characters (McKissack, Patricia C.), 138

Pratchett, Terry. *The Wee Free Men,* 144

Precious and the Boo Hag (McKissack, Patricia, and Onawumi Jean Moss), 139, 222

Prelutsky, Jack. *Poems of A. Nonny Mouse,* 144

Presenting Reader's Theater: Plays and Poems to Read Aloud (Bauer, Caroline Feller), 253

A Pride of African Tales (Washington, Donna L.), 155

The Prince of the Pond (Napoli, Donna Jo), 141

The Princess and the Pizza (Auch, Mary Jane), 113

Princess Furball (Huck, Charlotte), 129

The Princess Mouse (Shepard, Aaron), 149

"Prinderella and the Cince" (story), 105-107

Probuditi! (Van Allsburg, Chris), 200, 252

Pulling the Lion's Tail (Kurtz, Jane), 133

Pullman, Philip
   I Was a Rat!, 144
   The Scarecrow and His Servant, 144

Pulver, Robin
   Nouns and Verbs Have a Field Day, 221
   Punctuation Takes a Vacation, 221

Punctuation Takes a Vacation (Pulver, Robin), 221

Punia and the King of Sharks (Wardlaw, Lee), 50, 155

Puss in Boots (Kirstein, Lincoln), 133

Puss in Boots (Perrault, Charles, illus. by Fred Marcellino), 143

Putting the World in a Nutshell: The Art of the Formula Tale (Dailey, Sheila), 180

The Rabbit's Escape (Han, Suzanne Crowder), 126

Raccoon's Last Race (Bruchac, Joseph, and James Bruchac), 116

Rain (Stojic, Manya), 39, 251

"The Rainhat" (story), 94-104

"Rainstorm", 56

Raising Sweetness (Stanley, Diane), 208, 251

Raising Voices: Creating Youth Storytelling Groups and Troupes (Sima, Judy, and Kevin Cordi), 185

The Random House Book of Mother Goose (Lobel, Arnold), 135

Rapunzel (Zelinsky, Paul O.), 25, 158

Raschka, Chris. *Yo! Yes?,* 220, 249

Rascol, Sabina I. *The Impudent Rooster,* 144

Rathmann, Peggy
   Good Night, Gorilla, 249
   Officer Buckle and Gloria, 249

Rattletrap Car (Root, Phyllis), 145, 249

Raven (McDermott, Gerald), 138

Readers on Stage (Shepard, Aaron), 255

Readers Theater for Building Fluency: Strategies and Scripts for Making the Most of This Highly Effective, Motivating, and Research-Based Approach to Oral Reading (Worthy, Jo), 256

Read! Perform! Learn!: 10 Reader's Theater Programs for Literary Enhancement (Buzzeo, Toni), 253

Ready-to-Tell Tales: Sure-fire Stories from America's Favorite Storytellers (Holt, David, and Bill Mooney), 181

Red Riding Hood (Marshall, James), 136

Red Ridin' in the Hood: And Other Cuentos (Marcantonio, Patricia Santos), 18, 136, 226

The Remarkable Christmas of the Cobbler's Sons (Sawyer, Ruth), 147

Renfro, Nancy. *Storytelling with Puppets*, 180

Replay (Creech, Sharon), 227

The Revenge of the Witch. (Delaney, Joseph), 120

Rex, Adam. *Frankenstein Makes a Sandwich*, 145

Rietz, Sandra A.
   Storytelling Folklore Sourcebook, 184
   Storytelling: Process and Practice, 183

Riordan, Rick. *The Lightning Thief*, 145, 217, 249

Robin Hood (Hayes, Sarah), 127

Robinson, Fay. *Nathaniel Willy, Scared Silly*, 137

"Rockabye Baby" (song), 38

A Rocket in My Pocket (Withers, Carl), 156

Rockwell, Thomas. *How to Eat Fried Worms*, 201

Rodanas, Kristina. *The Blind Hunter*, 145

Rooster Can't Cock-a-Doodle-Doo (Rostoker-Gruber, Karen), 145, 249

Root, Phyllis. *Rattletrap Car*, 145, 249

Ros, Saphan. *Brother Rabbit*, 128

Rosen, Michael. *We're Going on a Bear Hunt*, 67, 145

Rosenthal, Amy Krouse. *Cookies: Bite-Size Life Lessons*, 46

Ross, Gayle. *How Turtle's Back Was Cracked*, 145

Rostoker-Gruber, Karen. *Rooster Can't Cock-a-Doodle-Doo*, 145, 249

Rotner, Shelley. *Action Alphabet*, 249

The Rough-Face Girl (Martin, Rafe), 136

Rounds, Glen
   Ol' Paul, the Mighty Logger, 145
   The Three Billy Goats Gruff, 145
   Three Little Pigs and the Big Bad Wolf, 146

Rowling, J. K. *Harry Potter and the Sorcerer's Stone*, 146

Rub-a-Dub Sub (Ashman, Linda), 238

Rubright, Lynn. *Beyond the Beanstalk: Interdisciplinary Learning Through Storytelling*, 184

Ruby (Emberley, Michael), 122

Ruby and the Sniffs (Emberley, Michael), 242

Rumford, James. *Dog-of-the-Sea-Waves*, 146

Rumpelstiltskin (Zelinsky, Paul O.), 26, 158

Rumpelstiltskin's Daughter (Stanley, Diane), 152

The Runaway Rice Cake (Compestine, Ying Chang), 118

Runny Babbit (Silverstein, Shel), 107

Rupp, Rebecca. *Journey to the Blue Moon*, 225

Ryan, Pam Muñoz. *Mice and Beans*, 146

Rydell, Katy. *A Beginner's Guide to Storytelling*, 185

Ryder, Joanne. *Earthdance*, 249

Sabuda, Robert. *Arthur and the Sword*, 146

Sachar, Louis. *Holes*, 249

Sacre, Antonio. *The Barking Mouse, 87,* 146, 208, 218, 230-236

Saint George and the Dragon (Hodges, Margaret), 128

Saint Patrick and the Peddler (Hodges, Margaret), 129

Salley, Coleen
   Epossumondas, 31, 146, 250
   Why Epossumondas Has No Hair on His Tail, 146

Sally Ann Thunder Ann Whirlwind Crockett (Kellogg, Steven), 131

Sam and the Tigers (Lester, Julius), 134, 222, 245

The Same Place But Different (Nodelman, Perry), 141

San Souci, Robert D.
   Cendrillon, 146
   Cinderella Skeleton, 250
   The Faithful Friend, 147
   Larger Than Life, 147
   Sister Tricksters, 147
   Sukey and the Mermaid, 147
   The Talking Eggs, 25, 147
   A Weave of Words, 147
   Young Arthur, 147

Sawyer, Ruth
   The Remarkable Christmas of the Cobbler's Sons, 147
   The Way of the Storyteller, 14, 185

Say, Allen. *Kamishibai Man*, 147

The Scarecrow and His Servant (Pullman, Philip), 144

Scared Witless: Thirteen Eerie Tales to Tell (Hamilton, Martha, and Mitch Weiss), 126

Scary Stories to Tell in the Dark (Schwartz, Alvin), 148

Schaefer, Carole Lexa. *The Biggest Soap*, 148

Schanzer, Rosalyn. *Davy Crockett Saves the World*, 148

Schimmel, Nancy. *Just Enough to Make a Story: A Sourcebook for Telling*, 98, 185

Schoolyard Rhymes: Kids' Own Rhymes for Rope Skipping, Hand Clapping, Ball Bouncing, and Just Plain Fun (Sierra, Judy), 150

Schwartz, Alvin
   And the Green Grass Grew All Around: Folk Poetry from Everyone, 148
   Busy Buzzing Bumblebees and Other Tongue Twisters, 148
   I Saw You in the Bathtub and Other Folk Rhymes, 148
   Scary Stories to Tell in the Dark, 148
   Tomfoolery: Trickery and Foolery with Words, 148

Scieszka, Jon
   The Frog Prince, Continued, 148
   Squids Will Be Squids, 148, 250
   The Stinky Cheese Man and Other Fairly Stupid Tales, 18, 149
   The True Story of the 3 Little Pigs, 14, 18, 149

Seedfolks (Fleischman, Paul), 207, 243

Seeger, Pete. *Abiyoyo*, 149

Serious Farm (Egan, Tim), 242

Seven Blind Mice (Young, Ed), 158
The Seven Chinese Brothers (Mahy, Margaret), 135
The Seven Chinese Sisters (Tucker, Kathy), 154, 208
Seven Spools of Thread (Medearis, Angela Shelf), 139
Shake-It-Up Tales!: Stories to Sing, Dance, Drum, and Act Out (MacDonald, Margaret Read), 183
Shannon, George
    Stories to Solve, 149
    True Lies, 149
The Shark God (Martin, Rafe), 50, 136
Shepard, Aaron
    Folktales on Stage, 255
    King o' the Cats, 149
    Master Man, 57, 149, 214
    The Princess Mouse, 149
    Readers on Stage, 255
    Stories on Stage, 255
The Shivers in the Fridge (Manushkin, Fran), 136, 216
Show Time at the Polk Street School: Plays You Can Do Yourself or in the Classroom (Giff, Patricia Reilly), 254
Shulman, Lisa
    The Matzo Ball Boy, 149
    Old MacDonald Had a Woodshop, 150
Shute, Linda. *Momotaro, the Peach Boy*, 150
Sidney Rella and the Glass Sneaker (Myers, Bernice), 14
Sierra, Judy
    Can You Guess My Name?, 150
    Fantastic Theater: Puppets and Plays for Young Performers and Young Audiences, 255
    The Gift of the Crocodile, 150
    Multicultural Folktales for Feltboard and Reader's Theater, 255
    Multicultural Folktales: Stories to Tell Young Children, 185
    Nursery Tales Around the World, 150
    Oryx Multicultural Folktale Series: Cinderella, 185
    Schoolyard Rhymes, 150
    Tasty Baby Belly Buttons, 150
    Twice Upon a Time: Stories to Tell, Retell, Act Out, and Write About, 185
    Wild About Books, 150
Silly Salamanders and Other Slightly Stupid Stuff for Readers Theatre (Fredericks, Anthony D.), 254
Silverman, Erica. *Big Pumpkin*, 90, 150, 195
Silverstein, Shel. *Runny Babbit*, 107
Sima, Judy. *Raising Voices: Creating Youth Storytelling Groups and Troupes*, 185
Simms, Laura. *The Squeaky Door*, 151
Singer, Isaac Bashevis. *When Shlemiel Went to Warsaw & Other Stories*, 151
Singh, Vandana. *Younguncle Comes to Town*, 151
Sir Gawain and the Loathly Lady (Hastings, Selina), 127
Sister Tricksters (San Souci, Robert D.), 147
Six Chinese Brothers (Cheng, Hou-Tien), 117
The Sleeping Beauty (Hyman, Trina Schart), 129
Sleeping Bobby (Osborne, Will, and Mary Pope Osborne), 142

Sloat, Teri. *Sody Sallyratus*, 74, 151
Slobodkina, Esphyr. *Caps for Sale*, 250
Sloyer, Shirlee. *From the Page to the Stage: The Educator's Complete Guide to Readers Theatre*, 255
Smith, Jeff. *Bone #1: Out from Boneville*, 226, 250
Smith, Lane
    The Happy Hocky Family Moves to the Country, 250
    John, Paul, George & Ben, 208, 209–211, 250
Snyder, Dianne. *The Boy of the Three Year Nap*, 151
So, Meilo. *Gobble, Gobble, Slip, Slop*, 74, 151, 200
Soap! Soap! Don't Forget the Soap! (Birdseye, Tom), 115
Sody Sallyratus (Sloat, Teri), 74, 151
Something from Nothing (Gilman, Phoebe), 124
The Sons of the Dragon King (Young, Ed), 252
Soto, Gary. *Chato and the Party Animals*, 251
Souhami, Jessica
    The Leopard's Drum, 151
    Mrs. McCool and the Giant Cuhullin, 151
    No Dinner!: The Story of the Old Woman and the Pumpkin, 151, 251
The Spider Weaver (Musgrove, Margaret), 140
The Spiderwick Chronicles, Book 1: The Field Guide (Black, Holly, and Tony DiTerlizzi), 115, 239
Spillman, Carolyn V. *Using Folk Literature in the Classroom: Encouraging Children to Read and Write*, 181
The Squeaky, Creaky Bed (Thomson, Pat), 154
The Squeaky Door (Simms, Laura), 151
Squids Will Be Squids (Scieszka, Jon), 148, 250
Stamm, Claus. *Three Strong Women*, 152
Stanley, Diane
    Bella at Midnight, 152
    The Giant and the Beanstalk, 152
    Goldie and the Three Bears, 152
    Raising Sweetness, 208, 251
    Rumpelstiltskin's Daughter, 152
The Star Maiden (Esbensen, Barbara Juster), 123
Steal Back the Mona Lisa (McCarthy, Meghan), 246
Steen, Sandra
    Car Wash, 251
Steen, Susan
    Car Wash, 251
Stella Louella's Runaway Book (Ernst, Lisa Campbell), 242
Stenson, Jane. The *Storytelling Classroom: Applications Across the Curriculum*, 184
Steptoe, John. *Mufaro's Beautiful Daughters*, 152
Stevens, Janet
    And the Dish Ran Away with the Spoon, 152, 251
    Cook-a-Doodle-Doo!, 152
    Coyote Steals the Blanket, 152
    The Great Fuzz Frenzy, 220
    Tops & Bottoms, 67, 153
Stillwell, Lydia. *Creative Drama for the Classroom Teacher*, 254
The Stinky Cheese Man and Other Fairly Stupid Tales (Scieszka, Jon), 18, 149
Stojic, Manya. *Rain*, 39, 251

Stolen Thunder (Climo, Shirley), 118

Stone Soup (Brown, Marcia), 115

Stone Soup (Muth, Jon J), 141, 247

Stories in Action: Interactive Tales and Learning Activities to Promote Early Literacy (Gordh, Bill), 181

Stories Neverending: A Program Guide for Schools and Libraries (Irving, Jan), 182

Stories on Stage (Shepard, Aaron), 255

Stories on the Move: Integrating Literature and Movement with Children, from Infants to Age 14 (Cohen, Arlene), 254

Stories to Play With: Kids' Tales Told with Puppets, Paper, Toys, and Imagination (Fujita, Hiroko), 80, 181

Stories to Solve: Folktales from Around the World (Shannon, George), 149

A Story, a Story (Haley, Gail E.), 126

The Story of Chopsticks (Compestine, Ying Chang), 118

The Story of Little Babaji (Bannerman, Helen), 208, 222, 238

Story Proof: The Science Behind the Startling Power of Story (Haven, Kendall), 181

The Storytellers (Lewin, Ted), 134

The Storyteller's Guide: Storytellers Share Advice for the Classroom, Boardroom, Showroom, Podium, Pulpit and Center Stage (Mooney, Bill, and David Holt), 63, 184

The Storyteller's Sourcebook: A Subject, Title, and Motif Index to Folklore Collections for Children, 1983-1999 (MacDonald, Margaret Read, and Brian W. Sturm), 184

The Storyteller's Start-Up Book: Finding, Learning, Performing and Using Folktales (MacDonald, Margaret Read), 183

Storytelling: Art and Technique (Greene, Ellin), 181

The Storytelling Classroom: Applications Across the Curriculum (Norfolk, Sherry, Jane Stenson, and Diane Williams), 184

Storytelling Folklore Sourcebook (Livo, Norma J., and Rietz, Sandra A.), 184

Storytelling for Young Adults: A Guide to Tales for Teens (De Vos, Gail), 180

Storytelling Games: Creative Activities for Language, Communication, and Composition Across the Curriculum (Lipman, Doug), 182

Storytelling: Process and Practice (Livo, Norma J., and Sandra A. Rietz), 183

Storytelling Professionally: The Nuts and Bolts of a Working Performer (Geisler, Harlynne), 181

The Storytelling Vine: A Source Book of Unusual and Easy-to-Tell Stories from Around the World (Pellowski, Anne), 184

Storytelling with Puppets (Champlin, Connie, and Renfro, Nancy), 180

Straight to the Pole (O'Malley, Kevin), 193, 247

Strauss, Kevin. *Tales with Tails: Storytelling the Wonders of the Natural World*, 185

Straw into Gold: Books and Activities About Folktales (Irving, Jan, and Robin Currie), 182

Strega Nona (DePaola, Tomie), 121

Sturges, Philemon. *The Little Red Hen (Makes a Pizza)*, 153

Sturm, Brian W. *The Storyteller's Sourcebook: A Subject, Title, and Motif Index to Folklore Collections for Children, 1983-1999*, 184

Subira Subira (Mollel, Tololwa M.), 140

Sukey and the Mermaid (San Souci, Robert D.), 147

Sunami, Kitoba. *How the Fisherman Tricked the Genie*, 153

The Sun Girl and the Moon Boy (Choi, Yangsook), 117

Super Simple Storytelling: A Can-Do Guide for Every Classroom, Every Day (Haven, Kendall), 181

Sure as Sunrise: Stories of Bruh Rabbit & His Walkin' Talkin' Friends (McGill, Alice), 138

Sutcliff, Rosemary. *Black Ships Before Troy!*, 153

Sutherland, Zena. *The Orchard Book of Nursery Rhymes*, 153

Swamp Angel (Isaacs, Anne), 67, 130

"The Swimming Pool Song" (song), 53

Swope, Sam. *Jack and the Seven Deadly Giants*, 153

Sylvia Long's Mother Goose (Long, Sylvia), 135

Taback, Simms

    Joseph Had a Little Overcoat, 153

    Kibitzers and Fools: Tales My Zayda (Grandfather) Told Me, 153

    There Was an Old Lady Who Swallowed a Fly, 74, 153

    This Is the House That Jack Built, 153

The Tailypo (Galdone, Joanna), 123

Tale of a Black Cat (Withers, Carl), 85, 156

The Tale of Despereaux (DiCamillo, Kate), 121, 202, 204, 217

The Tale of Rabbit and Coyote (Johnston, Tony), 130

The Tale of the Mandarin Ducks (Paterson, Katherine), 143

The Tale of Tricky Fox (Aylesworth, Jim), 114, 199, 238

Tales from Grimm (Gag, Wanda), 123

The Tales of Uncle Remus: The Adventures of Brer Rabbit (Lester, Julius), 134

Tales Our Abuelitas Told (Campoy, F. Isabel, and Alma Flor Ada), 116

Tales with Tails: Storytelling the Wonders of the Natural World (Strauss, Kevin), 185

Talkin' about Bessie: The Story of Aviator Elizabeth Coleman (Grimes, Nikki), 243

The Talking Eggs (San Souci, Robert D.), 25, 147

Tashjian, Virginia A.

    Juba This and Juba That: Story Hour Stretches for Large or Small Groups, 154

    With a Deep Sea Smile: Story Hour Stretches for Large or Small Groups, 90

Tasty Baby Belly Buttons (Sierra, Judy), 150

Teague, Mark. *Dear Mrs. LaRue: Letters from Obedience School*, 251

Telling Stories to Children (Ziskind, Sylvia), 186

Telling Stories to Children: A National Storytelling Guide (Lehrman, Betty), 182

Tell Me a Tale: A Book about Storytelling (Bruchac, Joseph), 180

Tell the World: Storytelling Across Language Barriers (MacDonald, Margaret Read), 183

Ten-Gallon Bart (Crummel, Susan Stevens), 240

Ten Suns (Kimmel, Eric A.), 132

"T for Tommy" (story), 81-87

The Terrible Eek (Compton, Patricia A.), 119

There Was an Old Lady Who Swallowed a Fly (Taback, Simms), 74, 153

Thiesing, Lisa. *The Viper*, 92, 154, 251

The Thing at the Foot of the Bed and Other Scary Tales (Leach, Maria), 133

This Is the House That Jack Built (Taback, Simms), 153

Thomas, Shelley Moore. *Get Well, Good Knight*, 154, 252

Thompson, Lauren. *One Riddle, One Answer*, 154

Thompson, Richard, 86-87

Thomson, Pat. *The Squeaky, Creaky Bed*, 154

The Three Billy Goats Gruff (Asbjørnsen, P. C.), 113

The Three Billy Goats Gruff (Rounds, Glen), 145

Three Cool Kids (Emberley, Rebecca), 122, 242

The Three Little Pigs (Marshall, James), 136

The Three Little Pigs (Moser, Barry), 140

Three Little Pigs and the Big Bad Wolf (Rounds, Glen), 146

The Three Little Pigs and the Fox (Hooks, William H.), 129

Three-Minute Tales: Stories from Around the World to Tell or Read When Time Is Short (MacDonald, Margaret Read), 183

"Three Myopic Rodents" (song), 40

The Three Pigs (Wiesner, David), 156

The Three Princes (Kimmel, Eric A.), 133

Three Samurai Cats (Kimmel, Eric A.), 133

The Three Sillies (Galdone, Paul), 124

The Three Sillies (Hewitt, Kathryn), 128

Three Strong Women (Stamm, Claus), 152

Tikki Tikki Tembo (Mosel, Arlene), 140

The Tinderbox (Andersen, Hans Christian, Adapt. and illus. by Barry Moser), 113

To Everything There Is a Season (Dillon, Leo, and Diane Dillon), 241

Tomfoolery: Trickery and Foolery with Words (Schwartz, Alvin), 148

Tomie dePaola's Mother Goose (DePaola, Tomie), 121

"Tongue Twister Song" (song), 58

Too Much Noise (McGovern, Ann), 138

Too Much Talk (Medearis, Angela Shelf), 246

Tooth-Gnasher Superflash (Pinkwater, Daniel), 192, 248

Tops & Bottoms (Stevens, Janet), 67, 153

Tortoise's Flying Lesson: Animal Stories (Mayo, Margaret), 245

Touch Magic: Fantasy, Faerie and Folklore in the Literature of Childhood (Yolen, Jane), 186

Toys Go Out (Jenkins, Emily), 130, 216

Traveling to Tondo (Aardema, Verna), 112

"Travels of a Fox", 199

The Trial of Cardigan Jones (Egan, Tim), 205, 208, 242

Tripp, Wallace. *A Great Big Ugly Man Came Up and Tied His Horse to Me*, 154

Troll Fell (Langrish, Katherine), 133

The Troll with No Heart in His Body (Lunge-Larsen, Lise), 135

Trouble (Kurtz, Jane), 133

True Lies: 18 Tales for You to Judge (Shannon, George), 149

The True Story of the 3 Little Pigs (Scieszka, Jon), 14, 18, 149

Tucker, Kathy. *The Seven Chinese Sisters,* 154, 208

Tucker Pfeffercorn (Moser, Barry), 140

The Turkey Girl (Pollock, Penny), 144

Twelve Tales from Aesop (Carle, Eric), 116

26 Fairmount Avenue (DePaola, Tomie), 1

Twenty Tellable Tales: Audience Participation Folktales for the Beginning Storyteller (MacDonald, Margaret Read), 184

Twice Upon a Time: Stories to Tell, Retell, Act Out, and Write About (Sierra, Judy, and Robert Kaminski), 185

"Twinkle, Twinkle?" (song), 40

The Two Bullies (Morimoto, Junko), 140

Two of Everything (Hong, Lily Toy), 129

Two Ways to Count to Ten (Dee, Ruby), 119

Untermeyer, Louis. *Aesop's Fables*, 154

The Uses of Enchantment: The Meaning and Importance of Fairy Tales (Bettelheim, Bruno), 179

Using Folk Literature in the Classroom: Encouraging Children to Read and Write (Goforth, Frances S., and Carolyn V. Spillman), 181

Vagin, Vladimir. *The Enormous Carrot*, 252

Van Allsburg, Chris. *Probuditi!*, 200, 252

Van Laan, Nancy. *In a Circle Long Ago*, 154

The Village of Round and Square Houses (Grifalconi, Ann), 125

"The Viper" (story), 91-92

The Viper (Thiesing, Lisa), 92, 154, 251

Waber, Bernard. *Bearsie Bear and the Surprise Sleepover Party*, 252

Waldherr, Kris. *Persephone and the Pomegranate*, 155

Walker, Paul Robert. *Big Men, Big Country*, 155

Walking Through the Jungle (Harter, Debbie), 244

Walk On!: A Guide for Babies of All Ages (Frazee, Marla), 193, 243

Wardlaw, Lee. *Punia and the King of Sharks*, 50, 155

Washington, Donna L. *A Pride of African Tales*, 155

Wattenberg, Jane. *Henny-Penny*, 155, 252

The Way of the Storyteller (Sawyer, Ruth), 14, 185

A Weave of Words (San Souci, Robert D.), 147

The Web Files (Palatini, Margie), 142, 222, 248

The Wee Free Men (Pratchett, Terry), 144

Weiss, Mitch

    Children Tell Stories: A Teaching Guide, 80, 181

Scared Witless: Thirteen Eerie Tales to Tell, 126
We're Going on a Bear Hunt (Rosen, Michael), 67, 145
"We're Going on a Lion Hunt" (chant), 65-67
Westcott, Nadine Bernard. *Peanut Butter and Jelly: A Play-Rhyme*, 45, 155, 196
What! Cried Granny: An Almost Bedtime Story (Lum, Kate), 135, 245
Wheeler, Lisa. *Old Cricket*, 155
When Birds Could Talk & Bats Could Sing (Hamilton, Virginia), 126
When Jaguar Ate the Moon (Brusca, María Cristina, and Tona Wilson), 116
When Shlemiel Went to Warsaw & Other Stories (Singer, Isaac Bashevis), 151
When the Lights Go Out: Twenty Scary Stories to Tell (MacDonald, Margaret Read), 184
Where's Pup? (Dodds, Dayle Ann), 241
Where's the Big Bad Wolf? (Christelow, Eileen), 117
Whipple, Laura. *If the Shoe Fits: Voices from Cinderella*, 28, 155
White, Carolyn. *Whuppity Stoorie*, 155
Who Hops? (Davis, Katie), 241
Who's Afraid of the Big Bad Book? (Child, Lauren), 117
"Who Took the Cookies from the Cookie Jar?" (chant), 46
Whuppity Stoorie: A Scottish Folktale (White, Carolyn), 155
Why Ducks Sleep on One Leg (Garland, Sherry), 124
Why Epossumondas Has No Hair on His Tail (Salley, Coleen), 146
Why Lapin's Ears Are Long and Other Tales from the Louisiana Bayou (Doucet, Sharon Arms), 121
Why Mosquitoes Buzz in People's Ears (Aardema, Verna), 15, 112
Why the Sky Is Far Away (Gerson, Mary-Joan), 124
The Wide-Mouthed Frog (Faulkner, Keith, and Jonathan Lambert), 80
"Wide Mouth Frog" (story), 75-80
Widget (McFarland, Lyn Rossiter), 246
Wiesner, David. *The Three Pigs*, 156
Wild About Books (Sierra, Judy), 150
The Wild Ducks and the Goose (Withers, Carl), 85
Wiley and the Hairy Man (Bang, Molly Garrett), 114
Willems, Mo
    Don't Let the Pigeon Drive the Bus, 197, 252
    Knuffle Bunny, 156, 192
    Leonardo the Terrible Monster, 220
    The Pigeon Finds a Hot Dog, 156
Willey, Margaret. *Clever Beatrice*, 156
William Tell (Early, Margaret), 122
William Tell (Fisher, Leonard Everett), 123
Williams, Diane. *The Storytelling Classroom: Applications Across the Curriculum*, 184
Williams, Linda. *The Little Old Lady Who Was Not Afraid of Anything*, 90, 156, 196, 252
"Will You Remember Me?" (riddle), 93
Willy the Dreamer (Browne, Anthony), 239
Wilson, Tona. *When Jaguar Ate the Moon*, 116

Wings (Yolen, Jane), 157
Winnie-the-Pooh (Milne, A. A.), 194
Wisniewski, David. *Worlds of Shadow: Teaching with Shadow Puppetry*, 256
Wisniewski, Donna. *Worlds of Shadow: Teaching with Shadow Puppetry*, 256
The Witches (Dahl, Roald), 204
The Witch's Walking Stick (Meddaugh, Susan), 139
With a Deep Sea Smile: Story Hour Stretches for Large or Small Groups Tashjian, Virginia A, 90
Withers, Carl
    A Rocket in My Pocket 156
    Tale of a Black Cat, 85, 156
    The Wild Ducks and the Goose, 85
Wolf, Joan M. *The Beanstalk and Beyond: Developing Critical Thinking Through Fairy Tales*, 185
The Wolf Who Cried Boy (Hartman, Bob), 127, 244
Wolkstein, Diane
    The Day Ocean Came to Visit, 156
    The Magic Orange Tree and Other Haitian Folktales, 7, 156
Womenfolk and Fairy Tales (Minard, Rosemary), 139
The Wonderful Shrinking Shirt (Anderson, Leone Castell), 113
Wood, Audrey. *The Bunyans*, 157
Worlds of Shadow: Teaching with Shadow Puppetry (Wisniewski, David, and Donna Wisniewski), 256
Worthy, Jo. *Readers Theater for Building Fluency: Strategies and Scripts for Making the Most of This Highly Effective, Motivating, and Research-Based Approach to Oral Reading*, 256
Wrede, Patricia. *Dealing with Dragons*, 157

The Year of the Dog (Lin, Grace), 134
Yeh-Shen: A Cinderella Story from China (Louie, Ai-Ling), 13, 135
Yep, Laurence
    The Dragon Prince, 157
    The Junior Thunder Lord, 157
    The Khan's Daughter, 157
Yolen, Jane
    Favorite Folktales from Around the World, 185
    Odysseus in the Serpent Maze, 157
    Passager: The Young Merlin Trilogy, Book 1, 157
    Pegasus, the Flying Horse, 157
    Touch Magic: Fantasy, Faerie and Folklore in the Literature of Childhood, 186
    Wings, 157
Yoshi's Feast (Kajikawa, Kimiko), 131
Young Arthur (San Souci, Robert D.), 147
Young, Ed
    Cat and Rat, 158
    Lon Po Po, 158
    Mouse Match, 24, 158
    Seven Blind Mice, 158
    The Sons of the Dragon King, 252
Younguncle Comes to Town (Singh, Vandana), 151

You Read to Me, I'll Read to You: Very Short Fairy Tales to Read Together (Hoberman, Mary Ann), 128, 207, 244

You Read to Me, I'll Read to You: Very Short Stories to Read Together (Hoberman, Mary Ann), 128, 207

Yo! Yes? (Raschka, Chris), 220, 249

Zelinsky, Paul O.
   The Maid and the Mouse and the Odd-Shaped House, 87
   Rapunzel, 25, 158
   Rumpelstiltskin, 26, 158
Zemach, Harve. *Duffy and the Devil*, 158
Zen Shorts (Muth, Jon J), 141
Ziskind, Sylvia. *Telling Stories to Children*, 186
Zomo the Rabbit (McDermott, Gerald), 138
Zoom Broom (Palatini, Margie), 248

About the Author

JUDY FREEMAN (www.JudyReadsBooks.com) is a well-known consultant, writer, and international speaker on all aspects of children's literature and storytelling. She is visiting lecturer in the School of Information and Library Science at Pratt Institute in New York City, where she teaches graduate courses on children's literature and storytelling. A former school librarian, she now spends her days reading, writing, and traveling the world to give seminars, workshops, speeches, and performances for teachers, librarians, parents, and children. Judy is a national presenter for Libraries Unlimited and for BER (Bureau of Education and Research). She served as a member of the Newbery Committee to select the Newbery Award book for the year 2000, and on the Sibert Committee for 2008.

Judy's popular companion books, *Books Kids Will Sit Still For: The Complete Read-Aloud Guide*, (Libraries Unlimited, 1990), *More Books Kids Will Sit Still For* (1995), and *Books Kids Will Sit Still For 3* (2006) are indispensable resources for literature-based classrooms. Her *Hi Ho Librario!: Songs, Chants, and Stories to Keep Kids Humming* (Rock Hill Press, 1997) is a book and CD full of her book-related songs and stories. Judy also writes about children's literature for periodicals including School Library Media Activities Monthly, NoveList, and School Library Journal's Curriculum Connections.

At home with her husband, Izzy Feldman, in Highland Park, New Jersey, she plays tennis, gardens, reads too many books, and plays fetch with Percy, her Ragdoll cat.

JUDY FREEMAN
CHILDREN'S LITERATURE CONSULTANT

JUDY FREEMAN (www.JudyReadsBooks.com) is a well-known consultant, writer, and speaker on children's literature, storytelling, and all aspects of librarianship. She is a visiting lecturer at the School of Information and Library Science at Pratt Institute in New York City, where she teaches courses on children's literature and storytelling. A national presenter for BER (Bureau of Education and Research), she also gives a variety of workshops and speeches throughout the United States and abroad for teachers, librarians, parents, and children. Judy served as a member of the Newbery Committee to select the Newbery Award book for the year 2000 and is on the Sibert Committee for 2008.

JUDY'S MANY COURSES, WORKSHOPS, & SPEECHES INCLUDE:
WINNERS!: A Closer Look at the Year's "Best" Books for Children
Books Kids Will Sit Still For: Children's Literature Every Teacher and Librarian Should Know
Literature and Library Skills: An Integrated Approach
Booktalking: Advertising Your Wares
Once Upon a Time: Storytelling, Creative Drama, & Reader's Theater for Grades PreK-6
Hi Ho Librario!: Songs and Chants to Keep Kids Humming

SCHOOL PROGRAMS FOR CHILDREN: The Musical Booktalk
Judy will give three one-hour assemblies for children, grades PreK–6, per day. She incorporates interactive storytelling, songs, poetry, creative drama, wordplay, and booktalks in a spirited exploration of the power of words, with lots of audience participation. Included are her annotated bibliography of her 100 favorite recent children's books (that you can easily duplicate as a handout for parents, teachers, and children) and a handout for teachers of songs, stories, and reading ideas as a follow-up to her program. If you are interested, Judy will be glad to give, at no extra cost, a one-hour after-school parent/teacher workshop on the latest best books for children, along with an annotated bibliography of all the titles she presents.

JUDY'S latest mega-book, *Books Kids Will Sit Still For 3* (Libraries Unlimited, 2006) and its popular companions *Books Kids Will Sit Still For: The Complete Read-Aloud Guide* (1990) and *More Books Kids Will Sit Still For* (1995) are indispensable resources for literature-based classrooms and libraries. (To order: 1-800-225-5800; www.LU.com.) Her *Hi Ho Librario!: Songs, Chants, and Stories to Keep Kids Humming* (Rock Hill Press, 1997) is a book and CD full of her book-related songs. (To order: ssocha@rockhillworks.com; 1-610-667-2375; www.rockhillworks.com.) Judy also writes book review columns for *School Library Media Activities Monthly*, *School Library Journal's Curriculum Connections*, and *NoveList*.

For further information about her programs:
JUDY FREEMAN
65 NORTH SIXTH AVENUE
HIGHLAND PARK, NJ 08904
732-572-5634 / E-mail: BKWSSF@aol.com / www.JudyReadsBooks.com